The Memory of the Civil War in American Culture

Edited by Alice Fahs & Joan Waugh

THE UNIVERSITY OF NORTH CAROLINA PRESS

Chapel Hill and London

© 2004
The University of North Carolina Press
All rights reserved
Manufactured in the United States of America
Set in Bulmer and Egiziano types
by Keystone Typesetting, Inc.

Several essays in this book have been reprinted in revised form from the following works:
David W. Blight, "Decoration Days," in David W. Blight, *Race and Reunion: The Civil War in
American Memory* (Cambridge, Mass.: Belknap Press of Harvard University Press, 2001), 64–97,
copyright © 2001 by the President and Fellows of Harvard College, used by permission of the
publisher; Gary W. Gallagher, "Shaping Public Memory of the Civil War: Robert E. Lee, Jubal A.
Early, and Douglas Southall Freeman," in Gary W. Gallagher, *Lee and His Army in Confederate
History* (Chapel Hill: University of North Carolina Press, 2001), 255–82, © 2001 by the University
of North Carolina Press, used by permission of the publisher; Patrick Kelly, "The Election of 1896
and the Restructuring of Civil War Memory," *Civil War History* (September 2003): 254–80, used
by permission of Kent State University Press; and Joan Waugh, *Personal Memoirs of U. S. Grant:
A History of the Union Cause*, Frank L. Klements Lecture Series, no. 12, James Marten, series ed.
(Milwaukee: Marquette University Press, 2003), used by permission of the publisher.

The paper in this book meets the guidelines for
permanence and durability of the Committee on Production Guidelines
for Book Longevity of the Council on Library Resources.

Library of Congress Cataloging-in-Publication Data
The memory of the Civil War in American culture / edited by Alice Fahs and Joan Waugh.
p. cm. — (Civil War America)
Includes bibliographical references and index.
ISBN 0-8078-2907-2 (alk. paper) — ISBN 0-8078-5572-3 (pbk. : alk. paper)
1. United States—History—Civil War, 1861-1865—Influence. 2. United States—History—Civil
War, 1861-1865—Historiography. I. Fahs, Alice. II. Waugh, Joan. III. Series.
E468.9.M54   2004
973.7′072′073—dc22   2004008919

cloth   08 07 06 05 04   5 4 3 2 1
paper   08 07 06 05 04   5 4 3 2 1

THIS BOOK WAS DIGITALLY PRINTED.

The Memory of the Civil War
in American Culture

CIVIL WAR AMERICA

Gary W. Gallagher, editor

Contents

Illustrations

The Memory of the Civil War
in American Culture

Alice Fahs & Joan Waugh

Introduction

he Civil War has never receded into the remote past in American life. The most momentous conflict in American history, it had a revolutionary social and political impact that continues to be felt today. The political firestorms of the 1980s and 1990s over the appropriateness of the Confederate battle flag flying over statehouses in Georgia, Mississippi, and South Carolina, for instance, demonstrate how deeply meaningful Civil War symbols remain in American politics, especially racial politics. The unveiling of Richmond's first and only statue to Abraham Lincoln in April 2003 brought forth a bevy of protesters. Although supporters of the life-size bronze sculpture of Lincoln and his son Tad emphasized the statue's symbolism for reconciliation, neo-Confederates waved signs bearing the slogan "Lincoln: Wanted for War Crimes." Indeed, in any given year since 1865 individuals and social groups have sought to legitimize claims, and even to redefine what is American, by evoking selective memories of the war. Such evocations have been—and continue to be—a powerful means of claiming membership in the nation as well as of denying others' claims to such membership.

This volume examines a variety of battles over the memory of the war during the last 135 years, finding in them important insights concerning our identities as individuals and as a nation. It recovers the racial and gender politics underlying numerous attempts to memorialize the war, provides new insights into how Lost Cause ideology achieved dominance in the late nineteenth century, and shows how contests over memories of the war were a vital part of politics during the civil rights movement of the 1950s and 1960s. One of the innovations of the volume is that it moves among a variety of cultural and political arenas—from public monuments to parades to soldiers' memoirs to political campaigns to textbook publishing to children's literature—in order to reveal important changes in how the memory of the Civil War has been employed in American life. By setting the politics of Civil War memory within this wide social and cultural landscape, it is able to recover not just the meanings of the war in various eras but also the specific processes by which those meanings have been created. Taken together, those cultural locations and processes form what Stuart McConnell has evocatively termed the "geography of Civil War memory."

That geography employs both literal and figurative dimensions involving physical and symbolic spaces. Processions, parades, and public ceremonies, for instance, have created theatrical public settings in which different social groups have asserted the legitimacy of their interpretations of the Civil War's meanings. Occurring in concrete physical settings, such ceremonies have also had important symbolic dimensions, as different groups have sought to affirm a specific language of memory attached to place. Similarly, the construction of Civil War monuments has involved not only a physical transformation of public space but also the creation and manipulation of a visual language of memory for specific ideological ends. Political campaigns, too, have employed the war's dramatic iconography as a legitimizing tool in public rallies and speeches. Finally, books have been both physical and symbolic spaces mapping out the contested historical and emotional terrain of the Civil War. Ulysses S. Grant's famous memoirs, late-nineteenth-century Southern textbooks, and children's Civil War fiction can all be seen as contributing to an ongoing argument over the war's meanings within American culture. At once material objects and symbolic spaces, such books have worked to connect individuals to larger regional or even national concerns.

Historians have not always linked the military and cultural history of the war, but this volume does so deliberately in order to produce new insights into the impact of the war within American life. The opening section of the book, for instance, focuses on the way the war's history was refought and reconfigured through the study of two military icons: General Ulysses S. Grant and General Robert E. Lee. Joan Waugh's essay on Grant's *Personal Memoirs* portrays the struggle of Grant and Northern veterans to keep the memory of the Union cause brightly lit even as the forces of reconciliation were dimming that light. In contrast, Gary W. Gallagher's essay demonstrates the success of Southern generals, and, later, Southern historians, to make the Confederate cause admirable through the deification of Lee. Both authors not only make clear the high stakes in the battle over the memory of the war but also reveal how book publishing became an arena in which that battle was fought.

The essays of James M. McPherson and Alice Fahs focus on books as an important location of Civil War memory. McPherson examines the largely successful effort by Southern textbook crusaders in the decades after the

　　　{ ALICE FAHS & JOAN WAUGH }

war to ease the bitter sting of defeat by replacing Northern versions of the war in schoolbooks. This crusade had significant repercussions for the way in which the history of the war was learned by later generations of Southerners. Surprisingly, the Northern press and public offered little opposition to the increasingly widespread positive view of the Confederate Lost Cause. In a study of popular children's war novels written both during and after the war, Fahs argues that a Northern embrace of Southern views of the war was in large part due to a prevailing racial ideology of masculinity, which emphasized the honor and courage of white soldiers on both sides.

Civil War monuments and public celebrations are the focus of two essays exploring how public commemorations have shaped collective memory and forged both a national and a sectional identity. In his essay on the politics of reunion, David W. Blight reveals that the establishment of Memorial Day centered around battles over the racialized meanings of Reconstruction in both the North and the South. Thomas J. Brown shows how a statue of John C. Calhoun, the brilliant advocate for Southern nationalism and a senator for South Carolina, became an embodiment of Lost Cause ideology by the time it was unveiled in the 1870s.

The next two essays turn explicitly to politics, offering new perspectives on how the Civil War affected the political landscape of the late nineteenth century. J. Matthew Gallman rescues an important figure from historical obscurity. Anna Dickinson, a young feminist firebrand for the Union and the first woman to speak to a joint session of Congress in 1864, played a significant role in the 1872 presidential election. Gallman shows how Dickinson's support of the liberal ticket headed by the newspaper editor Horace Greeley drew upon deeply contested memories of the war for the Northern public. Patrick J. Kelly's essay on veterans continues this examination of the war in the nation's political culture by focusing on the complex interplay between Northern veterans' patriotism, welfare demands, and the policies of the Republican Party. Both essays emphasize the power of evoking memories of the war to effect political agendas.

Contemporary concerns of race, class, and gender are showcased in the last essays of the book. LeeAnn Whites's piece chronicles how a 1930s monument honoring the courage of Missouri's Confederate soldiers became, by the 1960s, a symbol of racism and the center of debate over the appropriateness of such monuments in the late twentieth century. Jon Wiener's essay juxtaposes the planning and execution of the centennial of the Civil War from 1961 to 1965 against the profoundly unsettling period of American history driven by Cold War tensions and the second American civil rights revolution. Finally, in the epilogue Stuart McConnell provides an overview of the geography of memory in American culture, not only examining the variety of places where that memory has been constructed but also discussing the power politics underlying Americans' access to those important physical sites.

From 1865 to the present each new generation has actively reinterpreted the Civil War to support its own ideological agendas. As many of these essays reveal, only too often in the decades after the Civil War memories of that conflict were invoked to support racist agendas attempting to exclude African Americans from full participation in American life. In our own time, in contrast, it has become impossible to separate the history of slavery from the history of the Civil War era. Indeed, due to the concerted efforts of numerous groups who view the Confederate flag as a symbol of a slave regime rather than a part of a supposedly benign Southern "heritage," the flag has at long last been removed from the South Carolina statehouse. As that action reveals, and as this volume shows, the past is continually enlivened and renewed by the creativity of the present.

This book of essays evolved from a conference held at the Henry E. Huntington Library in San Marino, California. We thank Robert C. Ritchie, director of research, and his excellent staff, Carolyn Powell and Nancy Burrows, for making the riches of the Huntington Library available to scholars of the Civil War. We also express our deep appreciation to those who participated in the conference and who so graciously agreed to publish their papers in this volume. Finally, we thank David Perry, Paula Wald, Ruth Homrighaus, Becky Standard, and Mark Simpson-Vos of the University of North Carolina Press for their expert assistance.

Joan Waugh

Ulysses S. Grant, Historian

His troubles began on a festive holiday. Christmas Eve in 1883 was cold and rainy, and by late evening the sidewalk was frozen in front of Ulysses S. Grant's house on 3 East Sixty-sixth Street in New York City, not far from Central Park. Stepping out of a rented carriage, Grant slipped on the ice and sustained a painful injury. As the formerly robust general struggled to regain his health, another blow struck. In May 1884 he learned that Grant and Ward, an investment firm that held his fortune, had failed. Aged sixty-two, Grant was penniless.

Friends and supporters rallied around Ulysses and his wife, Julia. He was able to keep his residence but little else. In desperation he agreed to write an account of the battle of Shiloh for *Century Magazine*. He did it for the money at first but found that he liked the task. He decided to write more articles. One thing led to another, and before he knew it he had signed a book contract. A brief period of happiness ensued, but fate once again intervened. In the summer of 1884 Grant bit into a peach and was immediately seized with a terrible pain in his throat. A few months later his doctors confirmed the worst: he had a fatal throat cancer. Most men would have abandoned an ambitious writing project at such a time. Not Grant. Famed for his quiet determination on the battlefield, he decided to finish the manuscript before he died.

Through many months of indescribable agony Grant painstakingly recorded his role in the history of the great conflict. His family's financial future depended upon the successful completion of the books, and he would not let them down. But the writing also took on a special urgency; he felt an obligation to tell what he knew to be true about himself, about the war, about the United States. "I would like to see truthful history written," declared Grant. "Such history will do full credit to the courage, endurance, and ability of the American citizen soldier, no matter what section he hailed from, or in what rank."[1]

Grant wrote those words just a week or two into July 1885. In mid-June he traveled by train from the city to a wealthy supporter's summer cottage at Mount McGregor, a beautiful resort in the Adirondacks near Saratoga Springs. When he felt well enough, he liked to sit on the large and comfortable porch to read newspapers and enjoy the cool air. Grant reserved what little energy he had left for his memoirs. He fretted over the page proofs for the first volume, revising and pointing out errors that should be corrected. He continued working on the second volume, still in manuscript, adding pages, even chapters, and providing detailed commentaries.

A poignant photograph showed Grant writing intently while seated in a wicker chair on the porch at the Mount McGregor cottage. Swathed in scarves and shawls, with a woolen cap perched on his head, and propped up by a pillow, he was simply unrecognizable as the strong general who led the Union armies to victory. But a sharp observer of the image will note the resolution in his frail, ravaged countenance. Even as he faced death, Grant openly relished his role as a writer of history. As Bruce Catton described, Grant had become a "man of letters."[2] "I pray God," Grant wrote to his wife, "that [my life] may be spared to complete the necessary work upon my book."[3] His unfinished work kept him alive longer than his doctors had predicted. Grant died on July 23, 1885, two days after writing his last words.[4]

The posthumous publication in December of the two-volume *Personal Memoirs of U. S. Grant* (1,231 pages in total) proved a spectacular popular and critical success. The publisher, New York's Charles L. Webster and Company, eventually sold more than three hundred thousand sets. Within the first two years, royalties totaled over $450,000, bringing financial security to his widow and four children. With the publication of Grant's memoirs, "historian" could be added to his list of professions.

My essay explores the interpretative significance of Grant's *Personal Memoirs*. It does not present a detailed review or analysis of the narrative; rather, it offers an elucidation of the process that led to the completion of the massive work. In other words, I am concerned about the battle over the meaning of the American Civil War and Grant's role in that battle as a historian. I am defining "historian" broadly, as someone who is "a writer or student of history."[5] Grant's account of the war, above all, conveyed what he himself called "truthful history." It can be simply put. According to Grant, the Northern cause (based upon the sacredness of unionism and opposition to slavery) was the morally superior one. Grant challenged the idea, just beginning to take hold in the 1880s, that the Northern and Southern causes were equivalent. He reminded the country's citizens that "the cause

Ulysses S. Grant working on the Personal Memoirs.
(Courtesy of Library of Congress)

of the great War of the Rebellion against the United States will have to be attributed to slavery."[6]

Thus, the *Personal Memoirs* were written both to advance a larger truth, that of Union moral superiority, and to remind Americans of Grant's contribution to the victory that remade America into "a nation of great power and intelligence."[7] In Grant's mind the two purposes were linked. If the North's aims were union and freedom, then his reputation was forever secured. Few expressed Grant's thoughts better than his supporter Frederick Douglass: "May we not justly say, will it not be the unquestioned sentiment of history that the liberty Mr. Lincoln declared with his pen General Grant made effectual with his sword—by his skill in leading the Union armies to final victory?"[8]

Grant's importance as a symbol of unionism for his generation was undisputed. As a lieutenant general, as a general-in-chief, as a twice-elected president, as an international figure, as a private citizen, and as a dying hero, Grant sought actively to influence and shape the historical memory of the South's rebellion. That he identified himself with the "Union Cause" made it even more imperative to control the war's memory. Grant was a historian of the war as well as of the Union cause. Broke and discouraged in 1884, Grant turned the *Century* articles into the basis of his hefty memoirs. When he did that, he was emphatically not, as is sometimes portrayed, starting from scratch. Importantly, the volumes were the last stage of a process that began during the war and continued, gathering steam, in the decades of his postwar career. Grant explained his literary credentials in the following way:

> I have to say that for the last twenty-four years I have been very much employed in writing. As a soldier I wrote my own orders, plans of battle, instructions and reports. They were not edited, nor was assistance rendered. As president, I wrote every official document, I believe, usual for presidents to write, bearing my name. All these have been published and widely circulated. The public has become accustomed to my style of writing. They know that it is not even an attempt to imitate either a literary or classical style; that it is just what it is and nothing else. If I succeed in telling my story so that others can see as I do what I attempt to show, I will be satisfied. The reader must also be satisfied, for he knows from the beginning just what to expect.[9]

Grant's late-blooming literary masterpiece therefore represented a culmination, by one of the major figures in the conflict, of twenty-four years of thinking, writing, and talking about the meaning of the war for the United States. Finally, Grant's interpretation of the war was interwoven with and reactive to controversies and events—such as the development of the Lost Cause ideology and the publication of the *Official Records of the War of the Rebellion*—that shaped the writing of the civil war.[10]

:::

The Personal Memoirs: *A Background*

To understand the books' import, a brief background on the reception and reputation of the *Personal Memoirs of U. S. Grant* is necessary. In the 1880s there was an explosion of publications about the Civil War. Indeed, the amount of literature pouring forth from the presses seemed unstoppable: books, newspaper and magazine serials, and the conflict's official documents. Much of the material was military in nature—descriptive accounts of battles, fictional portraits of soldiers coming to grips with the war, biographies and memoirs of soldiers, unit histories—and it fed the public's insatiable appetite. Grant facilitated, and benefited from, this publishing phenomenon. For example, even before Grant's death, sixty thousand sets of the *Personal Memoirs* had been ordered by subscription, much to the astonishment of the ailing general. "General Grant," wrote an Ohio veteran and agent selling subscriptions for the books, "the people are moving *en masse* upon your memoirs."[11]

The reviews were effusive, and many compared the *Personal Memoirs* favorably with Caesar's *Commentaries*. Mark Twain, Grant's great friend as well as his publisher, pronounced, "General Grant's book is a great unique and unapproachable literary masterpiece."[12] The *Personal Memoirs* elicited praise from prominent journals and intellectuals. "Fifty years hence," wrote one reviewer, "the mind of the nation will distinctly recognize only two figures as connected with all that great upheaval, Lincoln and Grant."[13] Grant the historian was almost universally praised for his direct, simple, honest, and fair-minded portrayal of the Civil War and for his modesty in downplaying his own considerable role in bringing about Northern victory. Many readers observed that Grant's memoirs, above all other accounts of the war, told the "truth" about the nation's greatest conflict.[14] People were impressed by his ability to write a compelling narrative of the war's battles. His narrative seemed calm, measured, objective, and buttressed by solid documentation.[15] The *Personal Memoirs* sold briskly into the first decade of the twentieth century before falling into obscurity by the late 1920s and

1930s. It was no coincidence that Grant's reputation reached a nadir in those particular decades, as the popular culture celebrated the romantic image of the Confederacy epitomized in Margaret Mitchell's *Gone with the Wind* and immortalized in its movie adaptation.[16]

When interest revived in Grant's life and career, it sparked a reappraisal of his military and political record. Although the *Personal Memoirs* never again achieved its late-nineteenth-century best-seller status, modern scholars and critics turned to the books to help explain the man and the war. Edmund Wilson's assessment of the volumes as "a unique expression of national character" included a forceful argument for considering Grant as a writer who deserved to be included in the American literary canon. The editor of *The Papers of U. S. Grant*, John Y. Simon, asserted that the *Personal Memoirs* offered "candor, scrupulous fairness, and grace of expression."[17] Bruce Catton called the work "a first-rate book—well written with a literary quality that keeps it fresh." William McFeely, James M. McPherson, and Brooks D. Simpson have singled out Grant's memoirs as a historical and literary tour de force and all have written introductions to new editions.[18] In short, a strong consensus has emerged. The *Personal Memoirs* provide a literate, accurate, and indispensable resource for understanding the military and political history of the war that neither the professional historian nor the amateur can afford to ignore. But the work offers much more than that. For the modern reader, the *Personal Memoirs* can also explain two interrelated questions, "Why the North won" and "Why they fought." Not surprisingly, Grant's war experiences laid the foundation for his later writing efforts; his pen first captured those experiences in battlefield reports.

:::

Battlefield Reports

The history of the Civil War and its individual battles began as soon as the muskets and cannons fell quiet on the battlefield. The old saying "The pen is mightier than the sword" applies to the official reports that had to be written by the leading battle participants who had to justify their successes and failures to their military and political superiors. Grant's major (and minor) battles and campaigns from Fort Donelson to Shiloh to Vicksburg to Chattanooga to Cold Harbor had to be analyzed, explained, and defended, with blame cast and praise awarded to the major officers.

{ JOAN WAUGH }

The eminent editor of the Century series on the Civil War, Robert Underwood Johnson, was a close reader of numerous battles' conflicting accounts. In frustration, he turned to humor to explain the process. He observed that every battle has at least four points of view: that of the man who gets credit for the victory, that of the man who thought he should get the credit, that of the man who is blamed for the defeat, and that of the man who is blamed by the man who is blamed for the defeat. Out of such confusing elements, Johnson mused, history is written.[19] During the war, however, many reputations were advanced or damaged by the official reports, and if a high-ranking general was perceived as committing a serious blunder on the battlefield, he knew that his actions would be written up immediately and he could expect to be rebuked at best or, at worst, to be fired or court-martialed.

As a general Grant was no different than any other officer in the Civil War in this respect. Like other generals, he suffered from negative reports and evaluations as well as vicious attacks in the press. Like other generals, he cultivated certain politicians and reporters who would unfailingly support him and to whom he would explain and justify controversial actions. Grant's great supporter in Congress during the war was Illinois Republican Elihu B. Washburne.[20] Washburne made sure that Grant's accomplishments were brought to the attention of President Lincoln. By August 1863, with Vicksburg secured, Grant had emerged as Lincoln's favorite general. In that month Grant sent a crisp letter to the president informing Lincoln of his plans regarding the enrollment of black soldiers in the Union army. He added, "I have given the subject of arming the negro my hearty support. This, with the emancipation of the negro, is the heaviest blow yet given to the Confederacy." Those were exactly the words that Lincoln had been waiting to hear. Grant's wartime correspondence shows that he approached the ending of slavery as a practical problem to be dealt with as dictated by military necessities. Grant also judged the South harshly for slavery and often commented on the virtues of the free labor system. Grant's enthusiastic support, with both words and action, of Lincoln's emancipation policy endeared him to his commander-in-chief almost as much as his winning record on the field had.[21]

Grant became a master of writing clear and forceful battle reports, presenting his views so successfully that his superiors—President Lincoln, Secretary of War Edwin Stanton, and Lincoln's chief military advisor, Henry Halleck—rarely disputed them. An aide observed Grant at his desk during the war: "His work was performed swiftly and uninterruptedly. . . . His thoughts flowed as freely from his mind as the ink from his pen."[22]

The same clarity of thought that marked his official reports was also present in his instructions to his subordinates in written orders, telegrams, and letters. A member of General George Meade's staff remarked: "There is one striking feature of Grant's orders; no matter how hurriedly he may write them on the field, no one ever has the slightest doubt as to their meaning, or even has to read them over a second time to understand them." Examples of his superior prose—clear, incisive, and terse—abound.[23] During the Chattanooga campaign, Grant sent a brigadier general the following message: "Act upon the instructions you have, and your own discretion, and if you can do any thing to relieve Burnside, do it. It is not expected you will try to sacrifice your command, but that you will take the proper risks." Grant sent an urgent telegram to General Philip Sheridan after the battle of Cedar Creek: "If it is possible to follow up your great victory until you reach the Central road and Canal do it even if you have to live on half rations." In the midst of the bloody battle known as Spotsylvania, Grant dashed off a communiqué to Stanton that demonstrated his resolve to fight to the end: "We have now entered the sixth day of very hard fighting. The result to this time is much in our favor. Our losses have been heavy as well as those of the enemy. . . . I propose to fight it out on this line if it takes all summer."[24] Grant's farewell message to Union soldiers issued on June 2, 1865, was written with heartfelt precision: "By your patriotic devotion to your country in the hour of danger and alarm . . . you have maintained the supremacy of the Union and the Constitution, overthrown all armed opposition to the enforcement of the Law, and of the Proclamations forever Abolishing *Slavery*, the cause and pretext of the Rebellion, and opened the way to the Rightful Authorities to restore Order and inaugerate [*sic*] Peace on a permanent and enduring basis on every foot of American soil."[25]

The constant stream of reports, orders, and letters issuing from Grant's headquarters sharpened his perceptions of the larger issues of the conflict—loyalty, unionism, freedom, political democracy—as well as demonstrated his mastery of military strategy, thus uniting what General Horace Porter called Grant's "singular mental powers and his rare military qualities."[26] By the end of the war, Grant had accumulated a treasure trove of materials from his headquarters records to draw upon when he presented his 1866 "Report to Congress."

: : :
"Report to Congress"

In his "Report to Congress" Grant laid out for the nation's review the winning strategy of the war and how it was implemented for 1864–65. First: "I . . . determined . . . to use the greatest number of troops practicable against the armed force of the enemy." Second, he decided "to hammer continuously against the armed force of the enemy, and his resources, until by *mere attrition*, if in no other way, there should be nothing left to him but an equal submission with the loyal section of our common country to the constitution and laws of the land."[27] Was the phrase "mere attrition" Grant's admission that the North had won by sheer numbers and brute force? Did Grant diminish his own prowess as a military leader? Hardly. He immediately pointed out that no Northern military leader (except himself) had been able to use the numerical superiority in the most effective way to achieve total victory.

Moreover, Grant argued that the South, in fact, enjoyed significant advantages: a vast territory, a largely united and supportive population, and long lines of river and railroad commerce. The North, Grant remembered, had huge disadvantages: a fractured, disaffected population politically represented by the Democratic Party. The Democrats, he observed, had an excellent chance to win the 1864 presidential election and perhaps end the war on terms unfavorable to the Union. In addition, the 1862 voluntary enlistments were up and too many experienced soldiers had been honorably discharged and thus lost to the army when they were needed the most. In contrast, new voluntary enrollments were down. The people, he wrote, were sick and tired of the war. "It was a question," Grant reminded his readers, "whether our numerical strength and resources were not more than balanced by these disadvantages and the enemy's superior position."[28]

Presaging his later criticisms of the "marble man," Grant disparaged the generalship of his Southern counterpart, Robert E. Lee, the commander of the Army of Northern Virginia. Grant praised Lee's dignity at Appomattox Court House, the place where he accepted Lee's surrender on April 9, 1865. During the Overland campaign, however, Grant felt that Lee's defensive strategy had unnecessarily and tragically prolonged the war. Instead of meeting him face-to-face in battle, Grant claimed, "he acted purely on the defensive, behind breastworks, or feebly on the offensive immediately in front of them, and where, in case of repulse, he could easily retire behind them."[29] Grant wished the world to know that he and he alone of all the Northern generals had been fearless in Lee's presence.

The top Northern general also made clear his low opinion of the Confederate nation: "In the South, a reign of military despotism prevailed, which made every man and boy capable of bearing arms a soldier; and those who could not bear arms in the field acted as provosts for collecting deserters and returning them. This enabled the enemy to bring almost his entire strength into the field."[30] Grant concluded the report with a tribute to the armies he commanded and a call for reconciliation by stating, "Let them [Union soldiers] hope for perpetual peace and harmony with that enemy, whose manhood, however mistaken the cause, drew forth such herculean deeds of valor."[31]

Grant's 1866 "Report to Congress" provided the "larger truth" of the war that for him no new information or factual evidence would ever change: the Union had justice on its side; the cause of the war was slavery; Confederates had advantages that offset Union superiority in both numbers and resources; Northern soldiers fought just as well as Southern soldiers and under more difficult conditions; and Robert E. Lee's generalship was deeply flawed. Later, Grant would say of Lee: "I never could see in his achievements what justifies his reputation. The illusion that nothing but heavy odds beat him will not stand the ultimate light of history."[32] How wrong he was in this assessment.

:::

Influencing History

Grant continued in public service, first as general-in-chief of the U.S. Armed Forces (1865–68) and then as president until 1877. Although Grant could not devote time to writing the war's history during these years, he did expend much energy to advance what he considered to be the "truth" of the war for public edification. During his presidency he influenced the historical memory of the war in three ways. First, through the obviously symbolic nature of his position as the chief executive who was also the military savior of the Union; second, through his constant attention to veterans' needs and affairs; and third, through his enthusiastic sponsorship of military histories that reflected his viewpoint.

Scholars and students of Grant's career often pose the question, Why did the deliberately apolitical commander-in-chief accept the 1868 nomination for the presidency? Did he want to be president for the power or for the glory? Many have argued that Grant was unprepared, was naive, and, moreover, could not have chosen a path more likely to destroy his cherished reputation.

According to Brooks D. Simpson, the answer is simple and straightforward, like the man. Grant agreed to be president during this incredibly difficult time because he did not wish to leave the legacy of the war in politicians' hands. Grant explained his motives for accepting the nomination to his friend William Tecumseh Sherman: "I could not back down without, as it seems to me, leaving the contest for power for the next four years between mere trading politicians, the elevation of whom, no matter which party won, would lose to us, largely, the results of the costly war which we have gone through."[33] Simpson argued that Grant, throughout his presidency, remained steadfast in the belief that the goals of the war should be preserved in the policies of a firm Reconstruction that focused on establishing and protecting black economic and political rights. "My efforts in the future will be directed to the restoration of good feeling between the different sections of our common country," declared Grant in his second inaugural address. Those efforts, Grant made clear, included cementing the gains that had been made for African Americans: "The effects of the late civil strife have been to free the slave and make him a citizen. Yet he is not possessed of the civil rights which citizenship should carry with it."[34] Grant desired sectional harmony, but always in the service of remolding the South in the Northern, and thus the national, mold. Grant later wrote to Elihu Washburne: "All that I want is that the government rule should remain in the hands of those who saved the Union until all the questions growing out of the war are forever settled."[35]

: : :

The Union Cause versus the Lost Cause

By the time Grant left the presidency in 1877 his views seemed increasingly out of date. The American people were tired of Reconstruction. Northerners, whether they were Democrats or Republicans, were now more willing to trust Southern whites to protect black freedom, if not their right to vote, and to rule at home. The 1870s also witnessed the rise of a strictly Southern history of the Civil War that disparaged Grant's generalship.

The North's, and Grant's, interpretation of the war's righteousness was challenged in the decades after the war by an ideology about the Confederate nation called the "Lost Cause." The elements that define the Lost Cause are well known: the war was caused not by slavery but by states' rights; Southern armies were never defeated but instead were overwhelmed by numbers; the Southern soldier was brave and true, echoing the perfection of the patron saint of the Lost Cause, that courtly Virginia gentleman of impeccable lineage General Robert E. Lee. In the pages of the influential journal the *Southern Historical Society Papers* and in numerous speeches to Southern veterans' groups, Jubal A. Early, a former Confederate general, and his supporters actively and successfully promoted their version of "truthful history."

For the unreconstructed, it was not enough to idolize Robert E. Lee; Ulysses S. Grant's reputation had to be destroyed.[36] From the 1870s onward, myths about Lee and Grant assumed distinctly different trajectories. Lee's General Order 9, issued on April 10, 1865, provided his explanation for Confederate defeat and Union victory. In that farewell message, Lee honored his soldiers for having displayed "unsurpassed courage and fortitude" but argued that they had been "compelled to yield to overwhelming numbers and resources."[37] Taking his cue from General Order 9 as well as from conversations and correspondence with Lee himself, Early claimed in speeches and in print that Grant was a bloody butcher who was not even remotely equal to Lee as a military strategist or tactician. Moreover, he used an impressive array of facts and figures gathered exclusively to present the Confederate side of the story to the public.[38]

The negative portrayal of Grant that emerged not only tarnished Grant's national and international military stature but also increased Lee's, which was the true goal of this effort. Referring in part to the pro-Confederate histories that were critical of him, an irritated Grant said: "The cry was in the air that the North only won by brute force; that the generalship and valor were with the South. This has gone into history, with so many other illusions that are historical."[39] This seemingly unstoppable, and to Grant grotesque, adulation of Lee was neatly summed up by the English writer Matthew Arnold, who explained that in his view Grant "is not to the English imagination the hero of the American Civil War; the hero is Lee."[40] Just as Lee was presented as a flawless icon, so the Confederate cause was whitewashed. States' rights, not slavery, was elevated as the Southern cause worth living and dying for. Reflecting the sectional divide during the war, two sharply differing interpretations of the conflict emerged in full force only a decade after Appomattox.

Grant was aware that Lee's reputation was in some ways overshadowing his own. The growing influence of the Lost Cause owed much to the power of the criticisms hurled against Grant's hated Reconstruction policy in the South. From the pen of former Confederate general Dabney H. Maury in the influential *Southern Historical Society Papers* came a decidedly hostile evaluation of Grant's presidency: "In reviewing the history of this century it will be impossible to find a rule so barren of statesmanship . . . as Grant's has been. . . . It is uncharitable and of little profit to speculate upon the remnant of his life left to him. But we may well believe 'his [remaining] days will be few and evil.' "[41] White Southerners connected Grant's brutal generalship with his so-called imposition of Republican rule on the defeated region.

Grant, however, connected the war's goals—reunion and freedom—with an attempt, very imperfect, to make the South a place where black and white, Republican and Democrat could live together. He failed. "There has never been a moment since Lee surrendered," Grant remarked ruefully, "that I would not have gone more than halfway to meet the Southern people in a spirit of conciliation. But they have never responded to it. They have not forgotten the war."[42]

Over the next century understanding or appreciation of the Union cause steadily declined against the appeal of Southern nobility and romanticism. Although the Lost Cause ideology has been thoroughly discredited by scholars, it retains a powerful grip on popular imagination, albeit in a less racist form than it took during the last decades of the nineteenth century. The myth of Robert E. Lee is still immensely appealing to large numbers of Americans, and not just Southern Americans. Lee's brilliant generalship, his stainless character, his old-fashioned and gentlemanly style of warfare, and his noble acceptance of defeat commends him to us.[43] In contrast, the warfare conducted by Ulysses S. Grant, the "butcher," is repellent because it has been deemed modern. In his lifetime and afterward, Grant has been portrayed as having only luck on his side in the western theater and having only the advantage of vast numbers and unlimited resources in the eastern theater. The Southern journalist and Lost Cause historian Edward A. Pollard's cruel but widely quoted assessment of Grant as "one of the most remarkable accidents of the war . . . a man without any marked ability, certainly without genius, without fortune, without influence" has retained its force over decades of Civil War historiography.[44]

Much of Grant's negative image boiled down to the meaning assigned to the Union's numerical superiority. According to this view, a less talented general who has more soldiers can beat a more talented general who has fewer soldiers. Yet many historians have demonstrated the military advantage in holding the interior lines during the Civil War.[45] This advantage, used adeptly by Lee against a series of bumbling Union generals, made his small army more than equal to a larger one. Grant's genius was the opposite of Lee's. His great test came in successfully directing several armies comprised of almost a million soldiers over great swaths of the country. Grant struggled to make that point in many venues. It disturbed and distressed him to think that future citizens would downplay or forget about the hardships of the Union army (and of course his role) in winning the conflict. To some extent, his worst fears have been realized. Today, the revolutionary, progressive impact of the Union's victory is often downplayed, brushed aside, or ignored, especially in light of Reconstruction's failures. Perhaps that stance is appropriate for skeptical times. Grant and the generation of Americans who lived through the Civil War did not, as a rule, embrace either skepticism or moral relativism. That is what made the stakes so high and so meaningful in controlling the historical memory of the war for future generations.

To that end, Grant cultivated a special relationship, during and after his presidency, with Union veterans. A powerful interest group whose influence extended widely and deeply into the country's political, social, and economic sectors, the veterans who joined organizations such as the Grand Army of the Republic were the bulwark of the Republican Party for many years.[46] A review of President Grant's calendar and correspondence for just one year, 1873, provides compelling evidence of the enormous investment of time, energy, and passion on his part to keep the Union cause before the citizenry and before the judgment of history.[47] Although he accepted many fewer invitations than he received, Grant made frequent appearances at veterans' reunions and other commemorative occasions, striking a balance between the Union's eastern and western wings. On February 6, "the Great Commander" attended a meeting in Wilmington, Delaware; May 15 found him at an Army of the Potomac reunion in New Haven, Connecticut; on September 17 the veterans of the Army of the Cumberland enjoyed their former top general's presence at an event in Pittsburgh; while on October 15–16 Grant joined the two-day reunion of the Army of the Tennessee in Toledo, Ohio. He enjoyed being with "his old comrades in arms," declaring the meetings as being "attended . . . with a revival of old associations and sympathies, formed in such trying times."[48]

As president, Grant cemented his special relationship with veterans when he officially sanctioned a new holiday commemorating the deaths of Union soldiers. On May 21, 1873, Grant issued an order closing the govern-

{ JOAN WAUGH }

ment "in order to enable the employees of the Government to participate, in connection with the Grand Army of the Republic, in the decoration of the graves of the soldiers who fell during the rebellion." Grant did more than attend celebrations and support Decoration Day. He also answered innumerable letters from veterans asking for government pensions for injuries or losses. Grant also reviewed manuscripts and weighed in on some of the numerous controversies about the war.[49]

During his years as president Grant did not respond personally to criticisms of his military leadership. He did defend his reputation indirectly and by doing so influenced the writing of civil war history. As one historian commented wryly: "Grant's apparent indifference to what was said about him masked reality."[50] He lent his prestige, his oral recollections, and his collection of wartime materials to reporters and partisans who wrote important defenses of his generalship. The first significant volume to appear was that of Adam Badeau in 1868. Badeau, Grant's military secretary during the last year of the war, was in part responding to Edward A. Pollard's *The Lost Cause* and William Swinton's *Campaigns of the Army of the Potomac*, both published in 1866. Swinton, a Northern journalist banned by Grant during the war, agreed with Pollard and Jubal Early that Lee in the 1864 Overland campaign, although vastly outnumbered by the Union army, managed to outgeneral the blundering Grant. Then, instead of a certain and relatively painless victory, Lee forced the Union commander to settle for a costly siege at Petersburg. Not surprisingly, Swinton's work was highly praised by the Southern press and also by those in Northern circles unfriendly to Grant.

Badeau's book (eventually the three-volume *Military History of Ulysses S. Grant*, 1868–82), however, was bitterly denounced by that same Southern press, who was outraged by Badeau's claim (which was Grant's) that pro-Confederate historians inflated Union troop numbers while minimizing their own. Badeau's first volume in particular was the object of controversy in Northern newspapers allied with the Democratic Party, always hostile to Grant. One such attack claimed: "It is in everything but name the carefully prepared memoir of Grant, by himself." Calling the history a "panegyric and special pleading," the reviewer commented: "For his own good name and fame it is to be lamented that he did not put the task in more competent hands."[51] This unfriendly review provided evidence that Grant was almost as controversial within some parts of Northern society as he appeared to be in the South.[52] Nevertheless, he was most definitely the guiding force behind Badeau's history, and he expressed satisfaction that

Badeau had rebutted Swinton effectively and had put down the circle led by Early.

Other Grant partisans who wrote admiring accounts of his wartime achievements were Horace Porter and John Russell Young, a reporter for the *New York Herald*. Young accompanied the former president and his wife, Julia, on their two-year (1877–79) world journey. Grant gave Young a series of remarkable interviews in which he offered candid and controversial reflections on the art of war, Union and Confederate generals, other Civil War leaders, and important battles, particularly Shiloh. Young's recounting of the general's "conversations," published in the *Herald*, (and later in a book, *Around the World with General Grant*) were reviewed carefully by Grant.

Many of Grant's pronouncements caused controversy and discussion back home, including his thoughts about Lee's generalship. Grant's analysis printed in Young's interviews formed the basis for his evaluation of Lee found in the *Personal Memoirs*.[53] His assessment of Lee was harsh: "Lee was a good man, a fair commander, who had everything in his favor. He was a man who needed sunshine. He was supported by the unanimous voice of the South; he was supported by a large party in the North, he had the support and sympathy of the outside world . . . [and he] was treated like a demi-god."[54] Moreover, Grant rejected the Lost Cause claim that the two sides fought for equally honorable causes. Although Grant lauded the courage of Southern soldiers, he attacked the idea that only they were brave: "When I look for brave, noble characters in the war, men whom death has surrounded with romance, I see them in characters like McPherson, and not alone in Southern armies." He was also distressed by attacks on his character and military abilities and, by extension, on the typical Northern citizen soldier. "While I would do nothing to revive unhappy memories in the South," Grant declared, "I do not like to see our soldiers apologize for the war."[55]

Quite obviously, there was sharp contention over which version of history was "truthful." For Grant, as for others who wrote about the war in the two and a half decades immediately following 1865, there were "facts," which were verifiable, quantifiable, recoverable, objective, and rational. Grant sought the most accurate and up-to-date factual information with which to make his case. These facts could be retrieved from memory, conversations, written reports, letters, maps, telegrams, and diaries. Facts were supposedly objective and formed the narrative of history. There was

{ JOAN WAUGH }

also a "truth." Truth was derived from facts but not dependent upon them. Truth was subjective and morally based. Truth had a higher meaning. Truth was based in the facts but ultimately not answerable to them. Today, professional historians call truth "interpretation."[56]

That Grant read, digested, and was displeased with so many published accounts of the war was evident in his comment that they "only show how often history is warped and mischief made." Such writers "study out dispatches, and reach conclusions which appear sound . . . but which are unsound in this, that they know only the dispatches, and nothing of the conversation and other incidents that might have a material effect upon the truth." Grant concluded, "Wars produce many stories of fiction, some of which are told until they are believed to be true."[57]

:::

Official Records of the War of the Rebellion

Grant's comment was made at a time when more and more material with which to evaluate the war was being published. A monumental decision in favor of making the history of the war permanently accessible was handed down by the federal government in 1864. The goal was to publish the complete records (battle reports, telegraph messages, and so on) of all armies. The story of the funding, the debates over the records' location, and the intense editorial politics surrounding the publication of the 128-volume *Official Records of the War of the Rebellion* (*OR*) is almost as fascinating as the war itself. The editors of the *OR* selected materials to be published it deemed "significant, official, and produced during the war."[58]

A vast amount of paperwork was collected. The Civil War was the first conflict in which so many records were written and were required to be copied, recopied, and stored. Veterans and their organizations—who, along with military historians, were considered to be the buying public for the *OR*—supported the project with enthusiasm. By 1877 47 volumes were completed, and the first one was published in 1881. Needless to say, veterans were not the only ones to have befitted from the *OR*, as generations of professional historians have used it as an indispensable reference.

Equally momentous was the decision by the War Records Office to make this project as nonpartisan and as nonpolitical as possible. This dedication was present even before the project had officially begun. General Henry Halleck ordered Confederate records retrieved from the burning ruins of

Richmond, declaring them to be important to the conflict's history. Grant lent his strong support to the effort in an 1865 letter to Edwin Stanton: "If it is desirable to have all rebel documents Captured in Richmond and elsewhere in the South examined and notes made of their contents for convenient reference I would respectfully recommend Brig. Gn. Alvord . . . for the duty."[59] Throughout the 1870s and 1880s, over fifty tons of materials were stored in various buildings in the Washington, D.C., area.

From the beginning, then, the OR set a high professional standard of evenhandedness in the war's portrayal. Every effort was made to locate and include Confederate military records and publish them alongside the more voluminous Union records. The War Records Office hired former Union and Confederate officers as editors. Government officials formed a liaison with former Confederate brigadier general Marcus J. Wright, who scoured the South for hidden records. This liaison led to an agreement between the *Southern Historical Society Papers* and the War Records Office for "reciprocal free access" to each other's Confederate documents. Generally, the OR volumes were praised in the journal's pages.[60]

The influential publishing project's emphasis on fairness to both sides was echoed in the larger society's desire for reconciliation. As the extreme bitterness of the war years receded, another interpretation, or "truth," about the Civil War emerged. It took the least controversial elements from both perspectives in an effort to bolster an official national ideology upon which a majority of citizens could agree. This interpretation, rising in popularity by the 1880s, can be described as promoting "sectional harmony." Increasingly, the idea that slavery caused the war and that the Union army became a revolutionary instrument in bringing freedom to millions of slaves became an embarrassment to the South and therefore an impediment to reconciliation. As such, the African American presence before, during, and after the war was deemphasized.[61]

This denatured ideology encouraged a professional and nonpartisan style when writing the war's history. The emphasis on reconciliation was supported by important elements of the Northern and Southern press and public and to a more limited extent by veterans, especially in the Blue and Gray reunions that were regularly held on anniversaries of important battles. This less divisive explanation of the great conflict portrayed the two sides as equally honorable. Both sides fought for noble causes, and happily, for whites' sake, the still controversial issues of slavery and emancipation were rarely mentioned.

{ JOAN WAUGH }

The Century Series

The popular press both inspired and reflected reconciliation sentiment. Scribner's profited greatly with its well-received *Campaigns of the Civil War*. Then, in 1884, the first issue of the *Century Magazine*'s serial *Battles and Leaders of the Civil War* appeared. In the series the war's leading officers published their accounts of important battles. Conceived in the early 1880s, the series was run by editors Robert Underwood Johnson and Clarence Clough Buel, who explicitly demanded neutral contributions from their authors. Johnson later described the series thusly: "On the whole 'Battle and Leaders of the Civil War' is a monument to American bravery, persistence and resourcefulness, and has the additional distinction of having struck the keynote of national unity through tolerance and the promotion of good will. We rightly judged that articles celebrating the skill and valor of both sides would hasten the elimination of sectional prejudices and contribute toward reuniting the country by the cultivation of mutual respect."[62]

Although not every contributor held to these guidelines, most did, and the series was a smashing success if judged by the quality of the contributions and the extraordinary rise in subscriptions for the magazine. The publication of the series coincided with Grant's need to earn money for his family. A famous collaboration was born as Grant agreed to write four articles for the series, which ensured prestige and profits for the magazine.

: : :

Ulysses S. Grant, Historian

Grant had actually initially refused the editors' entreaties to be a participant, but early in the summer of 1884, broke from the failure of his last business enterprise, he agreed to write four accounts of major battles for $500 (later raised to $1,000). His first submission, "The Battle of Shiloh," was stilted and formal. Johnson disliked it immensely and begged Grant to adopt a more casual, entertaining style. Grant quickly rewrote the article to everyone's satisfaction. Its immediate success brought forth an offer from Johnson and the Century Publishing Company for an exclusive book from the general. But by this time several publishing firms were bidding for Grant's complete memoirs.

The same day that Grant learned he was ill with cancer, October 22, 1884, he verbally accepted the *Century* contract that provided him with 10 percent royalties on an expected subscription sale of twenty-five thousand sets. Mark Twain and his nephew and business partner, Charles Webster, counteroffered in December with a $50,000 advance and, to sweeten the deal, 70 percent of the profits. Grant could not refuse those terms, and he signed their contract on February 27, 1885, just five months before his death. Well before the contract was signed, however, Grant was working hard on his manuscript, which was going to be divided into two volumes (volume 1: birth to Vicksburg; volume 2: Chattanooga campaign to Appomattox).

Grant's work methods are well documented. With pen in hand and later through dictation, Grant provided the narrative structure of the books. Elsie Porter, daughter of Horace Porter, recorded that her father and Adam Badeau met with Grant daily in the summer of 1884. She vividly recalled Grant writing with his pencil "racing over his pad."[63] He usually worked from a table—in the kitchen or on the pleasant piazza overlooking the sea at his summer home in Long Branch, New Jersey, where he wrote the *Century* articles. Later, in the Grants' New York City brownstone, his writing table was set in a small room at the head of the stairs.

In Grant's final days in the cottage at Mount McGregor, when he was too weak to sit at a proper desk, a specially constructed lap table was made available to him. In all these places, Grant's surrounding "office" space was crammed with his maps, his primary materials, and his books. A friend and former Union general James Grant Wilson noted the obsessive nature of Grant's writing: "His mind was absorbed with the one subject of his military autobiography and a desire to be accurate in the most minute particulars. . . . In all matters aside from his book Grant took but a slight and passing interest."[64]

Grant's written or transcribed draft would then be passed along to his staff. Grant had a small group of researchers and assistants to help him revise, edit, check facts, correct dates, and procure other needed papers. "What part are you reading up and verifying?" he asked his son, Frederick Dent Grant, who was his principal assistant.[65] Other staff at various times included Adam Badeau; Horace Porter; Fred's wife, Ida Grant; Grant's two other sons, Ulysses Jr. and Jesse Grant; Harrison Tyrell, his personal valet; Nathan E. Dawson, his stenographer; and his two principal doctors, John H. Douglas and Henry M. Shrady. Mark Twain also played an important role in facilitating the publication of both volumes. In mid-March Twain

{ JOAN WAUGH }

checked the manuscript's progress almost daily, and by mid-April he was correcting the galley proofs for grammatical and other errors.[66]

Chronology is critical in understanding the evolution of the *Personal Memoirs*. From September 1884 to March 1885 Grant was able to work in a fairly productive and calm manner. The first volume was almost entirely handwritten by Grant before the worst of his illness set in and is generally considered to be superior to the second volume, which was largely dictated or written after he had lost his voice and was suffering from intense pain. The period from late March to his death in July was punctuated with constant medical crises, during which he was temporarily incapacitated. Indeed, the dosages of cocaine and morphine given by Grant's doctors often prevented him from working with a clear head. Drs. Douglas and Shrady demonstrated a great sensitivity toward Grant's desire to finish his work. They both expressed amazement at his dedication. Douglas recalled a typical consultation during which they "found the General engaged in writing. As we entered he raised his hand and said, 'I shall reach a period in a moment.' . . . After the consultation, he resumed his literary work, and I learned, at my evening visit, that he had worked in all four or five hours."[67] The two doctors, along with members of Grant's close circle (especially Fred and Harrison Tyrell), are to be credited with providing the controlled and supportive environment that allowed the desperately ill general to complete his memoirs.[68]

During this time Grant wrote, or directed Fred to write, letters to pertinent individuals seeking information about precise dates, movements, and details of various battles. He wrote to the war department as well, asking for specific maps or documents, which the department was only too happy to send to him. Clearly, writing his memoirs had become the major and only pleasurable activity during his illness, and as William McFeely observed, "The book was now his life."[69]

In April 1885 Grant headed off a potentially disastrous threat to the sales and reception of his history. Adam Badeau, his military biographer and hired assistant, became unhappy at his increasingly marginalized status within the Grant household. Badeau was a professional writer who rightly considered himself the expert on Grant's military career. He was contemptuous of the idea of Grant writing his memoirs and was bitterly at odds with Fred, who replaced Badeau as Grant's chief assistant. Badeau was worried that the publication of Grant's books would cut into his own books' profitability. Badeau told Grant that publication would damage "my reputation as your historian."[70] He demanded a renegotiation of his contract, which Grant refused. His unhappiness found its way into a newspaper article printed in the *New York World* that implied strongly that Badeau, not Grant, was the author of the forthcoming memoirs. Hurt and angry, Grant immediately wrote a rejoinder in which he unequivocally stated that "the Composition is entirely my own."[71] Badeau was fired from the project, and bitter feelings between him and the Grant heirs continued for many years. For Grant, however, the painful issue was resolved with satisfaction, and with continued support and perseverance, he was able to complete his memoirs.

:::

The Personal Memoirs of U. S. Grant: *An Evaluation*

The *Personal Memoirs* can be said to offer many things to many people. Grant's volumes are a history of the Civil War, an unmatched military narrative of the conflict, a carefully constructed autobiography of a man, a commentary on American character and institutions, and an exegesis of the Union cause. They provide a comprehensive and rich story of the war between the United States and the Confederate States of America. Grant's memoirs are far superior to any others published by leading military officials of the Civil War, including the books written by William Tecumseh Sherman and Philip Sheridan. The volumes follow the war chronologically, providing analysis and background on specific battles, overall military strategy, portraits of people, and description of events.[72]

Grant portrayed himself as a representative character of the North, the victorious nation. His writing style is simple and clear, even conversational at times. In adopting this style, he consciously invited the reader to appreciate the good, solid, if unspectacular virtues of the typical Northerner living in a free labor society. Volume 1 opens with a brief account of his family history. Grant took pains to point out his simple and rustic background, his trusting nature, and his unmilitary bearing. His personal simplicity endeared him to his soldiers and he retained their loyalty to his death. The same simplicity is present in his writing style and is similarly endearing. Grant continued the tale of his early youth by remarking that he did not at all want to go to West Point, but did so only because his father, Jesse, "rather thought I would go." He did middling well at West Point and was uncertain if he would continue in the professional army at all. As he points out, "A military life had no charms for me."[73]

Although Grant distinguished himself in the Mexican War of 1846–48, he did not support that effort, declaring the war "one of the most unjust ever waged by a stronger against a weaker nation." Yet Grant devoted many pages to the conflict, and his account is vivid, descriptive, and analytical. Grant's hero was not the tall, aristocratic Winfield Scott. Grant admired Scott's abilities, but his true model was the plain, simple soldier and later president Zachary Taylor, who rejected the pomp and circumstance of military life.[74] Most important, Grant revealed that the lessons he learned in Mexico had a much greater impact on him than did his four years at the U.S. Military Academy. "My experience in the Mexican war," he wrote, "was of great advantage to me afterwards. Besides the many practical lessons it taught, the war brought nearly all the officers of the regular army together so as to make them personally acquainted. It also brought them into contact with volunteers, many of whom served in the war of the rebellion afterwards."[75]

Slavery, interwoven with Grant's discussions of the causes and consequences of the Civil War, is addressed throughout the memoirs. In one such discussion Grant traced the Southern states' desire to expand their slaveholding territory to the war against Mexico, ending with this observation: "The Southern rebellion was largely the outgrowth of the Mexican war. Nations, like individuals, are punished for their transgressions. We got our punishment in the most sanguinary and expensive war of modern times."[76] Grant presented an articulate overview of the events that led to the outbreak of war in 1861. His position reflected exactly the antislavery position of the 1850s Republican Party. To protect slavery, the foundation of its prosperity, the South had to control the national government. To protect free labor, the North was compelled to prevent the extension of slavery. Secession and the rebellion that followed were treasonous and had to be stopped. The subsequent detailed unfolding of Grant's wartime career provides his firsthand view of the inexorable march toward slavery's end, first as a military and political necessity and then as a moral imperative.[77]

There were other issues to contend with in the *Personal Memoirs*. As the leading Union general, Grant was influential and so was his portrayal (both facts and truth) of the war, but by no means was it universally accepted either by Northerners or by Southerners. During and after the war, his actions sparked controversy, and criticisms of Grant's generalship—particularly surrounding the battle of Shiloh in April 1862 and the Overland campaign in the spring of 1864—appeared in newspapers, articles, and books.[78] Indeed, Shiloh is a good example of facts versus truth as played out in the *Personal Memoirs*. For his critics two charges could be leveled against Grant at Shiloh. First, Grant was unprepared for the Confederate attack on the morning of April 6, 1862. Second, his failure to prepare the ground defensively resulted in a devastating defeat that was only staved off by the timely arrival of General Don Carlos Buell's division, and thus the credit for the victory should have gone to Buell, not Grant.

Grant wrote a strong rebuttal based on his evidence: he was not surprised by the attack; he himself was all over the field deploying "green" troops and preventing disaster; Buell's troops, while welcome, did not "save" the battle because the Confederates clearly were going to be defeated the following day anyway. His account did not sway those who were already convinced otherwise. Facts were disputed bitterly in histories of the battle, and oppositional points of view remained entrenched.[79]

Grant mitigated his criticism of another general, Lew Wallace, when new information on Wallace's role at Shiloh came to light.[80] Grant never, however, wavered in his larger truth about Shiloh. First, Shiloh was the making of the western armies. Second, Shiloh convinced him that the South would not give up, even after suffering a string of terrible defeats: "Up to the battle of Shiloh, I, as well as thousands of other citizens, believed that the rebellion against the Government would collapse suddenly and soon, if a decisive victory could be gained over any of its armies. . . . [After Shiloh] I gave up all idea of saving the Union except by complete conquest."[81] This interpretation was very important to Grant in advancing his larger argument within the memoirs about Union motives and strategy. The "hard hand of war," Grant argued, was brought about by Southern intransigence: "The Northern troops were never more cruel than the necessities of war required."[82]

Understandably, Grant explained and defended his actions (as he could not during the war itself) against newspaper charges and coverage that he considered shoddy, inaccurate, and defeatist. Indeed, Grant's sensitivity to reporters and the impact of the press demonstrated a keen appreciation for the political nature of the Civil War. He constantly drew attention to the "big picture," never allowing his readers to forget that battlefield fortunes were linked to the home front. His explanation of the battle of Vicksburg was typical: "The campaign of Vicksburg was suggested and developed by circumstances. The elections of 1862 had gone against the prosecution of the war. Voluntary enlistments had nearly ceased and the draft had been resorted to; this was resisted, and a defeat or backward movement would have made its execution impossible. A forward movement to a decisive victory was necessary." Commenting on Lincoln's chances of reelection in

{ JOAN WAUGH }

1864, he stated that Sherman and Sheridan's "two campaigns probably had more effect in settling the election of the following November than all the speeches, all the bonfires and all the parading with banners and bars of music in the North."[83]

There is an obvious connection in the *Personal Memoirs* between Grant's personal memories, the era's social or historical memory (the memory of millions in a generation who shared war experiences), his ability to turn those experiences into meaningful narratives, and history (written accounts purporting to be objective).[84] A caveat: what ostensibly was an "autobiography" was not an intimate and personal revelation. Many embarrassments were left out. One can search in vain, for example, for any reference to his struggle with alcohol or his famous General Order 11 (December 1862) barring Jews from his command.

Grant used his memoirs to reflect on the motives and the behavior of his fellow officers and in doing so provided fascinating sketches of the many men with whom he served. One such man is Major General Gouverneur K. Warren, hero of Gettysburg and commander of the V Corps. Sheridan had relieved Warren of his command just before the battle of Five Forks in March 1865 with Grant's approval. Warren was personally humiliated and spent twenty of his postwar years trying to correct what he, and many others, felt was a gross injustice to his career.

Grant defended his and Sheridan's decision in the pages of his memoirs. He provided a close analysis of Warren's leadership flaws that led to his dismissal. "He was a man of fine intelligence, great earnestness, quick perception, and could make his dispositions as quickly as any officer, under difficulties where he was forced to act," Grant surmised. "But I had before discovered," Grant continued, "a defect which was beyond his control, that was very prejudicial to his usefulness in emergencies like the one just before us. He could see every danger at a glance before he had encountered it. He would not only make preparations to meet the danger which might occur, but he would inform his commanding officer what others should do while he was executing his move." Grant's was a harsh judgment. Although an honorable and talented officer, Warren could not be trusted to finish the job, and as Grant put it, "his removal was necessary to success." Warren was simply not capable of corps command: "I was very sorry that it had been done, and regretted still more that I had not long before taken occasion to assign him to another field of duty."[85] In portraying Warren's weaknesses Grant had summarized his own philosophy of leadership in the Civil War.

The *Personal Memoirs* ultimately failed to provide an evenhanded history, as much more attention was given to the western theater of the war than to the eastern theater. No time was spent on his two troubled terms as president, although his observations on the effect of Lincoln's assassination were trenchant and timely. Grant also did not leave any record of his thoughts on Reconstruction policy, although a hint came in the last chapter: "The story of the legislation enacted during the reconstruction period . . . is too fresh in the minds of the people to be told now."[86]

:::

Conclusion

The Personal Memoirs of U. S. Grant presented the moral, political, economic, and social argument for waging war against the rebellious states and touted the benefits of slavery's destruction for the Southern people. Yet, more often than not, Grant's *Memoirs* are also celebrated for the theme of reconciliation. In a often-quoted passage Grant commented: "I feel that we are on the eve of a new era, when there is to be great harmony between the Federal and the Confederate. I cannot stay to be a living witness to the correctness of this prophecy; but I feel it within me that it is to be so."[87] Embedded within the style and substance of Grant's *Memoirs* is a contradiction that was also played out in his public actions. On the one hand, Grant was the magnanimous victor of Appomattox who said, "The war is over. The rebels are our countrymen again."[88] The thrust of the war was reunion. On the other hand, Grant was the head of the Union army responsible for smashing the institution of slavery and bringing a revolution in race relations. There is no doubt that Grant deeply hoped for a permanent and genuine restoration of "great harmony" between North and South. But what exactly did he mean by expressing that desire? Did he mean that sectional peace (which all agreed was a good thing) should deliberately elide a still widely accepted belief among Northerners in 1885 that it was the Union, and not the Confederate cause, that was noble? Do the *Personal Memoirs* reflect this sentiment?

In his memoirs, Grant sought to bring back what he perceived was the reality of those causes, even as he promoted reconciliation—but on Northern terms. True enough, the *Personal Memoirs*, which was "dedicated to the American soldier and sailor," contained much about Civil War battles. The work noticeably highlighted the courage and valor of the soldiers on both sides. But by describing what happened on those battlefields, Grant

{ JOAN WAUGH }

tellingly emphasized that citizens can learn about the history of a nation, a nation that was forged anew at Appomattox with Union victory.

Thus, readers of *The Personal Memoirs of U. S. Grant* will note Grant's contempt for the Southern cause of slavery and for the general so associated with that cause, Robert E. Lee. He explained why the "complete conquest" was necessary to destroy slavery, save the Union, and restore harmony. The victor, not the vanquished, Grant claimed, should dictate the terms to end the war and should define the conditions for the reestablishment of peace and harmony within the Union. Grant's memoirs offered readers a stark and ugly depiction of a Southern society mired in backwardness and deeply tainted by slavery. The thrust of his history emphasized the best qualities of Northern free democratic society, deflecting serious criticism. He concluded that the modern war waged by the United States benefited, and would continue to benefit, the former Confederate nation: "The war begot a spirit of independence and enterprise."[89] Indeed, through his frequent tributes to Northern character and civilization Grant not only highlighted the superiority of wartime Union strength and resources but also asserted the ideological superiority of Northern free labor over Southern slave labor.

The essence of the *Personal Memoirs* went beyond a definition of autobiography, "the writing of one's own history."[90] The eminent military scholar John Keegan commented that Grant had provided "an enthralling history of one man's generalship, perhaps the most revelatory autobiography of high command to exist in any language." Grant's volumes were a deliberately triumphal narrative of the Civil War written from the viewpoint of the man most closely identified with bringing about Northern victory. But the individual merged with the event and the era, leading Keegan to conclude rightly: "If there is a single contemporary document which explains 'why the North won the Civil War' it is *The Personal Memoirs of U. S. Grant*."[91]

NOTES

1. Ulysses S. Grant, *The Personal Memoirs of U. S. Grant*, ed. Mary Drake McFeely and William S. McFeely (New York: Library of America, 1984), 169 (hereafter *PMUSG*). This edition combines both volumes of the original edition into one book.

2. Bruce Catton, "U. S. Grant: Man of Letters," *American Heritage* 19 (June 1968): 97–100.

3. U. S. Grant to Julia Dent Grant, July 8, 1885, box 2, series 10, Family Correspondence, Papers of Ulysses S. Grant, Manuscripts Division, Library of Congress, Washington, D.C.

4. My account of Grant's writing his memoirs is based partly on the following: Adam Badeau, *Grant in Peace: From Appomattox to Mount McGregor, a Personal Memoir* (Hartford: S. S. Scranton, 1887); Adam Badeau, "The Last Days of General Grant," *Century Magazine* 30 (October 1885): 919–39; Richard Goldhurst, *Many Are the Hearts: The Agony and Triumph of Ulysses S. Grant* (New York: Thomas Y. Crowell, 1975); William S. McFeely, *Grant: A Biography* (New York: W. W. Norton, 1982); *PMUSG*, 1162–70; Thomas Pitkin, *The Captain Departs: Ulysses S. Grant's Last Campaign* (Carbondale: Southern Illinois University Press, 1973).

5. *The American Heritage Dictionary of the English Language*, ed. William Morris (Boston: Houghton Mifflin, 1969). Autobiography as a genre is considered in the following: Joyce Appleby, *Inheriting the Revolution* (Cambridge, Mass.: Harvard University Press, 2000); Robert Folkenflick, ed., *The Culture of Autobiography: Constructions of Self-Representation* (Stanford: Stanford University Press, 1993); Jacquelyn Dowd Hall, " 'You Must Remember This': Autobiography as Social Critique," *Journal of American History* 85 (September 1998): 439–65; Charles Taylor, *Sources of the Self: The Making of Modern Identity* (Cambridge, Mass.: Harvard University Press, 1989).

6. *PMUSG*, 773.

7. Ibid., 779.

8. Frederick Douglass, "U. S. Grant and the Colored People: His Wise, Just, Practical, and Effective Friendship," speech given on July 17, 1872, in Washington, D.C., UCLA Special Collections, Westwood, Calif.

9. Grant quoted in Catton, "U. S. Grant: Man of Letters," 98.

10. Daniel Aaron, *The Unwritten War: American Writers and the Civil War* (1973; reprint, Madison: University of Wisconsin Press, 1987); James M. McPherson and William J. Cooper Jr., eds., *Writing the Civil War* (Columbia: University of South Carolina Press, 1998).

11. Edward E. Henry, Fremont, Ohio, Twenty-third Regiment Ohio Volunteers, to U. S. Grant, June 22, 1885, box 15, series 10, Family Correspondence, Papers of Ulysses S. Grant.

12. Mark Twain, "Rejoinder," in Matthew Arnold, *"General Grant" by Matthew Arnold, with a Rejoinder by Mark Twain*, ed. John Y. Simon (Kent, Ohio: Kent State University Press, 1995), 57. Twain was not only an admirer of Grant but also an investor in Charles L. Webster and Company and profited from the sales of the *Memoirs*.

13. Thomas W. Higginson, "Grant," *Atlantic Monthly* 57 (March 1886): 384–88 (quote on 384).

14. A small selection of favorable reviews are as follows: ibid.; "Grant's Memoirs: Second Volume," *Atlantic Monthly* 57 (September 1886): 419–24; *Harper's New Monthly Magazine* 72 (March 1886): 649–50; "Grant's Memoirs," *Nation* 42 (February 25, 1886): 172–74.

15. There were plenty of dissenters. Perhaps a few former Confederates bought the

Personal Memoirs as a gesture of goodwill toward the magnanimous victor at Appomattox. More of them probably agreed with the dismissive review given by the influential organ of the former Confederate officers, the *Southern Historical Society Papers*. That review described the *Personal Memoirs* as "a book full of blunders and flat contradictions of the official reports (both Federal and Confederate), and the future historian who attempts to follow it will be led very far astray from the real truth." "Book Notice," *Southern Historical Society Papers* 14 (1886): 574–76 (quote on 575).

16. Bruce Chadwick, *The Reel Civil War: Mythmaking in American Film* (New York: Alfred A. Knopf, 2001), and Jim Cullen, *The Civil War in Popular Culture: A Reusable Past* (Washington, D.C.: Smithsonian Institution Press, 1995), are two of the best books that include discussions of the impact of *Gone with the Wind* and the Lost Cause on American culture.

17. John Y. Simon, *Ulysses S. Grant: One Hundred Years Later*, Illinois State Historical Society Reprint Series, no. 1 (Springfield: Illinois State Historical Society, 1986), 245–56 (quote on 255).

18. The *Personal Memoirs* have never gone out of print. For discussion of the volumes' importance, see Edmund Wilson, *Patriotic Gore* (New York: Oxford University Press, 1962), 133; Bruce Catton, "Two Porches, Two Parades," *American Heritage* 19 (June 1968): 99; John Keegan, *The Mask of Command* (London: Jonathan Cape, 1987); and McFeely, *Grant*. Three contemporary recent editions of the *Memoirs* include *PMUSG*; *Personal Memoirs*, with an introduction and notes by James M. McPherson (New York: Penguin Books, 1999); and *Personal Memoirs of U. S. Grant*, with an introduction by Brooks D. Simpson (Lincoln: University of Nebraska Press, 1996).

19. Robert Underwood Johnson, *Remembered Yesterdays* (Boston: Little, Brown, 1923), 193.

20. This noteworthy relationship is chronicled in the Elihu Washburne Papers, Manuscripts Division, Library of Congress. See also Ulysses S. Grant, *General Grant's Letters to a Friend, 1861–1880*, ed. James Grant Wilson (New York: T. Y. Crowell, 1893). Grant's relationship with journalists is the topic of Harry J. Maihafer, *The General and the Journalists* (New York: Brassey's, 1998), and Sylvanus Cadwallader, *Three Years with Grant*, ed. Benjamin P. Thomas (1955; reprint, Lincoln: University of Nebraska Press, 1996).

21. Ulysses S. Grant, *The Papers of Ulysses S. Grant*, ed. John Y. Simon, 21 vols. (Carbondale: Southern Illinois University Press, 1967–), 9:196 (hereafter *PUSG*). For insightful discussion of Grant's relationship with Lincoln, see Gabor S. Boritt, ed., *Lincoln's Generals* (New York: Oxford University Press, 1994), and Joseph T. Glatthaar, *Partners in Command: The Relationships between Leaders in the Civil War* (New York: Free Press, 1994). Grant's stance on black soldiers is explored in Brooks D. Simpson, "Quandaries of Command: Ulysses Grant and Black Soldiers," in *Union and Emancipation*, ed. David W. Blight and Brooks D. Simpson (Kent, Ohio: Kent State University Press, 1997), 123–50.

22. Horace Porter, *Campaigning with Grant* (New York: Century, 1897), 7.

23. Meade's staff member quoted in Keegan, *Mask of Command*, 200. For a superb discussion of Grant's writing style from his battlefield reports to his memoirs, see James M. McPherson, *Drawn with the Sword: Reflections on the American Civil War* (New York: Oxford University Press, 1996), 159–73.

24. *PUSG*, 9:436–37, 10:422, 12:334.

25. Ulysses S. Grant, General Order 108, in *PUSG*, 15:120–21.

26. Porter, *Campaigning with Grant*, 514.

27. Ulysses S. Grant, "Report of Lieutenant-General U. S. Grant, of the United States Armies—1864-'65," in *PMUSG*, 781–848 (quotes on 781–82).

28. *PMUSG*, 781.

29. Ibid., 794.

30. Ibid., 783.

31. Ibid., 847–48.

32. John Russell Young, *Around the World with General Grant: A Narrative of the Visit of General U. S. Grant, Ex-President of the United States, to Various Countries in Europe, Asia, and Africa, in 1877, 1878, 1879*, 2 vols. (New York: American News, 1897), 2:459.

33. *PUSG*, 18:292.

34. *PUSG*, 24:61–62.

35. Grant, *General Grant's Letters to a Friend*, 103. By far the best analysis of Grant's career from 1865 to 1868 is Brooks D. Simpson, *Let Us Have Peace: Ulysses S. Grant and the Politics of War and Reconstruction, 1861–1868* (Chapel Hill: University of North Carolina Press, 1991). Two outstanding biographies on Grant have been published recently: Brooks D. Simpson, *Ulysses S. Grant: Triumph over Adversity, 1822–1865* (Boston: Houghton Mifflin, 2000), and Jean Edward Smith, *Grant* (New York: Simon and Schuster, 2001).

36. Two thoughtful and enlightening discussions of the controversies over Grant's generalship can be found in William A. Blair, "Grant's Second Civil War: The Battle for Historical Memory," in *The Spotsylvania Campaign*, ed. Gary W. Gallagher (Chapel Hill: University of North Carolina Press, 1998), 223–53, and Brooks D. Simpson, "Continuous Hammering and Mere Attrition: Lost Cause Critics and the Military Reputation of Ulysses S. Grant," in *The Myth of the Lost Cause and Civil War History*, ed. Gary W. Gallagher and Alan T. Nolan (Bloomington: Indiana University Press, 2000), 147–69.

37. Lee quoted in Emory M. Thomas, *Robert E. Lee: A Biography* (New York: W. W. Norton, 1995), 367.

38. Early's postwar career is analyzed in Gary W. Gallagher, "Jubal A. Early, the Lost Cause, and Civil War History: A Persistent Legacy," in *Myth of the Lost Cause*, 35–59.

39. Young, *Around the World with General Grant*, 2:459.

40. Arnold, *"General Grant,"* 11–12. Books on the Lost Cause include Thomas

{ JOAN WAUGH }

Connelly, *The Marble Man: Robert E. Lee and His Image in American Society* (New York: Alfred A. Knopf, 1977), and Gaines M. Foster, *Ghosts of the Confederacy: Defeat, the Lost Cause, and the Emergence of the New South, 1865 to 1913* (New York: Oxford University Press, 1987).

41. General Dabney H. Maury, "Grant as a Soldier and Civilian," *Southern Historical Society Papers* 5–6 (1878).

42. Young, *Around the World with General Grant*, 1:360.

43. For an effective rebuttal to the common assumptions about Lee, see Gary W. Gallagher, "An Old-Fashioned Soldier in a Modern War?: Robert E. Lee as a Confederate General," *Civil War History* 5–6 (December 1999): 295–312.

44. Pollard quoted in Simpson, "Continuous Hammering," 149. Two key published works that set a standard for the denigration of Grant's reputation are Jubal A. Early, "The Relative Strengths of the Armies of Generals Lee and Grant," *Southern Historical Society Papers* 2 (July 1876): 6–21, and Edward A. Pollard, *The Lost Cause* (New York: E. B. Treat, 1866). William McFeely disparages Grant's military ability in his acclaimed biography *Grant*, as does Ernest B. Furgurson in *Not War but Murder: Cold Harbor, 1864* (New York: Alfred A. Knopf, 2000).

45. Classic works portraying Grant in a highly favorable light are J. F. C. Fuller, *The Generalship of Ulysses S. Grant* (London: J. Murray, 1929); Bruce Catton, *Grant Moves South* (Boston: Little, Brown, 1960); and Bruce Catton, *Grant Takes Command* (Boston: Little, Brown, 1968).

46. Stuart McConnell, *Glorious Contentment: The Grand Army of the Republic, 1865–1900* (Chapel Hill: University of North Carolina Press, 1992), and Mary R. Dearing, *Veterans in Politics: The Story of the G.A.R.* (Baton Rouge: Louisiana State University Press, 1952), are the two classic works on Northern veterans.

47. The meetings are recorded in the calendar of *PUSG*, 24:xxi–xxii.

48. *PUSG*, 23:289.

49. For example, Grant read a portion of Adam Badeau's volume 2 on Grant's campaigns. See *PUSG*, 24:166–70; see also correspondence regarding the war actions of General David Hunter in ibid., 24:221.

50. Simon, *Ulysses S. Grant*, 253; see also James G. Barber and John Simon, *U. S. Grant: The Man and the Image* (Washington, D.C., and Carbondale: National Portrait Gallery and Southern Illinois University Press, 1985).

51. "HFK," *Philadelphia Times*, August 5, 1881. Early histories of the war provoking controversy include Adam Badeau, *Military History of Ulysses S. Grant*, 3 vols. (New York: D. Appleton, 1868–82); William Swinton, *Campaigns of the Army of the Potomac: A Critical History of Operations in Virginia, Maryland, and Pennsylvania from the Commencement to the Close of the War, 1861–65* (1866; new ed., New York: University Publishing, 1871); and Pollard, *Lost Cause*. Grant discusses Swinton in *PMUSG*, 486–88.

52. General William S. Rosecrans, dismissed by Grant after his loss to Confederate forces at Chickamauga, was an especially eloquent enemy of his former commanding

general. One example is his article "The Mistakes of Grant," *North American Review* 140 (December 1885): 580–99.

53. Young, *Around the World with General Grant*; Badeau, *Military History*. See also a fine new abridged edition: John Russell Young, *Around the World with General Grant*, ed. Michael Fellman (Baltimore: Johns Hopkins University Press, 2002).

54. Young, *Around the World with General Grant*, 2:459.

55. Ibid., 2:445.

56. For a thoughtful discussion of the modern historical profession, see Joyce Appleby, Lynn Hunt, and Margaret Jacob, *Telling the Truth about History* (New York: W. W. Norton, 1994).

57. Young, *Around the World with General Grant*, 2:293; *PMUSG*, 732.

58. Alan C. Aimone and Barbara A. Aimone, *A User's Guide to the Official Records of the American Civil War* (Shippensburg, Pa.: White Mane, 1993), 8.

59. Ulysses S. Grant to Edwin Stanton, May 29, 1865, in *PUSG*, 16:106.

60. One reviewer noted approvingly that *OR* volumes are "fair in the treatment of Confederate as well as Federal reports and documents." He advised the government, however, to drop the hated word "Rebellion" from the title. "Book Notice," *Southern Historical Society Papers* 11 (November 1883): 575–76.

61. For explication of the "whitewashing" of civil war memory, commemoration, and history, see David W. Blight, *Race and Reunion: The Civil War in American Memory* (Cambridge, Mass.: Belknap Press of Harvard University Press, 2001).

62. Johnson, *Remembered Yesterdays*, 208. See also Stephen Davis, "A Matter of Sensational Interest: The Century 'Battles and Leaders' Series," *Civil War History* 27 (4 December 1981): 338–49.

63. Elsie Porter Mende and Henry Greenleaf Pearson, *An American Soldier and Diplomat: Horace Porter* (New York: Frederick A. Stokes, 1927), 141.

64. James Grant Wilson, *General Grant* (New York: D. Appleton, 1897), 354.

65. Ulysses S. Grant to Frederick Dent Grant, undated in an envelope marked "Small messages written by U. S. Grant Gen'l and president to his son F. D. Grant, during last illness, July 1885," box 1, series 10, Family Correspondence, Papers of Ulysses S. Grant. Many letters in this collection document Grant's work in writing his *Memoirs*.

66. Albert Bigelow Paine, *Mark Twain, a Biography: The Personal and Literary Life of Samuel Langhorne Clemens*, 3 vols. (New York: Harper and Brothers, 1912), remains the best source for documenting Twain's professional and personal relationship with Grant.

67. John Douglas, June 3, 1885, "Journal," John H. Douglas Collection, Library of Congress; Horace Green, *General Grant's Last Stand: A Biography* (New York: Century, 1936); George T. Shrady, *General Grant's Last Days* (New York: DeVinne Press, 1908).

68. For an interesting discussion of the impact of Grant's bout with cancer on American society, see James T. Patterson, *The Dread Disease: Cancer and Modern American Culture* (Cambridge, Mass.: Harvard University Press, 1987), 1–11.

69. McFeely, *Grant*, 515.

70. Badeau quoted in Catton, "U. S. Grant," 98.

71. Grant quoted in ibid.

72. In addition to the works already cited, three others have helped me understand the full impact of Grant's writing: Henry M. W. Russell, "The Memoirs of Ulysses S. Grant: The Rhetoric of Judgment," *Virginia Quarterly Review* 66 (Spring 1990): 209; Elizabeth D. Samet, " 'Adding to My Book and to My Coffin': The Unconditional Memoirs of Ulysses S. Grant," December 29, 1999, paper in author's possession; and Michael W. Schaefer, *Just What War Is: The Civil War Writings of De Forest and Bierce* (Knoxville: University of Tennessee Press, 1997).

73. *PMUSG*, 29, 31.

74. Ibid., 41; Grant compared the styles of the two generals in ibid., 94–95.

75. Ibid., 129.

76. Ibid., 42.

77. Ibid., 142–51. Grant's conclusion also offers a lengthy explication of slavery as a cause of the war.

78. Controversies in the Overland campaign are well covered most recently by Blair, "Grant's Second Civil War," and Simpson, "Continuous Hammering." For Grant and the battle of Shiloh, see Simpson, *Ulysses S. Grant*, 119–46.

79. Ulysses S. Grant, "The Battle of Shiloh," in *Battles and Leaders of the Civil War*, ed. Robert Underwood Johnson and Clarence Clough Buel, 4 vols. (New York: Century, 1887–88), 1:465–87; Don Carlos Buell, "Shiloh Revisted," in *Battles and Leaders of the Civil War*, 1:487–536. An excellent overview of the battle and the controversies can be found in Jay Luvaas, Stephen Bownman, and Leonard Fullenkamp, *Guide to the Battle of Shiloh* (Lawrence: University Press of Kansas, 1996).

80. *PMUSG*, 236. There are many examples of Grant reconsidering his stance when presented with new information. See, for example, *PUSG*, 17:327–40; *General Ulysses S. Grant's Unpublished Correspondence in the Case of Fitz-John Porter* (New York: Martin B. Brown, 1884), and Kevin Donovan, "The Court-Martial of Fitz-John Porter," *Columbiad* 2 (Winter 1999): 73–97.

81. *PMUSG*, 246.

82. Young, *Around the World with General Grant*, 2:307.

83. *PMUSG*, 386, 511.

84. For a useful discussion of this literature, see Earl J. Hess, *The Union Soldier in Battle: Enduring the Ordeal of Combat* (Lawrence: University Press of Kansas, 1997). Outstanding examples of books that examine the memory of the war are Blight, *Race and Reunion*; Gary W. Gallagher, *Lee and His Generals in War and Memory* (Baton

Rouge: Louisiana State University Press, 1998); and McConnell, *Glorious Contentment.*

85. *PMUSG*, 701–2.

86. Ibid., 761.

87. Ibid., 779.

88. Grant quoted in Badeau, *Military History*, 3:608.

89. Ibid., 779.

90. *The Compact Edition of the Oxford English Dictionary*, vol. 1 (New York: Oxford University Press, 1971).

91. Keegan, *Mask of Command*, 202, 459.

Gary W. Gallagher

Shaping Public Memory of the Civil War
Robert E. Lee, Jubal A. Early,
and Douglas Southall Freeman

The former Confederate general Jubal A. Early and the historian Douglas Southall Freeman heavily influenced the way in which Americans have understood the Confederacy and the Civil War. Ardent Virginians and admirers of Robert E. Lee, Early and Freeman had much to do with creating the ironic situation in which the Rebel commander—rather than Ulysses S. Grant, William Tecumseh Sherman, or some other Union war hero—stands alongside Abraham Lincoln as one of the two most prominent figures of the conflict. Thomas L. Connelly, Alan T. Nolan, and other scholars have assessed Early's and Freeman's impact on the literature and on popular perceptions. These historians typically have functioned as rather harsh critics of the two Virginians, insisting that they exaggerated Lee's prowess and wartime reputation, overstated the importance of his operations within the Confederate war effort, and placed too much emphasis on Northern numbers as a factor in Union victory. In effect, runs a common argument, the work of Early and other Lost Cause writers, extended and strengthened by Freeman's scholarly publications in the 1930s and 1940s, self-consciously created an inaccurate version of the Confederacy's history and an explanation for its defeat that gained wide acceptance following the conflict and unfortunately has remained remarkably durable.[1]

These historians raise a number of important questions. Was Lee's heroic image a postwar creation? Did Early and Freeman exaggerate Lee's military influence? Did Northern human and material resources play the major role in defeating the Confederacy? And, finally, why do Early's and Freeman's principal interpretive points still have force? Any attempt to answer these questions leads to more important ones: Is it possible that arguments put forward to manage the memory of the Confederacy's war might be rooted in fact? If so, how can that be acknowledged without giving the appearance of also accepting the romance and apology characteristic of the larger Lost Cause interpretive tradition that cloaked the Confederacy in constitutional principle and denied the centrality of slavery to secession and the war? This essay cannot pretend to offer definitive answers to all these questions but it can, perhaps, point the way toward a reconsideration of some Lost Cause claims.

Robert E. Lee played a major role in shaping postwar perceptions of the Confederate experience. This aspect of his career, which contradicts the popular image of a conciliatory statesman who harbored little animosity toward the North and sought only to get beyond the war, has received less recognition than it deserves. In *Ghosts of the Confederacy: Defeat, the Lost Cause, and the Emergence of the New South, 1865 to 1913*, for example, Gaines M. Foster accords brief attention to this topic, observing that after Lee's death "several of the more ardent and unreconciled Confederate historians had good reason to believe they were following the lead of their commander." In fact, Lee worked hard to have his views placed on the public record. He explicitly and repeatedly stated that greater numbers explained the North's triumph, insisting that white Southerners should attempt to educate the world about Confederate valor and steadfastness. Lee's postwar comments mirrored his official and private correspondence during the conflict. His most famous wartime expression of this sentiment resides in General Order 9, dated April 10, 1865. Written by his staff officer Charles Marshall following a conversation during which Lee's "feelings towards his men were strongly expressed," this order pointed directly to Northern manpower and matériel as the crucial factors in requiring Confederate surrender: "After four years of arduous service, marked by unsurpassed courage and fortitude, the Army of Northern Virginia has been compelled to yield to overwhelming numbers and resources."[2]

In letters to Jubal Early and other former lieutenants shortly after the war, Lee stressed Northern numbers and the need to get the Confederate version of the war into print. The question of relative strengths occupied much of Lee's attention, but he also believed Northern commanders and their soldiers had destroyed civilian property wantonly and otherwise had subjected noncombatants to unnecessary suffering. He planned to write a history of the Army of Northern Virginia that would address what he considered salient features of the conflict, a task complicated by the loss of many official papers during his chaotic retreat from Richmond to Appomattox. He asked Early for information about various battles and campaigns, including "statistics as regards numbers, destruction of private property by the Federal troops, &c." Lee hoped to demonstrate the disparity in strength between the two sides, predicting that it would "be difficult to get the world to understand the odds against which we fought." "My only object," he stated in language that anticipated Early's and Freeman's later writings, "is to transmit, if possible, the truth to posterity, and do justice to our brave Soldiers." Lee himself stood ready to suffer criticism from Northerners. "The accusations against myself I have not thought proper to notice, or even to correct misrepresentations of my words & acts," he told Early. "We shall have to be patient, & suffer for awhile at least. . . . At present the public mind is not prepared to receive the truth." Lee assured another of his old subordinates that he had no thought of personal vindication in writing the army's history: "I want that the world shall know what my poor boys, with their small numbers and scant resources, succeeded in accomplishing."[3]

Such comments about Northern numbers and resources should not be interpreted to mean that Lee viewed the war as hopeless from the outset. Like Jefferson Davis and other civilian and military leaders, he understood that the weaker side had prevailed in conflicts such as the American Revolution. Union manpower and material bounty chastened him, but he believed the Confederacy could win the war by marshaling its men and matériel effectively, winning battles that would depress Union morale, and persuading the North that it would cost too much in lives and treasure to force the seceded states back into the Union. In the end, however, the Union's will proved sufficient. Lincoln and Grant provided exemplary leadership, and U.S. armies won victories at critical points (most especially following periods of deep Northern pessimism in the spring of 1863 and late summer 1864). The North found leaders who applied their greater resources to excellent effect, and Lee pronounced those resources a decisive factor in the war.[4]

Few men admired Lee more than Jubal Early, who throughout the war exhibited unquestioning devotion to his commander. Lee's letters to Early in 1865 and 1866 helped inspire the latter's dogged effort to create a published record that could convince future generations that Lee and his army deserved the highest praise. Early's *Memoir of the Last Year of the War for Independence in the Confederate States of America*, which appeared in 1866, emphasized points Lee had raised in his letters, highlighting the North's advantage in numbers and detailing Union depredations in the Shenandoah Valley in 1864. Early also may have interpreted Lee's comments about "accusations" and "misrepresentations" as a veiled invitation to defend his old chief against critics. Dismayed by what he considered unfair attacks on Lee, Early decided to persuade the public "to receive the truth," to use Lee's words, about the Confederate commander and his campaigns. In speeches, articles, letters to editors, and a huge correspondence with other former Confederates who were writing about the war, Early concentrated on a few crucial themes: Lee had been a general of unparalleled brilliance whose army carried the hopes of the Confederacy on its bayonets; Stonewall Jackson (whom Lee had called "my right [arm]" and "this great and good soldier")[5] stood just behind Lee in the Southern pantheon; Lee oversaw military operations that held at bay enormously more powerful Union forces, until finally, at the head of a much diminished army, he capitulated to Grant's well-supplied host at Appomattox; despite defeat, Lee and Jackson offered an ideal of Christian military leadership in which the white South could take continuing pride.

In late 1870, Early pursued the topic of manpower in reaction to Adam Badeau's assertion that Union forces had not enjoyed a significant advantage in numbers during the 1864 Overland campaign. A member of Grant's staff during the war, Badeau had published his argument in the *London Standard*, concluding that at the battle of the Wilderness "Lee had about 72,000 engaged, while Grant had 98,000 present for duty." Early's response, offered as a letter to the editor of the *Standard* and later reprinted in the *Southern Historical Society Papers*, insisted that Grant had commanded 141,000 soldiers to Lee's 50,000 and raised the specter of former Federal officers mounting "a persistent and systematic effort to falsify the truth of history." Early suggested an unflattering explanation for Badeau's figures: "That officers of Grant's army, after witnessing the terrible havoc made in their ranks by the small force opposed to them at the Wilderness, at Spotsylvania C[ourt] H[ouse], and at Cold Harbor, should over estimate the strength of that force, is not to be wondered at." Neither Early's nor Badeau's arithmetic was correct. Grant commanded roughly 120,000 troops and Lee 65,000 when their armies first came to grips on May 5, 1864.[6] Yet Early's basic argument, when stripped of hyperbole and anti-Northern rhetoric, is difficult to refute. Lee and the Army of Northern Virginia had faced intimidating odds during the 1864 campaign in Virginia.[7]

Early's famous address on the anniversary of Lee's birth in 1872 developed a cluster of durable Lost Cause themes. This speech portrayed Lee as without equal among history's noted captains. "It is a vain work for us to seek anywhere for a parallel to the great character which has won our admiration and love," stated Early. "Our beloved Chief stands, like some

*Jubal Anderson Early in 1869, the year before his exchange with Adam Badeau
about U.S. and Confederate strength during the campaign between Grant and
Lee. (Courtesy of Library of Congress)*

lofty column which rears its head among the highest, in grandeur, simple, pure and sublime, needing no borrowed lustre; and he is all our own." The Army of Northern Virginia had fought gallantly, insisted Early, before being "gradually worn down by the combined agencies of numbers, steam-power, railroads, mechanism, and all the resources of physical science." Northern might "had finally produced that exhaustion of our army and resources, and that accumulation of numbers on the other side, which wrought the final disaster." Despite defeat, white Southerners could look with pride to Lee and Jackson, "illustrious men, and congenial Christian heroes." "When asked for our vindication," affirmed Early, "we can triumphantly point to the graves of Lee and Jackson and look the world square in the face." Early closed by charging his audience with a "sacred trust" of "cherishing the memory of our leaders and our fallen comrades."[8]

Early's message of Confederate pluck and valor, as well as his direct assaults on Union writings about the war, struck a receptive chord among defeated white Southerners. One Mississippian looked to Ireland for a comparative example. "It was the dying wish of Young Emmet, the Irish patriot and martyr, that his epitaph should not be written until his country was free," remarked James F. Trotter in 1866. "The illfated patriot of our own land, General Early, has expressed nearly the same sentiment. . . . After correcting many gross errors in the official reports of the United States Officers, [he] begs that an impartial world may suspend any fixed judgment of our late struggle and its conflict until the time shall come for placing a true history before them." Like Early, Trotter alluded to Northern power and celebrated the Southern resistance, explaining that Confederates "laid down our arms when we could use them no longer and submitted to our destiny. . . . We have won true glory, for our struggle for liberty has no parallel in the history of the world."[9]

A determined and able controversialist, Early exerted enormous influence over Confederate historiography in the late nineteenth century. Many of Lee's old soldiers (as well as some who had served in other Southern armies) sent their manuscripts to him for approval before publication. Robert Stiles, a former artillerist in the Army of Northern Virginia who published his own reminiscences after Early's death, remarked that as "long as 'the old hero' lived, no man ever took up his pen to write a line about the great conflict without the fear of Jubal Early before his eyes." Early became widely accepted in the postwar South as the leading authority on Lee's army and its campaigns, and upon his death numerous newspapers and camps of the United Confederate Veterans lauded his accomplishments as what one set of the group's resolutions termed "a forceful and truthful writer of history." Among modern historians, Thomas L. Connelly has commented most strongly about Early's impact. Describing him as "the driving force behind the first Lee cult," Connelly characterized Early as "perhaps the most influential figure in nineteenth-century Civil War writing, North or South."[10]

Within twenty-five years after the surrender at Appomattox, Early and other Lost Cause warriors had managed to train the historical focus on Lee and his army rather than on Jefferson Davis and the Confederacy's political history. They helped create an interpretive framework within which military elements of the Confederate war would receive far more attention than any nonmilitary dimension. This proved immensely useful in presenting the white South's wartime experience in the best possible light. Far more attractive personally than Jefferson Davis, Lee could be examined within a martial setting largely free of the blighting influence of slavery. Lee's brilliance as a soldier, the undeniable odds he faced, and the totality of his eventual defeat invited sympathetic treatment of a type impossible with either the secessionists, whose ringing calls for a slaveholding republic in 1860–61 were problematical in a postemancipation era, or with the often messy political and social history of the Confederacy.

Douglas Southall Freeman shaped literature about the Confederacy and public understanding of Lee in the 1930s and 1940s much as Early had in the late nineteenth century. The longtime editor of the *Richmond News Leader* and holder of a Ph.D. in history from Johns Hopkins University (he received his degree in 1908 at the age of twenty-two), Freeman spent much of his boyhood in Lynchburg, Virginia, while Early lived in the city. The young Freeman absorbed Confederate lore from his father, a veteran of Lee's army who was named national commander-in-chief of the United Confederate Veterans in 1925. As a seventeen-year-old in 1903, Freeman experienced an epiphany while watching a reenactment of the battle of the Crater. The sight of twenty-five hundred veterans engaged in mock combat at Petersburg, he later explained, inspired him to determine "to preserve from immolating time some of the heroic figures of the Confederacy." Four years after his experience at the Crater, on the centennial of Lee's birth, Freeman expressed his feelings about the general to his mother: "Surely if there is an ideal in the Old South, it is Lee, he stands for all that was best and brightest there." Eighteen years later in a letter that revealed undiminished admiration for Lee, Freeman spoke of his hopes for the children of a woman who had corresponded with him: "May they grow up to cherish the

Douglas Southall Freeman at Westbourne, his home in Richmond. Volumes of R. E. Lee: A Biography *and* Lee's Lieutenants: A Study in Command *are among the books to his left. (Courtesy of Mary Tyler Freeman McClenhan)*

ideals of Lee! After those of the Saviour Himself, I know of none that are loftier."[11] Publication of his multivolume works *R. E. Lee: A Biography* and *Lee's Lieutenants: A Study in Command*, in 1934–35 and 1942–44, respectively, not only enabled Freeman to make good on his youthful resolution to honor Lee's soldiers but also thrust him into Early's old role as Lee's greatest champion.

Freeman's books reinforced themes that had been central to Lee and Early. Although his work rested on impressive research and took a far more detached approach than Early's speeches and writings had, it is easy to imagine that Freeman, laboring on his massive projects, had in mind Lee's expressed hope to "transmit, if possible, the truth to posterity, and do justice to our brave Soldiers." Numbers and resources stood at the center of Freeman's explanation for Confederate defeat in *R. E. Lee*: "Always the odds had been against him, three to two in this campaign, two to one in that. Not once, in a major engagement, had he met the Federals on even terms; not once, after a victory, had his army been strong enough to follow it up. . . . From the moment he undertook to mobilize Virginia until the last volley rolled across the red hills of Appomattox, there had been no single day when he had enjoyed an advantage he had not won with the blood of men he could not replace." Freeman concluded that "with poverty he faced abundance," and abundance won out. Unlike Early, Freeman admitted that "Lee himself had made mistakes"; however, those mistakes counted for little when arrayed against the general's accomplishments. "In the evils he prevented, as surely as in his positive military achievements," wrote Freeman, "when seen through the eyes of his subordinates as certainly as when one looks at him across the table in his tent, he is a great soldier and a great man. Twenty years' study of him confirms and deepens every conviction of that."[12]

Freeman seconded Early in placing Stonewall Jackson and the common soldiers who fought in the Army of Northern Virginia near Lee in a Confederate roll of honor. "The greatness of the Army was in its supreme command and in its infantry," Freeman noted. Of all the officers who fought in the eastern theater, "only two, Lee, the captain of the host, and his right arm, Jackson, are to be added to those of one's acquaintances, living or dead, real persons or the creation of literature, by whom one's own personal philosophy of life is shaped beyond understanding."[13]

Freeman's books won him a reputation as an unmatched interpreter of Confederate history. The *New York Times Book Review* offered representative praise for *R. E. Lee*. "You rise from the completed work," asserted the reviewer, "with the conviction that here is Lee's monument. . . . Dr. Freeman has left nothing for any after-sculptor to carve." T. Harry Williams, himself an immensely influential historian of the Civil War, observed in 1955 that "long before his life had ended, Douglas Freeman had become a name and a legend. To him was accorded the rare honor of being accepted, while still alive, as a great historian, as *the* authority in his field and of having his works acclaimed as classics that would endure permanently." Not long after Williams published his comments, Frank E. Vandiver, another major Civil War scholar, pondered "the question of Freeman's place in Civil War history," arguing that "he breathed new life into military and Civil War history, gave them popular as well as academic respectability, and lifted American biography to the level of literature."[14]

Passage of more than four decades since Williams and Vandiver wrote their assessments has done little to diminish Freeman's reputation. He remains the most widely known figure in the field of Confederate military history. Indeed, historians writing books about Lee or the Army of Northern Virginia often include something in their prefaces or introductions similar to what Emory M. Thomas wrote in *Robert E. Lee: A Biography*. "Freeman's four-volume study won a Pulitzer Prize in 1934 and has been 'the definitive Lee' ever since," stated Thomas in 1995. "For a long, long time Lee, essentially Freeman's 'Lee,' has been an American hero. This same Lee has been the patron saint of the American South."[15]

Treatment of Freeman's work in a trio of bibliographies published over a thirty-year span suggests the durability of his reputation. In 1969, Robert W. Johannsen—who rightly appreciated that Freeman was far more even-handed than recent critics would allow but scarcely could be termed a Lost Cause devotee—described *R. E. Lee* as a "classic example of the biographical form; exhaustively researched, vividly written, balanced, judicious and definitive in its portrayal of the Confederacy's greatest soldier." A decade later, Richard Barksdale Harwell, whose sympathies clearly did lie with the South, labeled *R. E. Lee* "a masterpiece of biography and of military history," adding that *Lee's Lieutenants* "stands in its own right as one of the great works of military history." In 1997, David J. Eicher's *Civil War in Books: An Analytical Bibliography* lauded both titles. Acknowledging Freeman's open admiration of Lee and his soldiers, Eicher nevertheless termed *R. E. Lee* a "classic work, characterized by brilliant writing" that is "a necessary part of any Confederate bookshelf." He similarly described *Lee's Lieutenants* as "a masterpiece of Confederate history" that deserves "to be read by all Civil War students."[16]

{ GARY W. GALLAGHER }

This evidence of Freeman's continuing influence brings me back to the question of how best to deal with many ideas he and Jubal Early put forward. Understandably reluctant to embrace a Lost Cause tradition that includes romantic and self-serving arguments, a number of historians have mounted a major critique of Early's and Freeman's works. Lost Cause interpretations, suggest these scholars, were formulated after Appomattox with the intention of placing Lee and the Confederates in the best possible light and continue to carry undeserved weight in Civil War literature.[17]

Several historians have questioned Early's and Freeman's portrayal of Lee (with Jackson playing the role of his strong right arm) as a supremely gifted soldier who towered above all others in the Confederate high command during the war. Although conceding that Lee possessed considerable military gifts, these scholars have suggested that postwar propagandizing by Jubal Early and a group of like-minded Virginians, rather than wartime accomplishment, accounts for much of the general's current reputation. Thomas L. Connelly and Barbara L. Bellows stated flatly that "Robert E. Lee's reputation as the invincible Confederate general was a postwar phenomenon." During the conflict, wrote Connelly elsewhere, the Confederate people would have lumped Lee together with Albert Sidney Johnston, Joseph E. Johnston, P. G. T. Beauregard, Stonewall Jackson, and others as commanders of approximately the same importance: "Not until the 1880s would Lee be regarded as the South's invincible general, the embodiment of the Confederate cause." William Garrett Piston, a student of Connelly, followed his mentor in arguing that "when he died on October 12, 1870, Lee was only one of a large number of Confederate heroes and was still second to Stonewall Jackson in the eyes of most Virginians." Carol Reardon's recent study of the image of Pickett's Charge in American history implicitly concurs with this view, alluding to Virginians who "directed postwar efforts to recast Robert E. Lee as the Confederacy's greatest hero." David W. Blight's work on Frederick Douglass and Civil War memory also weighed in on the question of Lee's reputation. Unreconstructed Lost Cause writers, stated Blight, most especially "the prototypical unreconstructed rebel" Early, "made Robert E. Lee into a romantic icon" as part of their larger effort to create a pro-Confederate version of the sectional crisis and the war.[18]

No scholar detected more flaws in Early's and Freeman's portraits of Lee than Alan T. Nolan. In *Lee Considered: General Robert E. Lee and Civil War History*, Nolan described what he termed "the manufactured 'history' of the Civil War that began to take form shortly after the fighting ceased" and grew out of "the combination of the war's actual contradictions and traumas and the postwar social rationalizations of the participants." From this process arose a "legend" that substituted "romance in place of realism" and engendered "radical distortions of critical facts." "Exalted himself," insisted Nolan, "Lee is also a visible sign of the elevation of the Lost Cause. The literature on Lee is symbolic of the South's postwar victory and the folk history of the war." Directing some of his sharpest criticism toward Freeman's *R. E. Lee*, Nolan labeled it the "paradigm of the historical treatment of Lee and his times," a "wholly adulatory account . . . setting forth every favorable fact and appealing story that could be reported and rationalizing any act that might be questioned." Selecting a classical allusion for his concluding sentence (and overlooking that Homeric heroes almost always possess major flaws), Nolan wrote that "Robert E. Lee is the Odysseus of an American *Odyssey*; but that *Odyssey*, like Homer's, is myth and legend, not history."[19]

The question of Northern manpower and material strength, which loomed so large in Lee's, Early's, and Freeman's thinking, also figures in several more recent studies. Gaines M. Foster contended that Early and his Virginia allies remain important because "their speeches and articles did help establish points that would be accepted by later veterans' movements and become part of the Confederate tradition." One of those points, chosen from an array of possible explanations, was that the South "succumbed only to overwhelming numbers and resources." David W. Blight also attributed to Early and other "die-hard" former Confederates a numbers-based strategy to deflect criticism from their war effort: "The Confederacy . . . was never defeated; rather, it was overwhelmed by numbers and betrayed by certain generals at pivotal battles (namely James Longstreet at Gettysburg)." A recent article on the Southern Historical Society supports Foster and Blight. "Lost Cause advocates held that the Confederacy had been overwhelmed by superior northern resources," noted Richard D. Starnes. The society's published *Papers*, over which Jubal Early exerted considerable editorial control, ran a series of pieces in 1876 designed to highlight the relative paucity of Southern resources and clinch a key Lost Cause argument; namely, that "brave southerners fought with great élan, ability, and success, considering the South's much smaller industrial base and its much smaller population."[20]

This scholarship offers a clear alternative to the interpretation of the Confederate war effort that Lee, Early, and Freeman hoped would prevail.

It has been useful in illuminating excesses on Early's and Freeman's parts, in demonstrating that a number of former Confederates worked hard to get their version of the war into the historical record as soon as possible, and in underscoring the influence of Freeman's published work.[21] Indeed, in the six decades between Early's first writings and publication of Freeman's massive biography, Lee had assumed a position so elevated as to cry out for revision. Any poll of lay readers almost certainly would have ranked him far ahead of Ulysses S. Grant as the greatest soldier of the Civil War—and perhaps ahead of all other generals in U.S. history. Moreover, Lee had been pictured as an opponent of slavery whose purity of motives raised him above most of his peers, when in fact he owned a few slaves and held quite conventional views about slavery for one of his time, class, and place. The explicit separation of Lee, who reasonably could be described as the central figure in Confederate history, from the institution of slavery proved invaluable to anyone seeking to offer a flattering assessment of the Southern experiment in nation building. By pursuing a "great man" version of history, Lost Cause warriors played to their strengths and neatly avoided a number of potential pitfalls. The revisionists performed a necessary service in forcing readers to reevaluate Lee's life and Confederate career.

Having said that, I will add that the revisionist scholarship suffers from its own flaws. Most obviously, it fails to acknowledge the degree to which much of what Lee, Early, and Freeman argued was grounded in wartime fact and accepted by participants on both sides during the conflict and in the half decade immediately after Appomattox—that is, before the Lost Cause literature began to appear in significant bulk.

I will make my final points as succinctly as possible, buttressing each with representative supporting evidence. First, critics of Early's and Freeman's portraits of Lee tend to misrepresent the general's stature during the war. This phenomenon arose in large measure from an understandable effort to combat some of the more extreme claims by Early especially. In Early's discussion of Confederate history, all other political and military figures except Stonewall Jackson seem to be little more than bit players. Yet in efforts to credit other leaders with their just position, a number of historians have misinterpreted Lee's relative importance. By the summer of 1863 at the latest, Lee was the most important Southern military figure, and he and the Army of Northern Virginia had become the principal national rallying point of the Confederate people. Moreover, his stature, along with that of his army, grew as the last two years of the war unfolded. The idea that Early and fellow Lost Cause warriors somehow plucked Lee out of a group of wartime peers and made him preeminent, and that Freeman perpetuated and embellished their cunning work, is simply wrong.[22]

Abundant wartime testimony leaves no doubt about Lee's commanding stature in the Confederacy. Four examples will suffice to make this point. A Georgia officer summoned Washington's name in a perceptive evaluation of the relationship between Lee and his soldiers. "General Robt. E. Lee is regarded by his army as nearest approaching the character of the great & good Washington than any man living," wrote Colonel Clement Anselm Evans during the difficult winter of 1864. "He is the only man living in whom they would unreservedly trust all power for the preservation of their independence." In a sentence at odds with the notion that Lee's image of perfection was a Lost Cause fabrication, Evans added, "General Lee has no enemies, and all his actions are so exalted that mirth at his expense is never known." Writing a few weeks after Evans, Lieutenant Colonel William Drayton Rutherford of the Third South Carolina described Lee's reviewing the First Corps. "Our venerable military father, Genl Lee, did us the compliment to come down and review us," began Rutherford, who described the event as "the most imposing pageant we have ever witnessed." Lee left the review amid "the shouts and tossing up of hats of the armed multitude. We all feel better after a sight of our grand chieftain. No one can excite their enthusiasm as he does. And no wonder, for such a noble face as he has, and such noble deeds as he has performed deserve admiration."[23]

The Macon, Georgia, *Christian Index* ran a sketch of Lee in July 1864 that understandably highlighted the general's well-known piety. "He is said to be never so busy that he cannot find time to study God's word, and offer earnest prayer for divine guidance and strength," averred this piece. "Gen. Lee (or 'Marse Robert,' as the boys familiarly call him,) is universally loved by the army. . . . Surely we should thank God for such a leader, while continued prayer ascends that he may be spared to the close of this conflict to reap the rich reward of his priceless services." In March 1865 a British visitor remarked about the degree to which Confederates invested their hopes in Lee: "*Genl R. E. Lee* . . . [is] the idol of his soldiers & the Hope of His country," wrote Thomas Conolly, a member of Parliament. "The prestige which surrounds his person & the almost fanatical belief in his judgement & capacity . . . is the one idea of an entire people."[24]

Many of Lee's opponents also elevated him to a special category among Rebel officers. For example, as late as March 24, 1865, with the Army of

Northern Virginia manifestly heading for defeat, veteran Northern soldier Wilbur Fisk cautioned that "we must bear in mind that we have not yet rendered it impossible for Gen. Lee to win another victory." Perhaps more tellingly, New Englander Stephen Minot Weld struggled to explain to his sister why he found it difficult to celebrate Lee's surrender at Appomattox. She had written several letters complaining of what he termed his "want of enthusiasm" about the climactic Union success. "To tell the truth, we none of us realize even yet that he has actually surrendered," admitted Colonel Weld. "I had a sort of impression that we should fight him all our lives. He was like a ghost to children, something that haunted us so long that we could not realize that he and his army were really out of existence to us. It will take me some months to be conscious of this fact."[25]

My second point concerns Northern human and material advantages as a principal cause of Confederate defeat. Far from being a postwar construction by Lost Cause warriors, allusions to Northern superiority in these categories abound in wartime Confederate writings, including Lee's. On January 10, 1863, for example, Lee wrote to the secretary of war about "the vast numbers that the enemy is now precipitating upon us." In the wake of Gettysburg, he betrayed deep concern in a letter to Jefferson Davis: "Though conscious that the enemy has been much shattered in the recent battle, I am aware that he can be easily reinforced, while no addition can be made to our numbers." Thirteen months later, with the armies locked in a grinding siege at Petersburg, Lee urged the secretary of war to do everything possible to reinforce the Army of Northern Virginia. "Without some increase of our strength," he warned, "I cannot see how we are to escape the natural military consequences of the enemy's numerical superiority."[26]

Lee understood that Union numbers would tell only if the Northern people remained willing to support the war. "Our resources in men are constantly diminishing," he wrote in June 1863, "and the disproportion in this respect between us and our enemies, if they continue united in their effort to subjugate us, is steadily augmenting." If anything, Jubal Early, who faced Union forces two-and-one-half or three times the size of his army in the 1864 Shenandoah Valley campaign, had an even stronger sense of how Northern numbers figured in military operations.[27]

Three women's accounts from 1865 suggest that civilians also blamed defeat on Northern material advantages. On the Georgia home front, Eliza Frances Andrews learned in late April of Lee's surrender and Joseph E. Johnston's armistice with William Tecumseh Sherman in North Carolina.

"It is all over with us now, and there is nothing to do but bow our heads in the dust and let the hateful conquerors trample us under their feet," she wrote in her diary. People no longer talked of "fighting to the last ditch; the last ditch has already been reached." Bitter toward England and France for remaining aloof and watching "a noble nation perish," Andrews explained the war's outcome in a single angry sentence: "We fought nobly and fell bravely, overwhelmed by numbers and resources, with never a hand held out to save us." The South Carolinian Harriet R. Palmer focused more specifically on Grant's numerical edge over Lee. "We know that Lee has surrendered," she recorded on May 3; he "had to evacuate Richmond and Petersburg and fought desperately but was outnumbered but not whipped. The Yankees brought nine columns against him. He repulsed eight with a terrible slaughter. Our loss was heavy, too. The ninth column broke through." Having affirmed Confederate resolve against massive odds, Palmer turned to the North's victorious general to clinch her point about numbers: "Grant behaved very nobly towards Gen Lee. Would not take his sword. Told him he was not whipped but was outnumbered." Catherine Ann Devereux Edmondston, a North Carolinian, echoed Palmer but without any flattering reference to Grant's nobility. "How can I write it? How find the words to tell what has befallen us?" she asked. "*Gen. Lee has surrendered*! Surrendered the remnant of his noble Army to an overwhelming horde of mercenary Yankee knaves & foreigners."[28]

Northerners understood their advantages as well. Abraham Lincoln's sense of frustration at the inability of larger Union armies to vanquish smaller Rebel opponents is well known. He worried about the Army of the Potomac's commander Joseph Hooker in this regard, as evidenced in his comments during a discussion with Hooker and General Darius Couch just before the Chancellorsville campaign. "I want to impress upon you two gentlemen," Lincoln told the officers, "in your next fight, put in all your men." The president clearly believed that proper application of Union resources would yield victory, and he watched with mounting frustration in 1862–63 as one after another of his commanders in the eastern theater failed to make effective use of available manpower.[29]

Other Northerners explained their triumph as a process of merely grinding down overmatched Rebels. Writing on the day of Appomattox, Colonel Charles S. Wainwright, a leading artillerist in the Army of the Potomac, implied that Lee and his army really never had been beaten. "The Army of Northern Virginia under Lee . . . today . . . has surrendered," observed Wainwright in language Early and other Lost Cause writers surely would have applauded. "During three long and hard-fought campaigns it has withstood every effort of the Army of the Potomac; now at the commencement of the fourth, it is obliged to succumb without even one great pitched battle. Could the war have been closed with such a battle as Gettysburg, it would have been more glorious for us; . . . As it is, the rebellion has been worn out rather than suppressed."[30]

Ulysses S. Grant also offered telling testimony on this point. In his final report on operations against the Confederacy, dated June 20, 1865, the Union hero inadvertently bolstered Southern arguments about the North's ultimate triumph. "The resources of the enemy, and his numerical strength, was far inferior to ours," stated Grant, although various factors, including the size of the Confederacy and daunting logistical obstacles, helped offset the Union's advantage. Grant's plan in 1864–65 sought to apply pressure across the strategic board, denying the Confederacy a chance to use its limited manpower most effectively. Grant determined "to use the greatest number of troops practicable against the Armed force of the enemy" and "to hammer continuously at the Armed force of the enemy, and his resources, until by mere attrition, if in no other way, there should be nothing left to him but an equal submission with the loyal section of our common country to the universal law of the land." Thus did Grant frame his orders during the last year of the conflict. How well the resultant campaigns achieved his ends would be for "the public, who have to mourn the loss of friends fallen in the execution, and to pay the pecuniary cost of all this, to say."[31] However the Northern people might choose to gauge Grant's performance, his report left little doubt that he believed manpower and resources had been indispensable to success.

How should Northern numbers and matériel figure in a consideration of the factors that underlay Confederate defeat? Any such reckoning must recognize the degree to which the war brought debilitating conflict to the Southern home front. Conscription, impressment, the tax-in-kind, and other such national measures fanned discontent and exacerbated class tensions. Increasing physical hardship also weakened some people's resolve. Thousands of soldiers deserted, and thousands of civilians behind the lines gave up on the Confederacy as the war dragged on (thousands of other white Southerners never had supported the Confederacy). Yet most Confederates remained quite resolute, at least until the autumn of 1864, in their determination to win independence. They capitulated only when large and well-supplied armies led by Grant, Sherman, and other Union commanders vanquished smaller and less-well-supplied Confederate armies and proved that they could move across the Southern interior virtually at will. Facing an enemy with seemingly endless reserves of well-supplied men commanded by talented officers determined to win, Confederates in and out of uniform grudgingly conceded the North's superiority and abandoned their hopes for independence.[32]

This brings me to the question of why some of Early's and Freeman's interpretations have retained vigor for so long. I believe a major factor is that Early and Freeman, as well as Lee on the question of Northern numerical and material advantages, built their arguments on solid foundations. All three men unquestionably hoped to place Lee, the soldiers in his army, and the Confederate nation in the best possible light. But Early and Freeman did not have to stray far beyond any reasonable definition of truth to portray Lee as a gifted general who was pivotal to Confederate hopes for victory; neither did they have to strain the evidence to show that Northern resources played a crucial—perhaps the crucial—role in defeating the Confederacy. I reiterate that this is not to suggest an inevitability of Union triumph—only to highlight superior numbers and matériel as part of an equation that included sound political and military leadership and continuing commitment on the part of the Northern populace.

Both Early and Freeman found a ready audience in the white South. Most former Confederates emerged from the war believing Lee had been an admirable and effective general who led brave troops in a gallant fight against long odds. They proved naturally receptive to Early's writings and speeches, and their descendants were equally quick to embrace Freeman's books.[33]

British readers similarly found the Lost Cause celebration of Lee attractive, as Matthew Arnold noted in his famous review of Grant's memoirs. "General Grant, the central figure of these *Memoirs*," remarked Arnold in his 1886 essay, "is not to the English imagination the hero of the American Civil War; the hero is Lee, and of Lee the *Memoirs* tell us little." Because Grant's *Personal Memoirs* focused on their author rather than on his Confederate antagonist, as well as because of Grant's corrupt presidential administration and failure to engage the British people's interest during a visit to England, explained Arnold, "the *Personal Memoirs* have in England been received with coldness and indifference."[34]

Perhaps more surprising is the degree to which many white Northerners during the war and its immediate aftermath expressed favorable interpretations of Lee, Jackson, and the men they commanded. During the fall of 1862, for example, the future Lord Acton noted that in Northern cities

"Stonewall Jackson is the national hero." Just after Jackson's death, the pro-Republican *Washington Daily Morning Chronicle*'s editor expressed relief at the removal of a major Rebel foe, but added that "every man who possesses the slightest particle of magnanimity must admire the qualities for which Stonewall Jackson was celebrated—his heroism, his bravery, his sublime devotion, his purity of character. He is not the first instance of a good man devoting himself to a bad cause." President Lincoln thanked the editor of the paper for the "excellent and manly article . . . on 'Stonewall Jackson.'"[35]

As for Lee and his soldiers, William Swinton's *Campaigns of the Army of the Potomac*, published in 1866, well before most Lost Cause authors had begun to write their works, suggests how generously some Northerners treated their former opponents. A wartime newspaper correspondent for the *New York Times*, Swinton praised the Army of Northern Virginia as "that incomparable infantry, . . . which for four years carried the Revolt on its bayonets, opposing a constant front to the mighty concentration of power brought against it." After a heroic struggle, wrote Swinton in a passage that doubtless would have elicited nods of approval from Lee, Early, and Freeman, "the army of Northern Virginia fell before the massive power of the North, yet what vitality had it shown! How terrible had been the struggle!"[36]

During the half decade after the war, Lee received considerable praise from many quarters in the North that prompted sharp comments from disapproving Northerners who saw him as a traitorous Rebel whose activities almost destroyed the Union. The day after Lee's death, George Templeton Strong commented about what he considered distasteful expressions of admiration for the former Confederate commander: "Died in Lexington, Virginia, the ex-Rebel General, Robert E. Lee, whom it is the fashion to laud and magnify as one of the greatest and best of men." Frederick Douglass opposed the Northern tendency to forgive former Confederates their sins and reacted more scathingly. "We can scarcely take up a newspaper," he complained, "that is not filled with *nauseating* flatteries of the late Robert E. Lee. . . . It would seem from this, that the soldier who kills the most men in battle, even in a bad cause, is the greatest Christian, and entitled to the highest place in heaven."[37]

Why so many Northerners in the 1860s chose to focus on Lee's and Jackson's piety and other attractive characteristics, as well as on the valor of the soldiers they commanded, perplexed and infuriated Frederick Douglass, as it certainly did many thousands of other Northerners.[38] For my purposes, it is enough to make the point that the attitudes so vexing to Douglass were formed before Early and the Lost Cause writers began to publish their work on the Confederacy. Like their white Southern counterparts, many Northerners obviously read the war and the roles of Lee and Jackson in a way that sustained much of what Early and Freeman would argue. They were not misled by crafty Lost Cause writers who had created a heroic, romantic set of arguments at odds with the facts.

Similarly, modern Americans interested in the Civil War can see that Early's and Freeman's interpretations make sense in many respects. Lee and his army were almost always outnumbered; Lee, with help from Jackson and others, forged a number of spectacular victories; and once Lincoln found Grant, a man who understood how to apply Northern resources, the Union's edge in men and matériel almost certainly would win the war if the Northern people remained committed to victory. In short, a major reason these elements of the myth of the Lost Cause continue to resonate is that they are not myths at all.

The idea that historians should take elements of the Lost Cause interpretation seriously is unsettling. It places us in the awkward position of having to concede some points to defenders of slavery and disunion. Such concessions might lead to confusion among students and lay readers about Lost Cause arguments that seek to recast the history of antebellum Southern society, secession, and the war without including slavery as a central factor. More ominously, it might provide fuel to those who find comfort in a vision of the Confederacy divorced from the ugly reality of the peculiar institution. Should we separate the various strands of the Lost Cause fabric in an effort to assess each individually? Or should we treat the whole as a dissembling effort by slaveholders, who had failed in their primary purpose to retain slavery, to salvage what they could by influencing the way in which future generations would define and comprehend the Confederacy?

Although the temptation to follow the latter course might be strong, I believe it is important to engage each part of the Lost Cause interpretation on its merits. Such an approach promises at least two positive results. First, it will yield a better understanding of a compelling example of how Americans have sought to create satisfactory public memories of major events. Second, and perhaps more important, a willingness to point out instances in which authors such as Early advanced arguments well supported by evidence will lend greater power to critiques of Lost Cause interpretations based on blatant twisting of the historical record. Such analysis will not give Lee, Early, and Freeman the last word about the Army of Northern Virginia and its operations, but it will help highlight the complexity of an important and fascinating dimension of the Civil War era.

NOTES

1. See Thomas L. Connelly, *The Marble Man: Robert E. Lee and His Image in American Society* (New York: Alfred A. Knopf, 1977); Thomas L. Connelly and Barbara L. Bellows, *God and General Longstreet: The Lost Cause and the Southern Mind* (Baton Rouge: Louisiana State University Press, 1982); Gaines M. Foster, *Ghosts of the Confederacy: Defeat, the Lost Cause, and the Emergence of the New South, 1865 to 1913* (New York: Oxford University Press, 1987); and Alan T. Nolan, *Lee Considered: General Robert E. Lee and Civil War History* (Chapel Hill: University of North Carolina Press, 1991).

2. Foster, *Ghosts of the Confederacy*, 51; Robert E. Lee, *The Wartime Papers of R. E. Lee*, ed. Clifford Dowdey and Louis H. Manarin (Boston: Little, Brown, 1961), 934; Charles Marshall, *An Aide-de-Camp of Lee: Being the Papers of Colonel Charles Marshall, Sometime Aide-de-Camp, Military Secretary, and Assistant Adjutant General on the Staff of Robert E. Lee, 1862–1865*, ed. Frederick Maurice (Boston: Little, Brown, 1927), 275–78. Marshall noted that he "made a draft [of General Order 9] in pencil and took it to General Lee who struck out a paragraph, which he said would tend to keep alive the feeling existing between the North and the South, and made one or two other changes" (278).

3. Robert E. Lee to Jubal Early, November 22, 1865, March 15, 1866, George H. and Katherine Davis Collection, Howard-Tilton Memorial Library, Tulane University, New Orleans; J. William Jones, *Personal Reminiscences, Anecdotes, and Letters of Gen. Robert E. Lee* (New York: D. Appleton, 1874), 180. On Lee's plans to write about the war in Virginia, see Allen W. Moger, "General Lee's Unwritten 'History of the Army of Northern Virginia,'" *Virginia Magazine of History and Biography* 71 (July 1963): 341–63.

4. For allusions to the American Revolution as an example for the Confederacy, see Robert E. Lee to Jefferson Davis, September 21, 1862, in U.S. War Department, *The War of the Rebellion: A Compilation of the Official Records of the Union and Confederate Armies*, 127 vols., index, and atlas (Washington, D.C.: GPO, 1880–1901), ser. 1, vol. 19, pt. 2, p. 143 (hereafter cited as *OR*; all references are to volumes in ser. 1); and Davis's speech at Mobile, Alabama, December 30, 1862, in Jefferson Davis, *The Papers of Jefferson Davis*, ed. Lynda Lasswell Crist et al., 11 vols. (Baton Rouge: Louisiana State University Press, 1971–), 8:587–89. For an argument that Lee believed defeat was inevitable, or at least highly likely, by the late summer of 1863, see Nolan, *Lee Considered*, chap. 6.

5. R. L. Dabney, *Life and Campaigns of Lieut.-Gen. Thomas J. Jackson (Stonewall Jackson)* (1866; reprint, Harrisonburg, Va.: Sprinkle, 1983), 717; Lee, *Wartime Papers*, 485. See also Jubal A. Early, *Memoir of the Last Year of the War for Independence in the Confederate States of America* (Toronto: Lovell and Gibson, 1866).

6. Badeau quoted in Jubal A. Early, *The Relative Strength of the Armies of Gen'ls Lee and Grant: Reply of Gen. Early to the Letter of Gen. Badeau to the London Standard* (n.p., [1870]), 1. In reprinting Early's piece in July 1876, the editor of the *Southern Historical Society Papers* termed the "relative strength of the Federal and Confederate armies . . . a matter of great importance. . . . Even our own people are in profound ignorance of the great odds against which we fought, while Northern writers have persistently misrepresented the facts." *Southern Historical Society Papers*, ed. J. William Jones et al., 52 vols. (1876–1959; reprint, with three-vol. index, Wilmington, N.C.: Broadfoot, 1990–92), 2:6–7. For the armies' strengths in early May 1864, see Gordon C. Rhea, *The Battle of the Wilderness: May 5–6, 1864* (Baton Rouge: Louisiana State University Press, 1994), 21, 34. On the exchange between Early and Badeau, see William A. Blair, "Grant's Second Civil War: The Battle for Historical Memory," in *The Spotsylvania Campaign*, ed. Gary W. Gallagher (Chapel Hill: University of North Carolina Press, 1998), 230–36.

7. Among other former Confederates who pursued the subject of numbers, Walter H. Taylor of Lee's staff stands out as particularly indefatigable. See especially his *Four Years with General Lee* (1877; reprint, Bloomington: Indiana University Press, 1962), 162–89. "Having for a long time supervised the preparation of the official returns of the Army of Northern Virginia, and having been permitted to make a recent examination of a number of those returns, now on file in the archive-office of the War Department at Washington," wrote Taylor in his preface, "I am enabled to speak with confidence of the numerical strength of the Confederate forces; my information concerning that of the Federal forces is derived from official documents emanating from the officers and authorities of the United States Government." Although Taylor's figures for the Army of Northern Virginia generally fell below the totals now accepted by scholars, he easily demonstrated that Lee frequently had fought at a striking numerical disadvantage. "Startling to some as the disparity in numbers between the two armies on certain occasions may appear," he observed in vintage Lost Cause language, "it is nevertheless established upon incontrovertible evidence, and makes pardonable the emotions of pride with which the soldier of the Army of Northern Virginia points to the achievements of that incomparable body of soldiery, under its peerless and immortal leader" (188). Grant also wrote about relative strengths, seeking in his memoirs and elsewhere to refute the idea that Lee had fought at a huge disadvantage. See Blair, "Grant's Second Civil War," 223–54.

8. Jubal A. Early, *The Campaigns of Gen. Robert E. Lee: An Address by Lieut. General Jubal A. Early, before Washington and Lee University, January 19th, 1872* (Baltimore: John Murphy, 1872), 45, 40, 44, 46.

9. James F. Trotter, "The Last Charge to the Court in Desota County, Miss., 1866," typed copy made from document in possession of Frank Hopkins, Holly Springs, Miss., April 1945, Southern Historical Collection, Wilson Library, University of North Carolina, Chapel Hill.

10. Robert Stiles, *Four Years under Marse Robert* (1903; reprint, Dayton, Ohio:

Morningside, 1977), 190–91; resolution from United Confederate Veterans camp on frames 234–35, reel 36, Jedediah Hotchkiss Papers, Library of Congress, Washington, D.C.; Connelly, *Marble Man*, 51.

11. Keith Dean Dickson, "The Divided Mind of Douglas Southall Freeman and the Transmission of Southern Memory" (Ph.D. diss., University of Virginia, 1998), 36, 38; Mary Tyler Freeman Cheek, "A High Calling: Douglas Southall Freeman and Robert E. Lee," in *Douglas Southall Freeman: Reflections by His Daughter, His Research Associate, and a Historian*, ed. Robert A. Armour (Richmond, Va.: Friends of the Richmond Public Library, 1986), 8; Douglas Southall Freeman to Ruth Davenport Deiss, December 14, 1935, collection of Jon Lowry (who kindly gave permission to quote from the letter). The most detailed biographical narrative is David E. Johnston, *Douglas Southall Freeman* (Gretna, La.: Pelican, 2002).

12. Douglas Southall Freeman, *R. E. Lee: A Biography*, 4 vols. (New York: Scribner's, 1934–35), 4:165–66, 4:167–69.

13. Douglas Southall Freeman, *Lee's Lieutenants: A Study in Command*, 3 vols. (New York: Scribners, 1942–44), 3:xxiii, 3:xxv.

14. *New York Times Book Review* quoted in Dickson, "Divided Mind," 118; T. Harry Williams, *The Selected Essays of T. Harry Williams* (Baton Rouge: Louisiana State University Press, 1983), 185; Frank E. Vandiver, "Douglas Southall Freeman, May 16, 1886–June 13, 1953," in *Southern Historical Society Papers*, 52:xiv.

15. Emory M. Thomas, *Robert E. Lee: A Biography* (New York: W. W. Norton, 1995), 13. Thirty years before Thomas published his life of Lee, Clifford Dowdey had admitted in the foreword to *Lee* (Boston: Little, Brown, 1965), that he "was awed at the prospect of trying to offer any supplement to Douglas Southall Freeman's definitive biography" (x).

16. Johannsen quoted in Allan Nevins, Bell I. Wiley, and James I. Robertson Jr., eds., *Civil War Books: A Critical Bibliography*, 2 vols. (Baton Rouge: Louisiana State University Press, 1967, 1969), 2:57; Richard Barksdale Harwell, *In Tall Cotton: The Two Hundred Most Important Confederate Books for the Reader, Researcher, and Collector* (Austin, Tex.: Jenkins, 1978), 21; David J. Eicher, *The Civil War in Books: An Analytical Bibliography* (Urbana: University of Illinois Press, 1997), 91, 333–34.

17. On the persistence of Lost Cause arguments, see Alan T. Nolan, "The Anatomy of the Myth," in *The Myth of the Lost Cause and Civil War History*, ed. Gary W. Gallagher and Alan T. Nolan (Bloomington: Indiana University Press, 2000), 11–34.

18. Connelly and Bellows, *God and General Longstreet*, 25–26; Connelly, *Marble Man*, 25–26; William Garrett Piston, *Lee's Tarnished Lieutenant: James Longstreet and His Place in Southern History* (Athens: University of Georgia Press, 1987), 117; Carol Reardon, *Pickett's Charge in History and Memory* (Chapel Hill: University of North Carolina Press, 1997), 84; David W. Blight, " 'For Something beyond the Battlefield': Frederick Douglass and the Struggle for the Memory of the Civil War," in *Memory and American History*, ed. David Thelen (Bloomington: Indiana University Press, 1990), 37–38. For a pair of less impressive works that make comparable argu-

ments about postwar efforts to build Lee's reputation, see Edward H. Bonekemper III, *How Robert E. Lee Lost the Civil War* (Fredericksburg, Va.: Sergeant Kirkland's Press, 1997), and John D. McKenzie, *Uncertain Glory: Lee's Generalship Re-examined* (New York: Hippocrene Books, 1997).

19. Nolan, *Lee Considered*, 171 (first through sixth quotes), 7 (seventh and eighth quotes), 174 (ninth quote).

20. Foster, *Ghosts of the Confederacy*, 58, 62; Blight, " 'For Something beyond the Battlefield,' " 37–38; Richard D. Starnes, "Forever Faithful: The Southern Historical Society and Confederate Historical Memory," *Southern Cultures* 2 (Winter 1996): 183.

21. That Freeman's multivolume works never have gone out of print suggests the degree to which they continue to influence readers. Both *R. E. Lee* and *Lee's Lieutenants* also have appeared in one-volume abridgments (the former in 1961 and again in 1991, the latter in 1998; James M. McPherson introduced the 1991 and 1998 editions), and Scribner's issued a three-volume paperback edition of *Lee's Lieutenants* in the late 1980s.

22. I have expanded on this point in much greater detail elsewhere. See *The Confederate War* (Cambridge, Mass.: Harvard University Press, 1997), especially chap. 3, and *Lee and His Generals in War and Memory* (Baton Rouge: Louisiana State University Press, 1998), 3–20.

23. Clement Anselm Evans, *Intrepid Warrior: Clement Anselm Evans, Confederate General from Georgia; Life, Letters, and Diaries of the War Years*, ed. Robert Grier Stephens Jr. (Dayton, Ohio: Morningside, 1992), 342–43; William Drayton Rutherford to "My own sweet one," April 30, 1864, typescript, Fredericksburg and Spotsylvania National Military Park Library, Fredericksburg, Virginia.

24. Macon (Ga.) *Christian Index*, July 1, 1864; Thomas Conolly, *An Irishman in Dixie: Thomas Conolly's Diary of the Fall of the Confederacy*, ed. Nelson D. Lankford (Columbia: University of South Carolina Press, 1988), 52.

25. Wilbur Fisk, *Hard Marching Every Day: The Civil War Letters of Wilbur Fisk*, ed. Emil Rosenblatt and Ruth Rosenblatt (Lawrence: University Press of Kansas, 1992), 318–19; Stephen Minot Weld, *War Diary and Letters of Stephen Minot Weld, 1861–1865* (1912; reprint, Boston: Massachusetts Historical Society, 1979), 396.

26. Lee, *Wartime Papers*, 388, 544, 844.

27. *OR*, 27 (3): 881.

28. Eliza Frances Andrews, *The War-Time Journal of a Georgia Girl*, ed. Spencer Bidwell Jr. (1908; reprint, Atlanta, Ga.: Cherokee, 1976), 171 (entry for April 21, 1865); Palmer quoted in Louis P. Towles, ed., *A World Turned Upside Down: The Palmers of South Santee, 1818–1881* (Columbia: University of South Carolina Press, 1996), 473–74; Catherine Ann Devereux Edmondston, *"Journal of a Secesh Lady": The Diary of Catherine Ann Devereux Edmondston, 1860–1866*, ed. Beth Gilbert Crabtree and James W. Patton (Raleigh: North Carolina Division of Archives and History, 1979), 694 (entry for April 16, 1865).

29. Lincoln quoted in Darius N. Couch, "The Chancellorsville Campaign," in

Battles and Leaders of the Civil War, ed. Robert Underwood Johnson and Clarence Clough Buel, 4 vols. (New York: Century, 1887–88), 3:155.

30. Charles S. Wainwright, *A Diary of Battle: The Personal Journals of Colonel Charles S. Wainwright, 1861–1865*, ed. Allan Nevins (New York: Harcourt, Brace, and World, 1962), 520–21.

31. Ulysses S. Grant, *The Papers of Ulysses S. Grant*, ed. John Y. Simon, 21 vols. (Carbondale: Southern Illinois University Press, 1967–), 15:165–66.

32. For a fuller explication of the arguments in this paragraph, see Gallagher, *The Confederate War*, especially chaps. 1 and 4.

33. On the receptivity of late-nineteenth- and twentieth-century Americans outside the South to Early's arguments, see Connelly, *Marble Man*, especially chaps. 4 and 6.

34. Matthew Arnold, *"General Grant" by Matthew Arnold, with a Rejoinder by Mark Twain*, ed. John Y. Simon (Kent, Ohio: Kent State University Press, 1995), 11–12.

35. Lord Acton quoted in Mark E. Neely Jr., Harold Holzer, and Gabor S. Boritt, *The Confederate Image: Prints of the Lost Cause* (Chapel Hill: University of North Carolina Press, 1987), 107; *Washington Daily Morning Chronicle*, May 13, 1863; Abraham Lincoln, *The Collected Works of Abraham Lincoln*, ed. Roy P. Basler et al., 9 vols. (New Brunswick, N.J.: Rutgers University Press, 1953), 6:214.

36. William Swinton, *Campaigns of the Army of the Potomac: A Critical History of Operations in Virginia, Maryland, and Pennsylvania from the Commencement to the Close of the War, 1861–65* (1866; reprint, Secaucus, N.J.: Blue and Grey Press, 1988), 16, 621–22.

37. George Templeton Strong, *The Diary of George Templeton Strong*, ed. Allan Nevins and Milton Halsey Thomas, 4 vols. (New York: Macmillan, 1952), 4:316; Douglass quoted in David W. Blight, *Frederick Douglass' Civil War: Keeping Faith in Jubilee* (Baton Rouge: Louisiana State University Press, 1989), 229.

38. On this point, see Blight, *Frederick Douglass' Civil War*, chap. 10.

James M. McPherson

Long-Legged Yankee Lies
The Southern Textbook Crusade

The most visible emblems today of the Civil War's continuing presence are thousands of monuments that stand on courthouse lawns or town squares from Maine to Texas—and, indeed, west to the Pacific Coast, where many Union veterans or their children moved in the decades after the Civil War. One of the most impressive Civil War monuments, of a Union soldier marching purposefully westward, can be found in Memorial Park, Pasadena, California. When this monument was unveiled on Memorial Day 1906, a veteran explained its symbolic significance to schoolchildren and bid them remember the sacrifices their grandfathers made so they could enjoy the heritage of republican liberty.[1]

Confederate veterans felt an even greater need to enshrine their deeds in stone or bronze and inspire future generations with the nobility of their cause. If the Confederacy had raised proportionately as many soldiers as the postwar South raised monuments, the Confederates might have won the war. Southern children played a more prominent role in the dedication ceremonies of these monuments than Northern children did. The climactic such event occurred in 1907 when three thousand children pulled a large wagon containing the statue of Jefferson Davis through two miles of cheering spectators to the site of the colossal Davis memorial on Monument Avenue in Richmond. According to an observer, the children hauled on "two lines of rope over seven hundred feet in length." In recognition of their sacred effort, "souvenir pieces of rope will be kept in their homes by many of the children through the years of the future."[2]

Children were ubiquitous at parades, rallies, and reunions of the United Confederate Veterans, United Daughters of the Confederacy, and Sons of Confederate Veterans. Indeed, the very names of the last two organizations expressed a determination to keep the Confederate heritage alive among the children of those who fought the war. Katharine Du Pre Lumpkin, born in Georgia as the youngest child of a Confederate veteran, remembered her first attendance at a United Confederate Veterans (UCV) reunion in 1903. The speeches made a great impression on the six-year-old girl, who recalled the occasion a half century later: "Even a child liked to listen, punctuated as they were every few moments with excited handclapping, cheers, stamping of feet, music. And such great men," including an Episcopal bishop who was a Confederate veteran. "Who there would not feel his Lost Cause blessed when so noble a man could tell them, 'We all hold it to be one of the noblest chapters in our history.' "[3]

Lumpkin's father was an officer in the UCV. He took her to many meetings during which she heard him exhort his colleagues to "educate the children! . . . Men of the South, let your children hear the old stories of the South; let them hear them by the fireside, in the schoolroom, everywhere, and they will preserve inviolate the sacred honor of the South." He practiced at home what he preached in public. All the time she was growing up, Lumpkin heard heroic tales of the war. One of her favorite memories was of formal debates that her parents organized among their children. These "debates" seem to have been rigged always to come out the same way, however, for she remembered "how the plaster walls of our parlor rang with tales of the South's sufferings, exhortations to uphold her honor, recitals of her humanitarian slave regime . . . and, ever and always, persuasive logic for her position of 'States Rights.' "[4]

Lumpkin's father relied on more than oral tradition. He "was ever in search of books to nurture us," she wrote. "One new set, I can recall, had, to be sure, lives of Lee and Jackson, but to our dismay also brought a life of Grant. We children were especially indignant at this affront," so her sister "snatched the Grant book away to hurl it into the woodshed as ignominious trash."[5]

Lumpkin's parents carried out the injunction of Sumner A. Cunningham, the founder and editor of *Confederate Veteran Magazine*, to create "living monuments" to Southern heroism. In 1909, at the close of a decade in which as many stone or bronze monuments had been dedicated as in all other decades combined, Cunningham noted with sadness that "year by year the ranks of the Confederate veterans are thinning; rapidly, the mothers of the cause are falling into their last sleep, and the time will be, only too soon, when at no convention, no meeting will there be left any who witnessed the great and wonderful struggle for liberty." Statues of Confederate soldiers were necessary to preserve the memory of this struggle, wrote Cunningham, but "shall no living monuments record the gallant dead?" The children and grandchildren of veterans must be these living monuments. "Let auxiliaries be formed of the eager children. In their fertile minds now is the time of planting if a harvest is to be reaped."[6]

In a grim reminder of those thinning ranks, the National Casket Company had become one of the principal advertisers in *Confederate Veteran Magazine*. In a brilliant stroke of the kind of dubious taste but effective advertising that we associate with our own time, this company entered the winning float in a Southern heritage parade in 1908. Two teenagers, one dressed as a Confederate officer and one as a plantation belle, stood on a float next to a casket atop a large funeral bier with the inscription "Your Sons and Daughters will forever guard the memory of your brave deeds."[7]

Confederate veterans and their wives had been aware of the need for living monuments well before Cunningham's editorial and the National Casket float. Soon after its founding in 1895, the United Daughters of the Confederacy (UDC) began to organize children's auxiliaries, most of which were named, appropriately, Children of the Confederacy. Their purpose, according to one UDC member, was "telling the Truth to Children." The "nobleness, the chivalry, the self-denial, the bravery, and the tireless endurance of the Confederate soldier should be instilled into every Southern child."[8]

The adult leaders of the Children of the Confederacy came up with several creative ways to accomplish this goal. One of the most effective was an "educational game" with fifty-two playing cards bearing portraits of Confederate officers and political leaders, the names of Confederate states and of victorious battles (with the definition of Confederate victories stretched a bit), and descriptions of other notable events. Called "The Game of Confederate Heroes," this pastime was a big hit. One woman who often played it with her children commented, "I always feel like weeping when I draw 'Robert E. Lee,' 'The Stars and Bars,' and 'The Cruise of the Shenandoah.' I find this an easy way of familiarizing the children with precious moments, and they all love to play the game."[9]

Another tactic was to have children recite poetry or speeches, supposedly of their own composition, on ceremonial occasions. At a reception in Charleston for Mary Custis Lee, General Robert E. Lee's daughter, the last of several children's speeches was offered by the youngest orator, seven-year-old B. William Walker, grandson of a Confederate general. Walker concluded with these words: Robert E. Lee "was a grand man. He loved God, and loved his country [which country was not specified], he loved all that was good and noble. . . . The name of Robert E. Lee will never die. It is written in history and the book of Life, and will live for ever." Mary

Lee was so moved by Walker's eloquence that she swept him up in her arms and kissed him. His response was not recorded.[10]

Alas, a serpent lurked in this Confederate Garden of Eden. The decades flanking 1900 were a period of expansion for public education at what we would today call the middle-school and high-school levels. Before this time, U.S. history had been part of the curriculum only in an occasional, unsystematic way. But by the 1890s the professionalization of history at the university level had come of age, and American history entered the curriculum in secondary schools. Publishers scrambled to produce textbooks for this new market. Most of their authors and nearly all of their publishers were located in the North—nine out of the ten leading U.S. history textbooks before 1900, according to one student of the subject, came from the North. Their point of view—to the extent they had one—tended to reflect the triumphant nationalism growing out of Union victory in the Civil War.[11]

Here was the serpent in the garden, warned Confederate veterans: Yankee textbooks in the schools introducing innocent Southern children to the knowledge of good and evil—mostly Northern good and Southern evil. The shocked chaplain general of the UCV reported that such books caused many Southern youths to "think that we fought for slavery. . . . This is really pathetic," for if schoolbooks continued to "fasten upon the South the stigma of slavery and that we fought for it . . . the Southern soldier will go down in history dishonored." This was only one of the "long-legged Yankee lies" in Northern books that invaded Southern homes, schools, libraries, bookstores, and news stands with "a horde of war literature so erroneous in statement of principle and fact . . . as to require on [our] part an immediate defense of [our] reputation by a prompt refutation of the errors thus widely sown in the minds of [our] children."[12]

As they had done in 1861, Southerners mobilized to repel this invasion. A principal motive for the UDC's founding was to counter this "false history," which taught Southern children "that their fathers were not only 'rebels' but guilty of almost every crime enumerated in the decalogue. . . . One of our main objects has been to put into the hands of our children a correct history."[13] Both the UDC and the UCV formed "Historical Committees" with the twofold purpose to "select and designate such proper and truthful history of the United States, to be used in both public and private schools of the South," and to "put the seal of their condemnation upon such as are not truthful histories."[14]

The historical committees might better have been termed censorship committees. In the 1890s they devoted more of their energies to condemning textbooks containing those long-legged Yankee lies than to promoting sound Southern books, in part because the latter were only beginning to appear. The UCV and the UDC directed state and local auxiliaries to form committees as well, to examine "every history taught in the schools of the state" and to determine whether "said books contain incorrect or inaccurate statements or make important omissions of facts, or inculcate narrow or partisan sentiments."[15]

Having found such unsatisfactory books, the committees could pursue either one of two courses or both. First, they could "enter into friendly correspondence with the authors and publishers of such books, with a view to correcting such errors, or supplying such omissions." This friendly correspondence should urge authors to make clear that "the cause we fought for and our brothers died for was the cause of civil liberty" and that Confederates were "a chivalric, intelligent, proud, liberty-loving people" who contended for "the most sacred rights of self-government" against "the clamor of a majority overriding the Constitution and demanding terms so revolting to our sense of justice" as to be intolerable.[16]

In general, these historical committees insisted on three broad themes as the sine qua non of textbook acceptability: secession was not rebellion but rather a legal exercise of state sovereignty; the South fought not for slavery but for self-government; and Confederate soldiers fought courageously and won most of the battles against long odds but were finally worn down by overwhelming numbers and resources. In sum, as the UCV historical committee expressed it in 1897, Southerners wanted their textbooks "to retain from the wreck in which their constitutional views, their domestic institutions, the mass of their property, and the lives of their best and bravest were lost, the knowledge that their conduct was honorable throughout, and that their submission at last . . . in no way blackened their motives or established the wrong of the cause for which they fought."[17]

Although the Grand Army of the Republic, the Union veterans' organization, also formed committees to promote its version of the war, the UCV and UDC committees were more determined, uncompromising, and persistent. As usual the wheel that squeaked loudest got the most grease. "Friendly correspondence" with Northern publishers had some results. Some publishers issued revised editions of their U.S. history textbooks in an effort to meet Southern criteria. Others put out separate editions for the Southern market.

But for most UCV and UDC history committees, these efforts were unsatisfactory. The books were still written by Yankees, "who are inimical

　　　　{ JAMES M. MCPHERSON }

to us, and who have permitted just enough of the truth to creep into their pages to make the lies stick and to place the Confederate soldier, as well as our entire people, in a false light before the world."[18]

Friendly correspondence having proved inadequate, the UCV vowed to "do everything in its power to encourage the preparation of suitable school histories and especially to encourage their publication by the building up of Southern publishing houses." This enterprise enjoyed considerable success. In 1895 the preeminent Southern educator Jabez L. M. Curry compiled a textbook entitled *The Southern States of the American Union*, published in Richmond. Unlike Northern books, which tended to "consign the South to infamy," wrote Curry in the introduction, his book demonstrated that the South was "rich in patriotism, in intellectual force, in civil and military achievements, in heroism, in honorable and sagacious statesmanship." Here was history as it should be written.[19]

Equally exemplary was *A School History of the United States*, first published in 1895, also in Richmond, written by a Virginian whose name announced her credentials: Susan Pendleton Lee. The abolitionists had branded slavery "a moral wrong," she wrote, but the Southern people knew that "the evils connected with it were less than those of any other system of labor. Hundreds of thousands of African savages had been Christianized under its influence—The kindest relations existed between the slaves and their owners. . . . [The slaves] were better off than any other menial class in the world." As for the Ku Klux Klan during Reconstruction, it was necessary "for self-protection against . . . outrages committed by misguided negroes."[20]

Armed with the increasing availability of these and several other textbooks by Southern authors, UCV and UDC committees met with local school boards and administrators to urge them to get rid of books that contained long-legged Yankee lies and substitute approved books by Southern writers. The UCV was a powerful lobby in Southern politics and the UDC enjoyed great prestige in Southern communities. Many school principals and school board members were Confederate veterans or the sons of veterans. The crusade to purge Yankee lies from the schools achieved great success. As early as 1902 *Confederate Veteran Magazine* ran an exultant headline: "False Histories Ousted in Texas."[21] In South Carolina the UCV history committee got a bill introduced in the legislature to ban any "partial or partisan or unfair or untrue book" from every school in the state and to punish anyone who assigned such a book with a five-hundred-dollar fine or one year's imprisonment. The bill did not pass, but school boards and teachers got the message. By 1905 a UCV leader in South Carolina could congratulate his colleagues that "the most pernicious histories have been banished from the school rooms."[22]

Other Southern states were not far behind. In 1904 the Mississippi legislature enacted a law requiring the state textbook commission to choose a uniform series of texts in which "no history in relation to the late civil war between the states shall be used in this state unless it be fair and impartial." Similar laws appeared on the books elsewhere. At least two states, North Carolina and Florida, appropriated funds to subsidize the production of "a Correct History of the United States, Including a True and Correct History of the Confederacy," in the words of Florida's law. Nearly all Southern states created state textbook commissions to prescribe textbooks for all public schools instead of leaving the choice up to local school systems, as most Northern states did—an interesting application of the state sovereignty these same textbooks maintained that the Confederacy stood for. Whether intended or not, one effect of this pattern of statewide adoptions was to compel national publishers to eliminate anything offensive to the South to avoid a state or regional boycott of their books.[23]

By 1910 the historical committee of the UCV expressed satisfaction with the results of its textbook crusade. "We do not fear the bookmaker now," the committee reported. "Southern schools and Southern teachers have prepared books which Southern children may read without insult or traduction of their fathers. Printing presses all over the Southland—and all over the Northland—are sending forth by thousands ones which tell the true character of the heroic struggle. The influence . . . of the South forbid[s] longer the perversion of truth and the falsification of history."[24]

The serpent had been banished from textbooks but still lingered in trade and reference books that might find their way into the hands of innocent youth. The UCV and the UDC led a charge against placing in public and school libraries such works "which are unkind and unfair to the South, which belittle our achievement, impugn our motives and malign the character of our illustrious leaders." Several state and local chapters formed committees to "recommend to the proper authorities the elimination of any books inculcating false history" from libraries.[25] One target of these committees was the *Encyclopedia Britannica*, which contained an article stating that slavery was exploitative rather than paternal and another maintaining that secession was revolutionary rather than constitutional. "Such a distortion of historical facts," bristled the UCV historical committee, "could emanate only from ignorance or malignity."[26]

{ JAMES M. MCPHERSON }

No book or author was either too important and powerful or too marginal and obscure to escape the censure of UCV and UDC watchdogs. Two examples come from 1911. A Confederate veteran happened that year to read Woodrow Wilson's *History of the American People*. In a brief reference to the famous naval battle between the USS *Monitor* and the CSS *Virginia* (*Merrimac*), Wilson wrote that the *Monitor* won the showdown. The outraged veteran fired off a letter of protest to Wilson and sent copies to Southern newspapers, which gave it wide publicity. "If this is the way a Virginia born historian writes her history, may God spare us from another such," he told Wilson, who was then governor of New Jersey and soon to run for president of the United States. "When one born of our own soil speaks untruthful history, it cuts deeper and makes a more insidious wound" than the "flaming slanders" of Yankee historians, who everyone knows are full of "overloaded prejudice and ignorance." A chastened Wilson wrote a letter of apology on the official stationery of the New Jersey executive mansion, expressing himself "very much mortified" by his mistake. Wilson's letter also was widely printed in the Southern press.[27]

While this exchange was taking place, a UCV committee discovered in a fourth-grade reader used in South Carolina schools a poem entitled "the Old Sergeant," which included a line describing the Confederate Army as a "dark, rebellious host." Using the tactics of "friendly correspondence," the UCV persuaded the Northern publisher, D. C. Heath, to replace the poem with the biblical story of Ruth, which the UCV found acceptable.[28]

If friendly correspondence and political activism by adults failed to purge false history, students themselves might take direct action. In 1894 a student in a Tennessee grammar school told her teacher, as a speaker at a UCV reunion described the incident, that "she didn't intend to study Mr. Higginson's history any more, that she had burnt her book up, for 'it made the Yankees win all the battles.' The other little girls in the class who were the daughters of the old soldiers burnt their books, too." Southern newspapers applauded this action; UCV camps passed resolutions of approval; and from Arkansas came a petition bearing five hundred signatures commending the girls, who "dared to take the first step toward writing a history that would do justice to the South."[29]

Two decades later the "historian general" of the UDC, Mildred L. Rutherford, who also described herself as the official state historian of Georgia, recounted an incident that occurred at an unnamed Southern college. The U.S. history text used there portrayed Jefferson Davis in an unflattering light. As Rutherford depicted it, the students "sent a committee to the teacher to request that the textbook be changed." The teacher refused. The students then went to the college president, who backed the teacher. The trustees declined to interfere. So, in Rutherford's words, the students "kindled a bonfire on the campus and into it every copy of that history was thrown." Rutherford commended their action and added that "the authorities were taught a lesson."[30]

As this incident suggests, while Confederate organizations had won the victory for true history in Southern public schools by the 1910s, private schools and colleges might still harbor Yankee textbooks. Therefore the UCV and the UDC could not rest on their oars. Rutherford made this point explicit in her address at the first UDC convention held outside the South in San Francisco in 1916. She claimed that 81 percent of Southern private schools "use histories which misrepresent the south."[31]

What this meant is unclear, for Rutherford's definition of "misrepresentation" was singular and her use of facts and figures was loose. Nevertheless, as historian general of the UDC she led a crusade to expand the surveillance by historical committees to shape up private institutions and prevent backsliding by public ones. In 1919 Rutherford published *A Measuring Rod to Test Text Books and Reference Books in Schools, Colleges, and Libraries*. The UCV Historical Committee adopted this measuring rod as a set of criteria for "all authorities charged with the selection of text-books for colleges, schools, and all scholastic institutions" and requested "all library authorities in the southern States" to "mark all books in their collections which do not come up to the same measure, on the title page thereof, 'Unjust to the South.'"[32]

Here are some of Rutherford's instructions to the historical committees:

Reject a book that speaks of the Constitution other than [as] a compact between Sovereign States.

Reject a text-book that . . . does not clearly outline the interferences with the rights guaranteed to the South by the Constitution, and which caused secession. . . .

Reject a book that says the South fought to hold her slaves.

Reject a book that speaks of the slaveholder of the South as cruel and unjust to his slaves.

Reject a text-book that glorifies Abraham Lincoln and vilifies Jefferson Davis.

Reject a text-book that omits to tell of the South's heroes and their deeds.[33]

{ JAMES M. MCPHERSON }

The UDC and the UCV also tirelessly promoted what Rutherford called the "Truths of History" in another of her pamphlets, in which she promised to present "a fair, unbiased, impartial, unprejudiced and Conscientious Study of History." Above all, she insisted, the historian must get her facts right, for the South had suffered from twisted facts and false history. Here are some examples of her "facts," culled from many of similar purport:

"Southern men were anxious for the slaves to be free. They were studying earnestly the problems of freedom, when Northern fanatical Abolitionists took matters in their own hands."

More slaveholders and sons of slaveholders fought for the Union than for the Confederacy (this fit awkwardly with assertions elsewhere that the Yankees got immigrants and blacks to do most of their fighting).

"Gen. Lee freed his slaves before the war began and Gen. Ulysses S. Grant did not free his until the war ended."

"The war did not begin with the firing on Fort Sumter. It began when Lincoln ordered 2,400 men and 285 guns to the defense of Sumter."

Union forces outnumbered Confederate forces five to one, not surprising when the Union population was 31 million while the Confederate population was only 5 million whites and 4 million slaves.[34]

Finally, Rutherford took great pains to describe Lincoln as a crude, vulgar, cynical tyrant who violated the Constitution at every opportunity. To support her portrait of Lincoln, she quoted James Ford Rhodes, perhaps the most influential Civil War historian of the time: Lincoln's "Emancipation Proclamation was not issued from a humane standpoint. He hoped it would incite the negroes to rise against the women and children. His Emancipation Proclamation was intended only as a punishment for the seceding States."[35]

This quotation is a total fabrication; Rhodes never wrote anything of the sort. Informed readers will recognize that every one of Rutherford's other "facts" and "truths" cited above are false—every one. Yet she was enormously influential in Southern education as well as in the UDC, and many of her "truths" found their way into approved Southern history textbooks, at least those below the college level.[36]

The discipline of history in Southern colleges partook to some degree in the professionalization occurring at the national level in the early twentieth century. Higher education, therefore, proved a tougher nut for neo-Confederates to crack, but crack it they did. As early as 1902 Professor William E. Dodd of Randolph-Macon College, who was a native of North Carolina and one of the few Southern liberals of his time, complained that Confederate veterans had imposed a straitjacket of censorship by requiring courses in American history to teach that "the South was altogether right in seceding from the Union" and "that the war was not waged about the negro." No serious scholarship was possible, wrote Dodd, "when such a confession of faith is made a *sine qua non* of fitness for teaching or writing history."[37]

But some professional historians who gave lip service to academic freedom were not above taking advantage of this climate of opinion. Professor Franklin L. Riley of the University of Mississippi and author of a U.S. history textbook publicly championed what the profession in those days called "scientific history" but privately told his agent to "hammer" a competing textbook in an Arkansas adoption struggle because the competitor gave more attention to Lincoln than to Davis and "devotes nearly 27 pages to 'the heroes who saved the Union' and only 7 pages . . . to only one Southern hero of the War—General Robert E. Lee."[38]

The cause célèbre in the college textbook wars began at Virginia's Roanoke College in 1910. A professor of history there, Herman J. Thorstenberg, a Northern-born son of Swedish immigrants, assigned Henry W. Elson's popular *History of the United States* as a textbook. A student whose father happened to be a Confederate veteran, a local judge, and a member of the college's board of trustees protested the book's treatment of the South and refused to attend class. Her father backed her up, brought the issue before the board, and publicized it in the local newspaper. From there it spread all over the South as the press and Confederate organizations seized upon the issue.

Not only was Elson a Yankee (from Ohio); he also had the temerity to suggest that Lincoln was a better man than Davis. But far worse was his treatment of the antebellum South, slavery, and the sectional conflict. Although he appeared to be evenhanded, holding Northern extremists like Charles Sumner and John Brown equally responsible with Southern fire-eaters for polarizing the sections, this apportionment of blame was unacceptable. Even more so was Elson's conclusion that the slavery issue was the main factor in provoking secession and war, which he called the "slaveholders' rebellion." But worst of all were two passages in which Elson quoted a sister of President James Madison, who had said that although "Southern ladies were complimented with the name of wife, they were only the mistresses of seraglios," and quoted another Southern woman who told

Harriet Martineau that "the wife of many a planter was but the chief slave of his harem."[39]

The uproar over this affair went on for almost two years. Citizens in Roanoke and in the nearby town of Salem, where the college was located, threatened mob violence against Thorstenberg and the college. The *Roanoke Times* thundered: "We would like to see a fire kindled on the campus and every copy of the book formally and carefully committed to the flames." The same newspaper later declared that "We had better have poison put into the food of our sons [and daughters] than to have them taught that their forefathers were heads of harems . . . and that the soldiers of the Confederacy fought to maintain human slavery."[40] The editor of the *Confederate Veteran Magazine* endorsed the determination of local citizens to "abolish their most cherished institution rather than tolerate such a book." UCV and UDC chapters all over the South took a position similar to the one expressed by the president of the Maryland UDC: "No history should be admitted into any school of the South until every sentence and word has been carefully scrutinized by competent and faithful Southern men, and the teacher who would commend such a book should be dismissed and advised that another climate would be conducive to his health."[41]

The faculty and president of Roanoke College offered a weak defense of academic freedom, but the matter became moot when Thorstenberg caved in to pressure from the board of trustees to stop using Elson's text. Meanwhile, UDC and UCV chapters discovered that the book was also used in several other Southern colleges, including the state universities of North Carolina, South Carolina, and Texas. But UDC leaders in those states soon reported "with great pleasure" that the book had been "discontinued" at these and other institutions. The following year a UCV officer in Tennessee gave the book a careful reading and discovered another problem: although "it is tinged with some make-believe of affection for the whites of the South, yet [it has] an uncontrollable love for the colored race and a desire upon the author's part, though unexpressed, to place them in every particular upon terms of equality with the better class of whites of the South."[42]

The UCV need not have worried that this unexpressed desire would continue to corrupt Southern youth. By the time Woodrow Wilson entered the White House as the first Southern-born president in nearly half a century, Elson's text had disappeared from Southern schools, along with any others that departed from the line laid down by the UCV and the UDC. The Lost Cause triumphed in the curriculum, if not on the battlefield. A North Carolinian educated in that state during the 1920s who later left the

South and eventually became dean of Yale Divinity School looked back on the books he had read in school: "I never could understand how our Confederate troops could have won every battle in the War so decisively and then have lost the war itself!"[43]

Neo-Confederate historical committees had done their work well. Nevertheless, the crusade could not end. Eternal vigilance was still the price of true history. Few members of the UCV remained by 1932, the last year of publication of *Confederate Veteran Magazine*. But the UDC and the Sons of Confederate Veterans remained vigilant. The Virginia chapter of the UDC expressed "shock" that year at the news that David Muzzey's all-time best seller among high school American history textbooks, described by the UDC as "atrocious" in its treatment of the South, had somehow been adopted by the Virginia textbook commission to replace a book by a native Virginian. The Sons of Confederate Veterans issued a "Call to Arms" to overturn this decision and return to "the purity of our history."[44] That quest for purity remains vital today, as any historian working in the field can testify.

NOTES

1. *Pasadena Evening Star*, May 29, 1906, March 27, 1937.

2. *Confederate Veteran Magazine* (hereafter *CVM*) 15 (1907): 199.

3. Katharine Du Pre Lumpkin, *The Making of a Southerner* (New York: Alfred A. Knopf, 1947), 118.

4. Ibid.

5. Ibid., 121–26.

6. *CVM* 17 (1909): 171.

7. *CVM* 16 (1908): 671.

8. *CVM* 6 (1898): 29.

9. *CVM* 11 (1903): 138.

10. *CVM* 15 (1907): 264.

11. Bessie Louise Pierce, *Public Opinion and the Teaching of History in the United States* (New York: Alfred A. Knopf, 1926), chap. 2; Frances Fitzgerald, *America Revised: History Schoolbooks in the Twentieth Century* (Boston: Little, Brown, 1979), 47–50, 227–28.

12. *CVM* 20 (1912): 512, 7 (1899): 507, 6 (1898): 476.

13. *CVM* 20 (1912): 440.

14. *Minutes of the Third Annual Meeting and Reunion of the United Confederate Veterans* (1892): 99.

15. *Minutes of the Ninth Annual Meeting and Reunion of the United Confederate Veterans* (1898): 147.

16. Ibid.; Basil Gildersleeve, "The Creed of the Old South," *Atlantic Monthly* 49 (January 1892): 87; *CVM* 5 (1897): 345.

17. *Minutes of the Eighth Annual Meeting and Reunion of the United Confederate Veterans* (1897): 46.

18. *CVM* 19 (1911): 26.

19. *Minutes of the Fifth Annual Meeting and Reunion of the United Confederate Veterans* (1894): 12; Curry quoted in Richard M. Weaver, *The Southern Tradition at Bay: A History of Postbellum Thought* (New Rochelle, N.Y.: Arlington House, 1968), 355.

20. Lee quoted in Pierce, *Public Opinion*, 162.

21. *CVM* 10 (1902): cover.

22. Herman Hattaway, "Clio's Southern Soldiers: The United Confederate Veterans and History," *Louisiana History* 12 (1971): 234–35; Lumpkin, *Making of a Southerner*, 127.

23. Pierce, *Public Opinion*, 39, 66–69, 162–63 (quote on 66); Fitzgerald, *America Revised*, 29, 35.

24. *Minutes of the Twenty-first Annual Meeting and Reunion of the United Confederate Veterans* (1910): 101.

25. *Minutes of the Twenty-second Annual Meeting and Reunion of the United Confederate Veterans* (1895): 15; *CVM* 19 (1911): 160.

26. *Minutes of the Sixth Annual Meeting and Reunion of the United Confederate Veterans* (1895): 23–24.

27. *CVM* 19 (1911): 561.

28. Ibid., 533.

29. *CVM* 4 (1896): 362.

30. Mildred L. Rutherford, "Historical Sins of Omission and Commission," in *Four Addresses* (n.p., 1916), 113–14.

31. Ibid., 112.

32. Mildred L. Rutherford, *A Measuring Rod to Test Text Books and Reference Books in Schools, Colleges, and Libraries* (n.p., 1919), 2–3.

33. Ibid., 5.

34. Mildred L. Rutherford, *The Truths of History* (n.p., n.d.); Mildred L. Rutherford, *The South Must Have Her Rightful Place in History* (Athens, Ga., 1923), 19; "The South in the Building of the Nation" (Washington, D.C.: 1912), in *Four Addresses*, 13; "Thirteen Periods of United States History" (New Orleans, 1912), in *Four Addresses*, 37.

35. Rutherford, *Truths of History*, 75.

36. In addition to holding several high offices in the UDC, Rutherford was a longtime teacher and administrator at a prominent Atlanta girls' school, the author of several textbooks on literature and history, and an officer or a board member for several women's organizations, including the national YWCA. See Edward T. James, ed., *Notable American Women*, 3 vols. (Cambridge, Mass.: Harvard University Press, 1971), 3:214–15.

37. William E. Dodd, "The Status of History in Southern Education," *Nation* 75 (August 7, 1902): 110–11.

38. Riley quoted in Gaines M. Foster, *Ghosts of the Confederacy: Defeat, the Lost Cause, and the Emergence of the New South, 1865 to 1913* (New York: Oxford University Press, 1987), 185.

39. *CVM* 19 (1911): 365.

40. *Roanoke Times* quoted in ibid., 148, 316.

41. Ibid., 319, 148 (Maryland UDC president).

42. Ibid., 194, 196, 275 (first and second quote); *CVM* 20 (1912): 443 (third quote). See also Foster, *Ghosts of the Confederacy*, 188–90.

43. Rollin G. Osterweis, *The Myth of the Lost Cause* (Hamden, Conn.: Archon Books, 1973), 113.

44. *CVM* 40 (1932): 128, 129, 157.

Alice Fahs

Remembering the Civil War in Children's Literature of the 1880s and 1890s

I n 1888 the immensely popular boys' author Oliver Optic (William Taylor Adams) decided to write a series of Civil War novels for boys, saying that "the call upon him to use the topics of the war has been so urgent, and its ample field of stirring events has been so inviting, that he could not resist."[1] Optic had already had a long and illustrious career as a boys' author, with numerous series such as the Yacht Club Series and the Onward and Upward Series selling handsomely for his longtime Boston publisher Lee and Shepard. By the turn of the century his publisher would boast that Optic had sold an astounding 2 million copies of his various juvenile works.[2]

For a popular author of juvenile works such as Optic to turn to the Civil War was not surprising; in the late 1880s adult fiction about the Civil War was also seeing a major resurgence, as numerous publishers capitalized on a revitalized public interest in the war. The famous 1884–87 *Century* magazine series of articles, stories, and reminiscences about the war, for instance, was an important sign of and a catalyst for this burgeoning popular culture of Civil War memory. This adult trend had its counterpart in the world of juvenile fiction, as numerous authors picked up their pens to reinvent and reimagine the war, whether in mainstream hardbound novels, in dime novels published as cheap pamphlets, or in stories published in weekly "story newspapers" such as *Street and Smith's New York Weekly*.

What makes Oliver Optic particularly interesting and instructive is that he had already published a group of popular Civil War novels for boys during and immediately after the war. These were what his publisher labeled the "Army and Navy Stories," and they included six volumes about two brothers, Tom and Jack Somers, one of whom was in the army, the other in the navy. Immediately popular when published from 1863 to 1866, these stories portrayed boy heroes engaged in exciting adventures facilitated by the new nation-state at war.[3]

Optic was not alone in publishing boys' war books during the Civil War.

Two major postwar authors of boys' books began their publishing careers with juvenile war novels: Horatio Alger Jr. published *Frank's Campaign* in 1864, while Harry Castlemon (Charles Austin Fosdick)—like Optic, enormously popular in the late nineteenth century as a writer of boys' adventure series—published his *Frank on a Gunboat* also in 1864. Other authors, too, weighed in with war juveniles: John Townsend Trowbridge, for instance, published his *Drummer Boy* in 1863 and his immensely popular *Cudjo's Cave* in 1864. A significant trend within wartime culture, the publication of war juveniles responded to boys' perceived interest in imagining themselves as part of the war; responded to parents' perceived desire to buy appropriate war books for their children; and performed the ideological function of integrating children into an imaginary world of war, portraying them as citizens of the new wartime state.[4]

When the war ended in April 1865 Optic had not yet finished his series, and "some of his friends," he later remembered, "advised him to make all possible haste to bring his war stories to a conclusion, declaring that there could be no demand for such works when the war came to an end." But as Optic commented with some pride in 1888, "the volumes of the series mentioned are as much in demand to-day as any of his other stories." Further, he had received "more commendatory letters from young people in regard to the books of this series than concerning those of any other."[5] Clearly Optic's Civil War stories maintained boys' interest during the postwar period. Other children's war novels first published during the war also retained their popularity, including the works of Harry Castlemon, who had himself fought during the war. As one reader named Franklin P. Adams remembered, "One Christmas morning in the late Eighties I found, under the tree, three brown-covered, gold-lettered volumes. I finished reading 'Frank on a Gunboat' before dark. . . . You whose grandfathers may have told you about the Civil War don't realize that we who were children in the Eighties got first-hand information about battles from participants; and 'Frank Before Vicksburg' and 'Frank on the Lower Mississippi' were wonderful. They were Adventure and they were History."[6]

If Optic's Civil War–era novels, like these other works, retained their popularity in the 1880s, why publish a new series of Civil War novels beginning in 1888? Clearly Optic and his publisher hoped to capitalize on a stunning resurgence of interest in the war at the end of the century. Other children's book authors, too, responded to this revitalized interest. Moreover, the market for new Civil War juveniles was potentially much larger

{ ALICE FAHS }

than it had been during the war itself, when Optic's books were necessarily marketed only to a Union audience. "From their nature," he commented about his earlier books, "the field of their circulation" had been "more limited."[7] Along with Optic, both Horatio Alger and Harry Castlemon published new Civil War series in this period; Alger wrote a set of stories for the *New York Weekly* in 1882, and Castlemon came out with a new group of novels during the 1880s and 1890s called Castlemon's War Series.

As Optic began to write the first of what would ultimately be twelve new Civil War novels—six novels in The Blue and the Gray Afloat Series and six novels in The Blue and the Gray on Land Series—he simultaneously began to reimagine the war in ways that corresponded to the changed political, social, and cultural climate of the late nineteenth century. The war Optic created in the 1880s and 1890s was not quite the same war that he had invented for his boyish readers during the war itself. Indeed, we can learn quite a bit about the shifting memory of the war within American culture by looking at the changes Optic made in his new fiction, especially in his representations of gender and race.

One major theme of boys' books published during the war was the necessity of redefining the individual's relationship to both family and nation. The war had occurred within a Victorian, maternalistic culture that celebrated domesticity, and the nation's demand that "her sons" leave home for the sake of "mother" country was a new form of national family drama explored over and over again in war fiction. Optic's 1863 *Soldier Boy*, for instance, opened with its sixteen-year-old hero, Tom Somers, shouting, " 'Fort Sumter has surrendered, mother!' " as he "rushed into the room where his mother was quietly reading her Bible."[8] This was an emblematic scene that simultaneously stressed the enthusiasm of youth, the "invasion" of the home by war, and the mother's role as her family's spiritual and moral guardian. It was a scene repeated in a wide variety of wartime literature.

Mothers' sacrifice of their sons, mothers' parting with their sons, and sons' longings for their mothers became themes within a wide range of poems, songs, and short stories published during the war. Sentimental songs, for instance, often focused on the intense bond between soldiers and mothers, as demonstrated in "Who Will Care for Mother Now?" (1863) and "Dear Mother, I've Come Home to Die" (1863).[9] For obvious reasons war juveniles tended to downplay soldiers' deaths, but they did over and over again portray partings from and reunions with mothers that were important structural elements.

Wartime juveniles did not tend to explore relationships between fathers and sons, however. John Townsend Trowbridge's *The Drummer Boy*, for instance, presented the young hero Frank Manly's father as a feeble figure: "His wife had become more the head of the family than he was, and every important question of the kind, as Frank well knew, was referred to her for decision."[10] In Castlemon's *Frank on a Gunboat*, the father was dead. In Optic's *Soldier Boy*, the father, a naval captain, was described as trapped in the South when war broke out and unable to return to his family. Mother-son relationships dominated the portrayal of family in these works, as plots centered around the drama of sons leaving their mothers for the sake of country.

In leaving home for country, however, these hero sons did not simply substitute one version of family for another; the army was not presented as an enveloping, maternalistic institution. True, wartime juveniles often featured father figures—older soldiers—who counseled young soldiers to avoid vices such as swearing, gambling, and smoking. But these father figures tended to be minor characters; the central drama of these stories lay elsewhere, in the ways in which the new nation facilitated glorious new individual adventures for boys. In *Soldier Boy*, for instance, Tom Somers experienced a series of picaresque adventures involving deception, cunning, derring-do, and—quite literally—gleeful thumb-nosing at the enemy —when he was accidentally cut off from his army unit. Such fiction imagined an adventurous new individualism encouraged by the state.

In his preface to *Soldier Boy* Optic stressed the new linkages between individual adventures and national goals: his work contained "the adventures of one of those noble-hearted and patriotic young men who went forth from homes of plenty and happiness to fight the battles of our imperilled country"; his book was a "narrative of personal adventure, delineating the birth and growth of a pure patriotism in the soul of the hero." He had endeavored to "paint a picture of the true soldier, one who loves his country, and fights for her because he loves her; but, at the same time, who is true to himself and his God, while he is faithful to his patriotic impulses."[11] In these statements we see not only the explicit linking of adventure and patriotism—a masculinist ethos that emerged strongly during the Civil War—but also an abiding Victorian concern with a deeply moral individualism.[12]

How did Optic's rendering of the war shift in the late nineteenth century? In The Blue and the Gray Series, the first volume of which was published in 1888, Optic also focused on adventure: indeed, what had been

{ ALICE FAHS }

a trend of Civil War fiction had by the 1880s become the sine qua non of boys' fiction. His depictions of family, however, had changed dramatically. His new works created an imagined world in which fathers reasserted their authority in the strongest possible terms. No longer were they weak, sickly, absent, or dead; on the contrary, Optic emphasized the link between fathers and national authority. Optic's 1888 *Taken by the Enemy*, as well as the subsequent volumes in this series (The Blue and the Gray Afloat) deserve some analysis on this point.

From the first page of *Taken by the Enemy* Optic placed paternal authority center stage. The novel opened not with the young hero of the series, Christy Passford, but with his father. " 'This is most astounding news!' " exclaimed Christy Passford's father, Captain Horatio Passford, in the book's first line. In direct contrast to the opening of *Soldier Boy*, the father, not the son, was the source of news about the war breaking out. This would be a minor point if the remainder of the novel focused on Christy—if, as in Civil War–era fiction, the young hero's individual adventures entirely structured the novel. But the father, Captain Passford, was a powerful figure throughout the six books of this series, so much so that in the final volume, *A Victorious Union*, Christy received his commission as lieutenant-commander not from a government official or a military superior but directly from his father. Christy's father became, quite literally, a stand-in for the state.

The reasons for this exceptionally strong linkage between paternal and national authority have everything to do with changing attitudes toward wealth and nationhood within late-nineteenth-century culture. In Optic's earlier Civil War series his young hero, Tom Somers, had come from a family of modest means; his father had left home to try to obtain money to pay a debt that threatened the family's precarious economic stability. Indeed, the only wealthy character in *Soldier Boy* had been depicted as a villain, a local "Squire" who threatened to foreclose on the Somers family home. A suspicion of wealth was thus an important subtheme of the story and reaffirmed antebellum republican values. Wealth and virtue might coincide, but wealth was certainly not a sign of virtue.

But that was 1864. In 1888 Optic described Christy Passford's father as "just returning from a winter cruise" in his "magnificent steam-yacht Bellevite."[13] Optic emphasized that "it would take more than one figure to indicate the number of millions" by which Captain Horatio Passford's "vast wealth was measured."[14] The blatant celebration of Passford's wealth throughout Optic's novel signaled the sea change that had occurred within American culture since the Civil War. What scholars have called the "incorporation of America" had reshaped the American landscape, both literally and figuratively; Optic participated in this celebration of big business, his characters speaking lines consonant with the ethos of the emerging gospel of wealth.[15] Indeed, the very state itself was imagined as dependent upon this new wealthy elite. The young Christy Passford, for instance, as "the heir of millions," had "given all his pay to wounded sailors and the families of those who had fallen in naval actions."[16] His father had donated the steamship *Bellevite* to the war effort. Christy Passford and his father were not so much supported by the state as propping it up. Optic had moved from celebrating forms of adventurous individualism that were facilitated by the state to celebrating a business individualism that held it together.

What Optic created in his late-nineteenth-century Civil War novels was a new "family romance" of the state.[17] He portrayed a masculinist world in which masculinity was revealed as much by outer signs of "virtue," such as wealth, as by the earlier Victorian inner virtues of character and self-determination that Optic had stressed in the 1860s. These late-nineteenth-century novels also offered a striking repudiation of maternal values: Optic did not portray Mrs. Passford, for instance, as a figure of strength within the Passford family but as a fussy, oversensitive mother who was guilty of a new late-nineteenth-century sin: overmothering. " 'Don't make a baby of me,' " Christy told his mother when she wanted to assist her wounded son (he had been wounded slightly in one arm, as happened frequently in war fiction that made wounds picturesque "badges of courage"); " 'Don't make me fall from my high estate to that of an overgrown infant, mother.' "[18] Such a comment was unimaginable in literature published during the Civil War, when poems and stories instead reiterated, with approval, the soldier's deep yearning for his mother's touch, his mother's caress.

Thus Optic's fiction revealed a remarkable shift in the way the war was imagined and remembered in the late nineteenth century, as an event in which the nation was formed through exclusively masculinist ties and masculinist values. During the war such an imagined exclusion of women was not possible, either ideologically or practically; after all, women's home front efforts had been necessary within a total war and by and large were celebrated as such during the war, at least after 1862. In articles and fiction women in particular had created an imagined war in which women's efforts and participation were highly valued. During and immediately following the war a smattering of juvenile fiction was also published that featured girl heroes (not as soldiers but as nurses or vivandières).[19] But the new gendered nationalism that took shape during the last years of the century

{ ALICE FAHS }

reimagined the Civil War within a markedly masculinist ethos. The children who read Optic's new fiction now found that the Civil War had always been a boys' war.

While the new imagined family of the state emphasized strong ties between fathers and sons, it also emphasized brotherhood among white soldiers. As numerous historians have pointed out, this was an immensely popular late-nineteenth-century theme, part of a literature of sectional reconciliation that found the true meaning of the war in an explicitly white supremacist ethos of bravery. It was precisely this white ethos of reconciliation (as David W. Blight has shown) that Frederick Douglass strenuously fought against during the 1880s, as he saw emancipation disappear as a central tenet of the war.[20]

Brotherhood among white Confederate and Union soldiers was, perhaps not surprisingly, also a major theme of Optic's late-nineteenth-century fiction. Optic hoped, he said, "to do more ample justice than perhaps was done before to those 'who fought on the other side.' "[21] While there were strong ideological reasons for this shift in meaning, there were also compelling marketing reasons within the book trade. Optic and his publisher were indeed at pains to make the books "fair" in their portrayals of the South, both in appearance and in content. The books' covers, for instance, offered material evidence of the warring sides' equal importance: they were literally divided down the middle into blue and gray sections, with Oliver Optic's name positioned in the middle, in gilt, to signal both the abiding ties between North and South and his own dispassionate stance (although one notes the blue spine). Not only did Optic assure his audience in a preface that he had "spent some time in the South" and had "always found himself among friends there," but he also within the series provided several awkward scenes of reconciliation between Northern and Southern white soldiers.[22]

In his 1893 *A Victorious Union*, for instance (the sixth book in The Blue and the Gray Afloat Series), a brave Confederate officer, many of whose men had just been killed in action by a young Union sailor named Christy Passford and his crew, congratulated Passford's parents on their son's bravery. " 'I am still a rebel to the very centre of my being,' " said Captain Rombold, the Confederate officer, " 'but that does not prevent me from giving the tribute of my admiration to an enemy who has been as brave, noble, and generous as your son. The brilliant exploit of Mr. Passford, I sincerely believe, cost me my ship, and at least the lives or limbs of a quarter of my ship's company. It was one of the most daring and well-executed movements I ever witnessed in my life.' "[23]

Optic further embroidered on this theme of mutual admiration by imagining that the Passford family invited Captain Rombold to stay with them while Rombold remained a prisoner of war in the North. At the end of this stay Optic recorded an exchange of flowery tributes more suited to the social niceties of the guest-host relationship than to the exigencies of war. " 'Though wounded I have passed four of the pleasantest weeks of my life,' " said Rombold, countered by Mrs. Passford's " 'We have been made happier by your presence with us than we could have made you.' "[24] The narrator approvingly commented, "Not a word about politics or the cause of the war had been spoken."[25] The incredulous reader might do well to remember that in another Civil War novel Optic remarked that he had not "felt called upon to invest his story with the dignity of history, or in all cases to mingle fiction with actual historic occurrences."[26]

With such polite scenes of mutual admiration, Optic directly reshaped the war's events to fit the new ethos of reconciliation emerging in the late nineteenth century. Political leaders and cultural commentators alike emphasized that a main meaning of the war was shared white bravery on the battlefield. Both Northern and Southern soldiers had fought heroically for their separate causes, according to this widespread interpretation, and such heroism was more important than sectional differences. On the grounds of white heroism a new version of nationalism could take shape.

If ideas of white heroism underlay emergent late-nineteenth-century ideas of nationalism, so too did related ideas of white supremacy over African Americans. Both Northern and Southern authors produced fiction in the late nineteenth century that denied blacks agency in the war's events, that reinterpreted slavery as a positive good under the right circumstances, and that presented black characters as laughable buffoons with little intelligence and no self-mastery. Such depictions especially emphasized African Americans' love of and need for white guidance at all times.

To some extent Northern authors had a less straightforward task in these racialized representations. Many Northerners, after all, had been against the institution of slavery even if they had been simultaneously opposed to an equal place—or, indeed, any place—for African Americans in American life. In the 1880s and 1890s, too, most Northern authors remained ideologically opposed to the institution of slavery on an abstract level; that is, they continued to believe that a system of perpetual human bondage was wrong. Nevertheless, many authors' opposition to slavery's practices softened con-

{ ALICE FAHS }

siderably as the century drew to a close. In the emerging and virulently racist culture of Jim Crow, a number of Northern authors indulged in a nostalgia for plantation slavery that had not seen expression during the war itself.

Oliver Optic, for instance, had not touched the subject of slavery in his wartime novels, although his racial thinking was apparent in the brief portrayal of an abject, whining "darkey" in *Soldier Boy*.[27] But most of that novel had instead been devoted to the depiction of a young soldier's thrilling adventures when cut off from his regiment in Virginia. In the 1890s, however, Optic foregrounded slavery in his new set of novels The Blue and the Gray on Land. In the first novel of that series, the 1894 *Brother against Brother; or, The War on the Border*, Optic made a strikingly conciliatory gesture to the South by vividly depicting a form of "good" slavery. Set in Kentucky, *Brother against Brother* featured a New Hampshire family transplanted South after inheriting the plantation Riverlawn. Far from using this plot device to expose or critique the evils of slavery, Optic instead mounted a stunning defense of slavery as a positive good when in the right hands.

The father of the family, Noah Lyon, was, "like the majority of the people of the North," instinctively "opposed to human bondage," Optic informed his readers; "but he had never been considered a fanatic or an abolitionist by his friends and neighbors. He simply refrained from meddling with the subject."[28] Lyon's first glimpse of the plantation he had inherited from his brother revealed a benign paternalistic world. As the family members entered the grounds of Riverlawn, they saw a "little village of negro houses, so neat and substantial that they deserved a better name than 'huts,' generally given to the dwellings of the slaves of a plantation. Each had its little garden, fenced off and well cared for. It was evident that the occupants of these cottages were subjected to few if any of the hardships of their condition." Moreover, as they were seen returning from the "hemp fields and horse pastures of the estate," they "seemed to be happy and contented, with no care for the troubles that were then agitating the State."[29]

In this pleasant setting, the overseer was virtually a Santa Claus figure: "His round face seemed to be overflowing with pleasantry and good nature."[30] The slaves were filled with love for and admiration of their white masters. "They had known and loved as a patriarch" their previous owner, and they all cheered the arrival of the new owner. "With pleasant smiles on their faces, all of them shouted, 'Glad to see you!' their enthusiasm being limited only by the vigor of their voices and the strength of their lungs."[31]

This depiction of a benign, pleasant form of slavery in *Brother against Brother* may at first seem to be a complete capitulation to a conservative Southern viewpoint—so much so that one might want to characterize the novel not as fiction of reconciliation but as fiction of submission. But there was more to Optic's depiction of slavery in the novel than a simple celebration of benign paternalism.

The centerpiece of the plot of *Brother against Brother* was an attack by Confederate "ruffians" against the staunch Unionists of Riverlawn. Without Union forces nearby to call upon for protection, the patriarch Noah Lyon decided to employ and arm slaves in defense of his plantation. No Southern novel written in the 1880s and 1890s imagined arming a group of African Americans. This was a specifically Northern rendering of the war that drew upon memories of black soldiering and on the surface suggested that Optic advocated a memory of the war as a struggle for black freedom— a meaning that most other white authors had long since dropped.

But Optic was far from advocating black soldiering or black freedom in a sustained way. Noah Lyon, for instance, explicitly rejected the idea of arming his slaves "to fight the battles of the nation." Instead, he explained that he armed them "to protect my wife and children and my property." "If a mob of fifty or a hundred or five hundred ruffians come over here to hang me and burn my house, shall I let them do so rather than employ the willing hands of men with black faces to defend myself?" he demanded.[32]

Optic admitted that slaves could be brave fighters: one character marveled that "the same number of white men of average ability could hardly have done better under similar circumstances." But the motives imputed to blacks to explain how well they fought always involved love of whites: "The negro was strong in his affections, and the feeling that they were fighting for the family who had used them kindly, and treated them with more consideration than they had been in the habit of receiving . . . was the stimulus that strengthened their souls and nerved their arms."[33]

In writing a novel that included black fighting, Optic gave a potentially radical twist to fictional memories of the war. In the 1880s and 1890s, few white Northern authors remembered African American fighting as an integral part of the war. But Optic interpreted that fighting in ways that also muted its radical impact. His fictional slaves fought well because they loved whites, not because their fighting might lead to emancipation. Thus in Optic's portrayal blacks continued to be fundamentally dependent, not independent, within American culture. In circumscribing black freedom and in carefully delineating black dependence, Optic participated in the

{ ALICE FAHS }

culture of reconciliation that celebrated white heroism in the war. Still, Optic's vision of reconciliation was not the same as that of Southern authors. In imagining Northerners as the only good slaveholders, in imagining African Americans fighting in Civil War skirmishes (although not as soldiers), and in celebrating a new corporate culture of immense wealth, Optic revealed his Northern origins only too clearly.

Southern authors imagined a different sort of reconciliation. Just as Optic seized on the opportunities offered by the late-nineteenth-century literary marketplace in publishing a new Civil War series, so too did the popular author Thomas Nelson Page, whose career flourished in the late 1880s and 1890s as he published a series of "plantation" stories in magazines such as *Century*. Page is usually remembered as an author of novels and stories for adults, including his 1898 novel of Reconstruction, *Red Rock*. But Page also published a variety of Civil War stories for children in national magazines and in books during this same period.

Like Optic, Page provided scenes of reconciliation between individual white Northerners and Southerners in his fiction. In his *Two Little Confederates*, which appeared serially in *St. Nicholas Magazine* in 1888 (the same year that Optic's first The Blue and the Gray novel appeared), a small Virginia boy, Frank, was the agent of reconciliation. A Union officer who questioned Frank about the whereabouts of Confederate soldiers was reminded of his own son: "The boy did not know that the big dragoon was looking down at the light hair resting on his arm, and that while he trod the Virginia wood-path, in fancy he was home in Delaware; or that the pressure the boy felt from his strong arms, was a caress given for the sake of another boy far away on the Brandywine."[34] When the officer died, Frank experienced a terrible loss, crying, " 'I don't want him to die! I don't want him to die!' "[35] Frank's family members not only buried the Union officer on the grounds of their plantation but also comforted his family members when, after the war, they came to retrieve his remains.

In Page's sentimental fiction, white children also served as avatars of white supremacy. In "A Captured Santa Claus," a Confederate officer was captured at home by a Union officer who had previously been the Confederate officer's prisoner. Both behaved with the elaborate courtesy that was a keynote of white reconciliation stories: " 'I have the honor to request your parole,' " said the Union general to the Confederate officer, speaking "with great politeness." He also expressed " 'the hope that I may be able in some way to return the courtesy which I formerly received at your hands.' "[36] The Confederate officer's son, Charlie, was not so polite to the Union officer, however, causing his mother to chastise him: " 'I am ashamed of you!—to be so rude!' "[37] But the Union officer did not take such rudeness amiss: " 'Let him alone, madam,' " said the Union general. " 'It is not rudeness; it is spirit—the spirit of our race.' "[38]

For Page, reconciliation between North and South was grounded in white supremacy. Elsewhere Page explicitly laid out his views on this subject, claiming "the absolute and unchangeable superiority of the white race," which he called "an inherent and essential superiority, based on superior intellect, virtue, and constancy." He did "not believe that the Negro is the equal of the white, or ever could be the equal." He claimed that "race superiority is founded on courage" as well as "intellect, and the domestic virtues, and in these the white is the superior of every race."[39]

Page put these beliefs into practice in a particularly insidious way in his juvenile fiction. Most commentators on Page have remarked on his benign view of slavery, his conception of an untroubled and affectionate relationship between slaves and their masters, his nostalgic celebrations of the supposed "idyll" of plantation slavery, his evocation of the loyalty of slaves even under the conditions of war. All these white supremacist beliefs can be found in Page's fiction, including his juvenile fiction, and they match the views of Optic to a great extent.

But some of Page's juvenile fiction reveals a less affectionate imagination of slavery as well as a more polemical adherence to the idea that African Americans were debased and degraded than was ever offered by Optic. The 1891 "Jack and Jake," for example, was a war story of two little boys— one white, one African American, with Jack the owner of Jake.[40] "Their names were always coupled together. Wherever you saw one, you were very apt to see the other—Jack, slender, with yellow hair, big gray eyes, and spirited look; and Jake, thick-set and brown, close to him, like his shadow." The story carefully laid out Page's white supremacist views: Jake was "dull" compared with Jack; he was doubting, irresolute, cowardly, reluctant to act, terrified of Yankees, willing at every moment to turn tail and run home. In contrast Jack was quick-thinking, courageous, generous, clever, loyal. At a crucial moment in the story, when they were being chased by Yankees and needed to ford a stream, Jake "was unstrung, and could not try it. He sat down and cried." Finally he tried to cross the water, but "clutched" at Jack. "Jack thought he had him safe. 'I've got you,' he said. 'Don't—' But before he could finish the sentence, Jake flung his arm around his neck and choked him, pulling him down under the water, and getting it into his throat and nostrils. Jack struggled, and tried to get up, but he could not;

{ ALICE FAHS }

Jake had him fast."[41] At the end of the story it was clear that Jake had drowned, while Jack had survived.[42]

It is hard to escape the symbolism here: Jake, Jack's shadow who had literally been weighing him down in the water, had been eradicated by the story's end. This "solution" to the question of what place African Americans should take in American life makes clear the often virulent racism that underlay the culture of reconciliation even—or perhaps especially—in children's fiction.

In the 1880s and 1890s Optic and Page shared a desire to reinvent a Civil War that emphasized an ethos of white reconciliation. As white soldiers admired one another's prowess and bravery, as Southern white children tugged at the heartstrings of white Union officers, a world of war emerged in which white unity predominated. In the service of this vision, both Optic and Page reinvented African Americans' role in the war, denying the reality of black soldiering while stressing how beneficial plantation slavery had been to African Americans' well-being.

Children's literature is often dismissed as a mere "step-child" of more important adult literature. There may be something to this view, but not necessarily when we think historically—when we think about the ways in which racial attitudes have been passed from generation to generation. "I luxuriated in the school of Thomas Nelson Page," one Southern reader later remembered of her childhood.[43] A copy of Page's *Among the Pines* at the Huntington Library in San Marino, California, bears the inscription "George S. Patton from his father, 1891." Another Huntington Library book, an Oliver Optic novel, carries Jack London's bookplate. Numerous other copies of these children's novels in libraries around the country still carry inscriptions from less famous parents to children for birthdays or Christmases. These inscriptions are signs of the potency of this literature in shaping the imaginations of children, whether in the South, where Thomas Nelson Page held sway, or in the North, where Page and Optic were popular authors. Though Page's and Optic's visions of reconciliation carried distinctive sectional accents, they were also united by an underlying consensus that the war had been—and should remain in memory—a white, masculinist experience in American life.

NOTES

1. Oliver Optic, *Taken by the Enemy* (Boston: Lee and Shepard, 1888), 7. For a listing of Optic's many series, see Dolores Blythe Jones, An *"Oliver Optic" Checklist:*

An Annotated Catalog-Index to the Series, Nonseries Stories, and Magazine Publications of William Taylor Adams (Westport, Conn.: Greenwood Press, 1985).

2. Oliver Optic, "Publishers' Preface," in *An Undivided Union* (Boston: Lee and Shepard, 1899), vi.

3. The books in this series, all published by Lee and Shepard (and its various permutations) of Boston, were *The Soldier Boy; or, Tom Somers in the Army: A Story of the Great Rebellion* (1863); *The Sailor Boy; or, Jack Somers in the Navy: A Story of the Great Rebellion* (1863); *The Young Lieutenant: or, The Adventures of an Army Officer: A Story of the Great Rebellion* (1865); *The Yankee Middy: or, The Adventures of a Naval Officer: A Story of the Great Rebellion* (1865); *Fighting Joe; or, The Fortunes of a Staff Officer: A Story of the Great Rebellion* (1865); and *Brave Old Salt: or, Life on the Quarter Deck: A Story of the Great Rebellion* (1866). For a complete publishing history of these works, see Jones, *An "Oliver Optic" Checklist*.

4. On juvenile literature published during the war, see James Alan Marten, *The Children's Civil War* (Chapel Hill: University of North Carolina Press, 1998). See also Alice Fahs, *The Imagined Civil War: Popular Literature of the North and South, 1861–1865* (Chapel Hill: University of North Carolina Press, 2001), especially chap. 8.

5. Oliver Optic, *Taken by the Enemy* (Boston: Lothrop, Lee, and Shepard, 1888), 5.

6. Jacob Blanck, *Harry Castlemon: Boys' Own Author; Appreciation and Bibliography* (New York: R. R. Bowker, 1941), xi.

7. Optic, *Taken by the Enemy*, 5.

8. Oliver Optic, *The Soldier Boy; or, Tom Somers in the Army: A Story of the Great Rebellion* (New York: Lee and Shepard, 1864; reprint, New York: Hurst, n.p.), 169, 11.

9. "Who Will Care for Mother Now?" (Brooklyn, 1863), Case Collection, Newberry Library, Chicago; "Dear Mother, I've Come Home to Die" (Brooklyn, 1863), Case Collection, Newberry Library, Chicago.

10. John Townsend Trowbridge, *The Drummer Boy* (Boston: J. E. Tilton, 1863), 9.

11. Optic, *Soldier Boy*, 5–6.

12. On Victorian values during this period, see Louise L. Stevenson, *The Victorian Homefront: American Thought and Culture, 1860–1880* (New York: Twayne, 1991), and Anne C. Rose, *Victorian America and the Civil War* (New York: Cambridge University Press, 1992).

13. Optic, *Taken by the Enemy*, 13.

14. Ibid.

15. Alan Trachtenberg, *The Incorporation of America: Culture and Society in the Gilded Age* (New York: Hill and Wang, 1982).

16. Oliver Optic, *A Victorious Union* (Boston: Lothrop, Lee, and Shepard, 1893), 279.

17. Lynn Hunt, *The Family Romance of the French Revolution* (Berkeley: University of California Press, 1992).

18. Optic, *A Victorious Union*, 266.

19. See, for instance, Jane Austin, *Dora Darling, the Daughter of the Regiment* (Boston: J. E. Tilton, 1864).

20. See David W. Blight, *Race and Reunion: The Civil War in American Memory* (Cambridge, Mass.: Belknap Press of Harvard University Press, 2001), and David W. Blight, *Frederick Douglass' Civil War: Keeping Faith in Jubilee* (Baton Rouge: Louisiana State University Press, 1989).

21. Optic, *Taken by the Enemy*, 6–7.

22. Ibid., 6.

23. Optic, *A Victorious Union*, 272–73.

24. Ibid., 289.

25. Ibid.

26. Oliver Optic, *On the Blockade* (Boston: Lee and Shepard, 1891), 7.

27. Optic, *Soldier Boy*, 169.

28. Oliver Optic, *Brother against Brother; or, The War on the Border* (Boston: Lee and Shepard, 1894), 67.

29. Ibid., 25.

30. Ibid., 47.

31. Ibid., 56.

32. Ibid., 244.

33. Ibid., 331.

34. Thomas Nelson Page, *Two Little Confederates* (New York: Charles Scribner's Sons, 1911), 123–24.

35. Ibid., 139.

36. Thomas Nelson Page, *Among the Camps; or, Young People's Stories of the War* (New York: Charles Scribner's Sons, 1891), 34.

37. Ibid., 36.

38. Ibid.

39. Thomas Nelson Page, *The Negro: The Southerner's Problem* (New York: Charles Scribner's Sons, 1904), 292–93.

40. "Jack and Jake" was first published as a serial in *Harper's Young People* 12 (October 13, 1891): 813–16, (October 20, 1891): 830–33, and (October 27, 1891): 846–49. It was then reprinted in *Among the Camps*.

41. Page, *Among the Camps*, 161–62.

42. " 'Where is Jake?' " Jack asked at the end of the story. But the adults around him "would not let him talk. They made him go to sleep" (163).

43. Katharine Du Pre Lumpkin, *The Making of a Southerner* (1946; reprint, Athens: University of Georgia Press, 1991), 123.

David W. Blight

Decoration Days
The Origins of Memorial Day in North and South

At the end of the Civil War the American people faced an enormous challenge of memorialization. Their war of limited aims in 1861 had become an all-out struggle of conquest and survival between the largest armies the Western Hemisphere had ever seen. Approximately 620,000 soldiers died in the war, 60 percent on the Union side and 40 percent on the Confederate. American deaths in all other wars combined through the Korean conflict totaled 606,000. Death and mourning were everywhere in America in 1865; hardly a family had escaped its pall. In the North 6 percent of white males aged 13–43 died in the war; in the South 18 percent of these were dead. Of the 180,000 African Americans who served in the Union army and navy, 20 percent perished. Diseases such as typhoid, dysentery, and pneumonia claimed more than twice as many soldiers as died in battle. The most immediate legacy of the war was its slaughter and how to remember it.[1]

Death on such a scale demanded meaning. During the war soldiers in countless remote arbors or on awful battlefield landscapes had gathered to mourn and bury their comrades, even as thousands remained unburied, their skeletons lying on the killing fields of Virginia, Tennessee, or Georgia. Women had begun rituals of burial and remembrance in informal ways well before the war ended, both in towns on the home front and at the battlefront. Americans carried flowers to graves or to makeshift monuments representing their dead, and so was born the ritual of "Decoration Day," known eventually as Memorial Day.

In most places the ritual was initially a spiritual practice. But soon remembering the dead, and what they died for, developed partisan fault lines. The evolution of Memorial Day during its first twenty years or so became a contest between three divergent, and sometimes overlapping, groups: blacks and their white abolitionist allies, white Northerners, and white Southerners. With time, in the North the war's two primary results—black freedom and the preservation of the Union—were rarely accorded equal space. In the South a uniquely Confederate version of the war's meaning, rooted in resistance to Reconstruction, coalesced around Memorial Day practices. Decoration Day, and the ways in which it was observed, shaped Civil War memory as much as any other cultural ritual did. The story of the origins of this important American day of remembrance is central to understanding how the reconciliationist legacies of the Civil War overtook the emancipationist ones.

Black South Carolinians and their Northern white abolitionist allies were primarily responsible for founding Decoration Day. In Charleston, South Carolina, where the war had begun, the first collective ceremony, involving a parade and the decoration of the graves of the dead with spring flowers, took place on May 1, 1865. The May Day event was the culmination of a series of extraordinary ceremonies in Charleston, where in the war's last months the planters' world and this jewel of a city were turned upside down. After a long siege, a prolonged and devastating bombardment, and numerous fires, the lower half of Charleston was in ruin by February 18, 1865, when it was finally evacuated. Forts Sumter, Moultrie, Ripley, and Castle Pinckney, ringing the harbor, had held out valiantly with small Confederate garrisons through more than a year and a half of siege and shelling.

From the battery at the harbor to Calhoun Street, Charleston had become the domain of mobs and anarchy. Above Calhoun Street, remnants of the city's white population (most had fled) tried to maintain a society through the long siege. By the end of 1864, wrote one of its chroniclers, Mrs. St. Julien Ravenal, the city had an "extraordinary appearance. . . . It was awfully biblical! . . . To pass from this bustling, crowded scene to the lower part of the town was . . . like going from life to death." Another Charlestonian called the lower section "a city of the dead." As the city was abandoned, fires broke out everywhere, including in the bales of cotton left in huge stockpiles in public squares that burned as if they were the funeral pyres of a dying civilization. Among the first Union troops to enter Charleston was the Twenty-first U.S. Colored Regiment; their commander, Lieutenant Colonel A. G. Bennett, received the formal surrender of the city from its mayor, and the troops helped put out fires in those first days of occupation. As the black soldiers marched up Meeting Street singing liberation songs, they left indelible memories on all who saw them.[2]

For Black Charlestonians this was a time of celebration and of ritual role reversals. On March 3 a large crowd of blacks gathered in Marion Square to watch as thirteen black women, elegantly dressed to represent the thirteen original states, presented the Union commander, General Quincy A. Gillmore, with a flag, a bouquet of flowers, and a fan for Mary Todd Lincoln. On March 29 approximately four thousand blacks marched in an unprecedented victory parade. Companies of soldiers were followed by tailors, coopers, butchers, sailors, and many other tradesmen. Eight companies of firemen marched, as did some eighteen hundred school children with their teachers, some of whom were from the Northern freedmen's aid societies that had been active on the Carolina coast for nearly two years. Then, dramatically, two carts rolled along in the procession, one carrying an auction block and an auctioneer selling two black women and their children. The second cart contained a coffin with a sign announcing the "death of slavery," and that "Sumter dug his grave on the 13th of April, 1861."[3]

In such collective public performances blacks in Charleston proclaimed their freedom and converted destruction into new life. In richly symbolic parades and other ceremonies they announced their rebirth; whatever the new order would bring in their lives, they drew a line of demarcation between past and present. These were days of awe and wonderment, of sorrow and gaiety. The freedpeople of Charleston had converted Confederate ruin into their own festival of freedom. They provided the images and metaphors, even the objects and places, with which to establish the earliest "theaters of memory" for the transition from slavery to freedom.[4]

On April 14 a celebration took place at the mouth of the harbor inside Fort Sumter. Four years to the day after the surrender of the fort, General Robert Anderson returned to Charleston with many Northern dignitaries to raise the flag he had lowered in 1861. Three thousand African Americans crammed on to the island fortress for the ceremony. In attendance were the abolitionist William Lloyd Garrison and President Lincoln's secretary, John G. Nicolay. Also among the throng was the former abolitionist and writer and now major in the Union army Martin Delany, as was the son of Denmark Vesey, the leader of a slave rebellion who was executed in Charleston in 1822. The former slave and boat pilot Robert Smalls was nearby aboard the *Planter* (which was filled with a contingent of freedpeople), the steamer he had commandeered and sailed out of Charleston to freedom during the war. Rev. Henry Ward Beecher was orator of the day. The audience heard Beecher condemn South Carolina's secessionists to eternal damnation. The South's "remorseless traitors" were held fully responsible for the war. Beecher promised them (as though they were in attendance) vengeance and that they would be "whirled aloft and plunged downward forever and forever in endless retribution." To other white Southerners, Beecher promised forgiveness and fellowship. Many in that special audience hoped for more guidance from Beecher about the confused and delicate questions of Reconstruction, but on that count they heard little in what unfolded as primarily a festival of victory, thanksgiving, and celebration. When hearing a regimental band play "John Brown's Body," Garrison, who two decades earlier had a price put on his life by the state of South Carolina, broke down and wept. Flowers were blooming everywhere amid the ruins of Charleston; for so many, remembrance at this early date was but a fragrance full of warring emotions. As the flag reached its height on the staff in the fort, guns all around Charleston harbor fired a salute. The grand day ended that evening at a banquet in the city as Anderson, among others, offered many toasts, some of which were to President Lincoln, who was that very night assassinated in Ford's Theater in Washington.[5]

During the next two weeks in Charleston, as elsewhere, mourning over Lincoln's death swept through the community of blacks and their Unionist and white abolitionist allies. Although Lincoln's death took prominence, death required attention all over the land. A Union quartermaster general's report shortly after the surrender at Appomattox noted that only about one-third of the Union war dead were interred in identifiable graves. The U.S. government instituted an elaborate program of locating and burying the Union dead all over the South in newly created national cemeteries, and by 1870 some three hundred thousand Northern soldiers were reinterred in seventy-three national cemeteries, with 58 percent of the remains identified. Retrieval and recognition of the Confederate dead took much longer due to inadequate resources. Early Reconstruction policies had not extended this program of reinterment to Confederates.[6] All this death on the battlefield, as well as the deaths of thousands of soldiers in prisons and hundreds of freedpeople in contraband camps, presented an overwhelming burden of memorialization.

Charleston had more than its share of this burden. During the war's final year the Confederate command in the city had converted the planters' Race Course (a horse racing track known as the Washington Race Course and Jockey Club) into a prison. Union soldiers were kept in terrible conditions, without tents or other coverings, in the interior of the track. At least 257 died from exposure and disease and were hastily buried without coffins in unmarked graves behind the judges' stand. After the city fell, Charleston's blacks, many of whom had witnessed the suffering at the horse track prison, insisted on a proper burial for the Union dead. The symbolic power of the race course was not lost on the freedpeople, and in conjunction with James Redpath and the missionaries and teachers of three freedmen's relief associations at work in Charleston, they planned a May Day ceremony that a *New York Tribune* correspondent called "a procession of friends and mourners as South Carolina and the United States never saw before."[7]

The "First Decoration Day," as this event came to be recognized in some circles in the North, involved an estimated ten thousand people, most of them black former slaves. During April twenty-eight black men from a local church built a suitable enclosure for the burial ground at the race course. In some ten days' labor, they constructed a fence ten feet high enclosing the burial ground and landscaped the graves into neat rows. The wooden fence was whitewashed and an archway was built over the gate to the enclosure. On the arch, painted in black letters, the workers inscribed "Martyrs of the Race Course." At nine o'clock in the morning on May 1 the procession to this special cemetery began as three thousand newly enrolled black school children marched around the Race Course, each with an armload of roses and singing "John Brown's Body." The children were followed by three hundred black women representing the "Patriotic Association," a group organized to distribute clothing and other goods among the freedpeople. The women carried baskets of flowers, wreaths, and crosses to the burial ground. The "Mutual Aid Society," a benevolent association of black men, next marched in cadence around the track and into the cemetery, followed by large crowds of white and black citizens. All dropped their spring blossoms on the graves in a scene recorded by a newspaper correspondent: "When all had left, the holy mounds—the tops, the sides, and the spaces between them—were one mass of flowers, not a speck of earth could be seen; and as the breeze wafted the sweet perfumes from them, outside and beyond . . . there were few eyes among those who knew the meaning of the ceremony that were not dim with tears of joy." While the adults marched around the graves, the children were gathered in a nearby grove, where they sang "America," "We'll Rally 'round the Flag," and "The Star-Spangled Banner."[8]

The official dedication ceremony was conducted by the ministers of all the black churches in Charleston. With prayers, the reading of biblical passages, and the singing of spirituals, black Charlestonians gave birth to an American tradition. In so doing they declared the meaning of the war in the most public way possible—by their labor, their words, their songs, and their solemn parade of roses and lilacs and marching feet on the old plant-

{ DAVID W. BLIGHT }

ers' Race Course. One can only guess at which passages of Scripture were read at the graveside on this first Memorial Day. But among the burial rites the spirit of Leviticus was surely there: "For it *is* the jubilee; it shall be holy unto you. . . . In the year of this jubilee ye shall return every man unto his possession."[9]

After the dedication the crowds gathered at the Race Course grandstand to hear some thirty speeches by Union officers, local black ministers, and abolitionist missionaries, all chaired by James Redpath, the director of freedmen's education in the coastal region. Picnics ensued around the grounds, and in the afternoon a full brigade of Union infantry, including the 54th Massachusetts and the 35th and 104th U.S. Colored Troops, marched in double column around the martyrs' graves and held a drill on the infield of the Race Course.[10] The war was over, and Memorial Day had been founded by African Americans in a ritual of remembrance and consecration. But the struggle to own the meaning of Memorial Day in particular, and of Civil War memory in general, had only begun.

According to a reminiscence written long after the fact, "several slight disturbances" occurred during the ceremonies on this first Decoration Day as well as "much harsh talk about the event locally afterward." But a measure of how white Charlestonians suppressed this founding from memory in favor of their own creation of the practice a year later came fifty-one years afterward, when the president of the Ladies' Memorial Association of Charleston received an inquiry for information about the May 1, 1865, parade. A United Daughters of the Confederacy official wanted to know if it was true that blacks and their white abolitionist friends had engaged in such a burial rite. Mrs. S. C. Beckwith responded tersely: "I regret that I was unable to gather any official information in answer to this."[11] In Southern and national memory the first Decoration Day was nearly lost in a grand evasion.

As a Northern ritual of commemoration, Memorial Day officially took hold in May 1868 and 1869, when General John A. Logan, commander-in-chief of the Grand Army of the Republic, called on all Union veterans to conduct ceremonies and decorate the graves of their dead comrades. In general orders issued each of the two springs, Logan called for a national commemoration unlike anything in American experience save possibly the Fourth of July. In "almost every city, village, and hamlet church-yard in the land," charged Logan's circular, those who died to "suppress the late rebellion" were to be honored annually "while a survivor of the war remains." On May 30, 1868, at a time of year when flowers were plentiful, in

183 cemeteries in 27 states funereal ceremonies were attended by thousands of people. The following year some 336 cities and towns in 31 states (including some in the South) arranged Decoration Day parades and orations. The observance grew manifold with time. In 1873 the New York legislature designated May 30 a legal holiday, and by 1890 every other Northern state had followed its lead.[12]

By the early 1870s and for at least two decades thereafter, as late spring arrived and flowers were in full supply, one could not live in or near an American city or village, North or South, and remain unaware of the ritual of decorating the graves of the Civil War dead. In most communities, women carried the primary responsibility of mobilizing people, including huge turnouts of school children, and gathering flowers for Decoration Day ceremonies. The Northern Women's Relief Corps (WRC), which evolved out of this memorial work in the 1860s and 1870s, claimed a membership of one hundred thousand by 1890, only seven years after its founding. The group's persistence kept Memorial Day focused on sorrow and loss in many communities into the late nineteenth century, when the holiday also became the occasion of amusement and sport. With time the WRC attracted women of varying persuasions—suffragists, antisuffragists, those who saw their roles as essentially moral and religious, and those who were political activists—but all, by and large, found unity in their duties as guardians of the memory of the Union dead.[13]

Because of Memorial Day, the ancient art of funereal orations and sermons gained a new life in America. The Decoration Day speech became an American genre that ministers, politicians, and countless former soldiers tried to master. In some communities these orations remained for decades primarily an occasion of sacred bereavement. But early on such speeches also assumed a political character; the dead and the lilacs were ever useful for the collective remembering and forgetting that Memorial Day helped foster.

Many widows and mothers at Memorial Day observances must have strained for forbearance during the endless expressions of joyous death on the altars of national survival. Northern speeches tended to be mournful, celebratory, and fiercely patriotic all at once. They mixed religion and nationalism in a victory cult that provided Northern Christians with a narrative through which to understand the sacrifice of their kin and friends. Their soldiers had died necessary deaths, they had saved the republic, and their blood had given the nation new life. In the Christian cosmology and the apocalyptic sense of history through which many Americans, white and black, interpreted the scale of death in the war, Memorial Day provided a means to achieve both spiritual recovery and historical understanding. In the cult of the fallen soldier a nineteenth-century manly ideal of heroism was redefined for coming generations. And, in a thousand variations, the Union dead—and soon the Confederate dead with them—served as saviors and founders, the agents of the death of an old social order and the birth of a new one. Memorial Day became a legitimizing ritual of the new American nationalism forged out of the war.

In Cincinnati in 1869 a crowd of thirty thousand people gathered in a cemetery to observe the decoration of 745 graves of that community's war dead. Among the processions was a disciplined line of hundreds of women, all dressed in "purest white" and carrying baskets of flowers. At a signal each woman stepped forward and cast her flowers on a grave. The scale of such an event would dwarf an All Saints' Day procession in some European cities. Ohio lieutenant governor J. C. Lee was orator of the day. In words modern anthropologists might endorse, Lee opened his speech: "Every act has its language, whether the act be of an individual, a society, a city, a state, or a nation, it has its language." Lee warned against the moral degeneration that the war's legacies might foster. Too many people understood the war, he maintained, as "nothing more than a material, visible matching of arms and physical force . . . [in which] nothing [was] achieved beyond that involved in a prize-ring." He reaffirmed that the central meaning of the war was that an "evil"—slavery—had been overthrown. The dead represented "something higher, something more enduring."[14] One has to read carefully to find such explicitly moral expressions, but good and evil, as well as the emancipationist legacy, were very much a part of early Memorial Day rhetoric.

Many Memorial Day ceremonies tingled with local and state pride, and all were collective expressions of genuine mourning. Some reflected the spirit of pastoral outings, as an observer indicated at the Antietam battlefield in 1869, describing small crowds "strolling" a landscape where "scarcely a scar made by the great conflict can be seen," yet where many knew those scars from published wartime photographs. The tradition of Memorial Day picnics began on these battlefields, not yet preserved as national parks, and in the ever-expanding rural cemeteries. To many orators the dead were not gone at all but survived in countless blood metaphors. "They are not dead," declared a speaker in Kenduskeag, Maine, in 1869. "The early manhood of this nation retains its majesty by their fall, and the black stain of slavery has been effaced from the bosom of this fair land by martyr blood." At many ceremonies a line of orphans marched in the cemetery procession, as in Baltimore, where some fifty children from the Union Orphan Asylum, led by their matrons, dropped flowers on their fathers' graves.[15]

However numbing the rhetoric, many a speech flowed with reconciliation as it honored the dead. In Little Rock, Arkansas, an 1869 orator, A. W. Bishop, pushed his audience to turn "from the past to the present" as quickly as they could. "The future is too full of opportunity," he said, "to be frittered away by a pointless antagonism." Reunion, especially its alleged permanence, was the theme of many Northern addresses in 1869 as well. In Mattoon, Illinois, an orator honored soldiers' heroism in the customary manner, reflexively denounced the rebellion, but then rejoiced with certainty that the nation had "secured a lasting peace" and had cemented a "common ancestry, one destiny, one heart."[16] Memorial Day rituals did their part in helping many Northerners become early believers in reunion, at least its ultimate necessity, while majorities still voted for the "bloody shirt."

Americans now had their Homeric tales of great war to tell. Within five years of the conflict speakers gave Union veterans their place in a direct line from Thermopylae to Gettysburg, from the "storied Wallace" and the Scottish tribes to "Sheridan's ride" and "Sherman's march to the sea." Americans now had a defining past of mythic battles, as the 1869 orator in Hornellsville, New York, put it, that would "stir the heart of the Irishman at home or abroad."[17] Such speeches undoubtedly inspired many veterans who heard them. These were tales of glory, epics they had lived and created, their future claim on the hearts and budgets of the nation. Thousands of those veterans would, in time, try their own hands at telling the story. Their individual narratives, which exploded as a reminiscence industry by the 1880s, were rooted in a decade and more of Memorial Day speechifying and monument dedications.

Many events and orators emphasized the democratic character of the war and its memorialization. To a minister in Ogdensburg, New York, in 1869, Union soldiers had broken down class barriers by their sacrifice. They did not come "from any one class or station of life, but from all," claimed L. L. Wood. "They came from the homes of refinement, of piety, and influence, as well as ignorance, poverty, and distress. They are all our own." In Wilmington, Delaware, in 1869 Memorial Day included an extraordinary interracial, interethnic, and interfaith procession to Brandywine Cemetery. Methodists, Episcopalians, Baptists, Unitarians, and Catholics marched together, representing the various churches of the city. White

GAR posts marched in the same parade with a black post, and the "Mount Vernon Cornet Band (colored)" kept step and time with the "Irish Nationalists with the harp and the sunburst flag of Erin." Rev. Fielder Israel of the First Unitarian Church, keeping alive a sense of the enemy of this composite gathering, broke from the conciliatory oratorical norm. Following the choir's rendition of the "Battle Hymn of the Republic," Israel laid the war's guilt squarely at the feet of Southerners, "the murderers of those whose memories we were here to honor."[18]

In other ceremonies sectional partisanship dissolved into celebration of the fallen's ethnic diversity. "Our adopted citizens from other lands have been more thoroughly Americanized . . . by the few years of war," remarked a Winona, Minnesota, speaker, "than they could have been by a long lifetime of peace." Sacred battlefields and hillsides full of graves gave some Americans an experience through which to define the nation as multiethnic and multiracial in a way they never could before. Indeed, a civic rather than an ethnic/racial definition of citizenship emerged in some Memorial Day oratory. "The gallant German . . . , the brave and generous Irishman, the sturdy Scandinavian," intoned the Minnesota minister, "and the various other nationalities who have fought by the side of our white and our black Americans . . . are by this fact forever identified with its destinies." This variation on the emancipationist legacy—the idea of a people's war for an expanding free labor society—was a real and abiding part of Civil War commemoration. In this vision the descendants of all the Union dead were "no longer strangers and foreigners, but are, by this baptism of blood . . . , consecrated citizens of America forever."[19] Decoration Day was, indeed, America's first multiracial, multiethnic commemoration. Along with emancipation celebrations, Memorial Day (and its derivatives) emerged as the Independence Day of the Second American Republic.

At Jefferson Barracks, in St. Louis, Missouri, on Memorial Day 1870, General I. F. Shepard spoke as the representative Yankee soldier remembering how emancipation evolved as a central result of the war. Slaves' freedom did not come by any simple playing out of destiny. Frail humanity had to be bludgeoned by divine power. Emancipation, claimed Shepard, "was heralded in the thunders of battlefields." It was a turning point in history "only second in sublimity to that upon Sinai's awful front, when the Decalogue was given in fire and smoke." Shepard then celebrated the war's transforming power as a victory over nativism. At length he identified the immigrant groups and declared the war unwinnable without the nation's "adopted sons." From the usual rhetoric about a new, single nationality "bathed" in baptismal blood Shepard moved to blacks, whom he characterized as pure victims of slavery, crushed but now the "ransomed menials" of the transforming war. Shepard's racist image of the freedpeople—a "differing species"—nevertheless portrayed them as benighted heroes, due their rights of "coequal privilege."[20] In such visions of the war's democratic legacy blacks had a place at Memorial Day processions, although that vision contained no plan yet for how an African American future would be secured.

At the dedication of a monument in the Soldiers' National Cemetery at Gettysburg on July 1, 1869, Reverend Henry Ward Beecher drew apocalyptic imagery, "heroic devotion," "mothers," and "orphans" into a single prayerful message to the next generation. "May the soldiers' children never prove unworthy of their fathers' name," pleaded Beecher. "Let them be willing to shed their blood, to lay down their lives, for the sake of their country." The transfer of a nationalistic legacy of heroism to the next generation took hold early. Veterans would struggle with this burden—as they laid it on their children—for decades. The orator at Gettysburg that day, Governor Oliver P. Morton of Indiana, left no doubts, however, about the meaning of the sacrifice. Morton linked Thermopylae not only to the fields of Gettysburg but also to emancipation and the Fifteenth Amendment (which had just passed Congress). A Yankee partisan who helped invent "bloody shirt" rhetoric, Morton refused to pay equal honor to the "rebel dead" and the Union dead. Of course, Southerners had fought with "courage," and he would "drop a tear to their memory." But his subject was war guilt more than the romance of heroism. "The rebellion was madness," declared Morton. "It was the insanity of States, the delirium of millions, brought on by the pernicious influence of human slavery." In his longwindedness, Morton was more Edward Everett than Abraham Lincoln; but his subject was precisely that of the former president six years earlier. "From the tomb of the rebellion a nation had been born again," Morton maintained. He gave the emancipationist meaning of the war full definition: "The rebellion, the offspring of slavery, hath murdered its unnatural parent, and the perfect reign of liberty is at hand."[21]

For white Southerners Memorial Day was born amid the despair of defeat and the need for collective expressions of grief. By 1866 local memorial associations, organized largely by women, took form in many Southern communities. Some new cemeteries were founded near battlefields, while existing ones in towns and cities were expanded enormously to accommo-

{ DAVID W. BLIGHT }

date the dead. In both sections, but especially in the South, the first monuments erected tended to be placed in cemeteries—the obvious sites of bereavement. By the 1890s hardly a city square, town green, or even some one-horse crossroads lacked a Civil War memorial of some kind. But through most of the Reconstruction years, the cemetery remained the public site of memorialization; obelisks and stone pyramids appeared as markers of the recent past that so haunted every community. Often directed by social elites who could fund monuments, the Southern "memorial movement . . . helped the South assimilate the fact of defeat without repudiating the defeated."[22] Memorialization functioned as a ritual process, a way of coping with loss on a profound scale. Elite women did much of the daily work of organizing memorialization, ostensibly keeping it in the realm of sentiment.

During Reconstruction Federal troops did very little to inhibit this process of Southern memorialization. Confederate Memorial Day had several independent origins in 1866. Different dates were recognized in different parts of the South. The Deep South tended to honor the dead on April 26, the day of Joseph E. Johnston's surrender to William Tecumseh Sherman, while communities in South and North Carolina adopted May 10, the anniversary of Stonewall Jackson's death. Virginia towns chose days ranging from May 10 to mid-June. The spectrum of dates caused some local ladies' memorial associations to compete over which days were most proper. By 1916 ten Southern states officially observed Memorial Day on June 3, Jefferson Davis's birthday. In both North and South, participants and orators often drew a comparison to the old Catholic European custom of All Saints' Day, on which whole villages and towns marched to churchyards to decorate the graves of generations of dead loved ones. After returning from decorating the graves of Confederate dead and reading a German novel that had described the custom in detail, Lizzie Rutherford of Columbus, Georgia, in 1866 recommended adopting All Saints' Day as a model. At the Winona, Minnesota, Memorial Day ceremony in 1869, Rev. William McKinley stood in the cemetery of the local Union dead and proclaimed: "This day may without impropriety be called our American All-Saints day."[23]

Memorialization could not forever be kept separate from civic life; it was itself part of the process of determining the meanings of the war and, therefore, inherently linked to the politics of memory. Some Southern orators tried hard to avoid "political utterances," but soon many began to connect the cause of Confederate independence with the struggle over

Reconstruction. Southern vindicationists may not have dominated Memorial Day oratory in the early years, but they certainly had their say. "Here let us look away from the gloom of political bondage," declared the Georgian Henry D. Capers in 1869, "and fix our vision upon a coming day of triumph, when principles, born of truth and baptized in the blood of our brothers, shall out live the persecution of a merciless enemy and the treachery of unhallowed ambition."[24] The postbellum war of ideas crept into the mournful processions and the silent grief on Southern Memorial Days and on many days in between.

By the early 1870s a group of former Confederate officers in Virginia had forged a coalition of memorial groups that quickly took over the creation of the Lost Cause tradition. They did so through print as much as through ritual commemorations. In 1866 former Confederate general Daniel H. Hill founded the magazine *The Land We Love*, a periodical devoted to demonstrating the skill and prowess of Confederate armies. By 1869 Hill's journal had become *Southern Magazine* and, most important, the Southern Historical Society (SHS) was founded as the vehicle for presenting the Confederate version of the war to the world. By 1876 the SHS had begun publishing its regular *Southern Historical Society Papers*, a series that ran for fourteen years under the editorship of a former Confederate chaplain, John William Jones. The driving ideological and emotional force behind the SHS was former Confederate general Jubal Early. Early had fled to Mexico at the end of the war and vowed never to return to his native Virginia under the U.S. flag. Despite such bluster and because of threatening poverty, Early returned to his home town of Lynchburg in 1869. He made himself, as Gaines Foster observes, into the "prototypical unreconstructed Rebel."[25] His principal aims were not only to vindicate Southern secession and glorify the Confederate soldier but also to launch a propaganda assault on popular history and memory.

With a millennial zeal and a conspiratorial vision, Early warned that Northern apologists were riveting deep into American memory a Unionist-emancipationist narrative of the war, an interpretation that portrayed Southern Confederates as traitors. He and his minions would do their best to burn such narratives out of Southern and national memory. Early saw this Unionist-emancipationist version of the war as a journalistic and pedagogical threat to destroy Southern honor, and he launched a counteroffensive.[26] The spirit of the Southern people would be redeemed, in Early's view, through the story of the irrepressible and heroic Confederate soldier. Black people would eventually have a place in the Confederate narrative,

{ DAVID W. BLIGHT }

but only as time-warped, loyal antebellum slaves. In the Confederate vision of the story, blacks would have to stay in the past, frozen in time, so that ex-Confederates could take their sick souls to a safe place for rehabilitation.

In 1873 Early and others gained control of the SHS and brought its operations to Virginia. At an August 14, 1873, meeting of some fifty-four delegates from twelve states in White Sulphur Springs, West Virginia, Early gave the keynote address. Attired in his uniform, with Confederate flag cuff links, Early forged defeat and victimhood into a passionate, heroic history. He argued that Confederate soldiers never lost on the battlefield and that secession had been right and honorable. At the "bar" of history, claimed Early, Southerners would "appear . . . as patriots demanding our rights and vindicating the true principles of the government founded by our fathers." The nobler side had lost the war, maintained Early, and its case had to be advanced boldly in the public memory. "The men who by their deeds caused so many battlefields of the South to blaze with a glory unsurpassed in the annals of the world," maintained Early, "cannot be so recreant to the principles for which they fought . . . as to abandon the tribunal to those before whose immense numbers and physical power alone they were finally compelled to yield from mere exhaustion." Early's targets included not only Northern historical writing and Memorial Day eulogies but also "their legislation and government policy."[27]

As former Confederates organized to vindicate their war experience and to forge the Lost Cause tradition, they sought a usable past in the coming battles over Reconstruction. As heroic victims of colossal Yankee machines and venal Republican tyranny they would have a well-rehearsed historical memory for the long struggle ahead. As the SHS published its battle accounts and vindications for the war, Southern terror succeeded on the ground, where myth-making held sway in the hearts and minds of citizens in overthrowing Reconstruction.

In the South monument unveiling days took on equal, if not greater, significance as rituals to that of Memorial Day. In Richmond, Virginia, on October 26, 1875, Confederate veterans by the thousands staged their first major coming out as a collective force. At the unveiling of the first significant monument to a Confederate hero, a standing statue of Stonewall Jackson sculpted by the British artist T. H. Foley, nearly fifty thousand people gathered for an unprecedented parade and a ceremony. As a public ritual and a mass statement of the meaning of Confederate defeat and Southern revival, the event had enormous political significance. A group of English citizens had funded and launched the effort to create the monument in 1863, shortly after Jackson's death. The sculptor, Foley, was preoccupied with many commitments and, fortuitously for Virginia, could not finish the work until the 1870s. It is hard to imagine such a ceremony in Richmond before 1874, when Republican Party rule was overthrown and former Confederate general James L. Kemper, who had been wounded in Pickett's Charge at Gettysburg, was elected the state's Democratic governor.[28]

The day dawned as balmy Indian summer in Richmond. The city was decorated and the parade route was festooned with flags, flowers, and streamers. Hundreds of doors and windows displayed portraits of Jackson. Everyday life and business were completely suspended; the stage was set for a public drama. Former Confederate general D. H. Hill described the scene as a "mournful but still a gala day." The crowds on the streets and on housetops watched the "imposing pageant," according to Hill, "with solemn faces and subdued feeling, as though looking at the funeral of the nation that died in 1865." Perhaps this was the celebratory funeral that the old Confederacy had been edging toward through nearly a decade of Memorial Days and resistance to Reconstruction. Despite the sunny skies, Hill found in the autumn leaves a "fading" and a "withering," "a requiem to the Lost Cause." Hill saw painful contrasts of the old and new everywhere in the procession. The flags' symbolism in particular caught his eye. "The battle-torn banners in the procession were conquered banners," Hill wrote. "The new, bright flags . . . were the flags of the conqueror. Those maimed and mutilated soldiers . . . were paroled prisoners. Those in tasteful uniforms were subjects of the conqueror. The flag that floats over the Capitol-grounds is the flag of the conqueror. The conquered banner is wrapped around the dead hero's body in the dead hero's grave." Deeply conscious of loss, Hill seems to have discovered in such a public display of remembrance a sense of what was truly gone. But in his commentary he also anticipated Robert Penn Warren's notion of how "in the moment of its death the Confederacy entered upon its immortality."[29]

At major intersections on the parade route, veterans, ladies' memorial associations, and "the indefatigable K.K.K." (Ku Klux Klan) had assembled artisans to construct arches and towers with elaborate decorations honoring Jackson. The largest arch, at Grace and Eighth Streets, included huge letters that read "Warrior, Christian, Patriot." Above the inscription was a painting representing a stone wall "upon which was resting a bare sabre, a Bible, and a Confederate cap." On either side of this arch stood two towers. "The most decided effect in any of the decorations," according to a journalist, "was produced by placing two Confederate soldiers, dressed in their

{ DAVID W. BLIGHT }

genuine, old, tattered Confederate garments, upon two pedestals just in front of each tower. They leaned upon reversed muskets, and were as immovable as statues; indeed, many people could not believe that they were living individuals."[30] Perhaps it was this sense of theater—living Confederate veterans in faded wool, standing as ersatz statues—that prompted D. H. Hill to hear the dirges for a dead nation.

One dispute among the planners of the Jackson statue unveiling nearly derailed the event. Governor Kemper was the grand marshal of the ceremonies and carefully planned the parade to the Capitol Square in Richmond. Kemper was nervous that "nothing shall appear on the 26th to hurt the party" (Democrats). He feared that the "least excess" in the Confederate celebration would give yet another "bloody shirt" to Northern Republicans, and he asked Confederate veteran leaders to show restraint in their displays of battle flags. Only days before the big event, Jubal Early wrote to Kemper complaining of rumors that black militia companies and civilians were to be "allowed in the procession." "I am inexpressibly shocked at the idea," said Early. He considered the involvement of blacks "an indignity to the memory of Jackson and an insult to the Confederates." Black Richmonders, totaling twenty to thirty thousand in Early's count, would swarm into the square, he believed, and whites would be forced to "struggle for place with buck negroes . . . anxious to show their consequence." Believing that blacks would wave "pictures of Lincoln and Fifteenth Amendment banners," Early threatened not to attend, and to urge other veterans to boycott the event, if Kemper executed the plan.[31]

In ferocious responses Kemper told Early to mind his own business and begged him to "stay at home." Black militia officers and ministers in Richmond had petitioned Kemper to take part in the procession. In an attempt to maintain racial "peace" in the city, the governor accepted the petitioners' request. The small contingent of blacks was placed at the extreme rear of a parade several miles long and comprised of dozens of white groups numbering many thousands of marchers. By the time the crowd assembled in the square for the unveiling speeches, Kemper felt certain that it would "have very far fewer negroes in it than would be there in case of no such formation." Since the blacks had promised to "humbly" honor Jackson, Kemper judged the situation as "calculated to vindicate our white people against Radical lies." To avoid any exhibition of racial mixing, Kemper even eliminated from the march the Virginia General Assembly, where a few black Republicans still served. Kemper kept the program as planned and Early attended, while washing his hands of any responsibility for its arrangements. The black militia companies, perhaps anticipating their humiliation, did not march. The only blacks who participated formally were a contingent of former slave workers in the Stonewall Brigade.[32] In the racial ordering fiercely disputed by these two former Confederate generals behind the scenes, we can see much of what was at stake in Southern memorialization as it went public. The position of blacks in this bitter dispute between the ultimate irreconcilable Confederate and a redeemer-reconciliationist governor remained utterly subordinate. One would eliminate blacks altogether from Confederate memory; the other would declare them loyal and dispatch them to the rear of parades. In the long history of Lost Cause tradition both got their wish.

As the immense crowd assembled at the state capitol grounds where the Jackson monument was to be unveiled, Kemper welcomed them as the Democrat-redeemer governor of Virginia. He announced that Jackson was a national hero, not merely a Southern saint, whose memory was to be a "common heritage of glory" for both the North and the South. The massive ceremony served as the South's reminder to the North of its insistence on "respect." The unveiling declared, in effect, that Reconstruction, as Northern Republicans had imagined it, was over. The monument, claimed Kemper, "stands forth a mute protest before the world against the rule of tyrants which, wanting faith in the instincts of honor, would distrust and degrade a brave and proud but unfortunate people, which would bid them repent, in order to be forgiven, of such deeds and achievements as heroes rejoice to perform." The whole event, declared Kemper, was the harbinger of "actual reconciliation" and the "equal honor and equal liberties of each section."[33] The war had been about sections, and the one conquered was back in the fold with much of its old leadership at the helm.

The Virginia legislature chose Rev. Moses Drury Hoge, pastor of the Richmond Second Presbyterian Church, as orator of the day. During the war, Hoge had given the daily prayer at the Confederate Congress and had served as a blockade runner as well as a chaplain at a Richmond training camp. Confederate defeat had apparently crushed Hoge psychologically in 1865. But ten years later, on that bright autumn day, he rose to the occasion and announced that Southerners were living in a "new era of our history." Preparing Lost Causers for the long haul, Hoge declared "defeat" the "discipline which trains the truly heroic soul." In his finale Hoge reached his most important theme: the overthrow of Reconstruction and the demand for a political return to a *status quo antebellum*. "If it be objected that we have already entered upon one of those political revolutions that never go backward," Hoge proclaimed, "then I ask, who gave to anyone the authority to say so?" Hoge summoned the audience to return to the old ways, to the old nation. Their duty in the new era was to return to "a Union as our fathers framed . . . the Constitution in its old supremacy."[34] Amid a massive performance of Confederate remembrance on this day, the Gettysburg Address and the Thirteenth, Fourteenth, and Fifteenth Amendments did not exist. In short, the civic meaning of emancipation fell among the litter on the streets of Richmond. As Southerners mourned their dead heroes and their dead Confederacy, they rejoiced in their emerging victory over the peace.

During the 1870s, perhaps as a way of escaping the rancor of Reconstruction politics, Northerners and Southerners began to participate together in Memorial Day rituals. Strikingly early, in 1867, Frances Miles Finch published in the *Atlantic Monthly* his widely popular poem "The Blue and the Gray," which gave to the cause of reconciliation verses expressing sweetness, mutual sympathy, and the universality of death and mourning. How true his simple lines must have seemed to the thousands who would hear them recited down through the years at Decoration Days and Blue-Gray reunions:

> Sadly, but not with upbraiding,
>   The generous deed was done;
> In the storm of the years that are fading,
>   No braver battle was won;—
>   Under the sod and the dew,
>   Waiting the judgment day;—
>   Under the blossoms, the Blue,
>   Under the garlands, the Gray.[35]

But beyond the pain and pathos of individual mourners, the emerging reunionism served many social and political aims.

In the South collective pride in the Confederate past returned in public outpourings on Memorial Days. That pride was often local as well as Southern. In Guilford, North Carolina, on Confederate Memorial Day (May 10) in 1873, John A. Gilmer, urging "pride" in "our own Guilford dead," invoked the memory of local commanders, regiments, and battles that had special associations for his audience. But mostly Gilmer celebrated the "rapidly returning sense of right in our own people." Southerners need no longer have any "hesitation" or "reluctance" about their Memorial Day, claimed Gilmer. The world had "*conceded* to Southern courage, Southern devotion, Southern skill, and Southern power, as displayed in that war."[36]

A year later, in Wilmington, North Carolina, on the federal Memorial Day, Albion Tourgee delivered a different, though conciliatory, address to a crowd of five thousand in the town's national cemetery. A former Union soldier, carpetbagger, and federal district judge in Greensboro, Tourgee was deeply committed to Reconstruction and to the rights of the freedpeople. In 1874 he was still embroiled in North Carolina politics, struggling to survive the terror of the Ku Klux Klan, and holding a dying Republican Party together. Tourgee would emerge later as one of the most eloquent proponents of the war's emancipationist legacy. But his Memorial Day effort in Wilmington in 1874 was, for him, extraordinarily generous toward former Confederates. He welcomed the former Confederates who had come to the ceremony that day as "those . . . who sit no longer on the 'sounding shore' of memory, and nurse the madness of the past—but as those who bow to the issue of war, and honor the valor which prevailed." Tourgee confronted the reality that the war had been one "between kindred —between brothers speaking the same tongue, worshipping the same God." It is doubtful that many former Confederates were comfortable with Tourgee's terms and sentiments of reconciliation. He lectured at some length on how slavery lay at the root of the war and that the "emancipation of the slave" had been a principal aim of the struggle and not, as had become "fashionable" to say, "forced upon the government." To the freedpeople in his audience, Tourgee declared the day their own. "These . . . are your dead," he announced. "They are those who fell in the wilderness between the Egypt of your bondage and the Promised Land of your freedom!"[37] On the ground in the South in a national cemetery at this interracial Memorial Day, the vexations and divisions of Civil War memory had become manifest.

In 1874–75 Union and Confederate veterans began to participate in Memorial Day exercises together in both the North and the South. In the wake of Memorial Day 1875 in North Carolina a black citizen in Raleigh, Osborne Hunter, anxiously observed in a letter to a newspaper "a noticeable spirit of reconciliation pervading the political atmosphere of both the Republican and Democratic parties of this state." In August 1874 the Democrats had regained power in North Carolina, and the highly racialized election had hinged, in part, on Southern resistance to federal enforcement of black civil rights. Until May 1875 blacks in Raleigh had always played a major role in Decoration Day ceremonies. That year they were discouraged

{ DAVID W. BLIGHT }

from participating, as the occasion was declared to be only a "soldier's turn-out." At the mark of a "decade in the history of freedom," concluded Hunter, Decoration Day seemed to be only an occasion for "ignoring the colored citizen and the colored voter."[38]

Up North Memorial Day orators began to strike chords of reconciliation, especially around the theme of shared soldiers' valor. On Decoration Day 1874 in Boston the Charles Russell Lowell Encampment of the Grand Army of the Republic assembled for a sermon in West Church by Rev. C. A. Bartol. In an effort entitled "The Soldier's Motive" Bartol honored the blind faith of warriors who forget themselves in devotion to a cause. Conviction, duty, and obedience with an "abandonment that neither reserves its resources nor counts the cost," declared Bartol, "is the all-surpassing reason for our approval and love." This theme, what Oliver Wendell Holmes Jr. would later term the "Soldier's Faith," would become a standard feature of memorial and reunion rhetoric. Within a decade of the war's end the soldierly virtue of devotion, whatever the cause, was well rehearsed as a means to sectional peace. Indeed, it became a rhetorical weapon of great potency in the retreat from and overthrow of Reconstruction.[39]

The disputed election of 1876 and the electoral crisis that culminated in the Compromise of 1877 brought the Republican Rutherford B. Hayes to the presidency as well as the final three Southern states not under Democratic control into that party's fold. Reconciliation seemed to sweep over the country's political spirit, as the Union survived another potential severing by sectional and partisan strife. Although it was hardly the first time that Northern and Southern commentators had declared the final conclusion to the issues of the war, the political settlement of 1877 handily took its place as the traditional "end" of Reconstruction (a label it has carried ever since).

On Memorial Day, May 30, 1877, New York City experienced an array of parades and ceremonies unprecedented since the formal inception of the holiday nine years earlier. Virtually every orator and editorial writer declared the day one of forgetting, forgiveness, and equality of the Blue and the Gray veterans. The *New York Herald* set the tone for the occasion two days in advance by offering a vision of an American character free of the burdens of the past: "The man whose memory dates back over a month is voted a bore, and accused of being interested in ancient history." With an unabashed sense of finality, the *Herald* declared that "all the issues on which the war of the rebellion was fought seem dead, and the late effort to manufacture political sentiment out of them was a signal failure. American eyes have a characteristic tendency to look forward and let the past be with itself." In this atmosphere of national reunion parade marchers thronged New York's streets and tens of thousands of citizens visited every cemetery in the region to lay flowers at the graves of the Union and Confederate dead.[40]

An "immense multitude" filled the streets of Manhattan to watch the Decoration Day parades. Detachments of city police, fire engine companies, the New York National Guard, the Association of Mexican War Veterans, and seventeen GAR posts assembled along Fourth Avenue between Sixteenth and Twentieth Streets. In each block several decorated floral wagons, a choir, a drum corps, and carriages for invited guests (some of whom were War of 1812 veterans) were positioned among the Civil War veterans. The parade was blessed with a late spring morning "so beautiful," reported the *New York Tribune*, "that it rested on the city like a benediction." Each detachment had a specific destination for the day's march—a cemetery or a monument in Brooklyn or lower Manhattan where participants would conduct ceremonies and lay the traditional flowers on graves.[41]

In Union Square and Madison Square floral decorations adorned the statues of George Washington, Abraham Lincoln, Marquis de Lafayette, and William H. Seward. The Lincoln statue drew the most attention and the most elaborate display of flowers. A laurel wreath perched atop Lincoln's head, and wisteria sprays, begonias, and greenery were wound around him; white carnations were used to write the word "Emancipation" across a panel in the center of the monument. As members of Abraham Lincoln Post Number Thirteen gathered, the black abolitionist and Presbyterian minister Henry Highland Garnet gave an opening prayer. A black militia group, the Skidmore Guards, occupied a prominent position in the ceremony, as did members of Garnet's congregation from Shiloh Church. The orator of the morning, General John Cochrane, a veteran of many battles and the vice presidential running mate of John C. Fremont in the 1864 election bid to unseat Lincoln from within the Republican Party, celebrated the recent national compromise, no doubt without any sense of irony, as "the birth of constitutional liberty." The restoration of home rule in the South and the cessation of hostilities between the sections was to Cochrane "a purely American emancipation. . . . A new nation burst into life, whose centennial glories embrace the liberalization of government." Cochrane spoke proudly about how three years before, in a ceremony at this very statue, the Abraham Lincoln Post members had advocated that "the graves equally of the Union and Confederate dead be decorated by loyal hands." Cochrane reminded his listeners that they should not lose their sense of which cause had been right and which wrong, but that as soldiers, the Confederates, dead and alive, were their "brothers."[42] On this day, the only meanings of the war given public airing were those that emancipated former foes to mutual honor and liberated the nation from division to a sense of political peace.

In late morning the New York parade headed south for twenty spectacular blocks on Fifth Avenue. One GAR post carried twelve stained and torn battle flags, and on the sides of one floral wagon a veterans' unit had displayed photographs of dead comrades. Following close behind all the hook and ladder companies of the fire department was a regiment of black troops, led by an African American marching band. After passing in front of a large grandstand on the west side of Madison Square and marching a short distance on Broadway, the parade turned and went down to the ferry docks on the East River. Parade marchers then rode ferry boats across to the Brooklyn shore, where via the Long Island Railroad and other conveyances they were transported to the Cypress Hills, Calvary, and Greenwood Cemeteries.[43]

A crowd estimated at nearly fifty thousand gathered along the roadways and near the Gothic arches at the entrance to Greenwood, one of the first such "rural" cemeteries designed in the United States. The long procession encircled the Soldiers' Monument (a typical symbol now in many cemeteries and town and city squares) erected in memory of the 148,000 New Yorkers who had served in the Union cause. As a band played intermittently between various prayers and speeches, individuals and family members walked forward from the crowds and placed wreaths at the base of the monument. The chief orator, Colonel A. W. Baxter, closed with an appeal for unity, calling all, "over the grave of buried bygones [to] rejoice that, now, as soldiers and citizens, we know no North, no South, no East, no West—only one country and one flag."[44] In the bucolic setting of Greenwood Cemetery, vast numbers of mourners stayed until nearly sunset.

At Calvary Cemetery, also in Brooklyn, similar ceremonies occurred amid huge crowds. The obliteration of sectional identity and animosity was the theme of poems and speeches. To the press the most striking feature of the Calvary ceremonies was that the day before a palmetto tree had been planted at the grave of a South Carolinian, James G. Kelly, a Confederate soldier buried in New York. The tree had been sent by friends from South Carolina, and the gesture seemed to many to capture the meaning of the occasion.[45] On these landscapes of Civil War memory devotion to the Lost Cause had already gained a special place in the American imagination—the alleged nobility of losers in a desperate struggle carried an enduring fascination in an age increasingly characterized by cynical politics, amoral machines, and the impersonal leviathan of industrialization. Political necessity combined with deep cultural need to produce an almost irresistible Decoration Day spirit of reunion.

Decoration Day 1877 in New York culminated with a special indoor event at the Brooklyn Academy of Music. The planning committee, dominated by Democrats, invited the prominent former Confederate general, lawyer, and Brooklyn resident Roger A. Pryor as orator of the evening. A committee member, Joseph Neilson, opened the proceedings with an explicit appeal for reconciliation. Neilson declared all the "causes" of the "late domestic contention" forgotten. As the voice of "healing," Pryor took the podium before an audience of nearly one thousand to deliver his extraordinary address, "The Soldier, the Friend of Peace and Union."[46]

Pryor, a Virginian, had been a fiery secessionist in 1861 and served in the Confederate Congress at the war's outset. He enlisted in the Confederate army and rose to the rank of brigadier general. Due to casualties his brigade was dissolved in 1863, whereupon Pryor reenlisted as a private in Fitzhugh Lee's cavalry and was captured near Petersburg in November 1864. In September 1865 Pryor, who would refuse a pardon until 1880, moved to New York, where Democratic Party friends helped him establish a legal career. He published articles defending the South's cause in the *New York Daily News*, sometimes under a pseudonym because he feared arrest. Republican newspapers referred to him as "the Rebel Pryor" for his advocacy of the Lost Cause. By the 1870s Pryor had gained membership in the Manhattan Club, a prominent Democratic Party organization, and began a long political career that would land him a seat on the New York Court of Common Pleas in 1890 and, in 1896, an appointment to the state supreme court. The man asked to be the chief speaker on Decoration Day in Brooklyn was the most prominent among a growing and influential group of what many called the "Confederate carpetbaggers" of New York and other Northern cities.[47] Pryor, along with his wife, Sarah Rice Pryor, who eventually became a significant writer and memoirist, never retreated from the righteousness of the South's cause even as they accepted some of the war's results.

As the embodiment of a sectional reunion forged out of business enterprise and a Reconstruction that sustained white supremacy, Pryor did not squander his opportunity in the spotlight. After thanking the organizers for their "overture of reconciliation," Pryor delivered an unreconstructed

Southerner's demand for recognition of the equality and nobility of the Confederate soldier as well as a ringing statement of the "needless war" doctrine that would become popular among some historians in the twentieth century. "The bloody work of secession," announced the former ardent secessionist, "was wholly the act of professed men of peace—the politicians." Soldiers were simply men of honor and duty serving the dictates of history and were, therefore, the suffering victims of fate. The Confederate veteran especially deserved the American people's sympathy. The orator touched a chord that would resonate for decades in Civil War memory. "From the reproach of conscious wrong the soldier of the South is free," declared Pryor.[48] The greatest heroes were those who fought for the cause lost; devotion alone merited a reunited nation's gratitude.

But Pryor did not restrict himself merely to the subject of the heroic soldier. Given such a forum, the Confederate partisan gave a full-throated condemnation of Reconstruction as "that dismal period—massacres of the helpless, violations of the ballot, usurpations of force on the popular will and the independence of the States." Pryor fashioned a beguiling version of the evil image of Reconstruction. The Reconstruction years were a time, he maintained, of "alien rule and federal domination by which sovereign states were reduced to the impotence of satrapies." The reunion now possible after the Compromise of 1877 was, therefore, a victory over Reconstruction, over racial equality, and over federal enforcement against the South. "Fallen it [Reconstruction] is at last," declared Pryor, "fallen like Lucifer never to hope again; fallen by the thunderbolt of the people's wrath."[49] Twelve years after Appomattox a former Confederate general and the voice of the Lost Cause explained to his Yankee audience, many of whom were Union veterans, that the South's vindication was really the nation's triumph. Pryor in effect announced, long live the new Union, saved from the Devil of radical Republicanism and black suffrage by Confederate veterans. This theme would continue to flourish in new literary and political forms over the next four decades.

Unlike many Memorial Day orators, Pryor did not hide the issue of race behind a rhetoric of reunion. The war had nothing directly to do with slavery, he proclaimed in what became an article of faith to Southern vindicationists and their Northern allies. Southerners were comfortably reconciled to the destruction of slavery because it had been only the "occasion not the cause of secession." Slavery was an impersonal force in history, a natural phenomenon subject only to divine control and therefore beyond all human responsibility. It was good while it lasted, but good once it was gone; no Southerner fought in its defense, and no Northerner died to end it. It just went away, like a change in the weather. Pryor declared with audacious confidence that "impartial history will record that slavery fell not by any effort of man's will, but by the immediate intervention and act of the Almighty himself; and in the anthem of praise ascending to heaven for the emancipation of four million human beings, the voice of the Confederate soldier mingles its note of devout gratulation."[50] In such selective and politically charged uses of memory, the devout could claim anything. Everyone responsible for slavery—and the war—had already achieved absolution, even a resurrection.

To Pryor, Southerners were the best Unionists because they understood fully how radical Reconstruction had been a scheme "devised to balk the ambition of the white race." Southerners knew best how their own "shelter and support" lay within the Union because they feared "the havoc and carnage of a war aggravated by a conflict between races and issuing inevitably in the catastrophe of a remorseful subjugation." The reunion taking hold by 1877 was none other than a national victory over the potential of a race war. As Pryor concluded his performance he folded "Grant and Lee[,] ... Stonewall and Sherman" into the same mystic remembrance and placed the future safety of the Union in the "blended memories" of Confederate and Union veterans. At the end of his speech, Pryor bowed before the "prolonged applause" of his New York audience.[51]

Following Pryor, former Union general Isaac S. Catlin delivered the evening's final address. In full sympathy with the former Confederate's speech, Catlin spoke of military pathos and glory, of the victimhood and heroism of all soldiers on both sides. "I love the memory of a soldier," said Catlin. "I love the very dust that covers his mouldering body." Catlin called on all to be "exultant" that slavery was dead. "Is this not enough?" he asked. "Is it not enough that we are all American citizens, that our country is saved, that our country is one?" In this doctrine of "enough," the emancipationist legacy of the war had become bad taste among gentlemen soldiers. The "divine doctrine of forgiveness and conciliation" was the order of the day.[52]

Dissent from this Blue-Gray, reconciliationist version of the war's memory, while now on the margins, had by no means been silenced. One year later, as though they had decided to invite a direct response to Pryor and his ilk, members of the integrated Abraham Lincoln Post of the GAR asked Frederick Douglass to address them in Madison Square on Decoration Day. As he did on so many occasions during the last quarter of his life, Douglass rose to the challenge with fire and indignation, offering an alternative, abolitionist-emancipationist memory of the war. "There was a right side and a wrong side in the late war," insisted Douglass, "that no sentiment ought to cause us to forget." As though he was answering Pryor in a debate, Douglass declared that the Southerner "must not glory in his shame, and boast his non-repentance." In Douglass's view the subject of Memorial Day should be the "moral character of the war." Sickened at the increasingly defensive posture of those Northerners who saw the war as a triumph for black freedom and the birth of a new republic, Douglass stood before Lincoln's statue and demanded that his audience "not be asked to be ashamed of our part in the war." The reconciliationists were using memory to send the nation down the wrong road to reunion, he believed. Douglass had no patience for endless tales of Southern woes. "The South has suffered to be sure," he said, "but she has been the author of her own suffering."[53]

Douglass called on his listeners not to cave in to pathos and sentiment, not to seek reunion in the mutuality of soldiers' sacrifice, hard as that might be in the climate of the late 1870s. In their processions to the graves, Douglass called white and black Union veterans to a different remembrance. The struggle had not been one of mere "sectional character," he asserted. "It was a war of ideas, a battle of principles[,] . . . a war between the old and new, slavery and freedom, barbarism and civilization." The war was "not a fight," he concluded, "between rapacious birds and ferocious beasts, a mere display of brute courage and endurance, but it was a war between men of thought as well as of action, and in dead earnest for something beyond the battlefield."[54]

In the passions evident in the speeches of Pryor and Douglass, the conflicted memory of the Civil War lived at the heart of American political culture. To mourn is to yearn for healing, but the extent of the healing often depends on the freedom and power of the mourners on the day after the grief ritual. By the late 1870s many Northern orators and commentators, even the most famous, clearly felt themselves on the defensive in the struggle over the war's memory. In an interview in 1878 Ulysses S. Grant complained about "historians" who kept rehearsing the argument that the Union forces had "overwhelmed the South" with numbers, especially foreign immigrants. Grant took umbrage at the claim that the Union had won with "hirelings and Hessians." "This is the way public opinion was made during the war," claimed Grant, "and this is the way history is made now. We never overwhelmed the South. . . . What we won from the South we won by hard fighting." Grant turned the argument around on Southern apologists and vindicationists in an ironic way. He complained that the "4,000,000 of negroes" who "kept the farms, protected the families, supported the armies, and were really a reserve force" were "never counted in any summary of the forces of the South."[55]

Moreover, General William Tecumseh Sherman, who was the orator for the 1878 evening ceremonies at New York's Booth Theater on Memorial Day, responded to the incessant demand that all the loss in life and treasure from the war "should be forgotten." Southerners had "long since been forgiven," Sherman answered. They were "our equals" in the councils of government and in "all attributes of citizenship." Indeed, the South's welcome back into the "family group," the general posited, might have "gone too far" and constituted "one of the great political questions now on trial." What Sherman, who was no friend of Reconstruction and black rights, would not yet extend to Southerners was an equal "measure of honor and glory" merely because their "motives were pure." He insisted that whatever else Southerners achieved in the reunion, they had to live with being on the "wrong" side in the war. "Abstract right and abstract wrong" mattered as a question of history, he maintained. Sherman insisted that Northerners not "tear from the history of our country the pages which record the great events from 1860 to 1865" and that they "never apologize for the deeds done."[56]

The fervor with which Americans practiced the rituals of Memorial Day began to fade in the late 1870s and early 1880s. "Graceful popular ceremonies," declared the *New York Tribune* in May 1878, no longer fit in a society characterized by "the pioneers of the prairie and the speculators in railway stock." Bitterness had waned, and as "individual sorrow for the fallen fades away," maintained the editors, Decoration Day "gradually loses its best significance." By 1880 the same paper editorialized on how Decoration Day had "become coarser and more blurred" in its meaning and how it had fallen into the "slough of politics." In the Gilded Age the *Tribune*'s editors claimed that the truly "loyal" would continue to honor the Civil War dead but also make every "effort to put out of sight the causes of the war, the hate and bitterness which we thought immortal." At stake now was the next generation and the social and moral order. Civil War memorialization should not be used for political purposes among the children born since the war, claimed the *Tribune*, but the sacrifice of soldiers should very much be used as lessons in morality and patriotism. "The days they [postwar children] have been born in are not heroic," declared the *Tribune*. "They are full of fraud, corruption, bargain, and sale. Men are not pushing to the battlefield to die for an idea; they are pushing into place." As an antidote to America's "sordid expertness in money-getting," the editors spoke for a large cross-section of the culture that now looked to the Civil War dead, as well as to living veterans, as the alternative to their unheroic age, as sources of honest passion, higher morality, something "noble and true . . . kept for our children." By the 1880s Americans needed a social and moral equivalent of war. They would achieve this, of a kind, in the realm of sentiment—in a resurgent cult of manliness and soldierly virtues recycled in thousands of veterans' papers, speeches, and reminiscences. Such a moral equivalent of war, however, came to exalt soldiers and their sacrifices but disembodied them from the war's causes and consequences. Returning to his home town of Lancaster, Massachusetts, to speak on Memorial Day in 1880, the veteran John D. Washburn announced that he could not speak of "abstract themes." "Even questions of present duty and the rights of man are too harsh," he said. The day was now reserved, in his view, only for "grateful love and tender recollection" of his dead comrades.[57]

Although it became dominant, such a mode of commemoration continued to spawn its dissenters during a turbulent contest over the meaning of Memorial Days and monument building. In Stillwater, Minnesota, in 1879 a veteran, Colonel Thomas F. Barr, offered his "utter dissent" from what he considered the "false sentimentality" of reconciliation based on a "blue and gray . . . fraternity." Echoing many of Frederick Douglass's postwar speeches, Barr insisted that "our tributes are not paid to courage. . . . It was no gladiatorial contest in which we were engaged—a test of physical prowess of sections. It was a death grapple between right and wrong." Barr was one Union veteran who believed too much forgiveness had been extended to the South. Identifying the destruction of slavery in particular as a central result of the war and the plight of the freedmen's rights as an ugly legacy, Barr argued that "treason" should have been "so punished . . . that it might never come to be eulogized as true loyalty."[58] More than one lost cause contended for space on the landscape of Civil War memory as the conflict receded into the past and into the realm of organized recollection mixed with imagination.

In the North of the 1880s Oliver Wendell Holmes Jr. came to represent as forcefully as anyone the dominant, nonideological mode of Civil War memory. The spirit of reconciliation as a method of forgetting had no greater spokesman than the great jurist from Massachusetts. Wounded at Antietam, horrified by what he called "an infamous butchery" at the battle of Fredericksburg in 1862, and worried for his own sanity during his experi-

ences of the Wilderness campaign in 1864, Holmes had resigned his commission before the war ended. Deeply troubled during the immediate aftermath of the war by his combat experiences, Holmes's changing attitudes
toward war mirrored the social climate. By 1884 Holmes was a regular
orator at Memorial Days and veterans' reunions. In Keene, New Hampshire, in 1884 he opened a Decoration Day address with the statement that
a young man had recently asked him why people still "kept up Memorial
Day." His memorable and writerly answer was not overtly about reconciliation, nor did he hint at the war's causes. The young needed to hear
veterans' stories, contended Holmes, because "the generation that carried
on the war has been set apart by its experience." In what are now famous
lines, Holmes spoke a kind of prose anthem of the American reunion:
"Through our great good fortune, in our youth our hearts were touched
with fire. It was given to us to learn at the outset that life is a profound and
passionate thing. While we are permitted to scorn nothing but indifference,
and do not pretend to undervalue the worldly rewards of ambition, we have
seen with our own eyes beyond and above the gold fields the snowy heights
of honor, and it is for us to bear the report to those who come after us." In
Holmes's vision Union and Confederate veterans were one in feeling and
experience. "The soldiers of the war need no explanations," Holmes declared. "They can join in commemorating a soldier's death with feelings
not different in kind, whether he fell toward them or by their side."[59]
Whoever was honest in devotion and courage was right. Such a mutual
feeling among soldiers on opposite sides has emerged from every modern
war. Holmes described many truths. But rarely from a civil war of such
violence and scale has such a reconciliation, forged in remembered valor,
taken hold so quickly and with such important political consequences.

The Holmesian mode of memory—passion and heroism immunized
from motive—did not go unchallenged as Memorial Day reached its twentieth anniversary. No one criticized Memorial Days devoted to Blue-Gray
reconciliation more than Albion Tourgee. In a series of articles in the
Chicago Inter-Ocean in 1884–85 called "The Veteran and His Pipe," Tourgee denounced and satirized a reunion based on soldierly honor alone.
Writing as a lone Union veteran speaking to his pipe, "Blower," Tourgee
dissented over and over from sectional reconciliation even if it meant the
obliteration of the emancipationist meaning of the war or, for that matter,
any other sense of ideology or cause. In a column entitled "Memorial Day"
Tourgee resented that the original name, "Decoration Day," had waned and
that the "festival of flowers" had been ransomed for "a little cheap lauda-

{ DAVID W. BLIGHT }

tion, in silly deference to a sickly sentimentality." The holiday had become one only of calculated forgetting, the veteran moaned into his pipe. "To dwell upon the hero's sufferings and ignore the motive which inspired his acts," he wrote, "is to degrade him to the level of the mercenary. Fame dwells in purpose as well as in achievement. Fortitude is sanctified only by its aim."[60]

The story of Civil War memory and the ritual of Decoration Days continued well beyond 1885 as the emancipationist legacy fought endless rear-guard actions against a Blue-Gray reconciliation that would sweep through American culture. Those who remembered the war as the rebirth of the republic in the name of racial equality would continue to do battle with the growing number who would remember it as the nation's test of manhood and the South's struggle to sustain white supremacy. Rituals such as Memorial Day parades, ceremonies, and speeches are the means by which real and ideal worlds meet in most cultures. As Clifford Geertz has written, "in a ritual, the world as lived and the world as imagined, fused under the agency of a single set of symbolic forms, turn out to be the same world."[61] Because the meaning of the Civil War remained so unsettled in American culture for so long, memorialization became just such a set of rituals whereby the dead continued to mingle among the living—in small stone monuments, symbolic bloody shirts, terrorists' white hoods, patriotic songs and speeches, veterans' fraternal bonds, women's Memorial Day committees, and, ultimately, in the concrete forms of election ballots.

NOTES

1. Maris A. Vinovskis, "Have Social Historians Lost the Civil War?: Some Preliminary Demographic Speculations," *Journal of American History* 76 (June 1989): 35–39; Drew Gilpin Faust, *"A Riddle of Death": Mortality and Meaning in the American Civil War*, Thirty-fourth Fortenbaugh Memorial Lecture, Gettysburg College (Gettysburg, 1995), 7–8; Thomas L. Livermore, *Numbers and Losses in the Civil War in America, 1861–65* (Bloomington: Indiana University Press, 1957).

2. Robert N. Rosen, *Confederate Charleston: An Illustrated History of the City and the People during the Civil War* (Columbia: University of South Carolina Press, 1994), 98–147 (Mrs. St. Julien Ravenal quote on 121).

3. Ibid., 152–53.

4. Raphael Samuel, *Theaters of Memory: Past and Present in Contemporary Culture* (London: Verso, 1994), especially 1:3–39. On the significance of ritual for collective memory, see Paul Connerton, *How Societies Remember* (Cambridge: Cambridge University Press, 1989), 6–71.

5. Justus Clement French, *The Trip of the Steamer "Oceanus" to Fort Sumter and*

Charleston, S.C., Comprising the Incidents of the Excursion, the Appearance, at that Time, of the City, and the Entire Programme of the Exercises of Re-raising the Flag over the Ruins of Fort Sumter (Brooklyn, 1865), 119, 65–69; Willie Lee Rose, *Rehearsal for Reconstruction: The Port Royal Experiment* (New York: Oxford University Press, 1964), 341–45; Rosen, *Confederate Charleston*, 150–53. See also "Replacing the Flag upon Sumter" from the narrative of an eyewitness, William A. Spicer, adapted by F. Milton Willis, in *Fort Sumter Memorial: The Fall of Fort Sumter, a Contemporary Sketch from Heroes and Martyrs*, ed. Frank Moore (New York: Edwin C. Hill, 1915), 29–46.

6. "Our Martyr and His Mourners," *New York Tribune*, May 13, 1865. On the federal reinterment program and the problem of death at the end of the Civil War, see Faust, *"A Riddle of Death,"* 10–18. On grief from psychological and symbolic perspectives, see Maurice Bloch and Jonathan Parry, eds., *Death and the Regeneration of Life* (Cambridge: Cambridge University Press, 1982), and Paul C. Rosenblatt, R. Patricia Walsh, and Douglas A. Jackson, *Grief and Mourning in Cross-Cultural Perspective* (New Haven, Conn.: HRAF Press, 1976). On the development of funereal practices in America, see David E. Stannard, ed., *Death in America* (Philadelphia: University of Pennsylvania Press, 1975), and James J. Farrell, *Inventing the American Way of Death, 1830–1920* (Philadelphia: Temple University Press, 1980). Some social historians have paid greater attention recently to the scale of death in the conflict. See especially Vinovskis, "Have Social Historians Lost the Civil War?" 36–39.

7. *New York Tribune*, April 8, 1865, May 13, 1865 (quote).

8. *New York Tribune*, May 13, 1865; *Charleston Daily Courier*, May 2, 1865. I encountered evidence of this first Memorial Day observance in "First Decoration Day," Military Order of the Loyal Legion of the United States Collection, Houghton Library, Harvard University, Cambridge, Mass. This handwritten description of the parades around the Race Course is undoubtedly based on the article by the *New York Tribune* correspondent named Berwick, whose name is mentioned in the description. The "First Decoration Day" author, however, misdates the *Tribune* articles. Other mentions of the May 1, 1865, event at the Charleston Race Course include Paul H. Buck, *The Road to Reunion, 1865–1900* (New York: Alfred A. Knopf, 1937). Buck misdates the event as May 30, 1865, does not mention the Race Course, gives James Redpath full credit for creating the event, and relegates the former slaves' role to "black hands [strewing flowers] which knew only that the dead they were honoring had raised them from a condition of servitude" (120–21). Whitelaw Reid visited the cemetery in Charleston founded on that first Decoration Day, making special mention of the archway and its words in his account of his travels through the conquered South: "Sympathizing hands have cleared away the weeds, and placed over the entrance an inscription that must bring shame to the cheek of every Southern man who passes: 'The Martyrs of the Race Course.'" Whitelaw Reid, *After the War: A Tour of the Southern States, 1865–1866* (1866; reprint, New York: Harper and Row, 1965), 69. James Redpath claimed much of the credit for the founding of Memorial

Day because of his role in the creation of the Race Course cemetery. Redpath did lead a group of ministers and missionaries who first visited the grounds and resolved to repair the site. See Charles F. Horner, *The Life of James Redpath and the Development of the Modern Lyceum* (New York: Barse and Hopkins, 1926), 111–18. At least two artists' depictions of the first Decoration Day at the Race Course exist, one by L. D. McMorris, in Horner, *Life of James Redpath*, 115, and the other an illustration from *Harper's Weekly* in 1867, reprinted in Rosen, *Confederate Charleston*, 155.

9. Lev. 25:12–13.

10. *Charleston Daily Courier*, May 2, 1865; *New York Tribune*, May 13, 1865. The *Daily Courier* named five black clergy, listed without their first names, who spoke at the ceremonies: Dickerson, Vanderhorst, Duncan, Miller, and Magrath.

11. Earl Marble, "Origin of Memorial Day," *New England Magazine* 32 (June 1905): 467–70; "Report of the President of the Ladies' Memorial Association, Charleston, S.C., June 5, 1916," 3, Ladies' Memorial Association Papers, South Carolina Historical Society, Charleston (hereafter SHS).

12. E. F. M. Faehtz, comp. *The National Memorial Day: A Record of Ceremonies over the Graves of the Union Soldiers, May 29–30, 1869* (Washington, D.C.: Headquarters, Grand Army of the Republic, 1870), 5–8; Buck, *Road to Reunion*, 120–21. On the disputed origins of Memorial Day, see Michael Kammen, *Mystic Chords of Memory: The Transformation of Tradition in American Culture* (New York: Alfred A. Knopf, 1991), 102–3; Cecelia Elizabeth O'Leary, *To Die For: The Paradox of American Patriotism* (Princeton: Princeton University Press, 1999), 3, 100–107; and Lloyd Lewis, *Myths after Lincoln* (New York: Press of the Readers Club, 1929), 304–19. Various towns claimed to have originated Memorial Day; Kammen makes special mention of Waterloo, New York. O'Leary writes that "the exact origins of the day may never be known" (103), but the Charleston event of May 1, 1865, deserves pride of place. On the symbolic meanings and uses of Memorial Day, see W. Lloyd Warner, *The Living and the Dead: A Study of the Symbolic Life of Americans* (New Haven: Yale University Press, 1959), 248–79.

13. On the Northern Women's Relief Corps, see O'Leary, *To Die For*, 89–106.

14. "Ceremonies at Cincinnati," in *National Memorial Day*, 789–90. Lee's speech confirms the thesis of Andrew Delbanco in *The Death of Satan: How Americans Have Lost the Sense of Evil* (New York: Farrar, Straus, and Giroux, 1995), 125–53. Delbanco sees the Civil War as the hinge of his argument that Americans steadily lost a sense of evil, of divine purpose in history, because of and in the wake of the bloodletting of 1861–65. The culture began to go spiritually flat, to embrace a doctrine of luck and chance, as it had to assess the meaning in who lived and who died as a result of such all-out war.

15. Faehtz, *National Memorial Day*, 249, 202, 21.

16. Ibid., 46, 112.

17. Ibid., 701–2. With what must have been at times awkward bluster, some orators found virtually no theme other than blood sacrifice. Rev. N. Mighill, in Brattleboro,

Vermont, rejoiced in how it is "sweet to die for one's native land. . . . They died, tens and hundreds of thousands, for dear fatherland" (710).

18. Ibid., 97–101.

19. Ibid., 710, 493.

20. I. F. Shepard, *Oration by Gen. I. F. Shepard, Adjutant-General of Missouri, Memorial Day, May 30, 1870, Jefferson Barracks, St. Louis, MO* (St. Louis: Missouri Democrat and Job Printing House, 1870), 7–12, Widener Library, Harvard University.

21. Oliver P. Morton, *Oration of Hon. O. P. Morton* (Gettysburg, 1870), 4–5, 13–14, 18–20, Widener Library, Harvard University.

22. See Gaines M. Foster, *Ghosts of the Confederacy: Defeat, the Lost Cause, and the Emergence of the New South, 1865 to 1913* (New York: Oxford University Press, 1987), 38–45 (quote on 45); "Reports of Memorial Day Exercises" at Magnolia Cemetery, compiled from the *Charleston Daily Courier*, 1866–82, Ladies' Memorial Association Papers. On the ritual process, see Clifford Geertz, *The Interpretation of Cultures* (New York: Basic Books, 1973), 87–169; Victor W. Turner, *The Ritual Process: Structure and Anti-Structure* (Chicago: Aldine, 1969); and Paul Connerton, *How Societies Remember* (Cambridge: Cambridge University Press, 1989), 41–71.

23. William McKinley, "Ceremonies at Winona," in *National Memorial Day*, 491. For the Rutherford reminiscence and the varied dates of Confederate Memorial Day, see Foster, *Ghosts of the Confederacy*, 42, and Charles Reagan Wilson, *Baptized in Blood: The Religion of the Lost Cause, 1865–1920* (Athens: University of Georgia Press, 1980), 28. The novel Rutherford read was Baroness Tautphoeus's *The Initials*. On Rutherford, see "Origin of Memorial Day: Miss Lizzie Rutherford's Idea, but Mrs. Williams' Achievement," in Lucian C. Wright, ed., *Georgia's Bi-centennial Memoirs and Memories* (Atlanta: by author, 1933), 274–77. On the origins of Memorial Day, see Martha E. Kinney, " 'If Vanquished I Am Still Victorious': Religious and Cultural Symbolism in Virginia's Confederate Memorial Day Celebrations, 1866–1930," *Virginia Magazine of History and Biography* 106 (Summer 1998): 237–66; and Margaret Inman Meaders, "Postscript to Appomattox: My Grandpa and Decoration Day," *Georgia Review* 24 (Fall 1970): 297–304.

24. Capers quoted in Foster, *Ghosts of the Confederacy*, 42; Geertz, *Interpretation of Cultures*, 112.

25. Foster, *Ghosts of the Confederacy*, 49–62 (quote on 55). Drawing on the work of the anthropologist Anthony F. C. Wallace, Foster persuasively contends that this early memorialization by former Confederates can best be understood as a "revitalization movement" (56). See also Anthony F. C. Wallace, "Revitalization Movements," *American Anthropologist* 58 (1956), 264–81. On the founding and character of the Southern Historical Society, see Richard D. Starnes, "Forever Faithful: The Southern Historical Society and Confederate Historical Memory," *Southern Cultures* 2 (Winter 1996): 177–94.

26. On the unionist-emancipationist narrative, see Daniel Aaron, *The Unwritten War: America Writers and the Civil War* (New York: Alfred A. Knopf, 1973), xiii–xiv. Aaron calls this conception of the war the "federal epic."

27. *Proceedings of the Southern Historical Convention, which Assembled at the Montgomery White Sulphur Springs, Va., on the 14th of August, 1873, and of the Southern Historical Society, as Reorganized, with the Address by Gen. Jubal A. Early, Delivered before the Convention on the First Day of Its Session* (Baltimore: Turnbull Brothers, n.d.), 27–28. On Early's role at the White Sulphur Springs meeting, see Charles C. Osborne, *Jubal: The Life and Times of General Jubal A. Early, CSA, Defender of the Lost Cause* (Baton Rouge: Louisiana State University Press, 1992), 434–36.

28. Rev. John William Jones wrote a reminiscence of Jackson and assembled a mass of documents, including speeches and press coverage of the monument unveiling in Richmond in 1875, as an appendix in John Esten Cooke, *Stonewall Jackson: A Military Biography* (New York: Appleton, 1876). See also ibid., 514–29, 537–45, and Wilson, *Baptized in Blood*, 18–24.

29. Hill quoted in Cooke, *Stonewall Jackson*, 574–76; Robert Penn Warren, *The Legacy of the Civil War* (1961; reprint, Cambridge, Mass.: Harvard University Press, 1983), 15.

30. Cooke, *Stonewall Jackson*, 570–72.

31. James L. Kemper to Mrs. D. Brown, October 7, 1875, Governor's Letterbook, and Jubal Early to Kemper, box 4, Executive Papers, Gov. James L. Kemper Papers, both in Virginia State Library, Richmond. See also Kemper to Early, October 11, 1875, and October 23, 1875, both in vol. 7, Jubal Early Papers, Library of Congress, Washington, D.C.

32. Kemper to Early, October 22, 1875, and October 23, 1875, both in vol. 7, Early Papers; Jack P. Maddex Jr., *The Virginia Conservatives, 1867–1879: A Study in Reconstruction Politics* (Chapel Hill: University of North Carolina Press, 1970), 192–93. Kemper and Early eventually reconciled to an extent. In November 1875 they were still working together to pay off bills from the Jackson statue unveiling. See Kemper to Early, November 15, 1875, and November 24, 1875, both in vol. 7, Early Papers.

33. Kemper quoted in Cooke, *Stonewall Jackson*, 545–47.

34. Hoge quoted in ibid., 548–49, 561, 564–65. On Hoge, see Wilson, *Baptized in Blood*, 21–23.

35. Frances Miles Finch, "The Blue and the Gray," *Atlantic Monthly* 20 (September 1867): 369–70. See also Buck, *Road to Reunion*, 122–26.

36. John A. Gilmer, "Memorial Address," Guilford, North Carolina, May 10, 1873, unidentified newspaper clipping, reel 18, Albion Tourgee Papers, Harvard University.

37. Albion Tourgee, "Memorial Address," Wilmington, North Carolina, May 30, 1874, two unidentified newspaper clippings, reel 18, Tourgee Papers.

38. Osborne Hunter, "Reconciliation with Vengeance," *Elevator* (black Raleigh newspaper), n.d., clipping, reel 18, Tourgee Papers. Hunter's letter includes an excerpt from an 1876 Memorial Day address by Tourgee delivered in Raleigh. A gathering of blacks did occur at an unidentified location in that year. Osborne Hunter is the brother of Charles N. Hunter, a Raleigh editor and schoolmaster.

39. C. A. Bartol, "The Soldier's Motive," May 30, 1874, in *Memorial Day Exercises of Charles Russell Lowell Encampment, Post Seven, G.A.R.* (Boston: J. A. Cummings, 1874), 7, 10–12, 14, American Antiquarian Society, Worcester, Mass. On veterans and the revival of soldiers' ideals, especially as a mode of reconciliation, in the postwar era, see Gerald F. Linderman, *Embattled Courage: The Experience of Combat in the American Civil War* (New York: Free Press, 1987), 266–97; Stuart McConnell, *Glorious Contentment: The Grand Army of the Republic, 1865–1900* (Chapel Hill: University of North Carolina Press, 1992), esp. 166–205; and Larry M. Logue, *To Appomattox and Beyond: The Civil War Soldier in War and Peace* (Chicago: Ivan R. Dee, 1996), 82–142.

40. *New York Herald*, May 29, 1877. On May 31, 1877, the *New York Tribune* opened its coverage of Decoration Day activities with the statement that across the country, North and South, "the spirit of reconciliation and peace seemed universal."

41. *New York Herald*, May 29, 1877, May 30, 1877.

42. Cochrane quoted in *New York Tribune*, May 31, 1877.

43. *New York Tribune*, May 31, 1877. On the political functions of parades and other public rituals, see Susan G. Davis, *Parades and Power: Street Theatre in Nineteenth-Century Philadelphia* (Philadelphia: Temple University Press, 1986), and John Bodnar, *Remaking America: Public Memory, Commemoration, and Patriotism in the Twentieth Century* (Princeton: Princeton University Press, 1992).

44. *New York Tribune*, May 31, 1877; *New York Herald*, May 31, 1877. On Greenwood and the rural cemetery movement, see David Charles Sloane, *The Last Great Necessity: Cemeteries in American History* (Baltimore: Johns Hopkins University Press, 1991), 44–127, and Stanley French, "The Cemetery as Cultural Institution: The Establishment of Mount Auburn and the Rural Cemetery Movement," in *Death in America*, 69–91.

45. *New York Herald*, May 31, 1877.

46. *The Proceedings of the Evening of Decoration Day, May 30, 1877, at the Academy of Music, City of Brooklyn, New York* (Brooklyn: Eagle Job and Book Printing Department, New York Bar Association, 1877), 4–5, AAS.

47. On Pryor, see Daniel E. Sutherland, *The Confederate Carpetbaggers* (Baton Rouge: Louisiana State University Press, 1988), 102–5; Sarah Rice Pryor, *My Day: Reminiscences of a Long Life* (New York: Macmillan, 1909), 280–82; Robert S. Holzman, *Adapt or Perish: The Life of General Roger A. Pryor, C.S.A* (Hamden, Conn., 1976), 90–92; and Mark Mayo Boatner, *The Civil War Dictionary* (New York: McKay, 1959), 674.

48. *Proceedings of the Evening of Decoration Day*, 8–9, 11. On the needless war school of interpretation, see Thomas J. Pressly, *Americans Interpret Their Civil War* (1954; reprint, New York: Free Press, 1962), 289–328.

49. *Proceedings of the Evening of Decoration Day*, 14, 15–16.

50. Ibid., 24–25 (quotes); *New York Tribune*, May 31, 1877.

51. *Proceedings of the Evening of Decoration Day*, 27–28.

52. Ibid., 29, 33.

53. Frederick Douglass, "Speech in Madison Square in Honor of Decoration Day," May 30, 1878, reel 15, Frederick Douglass Papers, Library of Congress. See also *New York Times*, May 31, 1878, and *New York Tribune*, May 31, 1878. Presiding over the ceremony at the Lincoln Monument was General Schuyler Hamilton, who, according to the *Tribune*, urged the crowd to "keep alive the memory of their dead . . . by burying past antagonisms." He, therefore, advocated the decoration of Confederate and Union graves with equal compassion. Douglass's speech, although from a prepared text, may have been directed, in part, against Hamilton's tone of reconciliation. On Douglass, Memorial Day speeches, and the memory of the war, see David W. Blight, "For Something beyond the Battlefield: Frederick Douglass and the Struggle for the Memory of the Civil War," *Journal of American History* 75 (March 1989): 1156–78.

54. Douglass, "Speech in Madison Square," 9–10.

55. Grant interview in *New York Tribune*, May 28, 1878.

56. Sherman speech in *New York Tribune*, May 31, 1878.

57. *New York Tribune*, May 30, 1878, May 30, 1880; John D. Washburn, *Memorial Address at Lancaster, May 29, 1880* (Worcester: Press of Charles Hamilton, 1880), 4, Widener Library, Harvard University.

58. Thomas F. Barr, *Memorial Address of Col. Thomas F. Barr, Judge Advocate, USA, Stillwater, Minnesota, May 30, 1879*, 4–5, American Antiquarian Society, Worcester, Mass.

59. Holmes's speech was delivered to the John Sedgewick Post Four, Grand Army of the Republic. It has been published under two titles. See Oliver Wendell Holmes Jr., *Dead Yet Living: An Address Delivered at Keene, N.H., May 30, 1884* (Boston: Ginn, Heath, 1884), 4, 11–12, U.S. Army Military History Institute, Carlyle Barracks, Pa., and "Memorial Day," in *Speeches by Oliver Wendell Holmes* (Boston: Little, Brown, 1934), 1–12. Excellent discussions of Holmes are found in George M. Fredrickson, *The Inner Civil War: Northern Intellectuals and the Crisis of the Union* (New York: Harper and Row, 1965), 218–21; Cruce Stark, "Brothers at/in War: One Phase of Post Civil War Reconciliation," *Canadian Review of American Studies* 6 (Fall 1975): 174–81; and Aaron, *Unwritten War*, 161–62.

60. Albion Tourgee, "Memorial Day," in *The Veteran and His Pipe* (Chicago: Homewood Publishing, 1902), 70–71, 77.

61. Geertz, *Interpretations of Cultures*, 112.

Thomas J. Brown

The Monumental Legacy of Calhoun

n Josephine Humphreys's delightful novel *Rich in Love*, official representations of John C. Calhoun epitomize the incompletely hidden past that shapes the present. The seventeen-year-old narrator, Lucille Odom, dismisses a textbook explanation of Calhoun's protest against the protective tariff as "a red herring" except insofar as it demonstrates "how men can dress greed as philosophy." But she takes a "consuming interest" in the Calhoun monument in Charleston. The statue atop the immense shaft brings the statesman alive for Lucille in an immediate and even intimate way. She cranes her neck to stare at "the deep brow, the wild mane." "I loved Calhoun's looks," she recalls. The virile figure inclines her to believe the legend that Calhoun was the true father of Abraham Lincoln. Unlike "the otherwise dry heart of politics," the supposed blood tie between Calhoun and Lincoln is to Lucille a living history of the Civil War era—animated by the irony, the generational tensions, and the "behind-the-scenes passion" that mark her exploration of her own past and her sexual awakening in a relationship with the historian married to her older sister.[1]

Recent scholars have joined Lucille Odom in finding that public monuments of the postwar South reveal more than might be expected from such sanitized expressions of established power. Many studies have observed that Southern monuments celebrated the Confederacy but promoted national reunion, denied the centrality of slavery to the sectional conflict but reinforced white supremacism, and saluted the Old South but facilitated rapid social change in the industrializing New South.[2] Although overlooked in this scholarship, the Charleston monument erected in 1896 is an important site in the commemorative landscape of the postwar South. The culmination of a campaign that began shortly after Calhoun's death in 1850, the monument offers an exceptional opportunity to trace shifts in Southern memory from the culture of secession to the heyday of the Lost Cause. Part of the distinctiveness of the opportunity is that the postwar South erected many monuments to Confederate military heroes but few monuments to the

John Massey Rhind, Calhoun monument, Charleston (1894–96).
(Courtesy of Library of Congress)

political architects of disunion. The Charleston project demonstrates that even in a tribute to an antebellum icon identified with the origins of the war, white Southerners preferred to recall their wartime experience and assert a broad claim of regional achievement rather than describe their shattered dream of a separate nation. As Lucille Odom suggests, however, that strategy did not divert all viewers of the monument from Calhoun's significance as a symbol of the Confederate idea.

Assessment of the uses of Calhoun's image converges with examination of the group that sponsored the Charleston monument, the Ladies' Calhoun Memorial Association (LCMA). Scholarship on Southern memory has disagreed about the date white women assumed leadership in commemorative activities and the extent to which they exercised meaningful power through these undertakings.[3] The LCMA's experience indicates that in one important Southern city women entered at an early stage into contests over public memory and asserted themselves more boldly after Appomattox. But they would not press their independence beyond the limits of white consensus, and they may have faced more constraints at the end of their project than they did at the beginning. Most vividly, the story of the LCMA shows that women believed deeply in the social value of their commemorative work. Although members of the LCMA doubtless would have been scandalized by Lucille Odom's reflections on Calhoun, they agreed with her conviction that "history was a category comprising not only famous men of bygone eras, but *me, yesterday*."[4] Their monument would commemorate both subjects.

Rollin Osterweis may have exaggerated in claiming that the apotheosis of Calhoun was to the emergence of romantic nationalism in South Carolina what the cult of Beethoven was to the development of romantic music in Europe, but the Nullifier was clearly a potent symbol during the 1850s. To be sure, his dominance had long irked potential rivals, and strategists soon abandoned some of his key positions. But while South Carolina politicians supported a monument to their state's hero less energetically than Daniel Webster's former lieutenants did, their comparative lethargy probably reflected their indifference toward urban monuments more than their ambivalence toward their longtime leader. A wide variety of factions sought to get right with Calhoun in almost every major political debate. His authority supported arguments for Unionism, cooperation, and separate secession; for participation in the national Democratic Party and isolation from it; for contentment with repeal of the Missouri Compromise and for insistence on a slave code for the federal territories; for and against the annexation of Cuba. When a spiritualist reported that he had made contact with Calhoun in the afterworld, one wag shrugged that nothing could have been less of a revelation than the received message: "I'm with you still." More surprising was the discovery that Calhoun had become an expert guitar player since his death.[5]

Extraordinary initiatives to enshrine Calhoun in the civic landscape accompanied these rhetorical invocations. Officials in Charleston and Columbia urged the Calhoun family to inter the senator at a site accessible to the public, and although one daughter correctly observed that "almost all the great men of the country are buried on their own places," widow Floride Calhoun surrendered her initial plan to lay her husband to rest at his famous Fort Hill plantation. After a compromise solution provided for temporary deposit of Calhoun's remains in Charleston pending action by the state legislature, the city staged a funeral long remembered as the grandest civic ceremony in its history. The procession from the city limits reportedly included "every white man in the city" and took two hours to pass the houses with windows respectfully shuttered and public buildings draped in mourning.[6] The unadorned stone in the St. Philip's churchyard inscribed simply "Calhoun" belied the continuing interest in creation of a magnificent symbolic space. William Gilmore Simms proposed final interment in Magnolia Cemetery at its dedication in November 1850, imagining Calhoun's tomb as the centerpiece in a garden of South Carolina memory. A week later Governor Whitemarsh B. Seabrook called on the legislature to purchase a lot adjacent to the statehouse and design a park around a suitable funerary shrine. That lot instead became the site for a fireproof archive and soon a new statehouse, in which remembrance of Calhoun figured prominently in the planning from the beginning of its construction, when Calhoun's valedictory speech in the Senate was the only document placed beneath the cornerstone.[7]

The arrival of Hiram Powers's statue of Calhoun in November 1850 complicated early planning for a monument. Originally commissioned in 1837 but not begun until funding solidified, the statue had left Italy shortly after Powers learned of Calhoun's death and had suffered considerable damage in the Fire Island shipwreck that claimed the lives of Margaret Fuller and her family. Its recovery and delivery to Charleston during the second meeting of the Nashville Convention dramatized the rebirth of Calhoun as an icon. One poet looked ahead hopefully to "Marble more quick than flesh—and Death more quick than life." Carolinians outraged by the Compromise of 1850 found significance in the fracturing of the scroll inscribed, pursuant to Calhoun's instructions and in simulation of his handwriting, "Truth, Justice, and the Constitution." The city council bought the statue from its sponsors and placed it on display in city hall while making preliminary arrangements to set it in an octagonal temple decorated by an interior frieze of the epic funeral procession.[8]

Despite this eagerness to embrace Powers's Calhoun, the composition did not win popular approval. While praised by some observers and reproduced in engravings and Parianware, "the incongruous blending of the Roman toga with the palmetto" also attracted ridicule as a portrait of Calhoun after emerging from his bath, wrapped in a sheet.[9] Frederick A. Porcher stressed in an important review that Powers's classical presentation violated the romantic principle that an artist portraying a hero "should strive to interweave his national character into his conception, and not assign to him a mere conventional greatness." "The first glance of curiosity satisfied, the statue stands unheeded, in the City Hall," Porcher reported, "and there it will stand, a monument of the public spirit of the citizens and of their disappointment. We have asked for our statesman, and have received a Roman Senator. . . . We have asked for our Calhoun, the Carolina planter, and have received an elaborately carved stone."[10] The city government quietly let the plans for an elaborate setting fade.

The conflict over Powers's work stimulated other proposals to commemorate Calhoun. On April 26, 1853, the third anniversary of Calhoun's funeral, the militia units and fire companies of Charleston organized the Calhoun Monument Association (CMA), which added support for a memorial over the next several months from other civic organizations. The project gained momentum in December 1853 when the state legislature defeated a resolution to fund a Calhoun monument in Columbia. Led by Benjamin F. Perry, the opposition maintained that only private contributions should go toward building the memorial. That challenge brought publicity to the recently announced plans of the CMA to launch its campaign formally on the following March 18, the anniversary of Calhoun's birth.[11]

The formation of the LCMA in January 1854 did not merely reflect support for the CMA but constituted a separate initiative that only partly shared the same motives and goals. The organizational roots of the LCMA could more accurately be traced to the Ladies Benevolent Society, traditionally the leading charitable outlet of elite Charleston women but recently waning as public institutions assumed increasing responsibility for care of the indigent.[12] Many of the founders of the LCMA were members of the Ladies Benevolent Society, including Mary Amarinthia Yates, the dominant spirit of the LCMA; her older sister, Isabel Snowden; longtime LCMA president Mary Robertson; Mary Yeadon and Eliza C. Palmer, the wife and adopted daughter of *Charleston Courier* editor Richard Yeadon; and Juliana Conner, whose husband, Henry W. Conner, was president of the Bank of Charleston.[13]

It was no coincidence that Yates first assembled the founders of the LCMA in her Church Street drawing room a few weeks after Ann Pamela Cunningham, writing to the *Charleston Mercury* as "A Southern Matron," began her campaign to save "the home and grave" of George Washington. Yates had attended school with Cunningham, and Cunningham's mother urged her to head the Mount Vernon campaign in Charleston. A commission as Cunningham's lieutenant may not have appealed to Yates, whom one co-worker later described as "always . . . trying to work everything her own way." Ideologically, the tributes to Calhoun and Washington began as rival projects with a common vision of women's role in politics, for Yates's separate course repudiated the Unionist symbolism of Mount Vernon.[14] The LCMA's initial appeal "To the Women of Carolina," written by the promising young author Esther B. Cheesborough, paralleled Cunningham's letter "To the Ladies of the South" by summoning women to remedy a failure of the legislative process, describing the undertaking as an extension of traditional female duties to preserve burial sites, and pointing to commemoration as an opportunity to instill virtue in children.[15]

Although it was a movement of privileged women claiming to build on conventional gender norms, the LCMA's entry into the public sphere was not without controversy. Cheesborough later recalled that "our grandmothers had confined their monumental efforts to the family graveyard, and some thought that their granddaughters had better do the same." Skepticism subsided, however, as the women provided reassurance that their initiative was "not simply a pretext or occasion for public display, or for an invasion of a province distinctively assigned to the sterner sex."[16] The CMA welcomed the LCMA chivalrously but did not pretend to recognize it as an equal. At the inaugural festivities on March 18, 1854, the fire companies, militia units, and other civic societies paraded to the ceremony through the streets of Charleston while the officers and members of the LCMA waited in a theater. The message was clear: men were to be the public actors; women were to be the passive supporters.[17]

The CMA soon began to make the central decisions about the project on the same premise, selecting a design and a site without consulting the LCMA. The design by the local architects Edward C. Jones and Francis Lee featured a Doric column with a suggested height of 150 feet topped by a twenty-foot-tall statue of Calhoun delivering a speech and supported by a base surrounded by statues of the female figures Wisdom, Justice, Truth, and Firmness. The last of these qualities particularly appealed to the CMA. As one competitor observed, the monumental column was traditionally associated with military glory, and the CMA proposed to represent the power of South Carolina by placing the monument near the waterfront to ensure that "the great scene of commercial labor and wealth is thus kept perpetually under the eye of him, who for many long years was the ac-knowledged master-spirit of the free trade policy." To raise the estimated $80,000 to $100,000 needed to build "the finger of might and strength," the CMA issued "An Appeal to the Planters of Carolina" while also con-tinuing to hope for legislative support.[18]

The LCMA pursued different strategies and targeted different constitu-encies. The women asked for no government funding and took no special notice of planters. Although the LCMA established a statewide board of directors and solicited contributions from every part of South Carolina, all the officers lived in Charleston and the organization sought primarily to mobilize local residents rather than to make the city a point of concentra-tion for the resources of a broader area. Charlestonians provided more than half of all donations to the project, which in turn comprised less than the funds raised by the LCMA through concerts, lectures, and other events; the "floral fairs" held in Charleston in 1855 and 1859 accounted for more than 40 percent of LCMA revenues excluding investment income. These ven-tures easily outpaced the fundraising efforts of the CMA, which repeatedly invited the LCMA to join forces during 1855–56. The women maintained their independence, however, and secured a legislative charter in December 1856.[19]

The LCMA's campaign thus assumed a prominent place among efforts in the 1850s to construct Carolinian identity through history and culture, sharing in the impulse behind the building of the new statehouse, the development of Magnolia Cemetery, and the founding in 1855 of the South Carolina Historical Society. "We are fast advancing towards the monumen-tal age of civilization," argued the *Charleston Courier*, "towards that stage of progress at which monuments become necessary to any free, intelligent people, who have had a past worth commemorating, or whose condition affords guarantees for a future." Cultural nationalists sought to ensure that

{ THOMAS J. BROWN }

South Carolina would pass this test. The LCMA received its largest donation from the classicist and local historian William J. Rivers, who compared South Carolina with the nation-state of Athens. William Gilmore Simms, recruited to aid the LCMA with a benefit performance of his play *Michael Bonham*, marked the occasion with an ode that began by connecting the project directly to the momentum for independence. "Nations themselves are but the monuments / Of deathless men," Simms declared.[20]

The LCMA's success in raising funds and political capital prompted some South Carolinians to suggest that the women honor Calhoun through the establishment of a school that would preserve his principles. The argument drew special force from the image of Calhoun as the personification of political thought. "He was all intellect—its very embodiment," one advocate wrote, "so that it would scarcely be just or true to represent him in any other way." The proposal shared much the same view of Calhoun as Powers, who had tried to show that "the concentrated energies of his powerful mind appear to glow, and sometimes to flash, from his face." The projected "Calhoun Institute," which would of course be restricted to young men, also resembled Powers's statue in envisioning the Nullifier as a model of active manhood. The sculptor chose not to depict the flowing locks famously captured in Matthew Brady's photograph of Calhoun because "where all is angular and masculine, long hair is effeminate and soft; it does not accord with the 'cast-iron man.' "[21]

The LCMA sought to commemorate neither the commercial power celebrated by the CMA nor the intellectual leadership admired by Powers and the proponents of a Calhoun Institute. The hero promoted by the women epitomized the creed of domesticity rather than the doctrines of state sovereignty; his true importance was "not identified with the prevalence or acceptance of any political dogma or philosophical tenets." Maintaining that "the great men who have marked history and have converted biography into history, have been greater in heart and in affections than in head or intellect," the women devoted their praise to Calhoun's "pure and unsullied heart," which—they declared—"repelled ever the allurements of place, and the fascinations of power." He represented the secessionist impulse not because he championed Southern interests or articulated Southern rights but because his domesticity defined his patriotism. Calhoun, the LCMA explained, "loved his country—his whole country—but God had given him the heart which sees and feels entirely and overpoweringly the nearer and in some respects plainer and humbler duties which begin at home and radiate in widening embraces." In this feminized conception of manhood it scarcely needed to be added that "his reverence and appreciation of womanhood, in its best and highest estate, was almost an idolatry."[22]

The LCMA gave form to these ideas in the steps it took toward building a monument. The women did not seek to build a grand setting for Powers's representation of republican intellect, as several entrants in the CMA design competition had urged. The LCMA members also showed little enthusiasm for the design selected by the CMA. Shortly before the war intervened, the Gentlemen's Advisory Committee of the LCMA recommended the commissioning of a bronze statue of Calhoun, perhaps referring to the model promoted by Henry Kirke Brown while he worked on sculptural ornamentation of the new statehouse. The women remained uncommitted, however, and the possibility that their monument would replace the tomb in the St. Philip's churchyard continued to be discussed.[23]

The LCMA expressed its goals more directly in selecting a site for the monument. Rejecting the CMA's site on the Battery as "a mere pleasure promenade," the women laid their cornerstone in Marion Square. The decision called on Charleston to fix its civic identity by looking inward rather than onto the harbor. The site of Marion Square had long been a symbolic space immediately outside the city limits; it was here that local officials had received Calhoun's body from the cortege that brought it from Washington. But five months later the municipality had annexed four outlying wards on Charleston Neck, asserting full control over an area disproportionately populated by free blacks deemed threatening to the slave regime. Placement of the Calhoun monument in Marion Square reinforced this extension of racial authority and envisioned a civic showcase in what Simms called "the only public square in Charleston that merits the title." Situated in front of the state military academy, the monument would "speak eloquently to the youths of the Citadel, prompting them to emulate the virtues of the great statesman."[24]

The cornerstone-laying ceremony showed the extent to which the LCMA had already succeeded in constructing a theater of political culture. The scheduling of the event for Palmetto Day highlighted the nationalist implications of the monument, as the anniversary of the battle of Fort Moultrie had become a festival of secessionism during the 1850s. The ladies chose as their keynote speaker Lawrence Keitt, a fire-eater who fervently demanded disunion as a nationalist imperative rather than as a mere remedy for violation of the federal compact. In pointed contrast to the CMA parade held four years earlier, the LCMA's ceremonies before a

{ THOMAS J. BROWN }

crowd estimated at twenty-five thousand emphasized that women shared in forging the new political community. As Esther Cheesborough proudly recalled a quarter century later, "Charleston saw what it had never seen before and what it has never seen since—a woman's procession" in which LCMA members occupied the lead carriages. The parade represented "the action of the women of Carolina endorsed by her men."[25] The monument remained to be built, but by the outbreak of the war the LCMA had defined a distinctive view of Calhoun that claimed a role for women in the formation of public values.

The Civil War muted the debate within South Carolina over Calhoun's image and framed a new exchange in which North and South agreed on the importance of Calhoun but disagreed violently on the value of his influence. The Charleston monuments to Calhoun—his tomb, Powers's statue, and the LCMA project—assumed significance as symbols of the meaning of the war. The ideological and physical attacks on these sites of memory offered the LCMA an opportunity to preserve the Southern past more dramatically than it had by raising funds in antebellum floral fairs.

Although not promoted as assiduously as George Washington, Calhoun enjoyed a prominent place in Confederate memory. Engravings after Matthew Brady's daguerreotype appeared on Confederate currency, Confederate bonds, and an unissued Confederate penny stamp. Powers's portrait also circulated widely. A painting of the statue stood atop the keystone of the Confederate arch depicted on the banner that hung behind the president's chair during the South Carolina secession convention in Charleston, and engravings of it decorated bonds issued by the Confederacy and notes issued by the Bank of the State of South Carolina.[26]

Calhoun loomed even larger on the Northern list of representative Southerners. *Harper's Weekly* featured a picture of Calhoun's tomb to illustrate a November 1860 report on the imminent secession of South Carolina, summarizing the Northern belief that the dead hand of Calhoun guided the South toward disunion.[27] Charlestonians recognized the threat implicit in this view by moving to protect their vulnerable symbols as Federal troops advanced. The city sent Powers's statue to Columbia for safekeeping in the old statehouse, and in the middle of the night on the Sunday after the evacuation of the Confederate defenses at Battery Wagner in September 1863, LCMA Gentlemen's Advisory Committee chairman Henry Gourdin and his brother, Robert, supervised the disinterment and hiding of Calhoun's remains.[28] As the Gourdins had anticipated, Northerners eventually did come to the grave in the St. Philip's churchyard. Walt Whitman reported that while working in a Union hospital at the end of the war he overheard a feverish young patient recently returned from Charleston describe to a more experienced soldier the surprisingly modest Calhoun monument. Whitman's veteran replied: "I have seen Calhoun's monument. That you saw is not the real monument. But I have seen it. It is the desolated, ruined South; nearly the whole generation of young men between seventeen and thirty destroyed or maim'd; all the old families used up—the rich impoverished, the plantations covered with weeds, the slaves unloos'd and become the masters, and the name of Southerner blackened with every shame—all that is Calhoun's real monument."[29] Similarly, William Lloyd Garrison and other abolitionists paid a visit to Calhoun's tomb after watching the U.S. flag restored at Fort Sumter. "Down into a deeper grave than this slavery has gone," Garrison declared, "and for it there is no resurrection."[30]

While the remembrance of Calhoun thus increased in importance, the LCMA became the organizational template for Confederate womanhood in Charleston. LCMA members formed the Soldiers' Relief Association of Charleston in July 1861, and a year later they applied their experience with the antebellum floral fairs to sponsor a Ladies' Gunboat Fair. "These daughters of Carolina are contributing towards the best and most enviable monument," observed the *Charleston Courier*, by aiding "a great movement, which is the crowning result of the teachings and utterances of Calhoun."[31] After evacuating Charleston, LCMA founder and treasurer Mary Amarinthia Yates, now Mary Amarinthia Snowden, supervised one of the most elaborate women's initiatives in support of the Confederacy, the Great Bazaar held in Columbia in late January and early February 1865. Snowden's immersion in war efforts prompted her mother to complain that "between looking after Calhoun money, hospital stores and the Bazaar," she "took no time to look after her children, and her own affairs."[32]

The advance of William Tecumseh Sherman ended the Great Bazaar prematurely and brought the transforming crisis of the LCMA. Amid the chaos in Columbia on the night of February 17, 1865, Snowden sought to save the LCMA assets, which consisted of antebellum purchases of municipal and railroad bonds and bank stock, with wartime interest invested in Confederate paper. Her escape from the burning city was a story that would be told time and again, with several different embellishments on the basic narrative. In one predictable version a faithful slave watched unseen while the treasurer and her sister hid the securities but did not betray their secret.

{ THOMAS J. BROWN }

TOMB OF JOHN C. CALHOUN, IN ST. PHILIP'S CHURCHYARD, CHARLESTON, SOUTH CAROLINA

Tomb of Calhoun. From Harpers Weekly, *November 24, 1860.*

In a variation that stressed the national unity underlying the American ordeal, Snowden claimed the personal protection of Sherman, whom she had supposedly met before the war at a wedding in which she was a bridesmaid and he was her groomsman.[33]

The consistent, crucial heart of the story, however, was that Snowden sewed the securities into her skirt and "carried, concealed on her person, the sacred fund."[34] The safeguarding of treasures within women's garments was an important trope in gendered narratives of Confederate identity, for it imagined the war as an encounter between Northern military advantage and loyal, resourceful Southern women who appealed to the restraints of morality. The sexual drama enacted in the ruse—the risk of search and exposure and the implied possibility of rape—assumed a new magnitude amid the breakdown of Southern male protection in Sherman's March. Snowden's private triumph during the sack of Columbia, one of the most often re- counted episodes of violence in the entire war and one particularly remem- bered as a sexual outrage, became a symbol of the ingenuity, the pluck, and the inviolate virtue of Confederate womanhood.[35]

The burning of Columbia not only provided the LCMA with a new significance but also helped to resolve its difficulties in envisioning the form of the Calhoun monument, for the fire that destroyed the old statehouse completely consumed Hiram Powers's ill-starred statue. Soon after the end of the war the LCMA decided that "the Monument should consist of a base and pedestal of native granite, surmounted by a bronze statue of Calhoun, similar to that of Powers's, which formerly stood in the city-hall at this place."[36] Although the antebellum LCMA had defined itself largely in opposition to the image of Calhoun that Powers had depicted, the connota- tions of the icon had changed. No longer the embodiment of severe, intel- lectual, masculine governance, it now represented the greatness of the South, dependent for its preservation on the efforts of Southern women.

The plan to replace Powers's statue notwithstanding, interest in Calhoun waned substantially after the Civil War. Although the Nullifier loomed large in the constitutional self-justification of an Alexander Stephens, LCMA supporters recognized "the now sleeping enthusiasm for the Great High Priest of State Sovereignty."[37] As longtime president of the Ladies' Memo- rial Association of Charleston, which like the Soldiers' Relief Association shared much of its governing nucleus with the LCMA, Snowden reflected the identification of the cause with its military heroes. The association marked the graves of Confederate soldiers buried at Magnolia Cemetery,

{ THOMAS J. BROWN }

reinterred another seventy-nine South Carolinians who had fallen at Gettysburg, put up a large monument in the cemetery honoring "The Defenders of Charleston," and annually led the ritual observance of Confederate Memorial Day. Snowden's chief project, however, was the Home for the Mothers, Widows, and Daughters of Confederate Soldiers. The Confederate Home, also supported by other LCMA stalwarts, brought the Calhoun monument into the center of a bitter conflict over civic memory, as the women tested the limits of their commemorative authority.[38]

Founded in October 1867 when Snowden and her sister mortgaged their house to make the initial rental payment for a large building, the Home for the Mothers, Widows, and Daughters of Confederate Soldiers did not long concentrate on the objectives summarized in its name. As relatively few mothers and widows moved into the Confederate Home, the institution gave its extra space to young women eager to attend school in Charleston and formed its own school in 1870. To establish the institution solidly, and looking ahead to the purchase of the building and its renovation to fit its educational use, Snowden proposed in October 1873 to devote the funds raised for the Calhoun monument to the Confederate Home.[39]

The suggestion sparked a vigorous debate over the next several months. Supporters of the plan argued that association of Calhoun with an educational institution would be "a living monument, suited to our great and solemn needs" and that support for the school would recall Calhoun's "supervision and fostering care" of the female seminary near Fort Hill, "one of the dearest works of his life." Opponents of the proposal strenuously denied that the institution could constitute a monument to Calhoun even if named after him. Snowden's allies rejoined that the act of incorporation establishing the LCMA did not constrain the form of the monument and pointed out that no public doubts had arisen during 1857–58 about the LCMA's authority to honor Calhoun by establishing a school of political science.[40]

As the antebellum parallel indicated, many objections to Snowden's plan owed less to zeal for a statue than to discontent with an educational monument that would benefit women rather than men. Even strict constructionists of the LCMA's mandate argued that if public opinion demanded an educational monument it should be a school for young men. They noted that the Citadel had remained closed since the Civil War, and they saw that the admission of the first African American student at South Carolina College in October 1873 would soon lead to white abandonment of the traditional training ground of state leadership. The most vitriolic spokesperson for this position was Calhoun's son-in-law, Thomas Green Clemson, who called on the LCMA to use the fund to help him found a school at Fort Hill that would save white Carolinians from "a race entirely distinct from ours . . . not capable of reaching a high degree of civilization." Calhoun offered the best possible model for this movement, and Clemson told Snowden that "It has long been my hope and desire, to connect his name with our regeneration." After Snowden declined, despite her sympathy with Clemson's goals, Clemson announced that the family firmly opposed her proposal. The difference between the two educational uses of the LCMA fund was that "Mr. Calhoun was peculiarly *manly*, and his example to our young men, of the greatest importance, and I must confess, frankly, that there is something inappropriate attached in my mind, to the idea of making a *female* school a memorial to his memory."[41]

The clash reflected not merely a contest for scarce resources but also the ways in which the transformation of the Confederate Home challenged gender conventions. Opposition to the LCMA proposal drew upon an uneasiness with the shift away from an institution that honored the Confederate dead by dramatizing and mitigating the isolation and helplessness of their mothers, widows, and orphans. Esther Cheesborough aptly summarized the implication that Southern women no longer lived in a world defined by male protection. "There was a time when the chivalry of our men prompted them to throw their velvet cloaks over the damp places of the world for the queens of home to step on," Cheesborough observed in a letter supporting Snowden's proposal. "The tender, chivalrous spirit is still there, but alas! the velvet cloaks are not; and to step over these damp places without hurt, our women must now wear the sandals of preparation."[42]

If the attempt to merge the Calhoun monument and the Confederate Home expanded considerably on the extent to which the LCMA had previously sought to combine remembrance of Calhoun with a statement about women's position in society, the resolution of the controversy revealed unwillingness to press independence beyond boundaries marked by the consensus of Charleston elites. Although the LCMA directors voted 36-7 in January 1874 to endorse Snowden's plan, the women decided to submit the legality of the proposal to their Gentlemen's Advisory Committee, which deadlocked on the issue, and then to the three surviving chancellors of antebellum South Carolina. Disdaining recourse to the current state judiciary, the arrangement ensured that Calhoun's admirers would not acknowledge the legitimacy of Reconstruction. When the arbitrators ruled by a 2-1 vote that the Confederate Home could not become the LCMA's monument to Calhoun, the women reverted to the less ambitious plan that had emerged from the ashes of the Civil War, the adaptation of Hiram Powers's statue.[43]

When the LCMA resumed work in 1876 toward the placement of a Calhoun monument in Marion Square, the path to completion seemed auspiciously direct. The program of the memorial was settled: it would be a bronze statue depicting Calhoun in modern dress but evoking Powers's lost sculpture and thereby recalling the burning of Columbia. The antebellum idea of incorporating a mausoleum no longer complicated the women's thinking, a decision that Thomas Green Clemson lambasted as a breach of trust when he unsuccessfully sought to move the remains of his father-in-law to Fort Hill in 1880.[44] Despite its ample resources and clear sense of direction, however, the LCMA would take twenty years to complete its undertaking. Before unveiling its permanent legacy in June 1896, the organization erected and destroyed a different monument that ironically sparked controversy primarily for its representation of Southern nationalism through the female form.

The monument that prompted this tempest was the work of Albert E. Harnisch, a young Philadelphia sculptor working in Rome to whom the LCMA awarded its commission on the recommendation of the Gentlemen's Advisory Committee in June 1879. Despite the Confederate poet Margaret J. Preston's warning that "it would make Calhoun stir in his grave if he were sculptured by a Northern chisel," sectionalism played little part in the selection. Local connections, however, were decisive. The expatriated Charleston artist Caroline Carson, a close friend of advisory committee chairman Henry E. Young, championed Harnisch in the highly informal selection process.[45] The committee claimed that it did not hold a competition because established artists would not enter such contests, although the LCMA could afford to offer attractive premiums and ultimately selected a sculptor who had never received a major commission. Harnisch had shown that he was willing to enter competitions: he had submitted flamboyant designs both for the Lee monument in Richmond, depicting Fame leading the general into Valhalla, and the National Freedmen's Memorial to Lincoln, dramatizing the rights of emancipated slaves by including figures to symbolize education, justice, and power.[46]

Harnisch's characteristically bold interpretation of the LCMA's charge presented an unequivocal monument to Southern nationalism. The composition depicted Calhoun moments after he had risen to his feet in the

Senate, his cloak falling onto his chair. In a gesture that classical oratory prescribed for the beginning of an address, the senator pointed forward with his slightly upturned right index finger.[47] This narrative of transition honored Calhoun both as a man of thought, conventionally seated, and as a man of action, customarily standing, and dramatized the realization of his political ideas. The chair, a traditional symbol of government authority, appropriately reflected his office as a representative of the sovereign state of South Carolina. The portrait anticipated Augustus Saint-Gaudens's more powerful treatment of corresponding themes in his *Standing Lincoln*; iconographically, at least, this Calhoun was Lincoln's older brother if not his father. Harnisch's Calhoun, moreover, embodied a distinct Southern race. As one visitor to the studio explained, the figure stood with toes inward, "like Southern people all over the world."[48] The allegorical figures surrounding the base of the monument reinforced Harnisch's central motif. The figures of Truth, Justice, and Constitution nodded toward Powers, as the LCMA commission required. The keynote to the sculptor's conception was the fourth allegorical figure, History, a sister to Antonio Tantardini's statue on Odoardo Tabaacchi's monument in Milan to Count Cavour. This acknowledged model for "the general plan of the whole" suggested a resonance in the lives of Calhoun and Cavour—aristocrats, intellectuals, politicians, architects of movements for self-government. Here was the romantic nationalism Frederick Porcher had sought in 1850.[49]

When the LCMA decided to take down Harnisch's monument, the official explanation would focus not on objections to the approved design but on flaws in its execution. The casting was poor; the style of coat worn by the statue had come into fashion after Calhoun's death; the exaggerated pointing finger "amounted to a deformity." Other observers noted that the chair was too large and obscured any view from the back. One critic called the work "a statue of an arm-chair, with a tall gentleman standing beside it."[50]

Long before Harnisch executed his design, however, the unveiling of his model in March 1882 excited attacks that struck more directly at the meaning of the monument. Most protests focused on the allegorical figures, which letters to newspapers savaged as "ridiculous," "inappropriate," "shabby-genteel," and "the style of ornamentation . . . seen on wedding cakes and candy castles."[51] The idealized nationalism that Harnisch adapted from the Cavour monument seemed frivolous to many South Carolinians. They sought not to represent a political or cultural dream of independence but to assert a status and power that defeat had obscured. The LCMA had already told Harnisch that it "hoped for something more imposing than the model suggests," and other detractors called for a statue "at a proper elevation" atop a high, commanding column.[52] Even after Harnisch had been at work for four more years, the LCMA debated instructing the sculptor to replace the allegorical figures with statues of William Lowndes, Langdon Cheves, Robert Y. Hayne, and Hugh Swinton Legaré. The serious consideration of this politically nonsensical proposal—Legaré openly regarded Calhoun as a "charlatan"—reflects the LCMA's indifference to antebellum ideological divisions and its eagerness to assert community claims to national respect.[53]

The dedication ceremonies held on April 26, 1887, demonstrated more clearly than Harnisch's work the LCMA's desire to promote reconciliation between the North and the South and among white South Carolinians. The LCMA could have carried forward the secessionist overtones of the cornerstone laying on Palmetto Day by holding the dedication two weeks later, on Confederate Memorial Day. Scheduling the dedication for the anniversary of Calhoun's funeral instead commemorated a legendary moment of civic unity in Charleston and recalled the nationwide expressions of respect for Calhoun upon his death. The unanimous choice for the orator of the day was L. Q. C. Lamar, who personified sectional reconciliation in addition to bearing Calhoun's mantle as the foremost Southern intellectual in politics. Recognizing the opportunity for a statement of intersectional harmony comparable to his eulogy of Charles Sumner, Lamar emphasized Calhoun's devotion to the Union and cheered the end of Reconstruction.[54]

Although Lamar's widely praised address demonstrated the value of the platform provided by the LCMA, the dedication ceremonies also revealed a challenge to women's authority over community memory. The parade to be held on the dedication day captured public enthusiasm far more than Harnisch's design or Lamar's oration, and merchants, veterans, and newspapers pressured the LCMA to reassign symbolically central roles. When the LCMA tried to avoid underwriting a "monster excursion" for all Confederate units in the state, the women came under vigorous criticism before succumbing to the force of New South boosterism. "Great Scott!" roared the *Charleston News and Courier*. "A half a dozen live, go-ahead, progressive men could take this thing in hand and make it the biggest thing of the century in Charleston, except, perhaps the Calhoun funeral and the earthquake [of 1886]."[55] The resulting pageant contrasted sharply with the cornerstone-laying ceremonies of 1858. Officers and directors of the LCMA again rode in the parade, but attention now focused on the veterans who marched at the front of the column.

Harnisch's work received mixed reviews. The LCMA signaled its continuing discontent in the commemorative book published after the dedication, which included several portraits of Calhoun but no pictures of the monument. Dissatisfaction with commissioned art was common in the boom of public sculpture that followed the Civil War, however, and while the *New York Times* acknowledged that Harnisch's effort "might easily have been a more artistic work," the newspaper concluded with resignation that "it will last a long time, and as it was built to perpetuate the name of Calhoun it will serve its purpose as well as if it were more beautiful."[56]

This forecast might have proven accurate had not the monument attracted ridicule from a different direction that focused on the compositional element most sensitive to the LCMA. "Blacks took that statue personally," recalled Mamie Garvin Fields, who was born in Charleston one year after the dedication. Updating the message that the annexation of Charleston Neck in 1850 had sent to free blacks in the area, Calhoun seemed to glare at each African American and say: "You may not be a slave, but I am back to see you stay in your place." According to local black memory, protesters struck back by defacing the statue so extensively that "whites had to come back and put him way up high, so we couldn't get him." Other evidence confirms that the decision in 1894 to replace Harnisch's work coincided with a surge in racialized concern about vandalism in the city, and specifically in Marion Square.[57] But whether or not protesters damaged the statue atop its thirty-three-foot-high base, they clearly undermined it with contempt. Harnisch had completed only one of the four allegorical figures in time for the dedication, and the unidentified woman sat at Calhoun's feet as in the Cavour monument. African Americans nicknamed the composition "Calhoun and He Wife," a label that became inseparably attached to the monument as racist parody converged with satire of Harnisch's artistic ambitions.[58] LCMA members and supporters could not have been amused that this image of subservient womanhood had resulted from their efforts to combine a tribute to Calhoun with a recognition of female influence.

Selected to create a replacement monument, John Massey Rhind furnished a design that conformed to the arguments raised from the outset against Harnisch's work, which the LCMA evidently sold for scrap bronze after it erected the new version in June 1896. At a total height of ninety feet, including its colossal statue of a caped and imperious Calhoun, Rhind's monument commanded respect without embodying political nationalism. Reliefs on the base depicted Calhoun replying to Webster in the Senate and as the secretary of war who reorganized the American military, identifying

{ THOMAS J. BROWN }

him not only with South Carolina and states' rights but also with the United States. Most important, reported *Harper's Weekly*, "the Rhind monument has no hint of a sibyl."[59] The allusion to Powers now took the form of palmetto trees in the base's corners and the inscription "Truth, Justice, and the Constitution" on the front of the base.

The LCMA no longer relied solely on this device, however, to indicate that the monument honored Southern womanhood as well as Calhoun. The inscription on the rear panel of the base only briefly noted Calhoun's "eminent statesmanship during the many years of his public life." Instead of elaborating on that achievement the text celebrated the fund-raising of the LCMA and recorded that "its treasurer Mrs. M. A. Snowden having charge of all its assets secured them about her person and thus saved them during the memorable night of the destruction of Columbia, S.C. by Sherman on the 17th February 1865."[60] The monument was thus explicitly self-referential, commemorating women's role in commemoration. The tribute was partly ironic, for the hope of the antebellum and early postwar period that the Calhoun monument might express a distinctive women's viewpoint had faded as white Southern memory consolidated. The LCMA's column and statue did not differ much from the design adopted by the CMA in 1854. But if the LCMA had not managed to reenvision Calhoun, it had given a lasting retrospective turn to the local tradition of elite women's voluntarism that extended from the antebellum Ladies Benevolent Society through the preservation movement of the 1920s.[61]

The LCMA had, moreover, placed one of the most significant ideological godfathers of the Confederacy in the living landscape of Charleston. The effect of that contribution is difficult to measure. Presumably the monument fostered some admiration for Calhoun and his principles, but few records of its impact are as vivid as local African Americans' testimony that they saw the statue as an emblem of white supremacism and the possibility of successful black resistance. In 2001 Jamaica Kincaid demonstrated the continuing power of the monument to focus vigorous debate by observing that the proximity of the statue to the city Holocaust memorial prompted her to reflect that Calhoun "was not altogether so far removed from Adolf Hitler."[62] The Calhoun monument has also cast its shadow into the ongoing controversy over proposals to commemorate Denmark Vesey in Marion Square. More clearly than the statues of Confederate soldiers erected across the South, the Calhoun monument has served as a reminder of the ideas at stake in the sectional conflict and particularly the issues of race and slavery at the heart of the Civil War. That glimmer of topics that public memory in the postwar South generally worked to forget has helped to stimulate alternative community memories and encourage thoughtful Charlestonians, like the fictional Lucille Odom, to ground their personal identities in an effort to uncover the past.

NOTES

The author would like to thank Alice Fahs, Joan Waugh, and the participants in the Huntington conference, as well as Fitz Brundage, Joan Cashin, Shirley Cook, Walter Edgar, James Loewen, Alex Moore, Jane Pease, William Pease, Leslie Rowland, Kirk Savage, Allen Stokes, and especially Ted Phillips for their help with this essay.

1. Josephine Humphreys, *Rich in Love* (New York: Viking, 1987), 46–47.

2. Landmarks in this scholarship include David W. Blight, *Race and Reunion: The Civil War in American Memory* (Cambridge, Mass.: Belknap Press of Harvard University Press, 2001); Gaines M. Foster, *Ghosts of the Confederacy: Defeat, the Lost Cause, and the Emergence of the New South, 1865 to 1913* (New York: Oxford University Press, 1987); and Kirk Savage, *Standing Soldiers, Kneeling Slaves: Race, War, and Monument in Nineteenth-Century America* (Princeton: Princeton University Press, 1997), 129–208. Grace Elizabeth Hale, "Granite Stopped Time: The Stone Mountain Memorial and the Representation of White Southern Identity," *Georgia Historical Quarterly* 82 (Spring 1998): 22–44, is a revealing look at similar themes in Southern memory after 1914.

3. Elizabeth R. Varon, *We Mean to Be Counted: White Women and Politics in Antebellum Virginia* (Chapel Hill: University of North Carolina Press, 1998), finds that the antebellum commemorative initiatives of elite Virginia women laid the foundations for their activities after the war. In contrast, LeeAnn Whites, *The Civil War as a Crisis in Gender: Augusta, Georgia, 1860–1890* (Athens: University of Georgia Press, 1995), describes women's postwar prominence in community remembrance as a striking reversal of their earlier exclusion from the public sphere. Whites's argument that the Lost Cause honored Confederate soldiers "in a public space that would of necessity be a feminized one" (179) also clashes with the position of Foster, *Ghosts of the Confederacy*, 26–32, 169–79, that the values of postwar remembrance did not substantially change traditional gender values, although commemorative activities expanded the public roles available to women. These opportunities for public activity and the organizational leadership of women are central to W. Fitzhugh Brundage, "White Women and the Politics of Historical Memory in the New South, 1880–1920," in *Jumpin' Jim Crow: Southern Politics from Civil War to Civil Rights*, ed. Jane Dailey, Glenda Elizabeth Gilmore, and Bryant Simon (Princeton: Princeton University Press, 2000), 115–39, which stresses the influence of white women over Southern memory during the period that Foster describes as a phase controlled primarily by veterans and business interests.

4. Humphreys, *Rich in Love*, 47.

5. *Charleston Daily Courier*, May 31, 1853 (quote), June 1, 1853; Rollin G. Osterweis, *Romanticism and Nationalism in the Old South* (New Haven: Yale University Press, 1949), 144. William W. Freehling, *Secessionists at Bay, 1776–1854*, vol. 1 of *The Road to Disunion* (New York: Oxford University Press, 1990), 515–19, emphasizes the irrelevance of Calhoun, but Bruce L. Dillenbeck, "The Decade after Moses: The Political Legacy of John C. Calhoun" (Ph.D. diss., Florida State University, 1990), documents the continued appeals to his authority. South Carolina College students went on strike in 1858 when the school president refused to declare a holiday on the anniversary of Calhoun's birth. See Daniel Walker Hollis, *University of South Carolina*, 2 vols. (Columbia: University of South Carolina Press, 1951–56), 1:209.

6. Martha Cornelia Calhoun to Anna Maria Clemson, May 20, 1850, Calhoun Papers Archives, University of South Carolina, Columbia (quote). "Narrative of the Funeral Honors Paid to the Hon. J. C. Calhoun, at Charleston, S.C.," in *The Carolina Tribute to Calhoun*, ed. J. P. Thomas (Columbia, S.C.: Richard L. Bryan, 1857), 65–82, recounts the ceremonies. For the contrast between this reverence of Calhoun and his distaste for Charleston, see Richard Hofstadter, "John C. Calhoun: The Marx of the Master Class," in his *The American Political Tradition and the Men Who Made It* (1948; reprint, New York: Vintage Books, 1974), 86–117.

7. William Gilmore Simms, "The City of the Silent," in *Magnolia Cemetery: The Proceedings at the Dedication of the Grounds* (Charleston, S.C.: Steam Power-Press of Walker and James, 1851), 53, 81; Whitemarsh B. Seabrook, "Message of the Governor of South Carolina to the Legislature," in *Carolina Tribute to Calhoun*, 330; John M. Bryan, *Creating the South Carolina State House* (Columbia: University of South Carolina Press, 1999), 55.

8. Richard P. Wunder, *Hiram Powers: Vermont Sculptor, 1805–1873*, 2 vols. (Newark: University of Delaware Press, 1991), 1:194–206, 2:26–28, 2:115–16; *Charleston Courier*, September 2, 1850, September 21, 1850, November 25, 1850; *Charleston Mercury*, September 13, 1850, November 21, 1850 (quote).

9. "Statue of John C. Calhoun, by Hiram Powers," *International Magazine of Literature, Art, and Science* 3 (April 1, 1851): 8 (quote); Wunder, *Hiram Powers*, 1:205.

10. Frederick A. Porcher, "Modern Art—Powers' Statue of Calhoun," *Southern Quarterly Review* 5 (January 1852): 109, 114.

11. *Charleston Courier*, April 26, 1853, December 8, 1853, December 12, 1853; *Charleston Mercury*, December 10, 1853, December 14, 1853, December 15, 1853, December 19, 1853.

12. Barbara L. Bellows, *Benevolence among Slaveholders: Assisting the Poor in Charleston, 1670–1860* (Baton Rouge: Louisiana State University Press, 1993), 166–67; Jane H. Pease and William H. Pease, *Ladies, Women, and Wenches: Choice and Constraint in Antebellum Charleston and Boston* (Chapel Hill: University of North Carolina Press, 1990), 122–23.

13. Clarence Cunningham, "A Sketch of the Foundation, Progress, and Work of the Ladies' Calhoun Monument Association, as Prepared from the Minute Books," in *A History of the Calhoun Monument at Charleston, S.C.* (Charleston, S.C.: Lucas, Richardson, 1888), 3–4, identifies the founders and officers of the LCMA. Margaret Simons Middleton, "A Sketch of the Ladies Benevolent Society, Founded 1813," in *Yearbook 1941, City of Charleston, South Carolina* (Charleston, S.C.: Walker, Evans, and Cogswell, 1942), 247–55, lists members of that organization.

14. *Charleston Mercury*, December 2, 1853 (first quote); Grace Brown Elmore, "Reminiscences," 38, typescript, South Caroliniana Library, University of South Carolina (hereafter SCL) (second quote); Yates Snowden to Mrs. W. M. Burney, September 28, 1928, enclosing Louisa Cunningham to Mary Amarinthia Yates, January 3, 1854, Mary Amarinthia Yates Snowden Papers, SCL.

15. *Charleston Courier*, February 1, 1854. On Cheesborough, see Daniel E. Sutherland, "The Rise and Fall of Esther B. Cheesborough: The Battles of a Literary Lady," *South Carolina Historical Magazine* 84 (January 1983): 22–34.

16. *Charleston News and Courier*, April 29, 1882 (first quote); "Woman's Tribute," unidentified newspaper clipping, March 18, [?], LCMA Scrapbook, Snowden Papers (second quote).

17. *Charleston Mercury*, March 18, 1854; *Charleston Courier*, March 20, 1854.

18. *Charleston Courier*, July 17, 1854, July 20, 1854, July 22, 1854, July 27, 1854, August 3, 1854, August 10, 1854 (quotes); *Charleston Mercury*, undated clipping, Snowden Papers.

19. Cunningham, "Sketch of the LCMA," 7–9, 16.

20. *Charleston Courier*, July 27, 1854 (first quote); William Gilmore Simms to Evert Augustus Duyckinck, March 27, [1855], in *The Letters of William Gilmore Simms*, ed. Mary C. Simms Oliphant, Alfred Taylor Odell, and T. C. Duncan Eaves, 6 vols. (Columbia: University of South Carolina Press, 1952–82), 3:372–73; William Gilmore Simms, "Charleston, the Palmetto City," *Harper's New Monthly Magazine* 85 (June 1857): 22 (Simms quote). On Rivers, see Wayne K. Durrill, "The Power of Ancient Words: Classical Teaching and Social Change at South Carolina College, 1804–1860," *Journal of Southern History* 65 (August 1999): 491–97.

21. *Charleston Mercury*, March 17, 1858 (first quote); Hiram Powers to Henry Gourdin, April 7, 1850, printed in *Charleston Mercury*, May 8, 1850 (second and third quotes). See also *Charleston Courier*, March 24, 1857, March 11, 1858, April 2, 1858, April 10, 1858, April 12, 1858, and April 13, 1858.

22. *Charleston Courier*, June 28, 1858. See also *Charleston Courier*, May 9, 1855, and for similar views by a woman who would later work with the LCMA leadership, see Mary Bates, *The Private Life of John C. Calhoun* (Charleston, S.C.: Walker, Richards, 1852). Kirsten E. Wood, " 'One Woman So Dangerous to Public Morals': Gender and Power in the Eaton Affair," *Journal of the Early Republic* 17 (Summer 1997): 237–75, notes that the Peggy Eaton affair dramatized Calhoun's deference to his wife, privileging of domestic morality above political ambition, and repudiation of

partisanship. The incident may have played a formative role in women's memory of Calhoun, but I have found no LCMA commentary on it.

23. Cunningham, "Sketch of the LCMA," 20–21; Henry Kirke Brown to Lydia Brown, March 31, 1858, May 23, 1858, May 25, 1858, June 1, 1858, and June 2, 1858, all in Henry Kirke Bush-Brown Papers, Library of Congress, Washington, D.C. On the relationship between the LCMA project and the final resting place of Calhoun, see *Charleston Mercury*, May 11, 1859, and *Charleston Courier*, August 16, 1859.

24. Simms, "Charleston, the Palmetto City," 12; *Charleston Courier*, April 29, 1882 (first quote). On the annexation, see John P. Radford, "Race, Residence, and Ideology: Charleston, South Carolina, in the Mid-Nineteenth Century," *Journal of Historical Geography* 2 (1976): 333–41. Kenneth Severens, *Charleston: Antebellum Architecture and Civic Destiny* (Knoxville: University of Tennessee Press, 1988), 252–55, describes the shift from the waterfront and rejection of early design proposals as a contraction of civic ambitions to become a capital of the South. This interpretation applies in some ways to the differences between the LCMA's decisions and the CMA's more outward-looking plans, although Severens's brief discussion does not address the LCMA's vision of Charleston. Severens also mistakenly identifies the present monument as the work erected in 1887.

25. *Charleston Courier*, April 29, 1882 (quotes); Alonzo Adams Vanderford to Cynthia Vanderford, July 5, 1858, Vanderford Papers, SCL. On Palmetto Day, see Robert Bonner, "Americans Apart: Nationality in the Slaveholding South" (Ph.D. diss., Yale University, 1997), 171–76; and Len Travers, "The Paradox of 'Nationalist' Festivals: The Case of Palmetto Day in Antebellum Charleston," in *Riot and Revelry in Early America*, ed. William Pencak, Matthew Dennis, and Simon P. Newman (University Park: Pennsylvania State University Press, 2002). On Keitt, see Eric H. Walther, *The Fire-Eaters* (Baton Rouge: Louisiana State University Press, 1992), 181–84.

26. Grover C. Criswell Jr. and Clarence L. Criswell, *Criswell's Currency Series*, 2 vols. (Passe-A-Grille Beach and St. Petersburg Beach, Fla.: Criswell's Publications, 1957–61), 1:1, 1:37, 2:3–4; "John Drinkwater's Poem about a Confederate Stamp," *Manuscripts* 6 (Spring 1954): 176–78; John Amasa May and Joan Reynolds Faunt, *South Carolina Secedes* (Columbia: University of South Carolina Press, 1960), 80; Wunder, *Hiram Powers*, 2:116.

27. *Harper's Weekly* 4 (November 24, 1860): 737.

28. "Exhumation of the Body of John C. Calhoun, 1863," *South Carolina Historical Magazine* 57 (January 1956): 57–58; May Spencer Ringold, "John C. Calhoun: Post Mortem," *Emory University Quarterly* 11 (June 1955): 98–102.

29. Walt Whitman, *Specimen Days* (1882; reprint, New York: New American Library, 1961), 106.

30. Garrison quoted in Henry Mayer, *All on Fire: William Lloyd Garrison and the Abolition of Slavery* (New York: St. Martin's Press, 1998), 582. For attacks on busts of Calhoun, see "The Dark Iconoclast," *Harper's Weekly* 9 (March 25, 1865): 178; and Bryan, *Creating the South Carolina State House*, 69.

31. *Charleston Courier*, March 18, 1862.

32. Yates quoted in Elmore, "Reminiscences," 34; Beverly Gordon, *Bazaars and Fair Ladies: The History of the American Fundraising Fair* (Knoxville: University of Tennessee Press, 1998), 97–99.

33. "Calhoun Statue in Heart of City," *Charleston News and Courier*, July 15, 1957; Cunningham, "Sketch of the LCMA," 14–15.

34. James G. Holmes, ed., *Memorials to the Memory of Mrs. Mary Amarinthia Snowden Offered by Societies, Associations, and Confederate Camps* (Charleston, S.C.: Walker, Evans, and Cogswell, 1898), 10.

35. Drew Gilpin Faust, *Mothers of Invention: Women of the Slaveholding South in the American Civil War* (Chapel Hill: University of North Carolina Press, 1996), 199, and George C. Rable, *Civil Wars: Women and the Crisis of Southern Nationalism* (Urbana: University of Illinois Press, 1991), 157, note repeated instances of women keeping valuables under their skirts. Another prominent example was the Confederate diplomatic papers that escaped seizure in the *Trent* affair. William Gilmore Simms, *Sack and Destruction of the City of Columbia, S.C.*, 2d ed., ed. A. S. Salley (Atlanta: Oglethorpe University Press, 1937), 47–53, 54–56, 65–69, vividly describes the sack of Columbia as a violation of Southern women. See also Francis Butler Simkins and James Welch Patton, *The Women of the Confederacy* (Richmond, Va.: Garrett and Massie, 1936), 238.

36. "Letter from Charleston," April 17, 1866, unidentified newspaper clipping, LCMA Scrapbook, Snowden Papers.

37. *Charleston News and Courier*, December 17, 1873.

38. F. A. Porcher, *A Brief History of the Ladies' Memorial Association of Charleston, S.C.* (Charleston: H. P. Cooke, 1880). On the Confederate Home, see the annual reports of the Home for the Mothers, Widows, and Daughters of Confederate Veterans, SCL.

39. *Charleston News and Courier*, October 20, 1873; Anna C. Clemson to Mary Amarinthia Snowden, October 28, 1873, Snowden Papers.

40. *Charleston News and Courier*, October 23, 1873 (first quote), November 18, 1873, December 9, 1873, December 17, 1873, January 9, 1874 (second and third quotes).

41. Mary Amarinthia Snowden to Thomas Green Clemson, December [?], 1873; Thomas Green Clemson to Mary Amarinthia Snowden, November 23, 1873 (quotes), and December 13, 1873, all in Snowden Papers; *Charleston News and Courier*, November 15, 1873, December 9, 1873, February 11, 1874.

42. Cheesborough quoted in *Charleston News and Courier*, undated clipping, LCMA Scrapbook, Snowden Papers.

43. *Charleston News and Courier*, January 21, 1874; Cunningham, "Sketch of the LCMA," 18–20.

44. Cunningham, "Sketch of the LCMA," 21; *Charleston News and Courier*, March 24, 1880, March 25, 1880. LCMA friends Robert N. Gourdin, Louis D.

{ THOMAS J. BROWN }

DeSaussure, and Henry D. Lesesne led the efforts that kept Calhoun's grave in the St. Philip's churchyard, where the state legislature put up a sarcophagus in 1884. Placed near the location at which Calhoun's remains were hidden during 1863–71, the reinscribed original tombstone became a monument calculated to recall the barbarity of an invasion that compelled such extreme measures.

45. Margaret J. Preston to Mary Amarinthia Snowden, June 10, [?], Snowden Papers; Caroline Carson to James Petigru Carson, February 11, 1880, April 7, 1882, May 20, 1883, and October 17, 1885, all in *The Roman Years of a South Carolina Artist: Caroline Carson's Letters Home, 1872–1892*, ed. William H. Pease and Jane H. Pease (Columbia: University of South Carolina Press, 2003), 110–11, 130–31, 143–47, 186–88. I am grateful to Jane Pease for pointing me to these and other letters by Carson, who also directed to Harnisch a commission from Charleston mayor William Ashmead Courtenay to sculpt a bust of Carson's father, James L. Petigru, for city hall. *American Architect and Building News* 6 (November 29, 1879): 172, shows a proposal by William Ware and Henry Van Brunt for the Calhoun monument.

46. Cunningham, "Sketch of the LCMA," 22; Savage, *Standing Soldiers*, 102–3; Sarah Shields Driggs, Richard Guy Wilson, and Robert P. Winthrop, *Richmond's Monument Avenue* (Chapel Hill: University of North Carolina Press, 2001).

47. John Stephens Crawford, "The Classical Orator in Nineteenth Century American Sculpture," *American Art Journal* 6 (November 1974): 65.

48. *Charleston News and Courier*, December 22, 1883.

49. Cunningham, "Sketch of the LCMA," 24–26 (quote on 24). Harnisch's citation of the Cavour monument as his model is particularly suggestive of a thematic parallel because contemporary French works provided more exact formal precedents. J. Q. A. Ward's similar monument to James Garfield in front of the U.S. Capitol, also dedicated in 1887, illustrates the currency of the portrait statue with allegorical figures around the base.

50. *Appendix to History of the LCMA*, offprint, SCL, 2 (first quote); *American Architect and Building News* 46 (December 22, 1894): 122 (second quote). See also *Columbia Register*, April 27, 1887.

51. *Charleston News and Courier*, March 13, 1882 (third and fourth quotes); *Columbia Register*, March 30, 1882 (first and second quotes).

52. Cunningham, "Sketch of the LCMA," 27; *Charleston News and Courier*, March 13, 1882.

53. Cunningham, "Sketch of the LCMA," 33; Michael O'Brien, *A Character of Hugh Légaré* (Knoxville: University of Tennessee Press, 1985), 251 (quote).

54. L. Q. C. Lamar, "Oration of the Hon. L. Q. C. Lamar," in *History of the Calhoun Monument*, 63–107. See also Wirt Armistead Cate, *Lucius Q. C. Lamar, Secession, and Reunion* (Chapel Hill: University of North Carolina Press, 1935), 464–67.

55. *Charleston News and Courier*, March 17, 1887. Don H. Doyle, *New Men, New Cities, New South: Atlanta, Nashville, Charleston, Mobile, 1860–1910* (Chapel Hill:

University of North Carolina Press, 1990), 159–88, describes the civic and commercial energies that shaped the dedication.

56. *New York Times*, April 27, 1887.

57. Mamie Garvin Fields, *Lemon Swamp and Other Places: A Carolina Memoir* (New York: Free Press, 1983), 57. See also Edmund L. Drago, *Initiative, Paternalism, and Race Relations: Charleston's Avery Normal Institute* (Athens: University of Georgia Press, 1990), 6. Karen Fields, "What One Cannot Remember Mistakenly," in *History and Memory in African-American Culture*, ed. Geneviève Fabre and Robert O'Meally (New York: Oxford University Press, 1994), 156–58, reflects on an unsuccessful search for nineteenth-century confirmation of the oral history. An article in the *Charleston News and Courier*, December 2, 1894, complains about vandalism and mentions defacement of the Washington Light Infantry monument but does not connect the problem to the decision to replace the Calhoun monument. The commissioners of Marion Square hired a keeper with police powers in the hope "that the nuisances and depredations now committed by goats, boys and night prowlers will be largely abated." *City of Charleston Year Book—1894* (Charleston, S.C.: Walker, Evans, and Cogswell, 1895), 195. After dedication of the new monument, the commissioners issued an ordinance prohibiting "the digging up of pebbles on the dull ground, the throwing of the same, or of rocks, brickbats, or other missiles; the marking, cutting, or otherwise injuring or defacing of the trees, tree boxes or fencing, or the Calhoun Monument." *City of Charleston Yearbook for 1896* (Charleston, S.C.: Lucas and Richardson, 1897), 257–58.

58. *Charleston News and Courier*, October 31, 1895, November 26, 1936; "The Calhoun Monuments," *Harper's Weekly* 41 (April 3, 1897): 343.

59. "The Calhoun Monuments," 343.

60. For the debate over the propriety of a previous version that described Snowden hiding the securities in her "petticoat," see *New York Times*, January 12, 1896.

61. On women's leadership in the preservation movement, see Stephanie Eileen Yuhl, "High Culture in the Low Country: Arts, Identity, and Tourism in Charleston, South Carolina, 1920–1940" (Ph.D. diss., Duke University, 1998), 28–47.

62. Jamaica Kincaid, "Sowers and Reapers," *New Yorker*, January 22, 2001, 41–42.

J. Matthew Gallman

Is the War Ended?
Anna Dickinson and the Election of 1872

On October 25, 1872, Anna Elizabeth Dickinson walked alone to the speaker's platform at New York City's Cooper Union. The weather was so terrible that evening that even the famed orator could not fill the house. But Susan B. Anthony and Elizabeth Cady Stanton were there along with various colleagues from the woman's rights movement. All the New York papers and most of the leading national journals sent reporters. They had gathered to hear what the woman who had once been dubbed "America's Joan of Arc" had to say about the upcoming election between Horace Greeley and Ulysses S. Grant.

The speech was a particularly dramatic one, delivered with the flair that audiences had come to expect from Dickinson. Historians have not paid much attention to Dickinson's words that day. In political terms she did not break new ground, nor did her words significantly affect the election results the following month. Nevertheless, the 1872 campaign—and the path that Dickinson took to her role in it—are a valuable window into how the memory of the Civil War shaped postwar politics and culture. Only seven years after Appomattox, all public events unfolded with the memory of the Civil War as a powerful backdrop, but the terms of that memory remained subject to interpretation and negotiation. Her audiences recognized Dickinson as a celebrated veteran of the sectional conflict, and thus, like the candidates themselves, the memory of her own wartime career framed the popular perceptions of her 1872 actions. Moreover, Dickinson, ever the clever orator, did her best to shape the popular recollection of the Civil War to support her chosen candidate. Anna Dickinson understood both the power and the potential malleability of historic memory.

Anna Dickinson had her first taste of the public arena in 1860 when, as an eighteen-year-old, she delivered "The Rights and Wrongs of Women" at a public forum in Philadelphia. The following February Dickinson returned to the same themes at Philadelphia's Concert Hall, where the famed abolitionist Lucretia Mott introduced the young orator to her first paying audience. Over the next four years Dickinson emerged as one of the nation's most charismatic, exciting, and controversial orators.[1] In the process she carved out a distinctive role for herself among American public women. Although a handful of female speakers had already broken the cultural barrier to women speaking before mixed audiences, Dickinson clearly exceeded their example, both in her tremendous national celebrity and in her emergence as an explicitly political speaker who covered partisan terrain where her radical colleagues chose not to tread.[2]

Dickinson first honed her rhetorical skills before abolitionist and woman's rights audiences, enjoying the early patronage of William Lloyd Garrison and Wendell Phillips. In 1863 Benjamin Franklin Prescott, the secretary of New Hampshire's Republican Committee, suggested to his colleagues that the fiery young orator might help the party, and soon Dickinson had signed on for twenty engagements across the Granite State. Dickinson proved to be a popular stump speaker and the victorious governor-elect Joseph A. Gilmore graciously credited her with helping ensure his victory.[3] She went directly from her successes in New Hampshire to speak for Republican candidates across the North, weaving radical convictions and political partisanship into performances that were sure to attract large audiences. Observers differed about whether she was beautiful or merely striking looking, but friend and foe alike were intrigued by what they saw. Her clothing, short-cropped curls, striking gray eyes, and almost every gesture seemed to attract comment. Whatever her prepared text, Dickinson was at her best when responding to hecklers, giving each performance its own special character.[4]

Following a celebrated excursion to Chicago's Northwest Sanitary Fair, the twenty-one-year-old received an invitation, signed by more than a hundred senators and members of Congress, to speak before the combined houses in Washington. After much negotiation the historic lecture was staged on January 16, 1864, in the hall of the House of Representatives. Dickinson initially performed true to form: attacking the Democrats, praising the Emancipation Proclamation, supporting the use of black troops, and critiquing the Lincoln administration's conciliatory stance toward the South. But, in characteristically dramatic fashion, Abraham Lincoln and Mary Todd Lincoln arrived in the audience just as Dickinson was itemizing the president's shortcomings. Whatever her initial inclinations, Dickinson opted to support the president for four more years.

The Washington lecture was certainly the highlight of her wartime ca-

{ J. MATTHEW GALLMAN }

Cabinet card of Anna E. Dickinson, photographed by Napoleon Sarony of New York City, circa 1870s. (Author's collection)

reer. For the next year and a half Dickinson continued to make her living on the lecture circuit, supporting the war effort and demanding racial justice while firing periodic salvos at the Lincoln administration. Despite her misgivings, as the election of 1864 approached Dickinson broke with her radical colleagues in endorsing the party's candidate and once again went on the campaign trail, nominally supporting Lincoln while emphasizing her disagreements with the Democrats and her hatred of the Confederacy.

With the war's end, Dickinson was in a quandary. Still in her early twenties, she was one of America's most famous women. She had come to enjoy and expect the fame, and her family—including her widowed mother, her sister, Susan, and several brothers—had grown dependent on her ample earnings. Moreover, the war had left her convinced that she had an important contribution to make in public life. Barred from elected office— and even access to the vote—Dickinson faced the limited options available to a public woman in postwar America. Between 1865 and 1872 she prospered as a leader on the booming lyceum circuit, delivering hundreds of public lectures across the country. In the process she was part performer, part writer, part businesswoman, and full-time ideologue. Each season required a new lecture; audiences measured success by the yardstick of past performances and against the work of contemporary competitors. Most of Dickinson's lectures tackled political topics, particularly concerning the rights of women, workers, and African Americans, but her most celebrated speech was on the life of Joan of Arc, a talk she introduced in 1870 and then reprised periodically for decades to come. Even her political lectures did not generally toe a particular reform line. Dickinson's "Demagogues and Workingmen" spoke up for the worker while alienating union leaders, and while she favored woman suffrage most of her lectures on women's issues concentrated on economic and social problems.

In 1868 as her companions in the suffrage movement battled for the franchise, Dickinson published a novel—*What Answer?*—which emphasized racial themes while essentially ignoring gender equality. Set in the midst of the Civil War, *What Answer?* featured a tragic interracial marriage between a white Union officer and a light-skinned Philadelphian who both fell victim to New York City's draft rioters. With this controversial narrative Dickinson was already experimenting with new perspectives on the war's memory. Rather than using her fiction to explore themes of sectional reconciliation or to wave a rhetorical bloody shirt at Northern Democrats or unreconstructed Southern whites,[5] Dickinson's novel recalled the heroism of black troops and the racial prejudice of Northern whites, calling on her readers to confront those memories and ongoing realities as they contemplated black suffrage.[6]

In the decade after the Civil War Dickinson maintained personal friendships and professional ties with a wide array of radical reformers and Republican Party regulars while following her own muse and her own fiscal needs in crafting her postwar career. An advocate for radical Reconstruction and black suffrage, she repeatedly took aim at President Andrew Johnson. In the meantime Dickinson remained a strong proponent of woman's rights, even while continuing to move out of the woman suffrage mainstream. During the war the leaders of the woman's movement had opted to set aside the suffrage agenda in favor of an emphasis on abolitionism. After the conflict as Congress contemplated legislation and amendments to enfranchise African Americans, the movement's leaders divided over the proper strategy. Should they insist that women, both white and black, be allowed to enter the voting booth alongside African American men or should they accept the argument—as offered by Wendell Phillips—that this was "the Negro's Hour"? Bitterly disappointed over the lost opportunity when the Fifteenth Amendment excluded women and divided by strategy and personality conflicts, suffragists split into two organizations in 1869: the American Woman Suffrage Association and the National Woman Suffrage Association.[7] Throughout much of these debates Dickinson sat uncharacteristically on the fence. Despite increasingly urgent letters from Susan B. Anthony, she refused to come out squarely for suffrage and, worse, she repeatedly dodged invitations to take a major organizational role in the movement.

Wherever Dickinson roamed it seemed as if admirers competed to host the charismatic orator. A dozen correspondents across the country wrote to her as an intimate friend. Among her extended circle were many of the nation's leaders in public life, including editors, publishers, authors, and politicians. When she was in New York she socialized with the brain trust behind the powerful *New York Tribune*, including Whitelaw Reid, Noah Brooks, John Hay, and the editor Horace Greeley himself. Reid and Dickinson were particularly close friends whose names were regularly romantically linked in the press; Brooks and Hay were both devoted admirers. Her Boston circle included the *Springfield Republican*'s Samuel Bowles, and during her frequent visits to Hartford she split her time between the home of Charles Dudley Warner, the editor of the *Hartford Courant*, and visits with various members of the extended Beecher clan. When the

Beecher-Tilton scandal broke (pitting Theodore Tilton against Rev. Henry Ward Beecher surrounding the charge that Beecher had committed adultery with Tilton's wife, Elizabeth) the muck that flew threatened to stain the lives and reputations of a host of Dickinson's friends, leaving her with a particular hostility to Victoria Woodhull and her sister, Tennie C. Claflin, whose newspaper had originally published the charges that had brought the scandal into the open.[8]

Often the personal and the political became intertwined as Dickinson navigated through her complex worlds. Her reluctance to throw her weight behind woman suffrage rather than black manhood suffrage certainly reflected her political beliefs, but she was undoubtedly also swayed by her loyalties to Charles Sumner and Phillips. In the meantime Dickinson's dealings with Susan B. Anthony were decidedly multilayered. Anthony's letters to Dickinson in the first months of 1868 suggest an urgency and a level of intimacy that is not present in their earlier correspondence. Perhaps their falling out had everything to do with Dickinson's refusal to rise to Anthony's woman's rights challenge, but some clues to Dickinson's reluctance lie in the unknown details of a complex personal relationship between two powerful women separated in age by a generation.[9] Meanwhile, Dickinson's ongoing relationship with her old friend and intellectual sparring partner Whitelaw Reid and his *New York Tribune* cronies meant that Dickinson was hearing the arguments against woman suffrage whenever she journeyed to New York. These and other relationships would come into play as the campaign season got underway in 1872.

The Republican Party was less than a generation old as the 1872 election approached. Thus, nearly all the party's leaders had memories of abandoning an established party and pursuing ideological and political agendas in a new coalition. By the end of his first term in office President Ulysses S. Grant had given many in the Republican Party ample reason to feel alienated and ready to once again turn to some other path. High on the list of Grant's sins was his ham-handed effort to annex Santo Domingo, despite the vigorous protests of Republican senators Charles Sumner—the chair of the Foreign Relations Committee—and Carl Schurz. Worse, upon losing the annexation vote Grant, who had earned his wartime fame by accepting heavy casualties while defeating an outgunned enemy, entered into open warfare with the embattled Sumner. Grant's Republican enemies were also deeply disappointed with charges of corruption and cronyism in the White House and the president's indifferent record on civil service reform. Lastly, news from the reconstructed South seemed unrelentingly bad and Grant's critics questioned whether he had the interest or ability to handle the problems.

Alienated by developments in their own party and unable to wrest control from Grant and his people, a key core of reformers—led by the likes of Sumner and Schurz—bolted from the Republican Party to form the Liberal Republican Party.[10] Convinced that a coalition of the nation's "best men," including right-minded Southerners, could return the nation to the proper path, the new party met in Cincinnati that May. Much to the surprise of most observers, the convention ended up nominating Horace Greeley. Greeley's nomination owed much to a deadlock between the leading candidates and more than a little to the deft stewardship of Greeley's young lieutenant, Whitelaw Reid.[11] Caught up in the desire to unseat the hated Grant, the Democrats nominated Greeley at their national convention, thus creating some particularly strange political bedfellows for the campaign to come. By nominating the highly idiosyncratic and controversial Greeley and allying with the Democrats, the upstart party faced an interesting set of political challenges. Although the former Whig element in the party had placed tariff reductions in the platform, their standard-bearer had an established record as a protectionist, leaving the Liberal Republicans with a two-pronged strategy stressing an end to corruption and reconciliation with the South. This proved a tough task, as the Republican cartoonist Thomas Nast persistently lampooned Greeley's call for clasping hands "across the bloody chasm" of war and the bulk of the abolitionist leadership that claimed the Republican Party's moral center refused to abandon Reconstruction despite their distaste for Grant.[12]

As she observed these developments, Anna Dickinson had to weigh a range of considerations. First, she had grown to dislike Grant with a venom born of public policy, personal distaste, and deep loyalty to the insulted Sumner.[13] Second, Dickinson had personal ties with many of the men who became part of the Liberal Republican leadership. In addition to Sumner (who was really less of a friend than a hero) and Schurz, Greeley, Reid, Theodore Tilton, and Samuel Bowles were all crucial players in the Liberal Republican insurrection. Charles Dudley Warner—one of her most consistent advisors—and most of the old abolitionists, in contrast, refused to abandon the Republican Party.[14] And, if Dickinson were to throw her considerable political weight behind the Liberal Republicans she would be almost alone among woman's rights advocates. The notorious Victoria Woodhull had launched a celebrated campaign for the presidency, drawing considerable support from defenders of woman's rights, while Anthony,

Stanton, and other suffrage leaders who could not stomach Woodhull eventually agreed to back Grant in exchange for his nominal support of woman suffrage. Meanwhile, Dickinson was acutely aware of the value of her good name and of her enduring public identity as a wartime patriot. Although she always spoke her mind and seemed to welcome controversy, Dickinson recognized that her reputation—built upon the public's memory of her wartime oratory—was her meal ticket and that her mother and sister depended on her earnings. Would there be a cost to backing the wrong candidate? Conversely, might there be substantial rewards to be earned by offering her services to those who could best afford them?

In the months leading up to the campaign Dickinson solicited advice from far and wide. For quite some time she toyed with a European tour, either as a tourist or as a professional speaker. But all the while she kept one eye on the political season to come. In March 1872 Oliver Johnson offered to help arrange a " 'political hoot' " in New York.[15] That same week Dickinson's brother John raised doubts about "pitch[ing] into the renomination of Grant 'til all the circumstances [are] considered," although her brother Ed added that if Anna were to get into the campaign she should do so early, "before delegates are chosen[,] otherwise you simply make a fuss, get abused & knocked, lose some influence & achieve nothing." Sister Sue worried that Anna would "only lose [her] popularity for no good by making a speech now."[16] Clearly Dickinson's political future was a hot topic for friends and family alike, with the latter particularly attuned to how a move against Grant might affect her hard-earned popularity.

On April 2 Dickinson temporarily broke her political silence with a public lecture in Pittsburgh. Still a month before the Liberal Republicans' convention, Dickinson surprised her audience by attacking President Grant while praising the efforts of the true Republican leadership of Sumner, Schurz, and Greeley, all converts to the new splinter party.[17] The crowd was large and Dickinson expressed pleasure with its responses despite scattered hissing at her more partisan attacks. Still, she was disappointed by the leading Republican papers—her old supporters—who barely mentioned the lecture, leaving it to the independent Liberal Republican editors and their new Democratic allies to sing her praises.[18] Her friends and advisors split on Dickinson's new stance. A jubilant Samuel Bowles wrote, "I am delighted that you have raised up your voice on this side" and reported that he had contacted Greeley about publishing her new speech. But the *Hartford Courant*'s Charles Dudley Warner—still a die-hard Republican—closed a note on May 11 with "You are now a democrat. I cannot write any more to a democrat now."[19]

The next week Dickinson delivered essentially the same lecture in Carlisle, Pennsylvania, followed shortly by a similar appearance at Philadelphia's Academy of Music. Carlisle's *American Volunteer* found the performance outrageous. "Anna Dickinson must be ruled out," the paper insisted. "She has the effrontery to stand up before a mixed audience, and declare that it was not Grant who saved the country, but the dead blue coats, and that he is not paying off the national debt, but the people. Was there ever such impudence?" In this context, Dickinson's "effrontery" was partially political, partially gendered—how dare she utter such sentiments before a "mixed audience"?—and partially an impudent refutation of the war's memory. Philadelphia's *Evening Bulletin* found the lecture "vastly inferior" to her recent lecture "Demagogues and Workingmen." And in more criticism that smacked of gendered dismissal, the paper suggested that "if the fair protestor desires to achieve any good result from her scolding, she must at least offer a reasonable and well-digested argument which will command respect and not ridicule." The *Evening City Item* was even less charitable, declaring that "a more complete political fizzle could scarcely have been obtained from any political Amazon," adding that perhaps Dickinson's bellicose demeanor was explained by her status as an unattached single woman.[20]

On April 19 Dickinson repeated her attack on Grant at New York City's Cooper Institute, two days after Grant's people had staged a large rally in the same hall. This time Dickinson, dressed elegantly in black silk, was introduced by her old friend Greeley, who proudly sat on the stage behind her as she spoke and soaked up rounds of applause from an enthusiastic audience. Anticipating themes that she would explore more fully on the eve of the election, Dickinson again called on her audience not merely to reflect on their memories of the Civil War but to rethink the meaning of those memories. "The war was only an act in a drama," she instructed. "What men did then they did not for the life or success of a party, but for the life and success of the nation." The question at hand was whether the next act should be left in the hands of the Republicans who gathered at Philadelphia or the new Liberal Republicans, who were really the proper heirs to the war's memory. So long as the Republicans clung to Grant as their man, Dickinson was prepared to seek answers from the Cincinnati convention.[21]

While she publicly attacked the Grant administration, Dickinson privately discussed her political options. Although fond of Greeley, Dickinson truly idolized Sumner and hoped that he would emerge as the Liberal Republican candidate, even while some of her politically savvy correspondents warned that Sumner carried too much baggage.[22] She declined an invitation to attend the Liberal Republicans' convention in Cincinnati that May, but followed the meetings carefully. When the nomination was announced Dickinson seemed ready to cast her lot with Greeley and the Liberal Republicans. "Hurrah for Us!" Dickinson wrote to Whitelaw Reid. "Next autumn I propose to do the best hooting I ever did in all my life in behalf of the good man and the good cause."[23]

Before long Dickinson once again began to have doubts. Family members and some friends counseled against damaging her reputation by casting her lot with the controversial Greeley. Some felt she would be better off sitting out this election, perhaps taking another stab at writing. In fact, in the midst of these political discussions Dickinson corresponded with Charles Dudley Warner for advice on publishers, book contracts, and the like.[24] The pressures came from all over and grew progressively more intense. On June 6 Dickinson barely missed separate visits from Reid and Bowles, two friends who had joined the Liberal Republican movement, and she received an unexpected call from Susan B. Anthony. Contradictory rumors flew. Liberal Republican advocate Laura Bullard heard that Dickinson had "given [her] . . . sanction to Grant & Wilson"; Republican senator M. S. Pomeroy wrote from Washington, "I read that you hurrah for Greeley!" In fact, in early June Dickinson had declined an invitation to speak for the Republicans and was still mulling over offers from the Liberal Republicans. Moses Coit Tyler chimed in from Michigan, "I'm waiting to be electrified by your tremendous Greeley speech—that one which you are working on now." But if she was working on a political speech Dickinson was still resisting any agreement with either party.[25]

In July Laura Bullard sent Dickinson an extended political analysis, declaring that Greeley was "no idol of" hers yet he was the right man for the moment. Moreover, she argued, "I want you to speak, not only for Greeley because of patriotic motives, but because of the woman question. It seems to me that men will be sooner aroused to the injustice of denying us the franchise, by the sight of such a woman as you acting & swaying an election, than in any other way."[26] Bullard invited Dickinson to visit her in Long Branch, New Jersey, but Dickinson recognized this as a ploy to get her to meet face-to-face with Greeley, something she was not yet ready to do. Ironically, by declining Bullard's invitation Dickinson was at her home in Philadelphia when Republican vice presidential candidate Henry Wilson dropped in. As she explained to her sister, "By avoiding one I fall into the claims of the other—By saying no to the would be President, I had to say yes to the would be ('tother) Vice President. By not accepting Mr. Greeley's invitation to spend Sunday at his house I had the pleasure of entertaining Mr. Wilson at my own."[27] The orator and the candidate shared tea while Dickinson heard Wilson's unsuccessful pitch to lure her into the campaign. Two days later Theodore Tilton invited Dickinson to come to New York to visit with Greeley, to which she responded: "Profoundly sorry but cannot come." If she went to see Greeley, she explained to her mother, "I would be in every paper in the country within twenty four hours." But she was not ready for such public pronouncements. "If I want to go with the campaign," she realized, "I will go with it, & get *paid* for it." If not, she would keep her own counsel.[28]

Faced with such heady invitations Dickinson threw herself into research for a new lecture while continuing to toy with her book project. Bowles could not resist giving her a difficult time: "So you turn aside from Greeley and from the girls and from heroes and martyrs and attack the labor conundrum! Audacious person!"[29] But in truth she had not yet turned aside from anyone so much as she had turned to more aggressive negotiations. "Do you want me to go into it," she asked Reid, "and if you do what will those vampires of the Com[mittee] pay me—the most, *very* most. Mind, I don't know that I will go at all," she added, "but I want to know on what ground I shall tread, if I do walk abroad."[30] In his response Reid recognized that he was at once friend, advisor, and political partisan. He deflected her requests for advice, pointing out, "You have many friends, whose counsels you are accustomed to consider, who earnestly deprecate your getting mixed up with it. . . . For myself, I am, of necessity, profoundly interested in the campaign, & therefore hardly a dispassionate adviser." But that having been said, he insisted, "I don't see how it could hurt you since ours is unquestionably the side that has the future with it." And turning to campaign logistics and fiscal strategy he suggested that Dickinson commit to "one or two elaborate speeches" for Greeley "at any price the Committee would pay, or without price. That is my idea of the political obligation of those who aspire to political leadership—obligation to the country, to their principles, to themselves. After that . . . I'd treat it purely as a business question, & work or not as the terms suited. But I can't reconcile it with my notions of political honesty or patriotism to make one's entrance on great national questions, on one side or the other, or even one's absolute silence depend solely on whether one got paid enough to break silence." Reid continued this extraordinary letter by alluding to their long history of personal squabbles and political bickering, concluding, "You used to rate me for being unsentimental, practical, indifferent to the sentimental demands of this or that Great Cause. Well, perhaps we've changed parts; & what I now write may seem a romantic idea of public duty that has no place in the calculations for a successful season. But it has always been my way of thinking." Thus, the crafty journalist tried to shape Dickinson's political future by calling upon her memories of their shared wartime past.[31] Oliver Johnson—another Greeley loyalist—penned an equally long and high-minded letter drawing on Dickinson's role as a beacon for all women: "I would have you make a speech so elevated and elevating that every one who hears you will be constrained to confess that your part is noble and every way worthy of a woman who aspires to lead and inspire man."[32]

Dickinson delayed her decision into August, assuring Reid that she was busy on other projects.[33] A concerned Greeley sought out Laura Bullard to find out why Dickinson had apparently changed her mind. Bullard explained that Dickinson made her living with her oratory and could not afford such ventures without compensation. The publisher-turned-candidate insisted that he had already authorized generous payment and was only awaiting news from Philadelphia.[34] But the negotiating dance continued for weeks. On August 7 Dickinson told Reid that she was writing a book for "a pot of money" while sitting out the election. But the following day she expressed uncertainty about book deals and admitted that although she lacked enthusiasm for the campaign her affection for Reid and Greeley might still win out.[35] As she continued her Hamlet-like indecision, Dickinson received advice from across the country. Even Dickinson's mother, always a bit unsettled by her public performances, entered the debate: "Dear daughter: please [do] not have any more to do with politicks [sic], political lectures and not much with politicians any more." We can only wonder if Mrs. Dickinson's views were swayed by a visit that afternoon from Wendell Phillips, an old mentor of Dickinson and no friend of the Liberal Republicans.[36]

Dickinson finally agreed to stand up for Greeley and the Liberal Republicans only to find that the party was unwilling to meet her price to speak in Maine, Pennsylvania, or Indiana.[37] For a time it seemed that Dickinson had finally thrown up her hands and abandoned the whole idea. She arranged for several newspapers to print short notices announcing that she would be sitting out the campaign while writing a book and that she would resume lecturing after the election.[38] Meanwhile, she told her mother and sister that she finally had a contract for a new book, promising a ten-thousand-dollar guarantee, which ensured that she would stay out of the campaign.[39]

A month later Bowles confided that he had heard from one of her "personal friends, high up in the Grant administration" that the Grant campaign was really behind the book deal as an effort to keep Dickinson off the stump for Greeley.[40] But if that had been the Republicans' devious plan, they had not properly reckoned on Dickinson's political drive and independent mind. By the end of September Dickinson and Reid were once again deep in negotiations about a Cooper Institute lecture planned for early October. The veteran lyceum speaker was still worried about her reputation, particularly given her recent falling out with James Redpath's speaker bureau and the loss of a few invitations because of her more controversial political stances. But this was no cynical careerist decision. "If you knew just how I stand towards a great many of my business people," she assured Reid, "you would understand that what I do I do with a bit, at least, of my life in my hand. If I pay such price I do it because conscience compels and because I believe I can be made of really great service to Mr. Greeley and a great cause, but to that end I need help."[41]

For much of October Dickinson worked away at the upcoming New York lecture that she was calling "Is the War Ended?"[42] But there was to be one more stumbling block before she reached the platform. The Republican leadership concluded that a full house was the highest priority and thus decided that the Cooper Institute lecture would be advertised with an unusually low twenty-five-cent admission. Dickinson was furious. Not only would the lowered price cut into her fee but the discounted rate also threatened to undercut her reputation as a speaker. Angry letters flew back and forth before Reid managed to talk his colleagues into raising the admission fee.[43] On October 22 the *New York Daily Tribune* published a letter from several prominent Liberal Republicans who officially called on Dickinson to break her silence on the campaign followed by Dickinson's response that she would do just that on the twenty-fifth of the month.[44] And so, after months of back-and-forth, the day of Dickinson's Cooper Institute lecture finally arrived.

Whereas in April Dickinson had been more interested in burying Grant than in praising Greeley, when she returned to the Cooper Institute in November she was playing the role of political partisan. And at the heart of her strategy was an elaboration on her earlier themes about how the Civil War should be remembered. In calling her lecture "Is the War Ended?"

Dickinson had adopted a clever rhetorical ploy. If the war was indeed over, then one might reasonably ask why the United States maintained a war footing in the conquered American South. Moreover, if the war was truly over then Ulysses S. Grant could not merely run for reelection on the basis of his war record. Rather, Dickinson insisted, he should be held accountable for his embarrassing record of cronyism and corruption. In short, she intended to challenge the Republican Party both on contemporary political terrain and on its claim to the bloody battlefields of the nation's memory.

Dickinson—the hired rhetorical gun—was at her best firing sarcastic shots at her political enemies and Grant made an easy target for her moral outrage. The president had, she declared, a "greater fondness for the smoke of a cigar and the aroma of the wine glass" than for the proper duties of the White House. After exhausting her ammunition on Grant's foibles, Dickinson shifted to praise for the Liberal Republicans and the Cincinnati convention. "He who runs to extinguish the flames of a house when the house is burning, does well," she acknowledged. But by that same token, "he who checks the flow of water when the flame is extinguished, does also well, because the water, continuing, swamps the house, ruins the furniture, and brings decay and rot into the house."[45] With this imagery Dickinson implicitly introduced another layer of memory into the debate. Four decades earlier William Lloyd Garrison had launched the *Liberator*, his great abolitionist newspaper, by promising that he would be uncompromising in his fight against slavery. "Tell a man whose house is on fire, to give a moderate alarm," he had written in 1831, "but urge me not to use moderation in a cause like the present."[46] Forty-one years later Dickinson seemed to be assuring her audience that the fire Garrison spoke of had been extinguished by emancipation, and thus the postwar years called for a more moderate approach. It was a particularly audacious act of historical appropriation since Dickinson well knew that the aging Garrison himself had refused to join his old abolitionist allies in jumping on the Liberal Republican bandwagon.[47]

As she turned to her central question, Dickinson constructed a complex case that the war was indeed over and that Grant and the Republicans were wrong for continuing to maintain a combative, fiscally wasteful posture toward the vanquished South. But how could the former abolitionist reconcile her calls for Southern home rule with her often-stated commitment to the political future—and physical safety—of the freedpeople? Following the logic of the Liberal Republicans Dickinson declared, "These blacks were slaves, then freemen, then citizens. Before the law they stand on a level with

　　　{ J. MATTHEW GALLMAN }

the whitest white man here. [Applause] That being the case there is no need and there should be no excuse for special legislation for any special class of people, since there is none such in the Republic. [Applause]." And following this logic further, "if they cannot defend themselves and exercise their right at the polls, then either we are in a state of war, and actual war power is brought to bear against them, and we ought to declare war and fight it out; or we are at peace, and being so, if millions of voters are unable to defend themselves . . . we might as well confess the experiment of the Republican Union is ended. [Applause]." If her audience wanted a return to war, so be it. If not, let the democratic process work its magic in the South. Let white Southerners craft policies to appeal to black voters, even if that might mean losses for the Republican Party.

In weaving her tale of what could and should be, Dickinson also imagined an alternative future shaped by another sort of memory: the memories that the young white Southerners of 1872 would take into their adulthood. Half the Southern voters, she pointed out, would be casting their first presidential ballot in 1872. Whereas the Southern white leadership remembered secession and war (and, she insisted, had become reconciled to defeat), "the boys, who never did anything, who were not born when the war began, those boys, and those men, have no such recollection, have no memories of combining against the Republic. All that they see is the wrong and bitterness of the Government which rules them." Thus, Dickinson argued, the election of 1872 was not only about how to understand the memory of the Civil War but also about how the next generation would remember what they did at the polls that year.

But the problem of memory was also much closer to home and less abstract for Dickinson and the Liberal Republicans. After all, President Grant was the Union's greatest war hero. Undaunted, Dickinson dismissed the president as "a man whose interest was first centered in a tap-yard; second in the blood he shed; and third in his cigar." As she geared up for more flowery invective, a voice from the audience cried out, " 'Who saved the country?' " The quick-witted Dickinson confronted this popular memory head on. It was "the men who fought under Gen. Grant" who won the war, she declared. And in fact those men "had learned their lessons of loyalty through twenty-five years of the columns of THE NEW YORK TRIBUNE." It was Horace Greeley, the *Tribune*'s editor, who deserved credit for fighting to break the chains of slavery, and now he stood for Republican constitutional principles. "History," she declared in offering yet another audacious twist on historic memory, "will write the record concerning us."

Dickinson was not content to claim that the nation owed a greater debt to the physically unimposing bespectacled editor than to the cigar-chomping hero of Vicksburg, Petersburg, and Appomattox. Before she closed she had to wriggle out of one other conundrum. How could she back a man who had opposed woman suffrage, when so many in the woman's rights leadership had aligned themselves with the Republicans? Part of the answer was simply that Grant's support of women smacked of cynical opportunism, backed by no real conviction or concrete action, so the suffragists should not hand over their political capital to such a man. But she did not stop there. Instead she turned again to the past, quoting Greeley's own words from 1860: " 'When the women of the United States shall desire this, not merely as a privilege, but as a responsibility, then I am willing to give it.' " Dickinson, ever the maverick, endorsed such harsh terms, adding, "We have enough supine and lazy and careless voters already."

The published responses to Dickinson's Cooper Institute lecture followed expected party lines, with several reports focusing on Dickinson's split with the other leaders in the woman's movement. The Democratic *New York World* led with the importance of Dickinson speaking to an enthusiastic audience "in opposition to her sisters of the suffrage-making organizations," while Grant supporters Elizabeth Cady Stanton and Sallie Devereaux Blake looked on from the audience. Conversely the *Boston Post* noted that while the familiar female leaders had ended their "meaningless flirtations" and backed Grant in exchange for a "ridiculously small bone," Dickinson was the "one woman who remains true to her honest convictions" in supporting Greeley.[48] The *Providence Journal* approached Dickinson and her lecture gingerly, noting that "Miss Anna Dickinson is a lady who makes lecturing a profession. . . . While we would treat all opponents with fairness," the *Journal*'s editors explained, "we confess to more than usual hesitation in dealing with a woman who has entered upon the domain of politics." Nevertheless, the newspaper managed to characterize Dickinson's lecture as "the most insipid and oft repeated slanders against General Grant, and an equally ludicrous and false glorification of Horace Greeley." The *Boston Journal* took the *New York Tribune* to task for celebrating "the sensational female declaimer" who was guilty of "demagogism." In contrast, Bowles's *Springfield Republican* celebrated the lecture as an "impressive plea for honest government and true national unity," adding that "in delivering it the most eloquent of American women has performed the noblest and most courageous actions of her life." Other critics found diverse ways to minimize Dickinson's significance. Waterbury, Connecticut's

{ J. MATTHEW GALLMAN }

Evening American suggested that the only remaining question was "who wrote it?" The mocking *National Republican* attributed the favorable coverage in the *Tribune* to Dickinson's personal relationship with Reid, "whom she rejected some time ago" and who "praises Anna in a gushing way in the *Tribune*, from which we infer that his angelic bosom is still torn by the tender passion."[49]

Dickinson's friends praised her performance even while acknowledging that it came with a cost. She had "[done] a noble thing in coming forward when Mr Greeley's chances seemed to be almost hopeless," gushed Carl Schurz. Laura Runkle, who had been in the audience, reported, "Everywhere I hear praises of your pluck and honesty even from Grant men, and, if it cost you loss, this winter as I hope it may not, it will be more than made up another year." Even her loyal Republican friends were impressed with the gesture. In early December Charles Dudley Warner, the always sardonic editor, wrote, "I thank the lord that I am so constituted that I love even geese, and Greeley people." Senator Ben Butler, who had a long-standing affection for Dickinson, told her that although he was disappointed that she made the speech he still thought it "the *bravest* thing done through the campaign."[50]

But what exactly had Dickinson done, and how and why had she done it? When she took the stage in support of Greeley, the war's memory was present in at least three senses. Most obviously, Dickinson's text was a direct confrontation with the Republican Party's claim to the war's memory. The Republicans' logic was powerful. The Republicans were the party of Lincoln, and President Grant had led the Union army to victory. A vote against the Republicans was a vote against fallen Northern soldiers and a martyred president. Thus, Grant's political enemies were wise to shift attention away from the war and toward his failings in office. Dickinson certainly took her shots at the Grant White House, but she also confronted the war's memory head on and claimed it for her side. If the war had indeed been won—as the Republican conquerors were proud of declaring—then why maintain a military presence in the South? If this was really a war for democratic principles and one of the results was the winning of suffrage for African American men, then why not let democracy run its course? And, most outrageously, Dickinson was not even willing to grant the president credit for winning the war. The soldiers, not the generals, really triumphed, and men like Greeley—who helped shape the popular will—deserved praise for the victory. Here was the old political pro making the best case that she could with the available material. While Greeley was proposing that Americans "clasp hands over the bloody chasm" and put the conflict behind them, thus effectively calling for national amnesia, Dickinson was suggesting new ways of remembering the war and its meaning that made such an approach more palatable.

At a very different level Dickinson's speech—and her tortured decision to give it—was all about her own memories of the war and its aftermath and an assortment of loyalties that dated to the war years. Her distaste with Grant ran deep, particularly because of his treatment of Sumner, and her friendships with Reid and other Liberal Republicans weighed into her decision. Still, Dickinson knew that her decision would disappoint Warner, Phillips, Garrison, and a host of old allies, thus making the decision that much more difficult. At bottom, Dickinson was drawn into the campaign because of her own sense that she belonged in the political arena. And that sense of self was born in her own memories of youthful wartime successes and the recollection of a time when thousands flocked to hear her opinions on affairs of the day. This can be read in various ways. On the one hand, Dickinson had a large ego that thrived on the attention and praise she received as an important political player. On the other hand, she was a woman of powerful convictions that she felt deserved public airing. In a political world that offered her few opportunities to effect change, how could she turn down such a fine pulpit?

This raises a further tier in this tableau of memory. Rather than concentrating on what Dickinson said or why she said it, perhaps we should shift our focus to the collective memory of the people in that New York audience. As a Boston reporter explained, Dickinson's appearance "recalled vividly the days of the war, not so very far away, when her woman's voice rang out through the country in defense of all that was just and noble, and in bitter denunciation of wrong."[51] Dickinson, like Grant, was a veteran of the Civil War. And like many other war heroes she had built her postwar career on her celebrated actions as a patriotic youth. Even those reporters who came to ridicule recognized the political significance of Dickinson's endorsement of Greeley. That both camps battled for endorsements from leading women, and trumpeted those successes, was an acknowledgment of women's expanded public role. That increased political voice was in no small part a further legacy of the Civil War and particularly of Dickinson's celebrated role in wartime politics.

Dickinson's continuing importance as a public woman was not lost on her many female friends. As one friend and admirer wrote, "Don't forget that you owe it to all us women who are dumb, and for whom you speak, who are in obscure places, and for whom you stand, who find in you the ripe, beautiful, missing expression of full womanhood, to be always at your best in all of your spoken and written words—So much of the future of women lies in your white hands, so heavy a burden of the needs rests on your girlish shoulders."[52] Almost a decade after the war Dickinson still played an important symbolic role in American public life.

Things went badly for the Liberal Republicans in the election of 1872 and far worse personally for Horace Greeley. On October 30 Greeley's wife passed away, and within a month a distraught Greeley followed her to his grave, but not before Dickinson visited him one last time at the *Tribune* office.[53] Anna Dickinson was thirty in 1872. She would remain in and out of the public eye for another two decades as a lecturer, author, occasional stump speaker, and—for a time—a celebrated actress and playwright, but she never really recaptured the fame or popularity of her earlier years. By the late 1880s Dickinson was poor, seemingly mentally unstable, perhaps an alcoholic, and generally in terrible shape. In 1891 her sister, Susan, arranged to have Dickinson committed to a hospital for the insane. Dickinson successfully won her freedom and then spent much of the next several years in a series of court battles against those who had had her committed and against an assortment of newspapers—including many of her old supporters—who had trumpeted her insanity. She died in quiet obscurity in 1932, largely forgotten by her contemporaries. In her final years she spent much of her time filling scrapbooks with clippings and writing long letters in a seemingly futile attempt to etch her name more deeply into the nation's memory.

NOTES

Preliminary research for this project was supported by a fellowship from the National Endowment for the Humanities. I would like to thank Joan Waugh and Alice Fahs and the participants in the Huntington Library's conference "The Memory of the Civil War in American Culture." I would also like to thank two anonymous readers for their suggestions.

1. This essay is part of a larger biographical study of Anna Dickinson (forthcoming from Oxford University Press). For a short essay emphasizing Dickinson's war years, see J. Matthew Gallman, "Anna Dickinson: Abolitionist Orator," in *The Human Tradition in the Civil War and Reconstruction*, ed. Steven E. Woodworth (Wilmington, Del.: Scholarly Resources, 2000), 93–110. Dickinson's papers are housed in the

Anna E. Dickinson Papers at the Library of Congress, Washington, D.C., and available on microfilm (hereafter AED Papers). The only published biography is Giraud Chester, *Embattled Maiden: The Life of Anna Dickinson* (New York: G. P. Putnam's Sons, 1951). James Harvey Young, who wrote a dissertation on Dickinson's wartime career and several important articles on various aspects of her life, authored a Dickinson biography in the late 1940s, "Anna Elizabeth Dickinson," that has never been published. I am indebted to Young for permission to inspect both this manuscript and his research notes in the James Harvey Young Papers, Special Collections, Emory University, Atlanta, Georgia.

2. Karyln Kohrs Campbell, ed., *Women Public Speakers in the United States, 1800–1925: A Bio-critical Sourcebook* (Westport, Conn.: Greenwood Press, 1993). See also Karyln Kohrs Campbell, *Man Cannot Speak for Her*, 2 vols. (Westport, Conn.: Greenwood Press, 1989).

3. Benjamin Franklin Prescott to Anna Elizabeth Dickinson (hereafter AED), January 29, 1863, AED Papers; Young, "Anna Elizabeth Dickinson," chap. 3, pp. 1–7.

4. On Dickinson's rhetoric and popular responses, see J. Matthew Gallman, "An Inspiration to Work: Anna Elizabeth Dickinson, Public Orator," in *The War Was You and Me: Civilians in the American Civil War*, ed. Joan Cashin (Princeton: Princeton University Press, 2002), 159–82; and J. Matthew Gallman, "Anna Dickinson, America's Joan of Arc: Public Discourse and Gendered Rhetoric during the Civil War," in *American Public Life and the Historical Imagination*, ed. Wendy Gamber, Michael Grossberg, and Hendrik Hartog (Notre Dame: University of Notre Dame Press, 2003), 91–112.

5. See Nina Silber, *The Romance of Reunion: Northerners and the South, 1865–1900* (Chapel Hill: University of North Carolina Press, 1993).

6. Anna Elizabeth Dickinson, *What Answer?* (Boston: Ticknor and Fields, 1868). See also J. Matthew Gallman, "Introduction" to *What Answer?* by Dickinson (1868; reprint, Amherst, N.Y.: Humanity Books, 2003), 7–28.

7. See Ellen DuBois, *Feminism and Suffrage: The Emergence of an Independent Women's Movement in America, 1848–1869* (Ithaca: Cornell University Press, 1978).

8. See Barbara Goldsmith, *Other Powers: The Age of Suffrage, Spiritualism, and the Scandalous Victoria Woodhull* (New York: Alfred A. Knopf, 1998).

9. Susan B. Anthony to AED, various correspondence, AED Papers. Jean Baker discusses the Anthony-Dickinson relationship in her forthcoming book *Founding Sisters*.

10. The standard history of the Liberal Republican Party is still Earle Dudley Ross, *The Liberal Republican Movement* (1919; reprint, New York: AMS Press, 1971). See also Richard Allan Gerber, "The Liberal Republicans of 1872 in Historiographic Perspective," *Journal of American History* 62 (June 1975): 40–73, and the sources cited below in notes 11 and 12.

11. Matthew T. Downey, "Horace Greeley and the Politicians: The Liberal Republican Convention in 1872," *Journal of American History* 4 (March 1967): 727–50.

12. James M. McPherson, "Grant or Greeley?: The Abolitionist Dilemma in the Election of 1872," *American Historical Review* 71 (October 1965): 43–61.

13. On Dickinson's feelings for Charles Sumner, see AED to Mary Dickinson, February 2, 1871, AED Papers.

14. McPherson, "Grant or Greeley?"

15. Oliver Johnson to AED, March 8, 1872, AED Papers.

16. John Dickinson to AED, March 7, 1872; Sue Dickinson to AED, March 13, 1872; and Ed Dickinson to AED, March 19, 1872, all in AED Papers.

17. *Pittsburgh Daily Post*, April 3, 1872, clipping in Dickinson scrapbook, AED Papers.

18. AED to Susan Dickinson, April 3, 1872, AED Papers.

19. Samuel Bowles to AED, April 5, 1872, AED Papers; Charles Dudley Warner to AED, May 11, 1872, copy in Young Papers.

20. *Carlisle (Pa.) American Volunteer*, April 11, 1872; *Philadelphia Evening Bulletin*, April 12, 1872; *Philadelphia Evening City Item*, April 12, 1872, clipping in Dickinson scrapbook.

21. *New York World*, April 20, 1872; *Springfield Republican*, April 20?, 1872; *St. Louis Dispatch*, April 20, 1872; *Boston Post*, n.d.; *New York Sun*, April 20, 1872; and several unidentified newspapers, April 1872, all clippings in Dickinson scrapbook.

22. Laura Bullard to AED, April 5, 1872; and Melinda Jones to AED, April 6, 1872, both in AED Papers.

23. AED to Whitelaw Reid, May 11, 1872, Whitelaw Reid Papers as cited in Giraud Chester notes, AED Papers.

24. Laura Bullard to AED, May 31, 1872, July 14, 1872, August 9, 1872; Robert Callyer to AED, July 28, 1872; "Little Brownie" (Ele Brown) to AED, July 29, 1872; and Charles Dudley Warner to AED, May 9, 1872, and May 11, 1872, all in AED Papers.

25. Laura Bullard to AED, June 6, 1872; M. S. Pomeroy to AED, June 7, 1872; Moses Coit Tyler to AED, June 30, 1872; Henry Wilson to AED, June 11, 1872; and AED to "Dicky" (Susan Dickinson), June 7, 1872, all in AED Papers.

26. Laura Bullard to AED, July 7, 1872, AED Papers.

27. AED to "My Dear Badness," July 14, 1872, unidentified letters folder, AED Papers. This letter is almost certainly to Susan Dickinson.

28. AED to Mary Dickinson, July 12, 1872, July 15, 1872; AED to Susan, July 10, 1872; Susan to AED, July 11, 1872; and Theodore Tilton telegram to AED, July 12, 1872, all in AED Papers. All quotations are from Dickinson's July 12, 1872, letter to her mother.

29. Samuel Bowles to AED, July 15, 1872, AED Papers.

30. AED to Whitelaw Reid, July 23, 1872, Whitelaw Reid Papers as cited in Giraud Chester notes, AED Papers.

31. Whitelaw Reid to AED, July 30, 1872, AED Papers.

32. Oliver Johnson to AED, July 30, 1872, filed under "unidentified fragments," AED Papers. Identified by handwriting and return address.

33. AED to Whitelaw Reid, August 2, 1872, Whitelaw Reid Papers as cited in Giraud Chester notes, AED Papers.

34. Laura Bullard to AED, August 3, 1872, AED Papers.

35. Ibid.; AED to Whitelaw Reid, August 7, 1872, August 8, 1872, Whitelaw Reid Papers as cited in Giraud Chester notes, AED Papers.

36. Mary Dickinson to AED, August 16, 1872, AED Papers.

37. Whitelaw Reid to AED, August 22, 1872, AED Papers.

38. For the newspaper notices, see *New York Independent*, August 27, 1872; *New York Golden Age*, August 31, 1872; *New York Daily Tribune*, August 30, 1872; *Pittsburgh Evening Chronicle*, August 28, 1872; and several unidentified newspapers, all clippings in Dickinson scrapbook. For correspondence demonstrating that Dickinson was behind these notices see Wm[?] Hayes Ward to AED, August 26, 1872; Oliver Johnson to AED, August 27, 1872; AED to Susan Dickinson, August 30, 1872; and Susan Dickinson to AED, September 2, 1872, all in AED Papers.

39. AED to Susan Dickinson, August 26, 1872, and AED to Mary Dickinson, August 27, 1872, both in AED Papers.

40. Samuel Bowles to AED, September 27, 1872, AED Papers.

41. AED to Whitelaw Reid, October 3, 1872, Whitelaw Reid Papers as cited in Giraud Chester notes, AED Papers. For lost lecture opportunities, see Sue Warner to AED, September 28, 1872; and Moses Coit Tyler to AED, October 2, 1872, both in AED Papers.

42. AED to "Birdie" Warner, October 4, 1872, copy in Young Papers; Susan Dickinson to AED, October 7, 1872, AED Papers.

43. AED to Mary Dickinson, October 6, 1872, AED Papers; AED to Whitelaw Reid, October 7, 1872, Whitelaw Reid Papers as cited in Giraud Chester notes, AED Papers; Whitelaw Reid to General John Cochrane, October 4, 1872, Whitelaw Reid Letter Books, Whitelaw Reid Papers, microfilm, Library of Congress; Whitelaw Reid to General John Cochrane, October 9, 1872, AED Papers; AED to Susan Dickinson, October 9, 1872, AED Papers; Whitelaw Reid to AED, October 10, 1872, AED Papers; [Laura Bullard?] to AED, October 10, 1872, miscellaneous letters, AED Papers; Susan Dickinson to AED, October 11, 1872, AED Papers; E. P. Bullard to AED, October 13, 1872, AED Papers; Whitelaw Reid to AED, October 24, 1872, AED Papers; AED to Whitelaw Reid, October 24, 1872, Whitelaw Reid Papers as cited in Giraud Chester notes, AED Papers.

44. *New York Daily Tribune*, October 22, 1872, clipping in Dickinson scrapbook.

45. Several newspapers reported detailed accounts of the speech. The excerpts throughout come from the *New York Sun*, October 25, 1872, clipping in Dickinson scrapbook.

46. *Liberator*, January 1, 1831.

47. McPherson, "Grant or Greeley?"

48. *New York World*, October 26, 1872; *Boston Post*, October 30, 1872, clipping in Dickinson scrapbook.

49. *Providence Journal*, October 29, 1872; *Boston Journal*, October 29, 1872; *Springfield Republican*, October 28, 1872; *Waterbury (Conn.) Evening American*, October 26, 1872; and *National Republican*, n.d., all clippings in Dickinson scrapbook.

50. Carl Schurz to AED, November 3, 1872; Laura Runkle, November 7, 1872; Charles Dudley Warner to AED, December 21, 1872; and AED to Mary Dickinson, November 14, 1872, all in AED Papers. Dickinson quoted Butler's sentiments in her letter to her mother.

51. *Boston Post*, October 30, 1872.

52. Laura Runkle to AED, August 27, 1872, AED Papers.

53. AED to Susan Dickinson, November 8, 1872, AED Papers.

Patrick J. Kelly

The Election of 1896 and the
Restructuring of Civil War Memory

Gilded Age Republicans were notorious for attacking their Democratic opponents by waving the bloody shirt, a campaign tactic designed to activate the historical remembrance of the Civil War among Northern voters. Carefully selected, the wartime memories used by bloody-shirt Republicans became as familiar as the Scriptures: Lincoln's party held firm in the face of secession while the treasonous wartime Democratic Party was hijacked by Southern fire-eaters during the secession crisis and closely associated with Northern Copperheads during the fighting itself. They also dramatically recalled the suffering of Union soldiers, especially prisoners of war, in the struggle to save the nation. Speaking directly to the North's enormous cohort of Union veterans, GOP candidates exhorted, "Vote as you shot." The tactic of waving the bloody shirt, always controversial within the party—many thought its heated rhetoric needlessly inflamed sectional tensions—became even more contested in the 1880s when the rhetorical focus shifted toward memories of the GOP's role in emancipation and in securing African Americans the right to vote. The last stand of bloody-shirt Republicans came in January 1891 with the defeat in Congress of the Force Bill, legislation designed to use U.S. military power to enforce black suffrage in the South. By 1896, then, the time when Republican Party candidates could marshal remembrance of the Civil War to win elections seemingly had ended.[1]

Yet a striking feature of the momentous 1896 presidential campaign was the role that Civil War–era memory played in the successful effort of William McKinley to defeat William Jennings Bryan. By the mid-1890s the GOP was led by a new generation intimately associated with the emergent corporate capitalist elite—most notably Mark Hanna, a successful Cleveland industrialist, McKinley's closest advisor, and his presidential campaign manager—and its political language had shifted away from the racial commitments of the previous generation of party leaders. Stunned by Bryan's nomination and alarmed by his appeals to both rural and working-class laborers, the 1896 Republican campaign architects crafted an electoral strategy that emphasized a renewed nationalism based on sectional reconciliation. Speaking to a group of Confederate veterans while visiting his Canton home in October 1896, McKinley articulated the new Republican creed when he proclaimed, "Let us remember now and in all the future that we are Americans, and what is good for Ohio is good for Virginia."[2] Tragically, however, the party's shift from a sectional to a national strategy was predicated upon Republicans' acceptance of the racial apartheid that by the mid-1890s had taken firm hold in the South. Most tellingly, the 1896 Republican platform for the first time since the end of the Civil War omitted any demand that the federal government use its military power to guarantee black suffrage in the South. This omission, the *New York Times* noted approvingly, was an important indication of McKinley's "sagacity . . . in depreciating sectional division and appealing to a common patriotism to protect the Nation's honor."[3] In 1896, then, GOP leaders, indifferent to the intensified attacks on the social and political rights of African Americans and eager to promote a patriotic nationalism based on the reconciliation of whites in the North and the South, distanced the party from its historical role in revolutionizing U.S. race relations during the Civil War and Reconstruction.

In restructuring the public remembrance of the Civil War to further its nationalist message, the McKinley campaign mobilized a potent but racially neutral historical memory, the secession crisis of 1861. In comment typical of GOP rhetoric, Henry Cabot Lodge wrote shortly after Bryan's nomination that those aligned against the Democratic candidate were "fighting to save the country from a disaster which would be only second to 1861."[4] A Bryan presidency posed a renewed threat to national solidarity in two ways. First, his pro-silver monetary policies promised once more to tear the nation apart along sectional lines. Writing in the *North American Review*, Republican senator William E. Chandler argued that the Democratic convention "deliberately, in the year 1896, undertook to organize the solid South with a few states of the West, to menace the prosperity of the North and East, by as wicked a movement as that after which it was deliberately patterned, the Southern rebellion of 1861."[5] For the millions of Americans who remembered the staggering amount of death and destruction resulting from the Civil War, the dangers of sectional division remained very real. In 1896, however, McKinley's campaign paired sectional conflict with a new and deeply ominous threat to a nation undergoing rapid urban and industrial growth: class warfare.

Seizing on Bryan's statement that the "sympathies" of the Democratic Party "are on the side of the struggling masses," prominent McKinley supporters accused the Democratic candidate of fomenting social strife among the expanding population of working-class Americans.[6] In October 1896 John Ireland, archbishop of St. Paul, issued a public letter, reprinted and widely circulated by the Republican National Committee, cautioning that the "movement which had its expression in the Chicago [Democratic] convention . . . is, in its right logical effects, revolution against the United States: it is secession, the secession of 1861." Ireland concluded with the grim warning, "The war of class against class is upon us." Speaking at a rally in New York City a few nights before the election, General Horace Porter reminisced, "During the heroic age of the country, in 1861, the old soldiers went to the front to save the nation's life." But, he warned, the times "were more perilous" than in 1861. "The only words in the English language that can describe the threatened situation are 'redhanded anarchy.' "[7]

The GOP's restructuring of Civil War memory to include the dangers of class division was especially concentrated in the key electoral battleground states of the Midwest: Illinois, Indiana, Michigan, Wisconsin, and Ireland's home state of Minnesota. The Midwest had seen some of the most violent labor strife of the 1890s. This region also was home to one of the largest concentrations of Union veterans in the nation, a key GOP constituency. By stirring historical remembrance of the secession crisis of 1861 in this and the country's other regions, the Republican Party was able to position itself as the patriotic defender of the nation-state against political forces that in 1896, or so McKinley and his campaign surrogates claimed, threatened to divide the country along the explosive fault lines of section and class.

The party's use of a wartime remembrance that elided emancipation and evoked instead the public memory of sectional divide supports David W. Blight's argument that in the battle to define the historical meaning of the Civil War the "inexorable drive for reunion . . . trumped race." Unlike the nation's white population, African Americans viewed the secession crisis of 1861 as a largely positive historical event because the Civil War marked the beginning of the end of chattel slavery. During the secession winter Frederick Douglass's great fear was not war between North and South; he feared that white politicians would leave the institution of slavery intact by agreeing to "peaceful disunion." Soon after Southern artillery shelled Fort Sumter, the brilliant African American physician and abolitionist James McCune Smith wrote, "Circumstances have been so arranged by the degrees of Providence, that in struggling for their own nationality they [white

{ PATRICK J. KELLY }

Northerners] are forced to defend our rights."[8] In the decades after the Confederate surrender Douglass and other African American leaders articulated what Blight calls an "emancipationist" memory of the Civil War, a vision that defined the conflict as a struggle for black freedom, citizenship, and constitutional equality. The emancipationist vision of the Civil War, however, ran counter to strong reconciliationist currents in the national culture, and as early as 1875 Douglass wondered aloud, "If war among the whites brought peace and liberty to blacks, what will peace among the whites bring?"[9]

Douglass's apprehension proved justified. By the mid-1890s, Blight argues, the "forces of reconciliation [had] overwhelmed the emancipationist vision in the national culture . . . [and] delivered to the country a segregated memory of the Civil War on Southern terms."[10] In the powerful and well-financed McKinley campaign's drive to gain control of the White House nationalist rhetoric played an important role in solidifying the reconciliationist vision within American culture. With very few exceptions white America remembered the sectional crisis of 1861 as a national catastrophe. Drawing from this well of collective memory, the Republicans in 1896 attacked Bryan's monetary policies by deploying a historical remembrance that highlighted the perils of sectional division while at the same time ignoring the party's role in the transformation of race relations during the Civil War and Reconstruction.

Sectionalism, then, remained a vitally important national concern in 1896, and Blight offers a convincing argument that white America's acceptance of a reconciliationist memory of the Civil War played a key role in facilitating sectional reunion by World War I. In addition to sectionalism, however, by the mid-1890s, a period marked by industrial depression and violent labor conflict, many Americans were also deeply concerned about an emerging threat to the nation's solidarity, class warfare. Seizing upon Bryan's convention statement that the Democratic Party sided with the "struggling masses" against the "idle holders of idle capital," Republicans accused the Democratic candidate of fomenting civil strife and deployed the public recollection of 1861 as a stern warning against social division.[11] Focused on race as "the central problem of how Americans made choices to remember and forget about their Civil War," Blight's model deemphasizes the capacity of the McKinley campaign to restructure the memory of the Civil War to buttress the GOP's combined goals of sectional and class solidarity.[12] Establishing the links among public memory, campaign strategy, and partisan ideology will reveal a Civil War memory that warned against sectional division and, transcending race as the "central problem" of wartime remembrance, allowed the Republican Party to brand political protest against America's growing social and economic inequalities as unpatriotic threats to national unity.

In July 1896 when Democratic Party members gathered in Chicago to nominate their candidate for president, the United States was a nation in distress. The repercussions of the business depression that began with the Philadelphia and Reading Railroad Company's bankruptcy in February 1893 continued to haunt the nation's economy, with an estimated 15 percent of the workforce still unemployed in 1896. With hard times came social and political unrest. In 1894 a group of jobless workers, under the leadership of Jacob S. Coxey, marched to Washington demanding federal assistance. Coxey's desperate "army" of the unemployed was easily dispersed but, paired with the nation's growing industrial labor unrest—in 1894, the year of the great Pullman Strike, there were one hundred industrial work stoppages averaging nearly fifty days in length and involving nearly forty-six thousand workers—his movement alarmed many middle- and upper-class Americans.[13] Labor agitation, however, was only one problem facing the comfortable classes in 1896. In the 1890s the Populist movement demanded stronger government intervention into the economy, including the free coinage of silver at a ratio of sixteen to one with gold. Gaining the support of millions of Americans in the West and South, the Populists offered a powerful agrarian challenge to the two-party system. In 1896, then, the political status quo was under attack in both the industrial and the agricultural areas of the United States. It is no wonder that as the presidential election approached many Americans feared that the nation was, once more, about to tear itself apart.[14]

If the United States was a nation in distress in July 1896, the Democratic Party was a political organization in disarray. In 1892 the Democrats captured control of the executive and legislative branches of the federal government for the first time since 1856. As a consequence of hard times, however, the party suffered staggering congressional losses in the midterm elections of 1894. By the summer of 1896 discontent with Grover Cleveland and the conservative Bourbon Democracy was rampant among the party faithful, and a new generation of party leaders had emerged. One such leader was Senator Ben Tillman of South Carolina. Speaking in favor of the free coinage of silver at the Chicago convention, Tillman maladroitly interjected the memory of the Civil War into the 1896 campaign.

{ PATRICK J. KELLY }

In the words of his biographer Stephen Kantrowitz, Tillman regarded bimetallism as a "bridge between disaffected producers in the Democratic South and their brethren in the Republican West." The senator believed that this regional alignment would "redefine American sectionalism and rally white producers everywhere against their common enemies in the seats of monopoly [and] finance." Tillman's attempt to redefine sectionalism in Chicago, however, proved disastrous. Speaking during the early part of the convention, days before Bryan's surprising nomination, Tillman opened with the words, "I come from the South, from the home of secession." This defiant opening startled his listeners, who greeted his remarks with loud hisses from the convention floor. The senator's statements haunted the Democratic national campaign until election day. But there were more surprises to come.[15] Raising his voice to be heard over shouts of disapproval from members of his own party, the undaunted Tillman continued, "Some of my friends from the South and elsewhere have said that this is not a sectional issue. I say it is a sectional issue." "We of the South," he continued, "have turned our faces to the West, asking our brethren of those States to unite with us in restoring the government, the liberty of fathers, which our fathers left us."[16] Tillman left the speaker's podium to a torrent of boos; Kantrowitz argues that this speech "destroyed his chances to become a national candidate," but the damage to the party was at least as severe.[17]

Coming from a senator representing South Carolina, Tillman's intemperate remarks on secession and section offered opponents of bimetallism an opportunity to attack free silver as both financially unsound and a new threat to national unity. They wasted no time in exploiting the opening. On July 9, the day before Bryan's nomination, the staunchly Republican *Chicago Tribune* editors warned that the convention's "Southern fire-eaters . . . are just as rancorous now as they were in 1861, when they repudiated their debts, confiscated Northern private and Union national public property, and proceeded upon their mad effort to destroy the republic."[18] Conservative Democratic newspapers, angry at the convention's rejection of Grover Cleveland's sound money policies, joined in the attack. The *Chicago Chronicle*'s editors argued that the "hothead silver leaders of the South . . . are of the same class who got the South to pass the secession ordinances in 1860–'61 and followed it by repudiation of public and private debts due the North." The *Chronicle* editors concluded ominously, "History repeats itself, and threatens a renewal of its calamitous episodes."[19] Even before Bryan's dramatic nomination, then, the proponents of sound money seized the opening provided by Tillman by aggressively reviving the public memory of the 1861 secession crisis as a new front in their determined attack against the free coinage of silver.

Although it became apparent during the convention that the Democratic Party would renounce the sound money policies of Grover Cleveland, the party's nomination of William Jennings Bryan still came as a shock to most Americans, including the leadership of the Republican Party. The Republicans had nominated William McKinley as their presidential candidate earlier that summer and planned a campaign centered on the message that protective tariffs would return economic prosperity by protecting American jobs and wage scales. Hearing the news of Bryan's nomination while yachting off the New England coast, McKinley's campaign manager, Mark Hanna, telegraphed the candidate, "The Chicago convention has changed everything. . . . With this communist spirit abroad the cry of 'free silver' will be catching."[20] Hanna quickly regained his balance and even mocked other Republicans who were panic-stricken at the possibility of Bryan's election as "just a lot of damn fools," but even he was startled when the advance "sixty-day" polls he commissioned indicated that Bryan held a lead over McKinley. Reflecting the fluid political situation, Josiah Quincy wrote in the August issue of the *North American Review*, "With the old political fences so completely down, and in the face of conditions so chaotic, there is no warrant for any assurances as to the result of the election in November."[21] The prospect of a Bryan victory seemed, for a short time at least, very real to contemporary observers, and in response the anti-Bryan "counter-crusade" began organizing its extraordinarily well-financed and well-coordinated assault on the Democratic candidate.[22]

After the election, the GOP's national campaign committee reported that it had raised and spent nearly $4 million between July and November 1896; however, by some estimates, the party had spent more than $16 million electing McKinley.[23] Most of this unprecedented campaign money came from the nation's corporate elite who, genuinely alarmed by Bryan's nomination, flocked to the McKinley banner. One of McKinley's most powerful supporters was the railroad magnate James J. Hill, a conservative Democratic political ally and close friend of Grover Cleveland. Outraged by the Democratic convention's renunciation of the sitting president and his pro-gold policies, Hill energetically opposed the Bryan campaign. In mid-July he wrote to J. P. Morgan, "I feel it is very important that the sound money men not waste a single day in getting to work." Hill, whose railroads purchased coal from Hanna's mines, introduced Hanna to New York City's leading industrialists and financiers.[24] In mid-August Hill accompanied Hanna "on a tour through the high places of Wall Street, and during the next five days they succeeded in collecting as much money as was immediately necessary."[25] John McCall, president of New York Life Insurance Company, authorized a $50,000 contribution to the GOP.[26] J. P. Morgan Bank and Standard Oil contributed $250,000 each to the McKinley campaign. Declaring, "I can see nothing else to do, to serve our Country and our honor," John D. Rockefeller sent Mark Hanna a personal check for $2,500.[27] The $500,000 contributed to the party by Standard Oil and the House of Morgan alone constituted more than the entire campaign chest of the Democratic Party in 1896. Well organized under the watchful eye of Hanna, the GOP's "educational" campaign hired more than one thousand speakers to address targeted audiences throughout the United States and printed and distributed tens of millions of pieces of campaign literature, in up to a dozen languages, for distribution to voters. At the end of the campaign Theodore Roosevelt complained to a GOP official that Hanna had advertised McKinley "as if he were patent medicine."[28]

Given the Republican Party's overwhelming advantage in money and organization and the weakness of a Democratic Party that bore the onus for the depression of the 1890s while being split over the nomination of Bryan, McKinley's election was not surprising. The GOP's aggressive deployment of Civil War memory was but one of many factors propelling McKinley into the White House. In addition to electing party candidates, however, presidential campaigns are in part mass movements of political education that exert great influence on the nation's understanding of its past. The makers of campaign rhetoric are architects of national and political consciousness, and presidential campaigns, especially in watershed elections such as 1896's, are part of the continuing process of nation building and, in post–Civil War America, nation rebuilding. The overarching theme of McKinley's "shrewd campaign," in the words of Bryan's biographer LeRoy Ashby, emphasized "unity rather than social and regional conflict."[29] In crafting a campaign of national solidarity, GOP tacticians quickly deployed a historical recollection that reminded voters of national division's perilous consequences. In selecting this remembrance, the McKinley campaign, a political organization with the power to advertise its nationalist message into virtually every household, fundamentally restructured the meaning and memory of the Civil War in American culture.

In 1896 the Republican Party waged its campaign of memory along two fronts. The first was the party's charge that Bryan's pro-silver policies endangered national unity by pitting the North and East against the South and West. Days after Bryan's nomination McKinley attacked the Democratic candidate by evoking public remembrance of the Civil War. "Then section was arrayed against section," McKinley declared. "Now men of all sections can and will unite to rebuke the repudiation of our obligations and debasement of our currency." The *New York Times* editors noted approvingly that in his speech McKinley had "drawn clearly" the "parallel between the duties imposed by the civil war and those imposed" by free silver supporters. "He is moderate in saying," the *Times* editors concluded, "that never since that time have honest Americans had a 'greater duty.'"[30]

Bryan, like Tillman and most other supporters of bimetallism, envisioned a political coalition from the West and the South working together in the fight against the gold standard. Unlike Tillman, Elizabeth Sanders argues, Bryan "assiduously counseled tolerance and avoided divisive social issues."[31] Realizing that Republican charges of sectionalism were damaging his campaign, Bryan insisted that the Democratic platform was "not the platform of section. It is the platform of our common country, and appeals to those who love mankind to rise to its defense." Unlike his opponent, Bryan rarely discussed the war and, offering a different historical memory to voters, he argued that his party "breathes the spirit of the Declaration of Independence."[32] Bryan's reluctance to stir voters' memories of the Civil War echoed the desire of Populist leaders from earlier in the decade who, unsuccessfully, urged Americans to bury the passions generated from this fratricidal conflict.

Bryan ran for president on both the Democratic and the Populist tickets. In the early 1890s, however, the Populist Party existed solely as an independent third-party movement facing the immense challenge of appealing to Northern voters while simultaneously attracting white voters in the Democratic stronghold of the "Solid South." Determined to focus the nation's attention on the rapidly expanding economic and social dislocations resulting from the rise of unregulated corporate finance and industrial capitalism, Populist leaders called on American voters to transcend the sectional divisions growing out of the Civil War and Reconstruction. Leonidas Polk, president of the Southern Alliance, argued in 1891 that the modern struggle was not the conflict of twenty-five years ago, "but the gigantic struggle of today is between the classes and the masses." He concluded, "In the appalling presence of such an issue, buried and forgotten forever be the prejudices, animosities, and estrangements of that unfortunate war."[33] The party's 1892 Omaha platform argued that "the civil war is over . . . and every

{ PATRICK J. KELLY }

passion and resentment which grew out of it must die with it, and that we must be, in fact, as we are in name, one united brotherhood of free men."[34] That year the Populists, attempting to neutralize the politics of sectionalism and attract Southern voters, fielded a Blue-Gray ticket headed by Union veteran general James B. Weaver of Iowa as its presidential candidate and, as his running mate, Confederate veteran James G. Field of Virginia. In 1892 the Populist Party tried to convince voters to focus on current economic struggles; in 1896 Bryan, who rarely mentioned the war, adopted the same tactic.

Ultimately, however, Bryan's attempt to overcome sectionalism by restraining public recollection of the war was no match for his opponent's tactics. Possessing vastly greater resources, the McKinley campaign promoted sectional unity in the opposite manner, by mobilizing a remembrance of the Civil War that attacked Bryan's monetary policies by linking free silver with regional conflict. Prominent Union army veterans were especially useful in the Republican effort to link the memory of sectional conflict with free silver. In September former Union major general Daniel Sickles argued in a speech that Bryan and "many of his supporters are trying to combine the South and West against the North and East. This is sectionalism—of which the rebellion was the offspring."[35] A few days later Sickles, who had lost his leg to a combat wound during the battle of Gettysburg, was the featured speaker in a giant veterans' rally for McKinley. Speaking to the aging Billy Yanks, Sickles argued:

> The rebellion grew out of sectionalism and the veterans who are here and their comrades all over the land know too well what it cost us to put that rebellion down. Five hundred thousand lives and uncounted millions of treasure. A million homes left desolate. Widows, sisters, fathers, and mothers bereft. Our country covered with graves of the noble heroes sacrificed to maintain and preserve our unity. We cannot tolerate, will not tolerate, any man representing any party who attempts again to disregard the solemn admonitions of Washington to frown down every attempt to set one portion of the country against another.[36]

Widely reprinted in the nation's newspapers, Sickles's grim warning of sectional conflict's dangers was typical of the emotional rhetoric utilized by an aggressive Republican campaign determined to wield the Civil War's historical memory in its assault on Bryan's economic plank.

In selecting a memory designed to stamp Bryan's free-silver policies as dangerously divisive, his opponents were careful to portray the affable

Nebraskan as a mere figurehead, a dupe controlled by Southern politicians who were, like the fire-eaters of 1861, leading the nation into disaster. According to the Republican campaign narrative, national unity was being threatened by a sinister scheme hatched by radical Southern political leaders, a group that, in 1896, consisted of Tom Watson of Georgia—Bryan's running mate on the Populist ticket—Marion Butler of North Carolina, and, most notoriously, Tillman. The South Carolinian literally became the poster child of sectionalism: clutching his trademark pitchfork, he often appeared alongside Bryan in hostile political cartoons during the summer and fall of 1896. Speaking in Iowa, the ubiquitous Sickles, useful to McKinley because he was a conservative Democrat deeply opposed to bimetallism, noted: "I could not permit Jeff Davis to make a platform for me in 1861. I cannot permit Tillman to do so in 1896."[37]

The former Confederate president, of course, did not make a platform for Sickles, or anybody else for that matter, in 1861. Sickles's statement illustrates the practice, characteristic of the McKinley campaign, of merging memories of the 1860 election campaign with the 1861 secession crisis. Historical accuracy aside (in 1860 Davis was considered a moderate on secession), the important link between these two events in the GOP's campaign narrative was the allegation that in both 1861 and 1896 the people of the South were held hostage by the disastrous policies of a radical political leadership determined to wreck the Union. This attack on the Southern political elite offered a tactical advantage to the Republican campaign by separating the Southern people from the actions of the region's political leadership. Holding a tiny group of Southern political leaders responsible for secession absolved the vast majority of white Southerners from responsibility for the Civil War.

In the Republican efforts to reunite North and South the memory of 1861 offered another great advantage. It allowed the McKinley campaign to talk about the Civil War without talking about race. Focused on the memory of the secession winter—a historical event that occurred long before the war evolved into what Lincoln referred to as a "remorseless and revolutionary struggle"—the GOP was able to bracket off from public memory the racially charged historical issues of slavery, emancipation, and the crucial role African Americans played in the struggle to save the Union.[38]

The omission of race from the party's public remembrance of the war demonstrates the triumph of what Blight has named the "reconciliationist" vision of the Civil War. Like many Republicans of his generation, McKinley began his political career as a vocal advocate of African Americans' rights.

As governor of Ohio, for instance, he left his New Orleans hotel after its management refused to allow a black delegation to meet with him. After the 1891 defeat of the Force Bill, however, McKinley abandoned his commitment to black equality in favor of a nationalist agenda predicated on the reconciliation of whites in the North and the South.[39]

After McKinley's nomination, African American newspapers gratefully recalled his prior support for black rights. Editors of the *Freeman*, a black newspaper based in Indianapolis, argued that McKinley had always "leaned toward this portion of humanity," and they vigorously supported his candidacy. What editors of black newspapers such as the *Freeman* did not realize, or what they were unwilling to admit, was that by 1896 McKinley had quietly distanced himself from the social and political struggles of African Americans living in the former Confederate states. Writing in 1916, McKinley's biographer Charles S. Olcott approvingly summed up McKinley's attitude toward the white South: "The demand for 'rights' gave way to brotherliness, and the desire to coerce melted before a flame of deep patriotism."[40] McKinley's desire for a patriotic reconciliation among white Americans at the expense of Southern blacks was reflected in the 1896 Republican platform, a document that was silent about federal protection for African American voting rights. In October the *New York Times* noted with satisfaction, "It is safe to say that the era of Force Bills and Federal interference [in Southern elections] has passed." The "fear of Force Bills," the *Times* editors argued, had kept the "South solid . . . and Major McKinley has given one indication of his sagacity [by] depreciating sectional division and appealing to a common patriotism to protect the Nation's honor."[41] Working for a candidate who was, in Blight's words, an "inveterate conciliator, especially toward the South," McKinley's campaign strategists attacked Bryan's pro-silver policies through a memory of the Civil War that highlighted the common danger of sectional division while erasing a remembrance of that conflict as revolutionizing, for a short time at least, U.S. race relations.[42]

Given the social unrest of the 1890s, in fact, the Republican Party had no desire to stir up any memory that smacked of revolutionary change. In the previous decade the nation had witnessed three epic battles in the war of labor against capital—the Haymarket affair and the Homestead and Pullman strikes—as well as numerous local skirmishes. The business depression that started in 1893 showed no signs of easing in 1896, and that year nearly 15 percent of urban workers remained unemployed. The Democratic convention is most often remembered for Bryan's sensational "Cross of Gold" speech, but in attempting to create a farmer-worker coalition the party's platform did not focus exclusively on the question of free silver. At the instigation of the party's urban-based reformers, including Illinois governor John Peter Altgeld, the Democratic Party decried the practice of suppressing strikes with federal court injunctions.[43] Bryan's opponents found his appeals to urban workers as alarming as his appeals to farmers. When, in his speech accepting the Democratic presidential nomination, Bryan defined the contest as a conflict between the "idle holders of capital" and the "struggling masses" and declared that the "sympathies of the Democratic Party . . . are on the side of the struggling masses," he thrilled the convention but terrified many Americans.[44] Soon after Bryan's nomination Mark Hanna wrote to McKinley, "I consider the situation in the West quite alarming, as business is going all to pieces and idle men will multiply rapidly."[45] Determined to halt the Bryan bandwagon in its tracks, the McKinley campaign opened the second front in the war of memory against the Democratic campaign, one that paired the dangers of sectional division with an ominous new threat to national unity, the conflict between labor and capital.

Again and again during the summer and fall of 1896 anti-Bryan periodicals argued that a victory by Bryan would, in the words of *Harper's Weekly*, "mean national dishonor, the triumph of ignorance [and] a sectional and class war upon vested rights." The *New York Mail and Express* called Bryan's campaign a "hysterical declaration of a reckless and lawless crusade of sectional animosity and class antagonism."[46] In attacking the Democrats' platform as a document bent on setting the haves against the have-nots, Bryan's opponents often refrained from personally attacking the candidate himself. Instead, they focused upon another Democrat reformer, Illinois governor John Peter Altgeld. Much as the Republican press made Tillman the national symbol for "sectionalism," it painted Altgeld as the symbol of "anarchy." Praising Archbishop John Ireland, for example, one of McKinley's strongest supporters, the *New York Times* editors commented, "Like a patriotic American he rebukes the attempt of BRYAN and ALTGELD to array class against class, and the attempt of TILLMAN to array section against section."[47] The image of Altgeld standing beside Tillman and Bryan often appeared in cartoons lampooning the Democratic campaign. The names of Bryan, Tillman, and Altgeld were regularly denounced in the same sentence with dangers to national unity. In early October, *Harper's Weekly* concluded, "well seconded by Senator Tillman and Governor Altgeld—Mr. Bryan's natural allies are the enemies of the state, the conspirators against the existing order. He would set the land on fire with class hatred

{ PATRICK J. KELLY }

and sectional strife."[48] In the campaign of memory against the 1896 Democratic campaign, then, sectional and class division were closely linked, with Tillman serving as a surrogate for sectional strife and Altgeld as a surrogate for anarchy and class warfare.

Having paired sectional and class conflict as twin dangers to national unity, it was but a short step for Bryan's opponents to turn to the memory of secession as a means of attacking the Democratic campaign. In this effort Altgeld, like Tillman, was a natural target. He was the most prominent left-leaning politician of his day—closely allied with Hull House. Altgeld had appointed Florence Kelley as Illinois's chief factory inspector and Julia Lathrop to the State Board of Charities. In the words of Morton Keller, Altgeld "rode to power on the first wave of urban Democratic liberalism."[49] Soon after his election as governor he gained infamy among the property-owning classes by pardoning four anarchists convicted for their role in the Haymarket affair. In 1894 Altgeld, who wanted more time for Illinois authorities to resolve the Pullman strike, vigorously protested Cleveland's decision to order federal troops into Chicago and sent a widely publicized telegram to the president arguing that "local self-government is a fundamental principle of our Constitution."[50]

The governor's public rebuke of President Cleveland combined with his defense of local self-determination immediately stirred memories of the South's defiance of the federal government during the secession crisis among the nation's newspaper editors. The *Philadelphia Telegraph* denounced Altgeld's telegram as "an affront more abominable than the degradations submitted to by James Buchanan at the hands of Southern secession." The *Indianapolis American Tribune* editors argued, "This is the same States Rights rot that was the cause of the rebellion."[51] The spontaneous outpouring of Civil War memory in reaction to Altgeld's dispute with Cleveland illustrates how easily the public's feelings about secession could be brought to a boil. Two years later, following the takeover of the Democratic Party by reformers such as Bryan, Altgeld, and Tillman, McKinley's supporters mobilized the memory of 1861 in a more organized manner by accusing Democratic politicians of fomenting civil war along class as well as regional lines.

Altgeld was instrumental in securing Chicago as the site for the 1896 Democratic convention. Unlike Tillman, however, he made no inflammatory speeches. Instead, he played a key behind-the-scenes role in assuring that the Democratic platform called for the abolition of court injunctions against labor unions and, in a thinly veiled censure of Cleveland's actions during 1894, denounced the "arbitrary interference by Federal authorities in local affairs as a violation of the Constitution."[52] Describing the trajectory of the 1896 campaign in early November, the *New York Times* pointed to the adoption of the Democratic platform as a crystallizing moment of the presidential election. The editors argued, "When to the declaration for unlimited coinage of silver [was] linked . . . the . . . practical endorsement of the Altgeld doctrine of State rights and riot, and appeals to class and sectional passion," the line of battle was drawn. Echoing attacks during the Pullman crisis, newspapers and magazines opposed to Bryan wasted little time reminding voters that during the secession winter Southern Democrats had offered similar arguments against federal power's reach. In September editors for *Harper's Weekly*, fierce opponents of the Democratic Party, argued, "In 1861 some of the States undertook to enforce the doctrine that the Federal government had not the power to prevent them from leaving the Union. Their attempt was defeated after a terrible war." The Democratic platform, the editors continued, "seeks to revolutionize the government by destroying the results established by the war of secession; for if [it] is right, Mr. Lincoln was wrong when he sent his troops into the South to restore the supremacy of the laws of the Union and to protect the property of the United States."[53] Perhaps the most damning statement against the Democratic platform came in October, however, when John Ireland, archbishop of St. Paul, publicly denounced Bryan's candidacy.

As part of its campaign of national unity, one scholar argues, the McKinley campaign "openly courted" Catholic voters, and one of the "major developments of the campaign was the announcement by Archbishop Ireland of the St. Paul diocese that he supported McKinley."[54] Ireland's letter ritually attacked the Democracy's support of bimetallism. Significantly, however, Ireland declared the "monetary question . . . a secondary issue in the campaign." For Ireland, free silver "has its importance, but it is of minor importance in the presence of other questions which are brought into issue." Turning to the real meat of his argument, Ireland insisted that the Democratic platform's denunciation of federal interference in local affairs was "the old secession doctrine that states are independent of the national government at Washington." "The movement," Ireland continued, "which had its expression in the Chicago convention . . . is in its logical effect, revolution against the United States; it is secession, the secession of 1861, which our soldiers believed they had consigned to eternal death at Appomattox." Reaching across the Atlantic to revive the public's memory of the social convulsion of the Paris Commune of 1871, Ireland warned his readers, "The war of class against class is upon us. . . . Many adherents of the movement do not perceive its full meaning: but let them beware. They are lighting torches, which, borne in the hands of reckless men, may light up the country in the lurid fires of a commune."[55] Widely reprinted in newspapers throughout the United States, Ireland's apocalyptic prophecy that Bryan's election would trigger a new civil war pitting class against class created a public sensation. A Methodist minister in California wrote the archbishop that a reading of Ireland's letter during his Sunday sermon "brought the whole congregation to its feet."[56] Bryan's supporters, in contrast, were furious at Ireland's overheated attacks on the Democratic candidate. William Randolph Hearst, publisher of the *New York Journal* and one of Bryan's most powerful backers, sent an angry cable to the Vatican's secretary of state demanding to know if Ireland was speaking officially for the Roman Catholic Church.[57]

The story behind the well-coordinated production and publication of Ireland's statement offers a striking opportunity to explore how, in the words of John Bodnar, political elites "selectively retrieve" historical memories to "advance [their] concerns by promoting interpretations of the past and present reality that reduce the power of competing interests that appear to threaten the attainment of their goals."[58] Ireland was a close associate of James J. Hill. The wealthy and powerful Hill, whose Great Northern Railroad was headquartered in St. Paul, was an energetic supporter of McKinley. Concerned about McKinley's election chances in the Midwest, the railroad magnate had written J. P. Morgan in July to urge "those who are to manage the McKinley campaign that they should get to work *at once* and open the fight in St. Louis, Chicago, and all the leading Western cities and drive back the wave that is rising over the doubtful states." Hill performed a number of invaluable favors for the McKinley campaign in the region. Among these was his request to Ireland that the archbishop issue a statement denouncing Bryan. On September 30 Hill alerted Mark Hanna, "We are giving Archbishop Ireland, through a non-partisan letter signed by twenty representative men, an opportunity to state his views fully, which he is prepared to do, and I am sure he will cover the ground, stripping the [Democratic] platform to the bone."[59] Nearly two weeks later, on October 11, Ireland's statement was released.

Why did the archbishop agree to publicly attack the Bryan campaign? In his careful study of this affair Marvin R. O'Connell notes that although Ireland's letter represented his personal views, the public statement was "extracted" from him by Hill as "partial payment for favors rendered [to

Ireland] and favors he hoped for." Although Ireland never admitted to the origins of his public denunciation of Bryan, he certainly never regretted his role in the campaign. After looking into his actions Vatican officials signaled Ireland their pleasure at this manifestation of his political clout, and soon after the election the archbishop was invited to McKinley's home in Canton, where he fought for the inclusion of a Roman Catholic in the president-elect's cabinet.[60]

The national dissemination of Ireland's dire warning that the Democratic platform was the "secession of 1861" was as well coordinated as the letter's production. Circulated by wire reports, the archbishop's letter was reprinted on the front pages of many newspapers the day after its release. Just as significantly, the Republican National Committee, thanks to Hill's communication to Hanna, had nearly two weeks to prepare its strategy for taking advantage of Ireland's statement and immediately set to work printing the letter in pamphlet form, ultimately distributing more than 250,000 copies to voters.[61] As the archbishop's words circulated through the national media, the cover story concocted by Hill—that Ireland had offered his remarks only at the request of a nonpartisan group of prominent Minnesotans—was accepted without question. Editors for the *New York Times* commented that the "respect in which the Archbishop is held in his own diocese is attested by the fact that the public expression of his opinion on the political issue was not volunteered by him, but was elicited by written request for it, signed by twenty-seven of the leading citizens of Minnesota and representing both political parties."[62] One historian has observed that the "crafters of memory are eager to erase the origins of the memories they promote," and this was certainly true of Hill's role in the production and circulation of Ireland's famous attack against Bryan.[63]

By September, the month Hill asked Ireland to issue his statement, the focus of the McKinley campaign had turned to the midwestern states of Illinois, Ohio, Indiana, Michigan, Wisconsin, and the archbishop's own Minnesota. Republican Party strategists considered these states the key to victory and feared that the loss of any state in the region would prove disastrous for the campaign. Indiana and Illinois, for example, had both gone for Cleveland in 1892. As the *Review of Reviews* noted about the election, "The East is conceded to McKinley, the South and extreme West to Bryan. The Central Western states are the battleground of the campaign."[64] Hanna himself chose Chicago as the site of the Republican national campaign headquarters. Leaving New York for Chicago in early October, Hanna announced that the "battleground is in the Middle West-

{ PATRICK J. KELLY }

ern States" and in this region the "hardest campaigning is to be done."[65] Given the GOP's obsession with winning the Midwest, the solicitation of an anti-Bryan statement from the Roman Catholic archbishop of St. Paul was a smart political tactic. Ireland's use of historical memory of the "secession of 1861" reflected the McKinley campaign's determination to win the Midwest by linking the Democratic candidate with Civil War Rebels.

The decision to attack Bryan by supersaturating the battleground states of the Midwest with wartime remembrance came, in part, because of the area's large bloc of voters critical to the election: nearly four hundred thousand Union veterans.[66] Prodded by veterans' newspapers, the North's former soldiers, especially midwestern veterans, saw frightening parallels between the labor upheavals of the 1890s and the Civil War. Chicago was a hotbed of labor unrest, and the violent Pullman strike angered many soldiers. At the height of the Pullman crisis members of a Grand Army of the Republic local post wrote Chicago's mayor to volunteer the services of its two hundred men. "We were among those who responded to the call of our country in 1861 to defend our flag," the members of Abraham Lincoln Post Ninety-one wrote. "We, therefore, now offer ourselves as ready to respond to a call from you to defend the fair name of our city."[67] The *Chicago Tribune* wrote during the same period that the "soldiers of 1861 are as ready to fight the Anarchist rebels north of the Ohio as they were secession rebels south of it."[68] Veterans' newspapers, usually no friend of Cleveland, were virtually unanimous in praising the president's decision to put down the strike through force.

For many midwestern veterans the growing influence of Altgeld, who angered veterans by pardoning the Haymarket anarchists and by challenging the legality of Cleveland's actions during the Pullman strike, offered a threat to law and order potentially as dangerous as the crisis they had faced a generation earlier. Phillip S. Paludan has argued that many Northerners resisted secession in 1861 because they viewed it as a crisis of law and order. "Again and again," Paludan wrote, "newspaper editors and political leaders discussed the degree to which secession was likely to produce disorder, anarchy, and general disrespect for democratic government."[69] Speaking at a rally of Union veterans in Chicago, one prominent veterans' spokesperson declared, "We are told in the Chicago platform, in vague language, but easily read between the lines, 'You may have more Chicago riots.' You may have them here, or in New York, or in Boston [and if] your Governor chooses to turn a deaf ear to the appeals of the people for protection of their rights of personal property, you are told, under those circumstances, 'Let havoc have its way.' "[70] Stuart McConnell, writing about the political philosophy of the Grand Army of the Republic (GAR), suggested that "when push came to shove the GAR was always to be found in the camp of order and property rights." GAR nationalism, he argued, "combined allegiance to a liberal capitalism of a distinctly antebellum variety . . . and loyalty first to the nation state rather than to race, class, gender, region, religion, or any other particularism. Operating within an established state, it functioned not only as an endorsement of that state but also as a negative statement about potential alternative nationalisms that sought to alter it."[71] The political views of powerful veterans' organizations such as the GAR, then, meshed perfectly with the memory of the Civil War promoted by the Republican Party. Because of its high concentration of Union veterans, the Midwest offered the party the chance for its reconfiguration of Civil War memory to reach its greatest intensity in promoting a patriotic unity between the nation's economic classes.

Writing soon after Bryan's nomination, editors for the *Chicago Tribune* predicted that veterans would "recognize the danger which confronts the country from an anarchical, repudiating, and revolutionary mob, and they will do their duty in 1896 as they did it from 1861 to 1865. They will help again save the country." Prominent Union veterans joined in this attack. Former Union general Franz Sigel argued that Bryan's election would result in the "subversion of the social order, a war of the masses against classes for the possession of wealth." Aiming at the North's veterans, the *Harper's Weekly* editors concluded: "We do not believe that the honest farmers and working men of this country, from whose ranks came the great mass of Union soldiers, are ready to join this motley throng in its assaults upon the institutions which they once defended."[72] McKinley's supporters thus linked the breakdown of law and order in 1861 with the nation's labor unrest in the more recent past to gain the veteran vote.

The Republican Party, however, had another tactic in its campaign of memory aimed at the North's veterans—one that combined historical recollections of 1861 with economic self-interest. The "public liaison" between the GOP and the GAR was, in the words of one scholar, "about as secret as the relations between Lord Nelson and Lady Hamilton and just as understandable."[73] The Republican alignment with the GAR, one of the most successful special-interest groups in U.S. history, was based as much on hard economic calculations as on emotional appeals to wartime memories. What drew Union veterans again and again to the GOP was the combination of a calculated deployment of Civil War remembrance and the ability to

{ PATRICK J. KELLY }

deliver a remarkably generous array of benefits. The economic battle for the veteran vote focused around federal entitlements: government jobs for former soldiers, a system of institutional care for war-disabled and indigent vets, and, above all, the expansion of the number of veterans eligible for pensions. In each of these areas the GOP delivered. In 1882, for instance, nearly half the Republican patronage appointments in Washington went to Union veterans. For institutional care and pensions the party's achievements were even more impressive. By the mid-1890s, for instance, nearly one hundred thousand former soldiers had sought shelter in a branch of the National Home for Disabled Volunteer Soldiers, the federal institution created for the care of elderly veterans, and 65 percent of the surviving cohort of Union veterans received a pension check from Uncle Sam.[74] In the mid-1890s, then, the GOP was largely responsible for creating a comprehensive Union veterans' welfare state.

By 1896, however, the ties between organized veterans' groups and the Republican Party were seemingly attenuating. The Dependent Pension Act of 1890, a great victory for the GAR, offered a pension to "every discharged soldier of ninety days' service who suffered from any disability that incapacitated him for manual labor, no matter what his financial situation and no matter how the disability had been incurred." This legislation virtually granted the North's aging veterans what was closest to their heart's desire: a service pension system. Between 1890 and 1896 the number of former Union soldiers receiving a quarterly pension check from the government jumped from 537,944 to 970,678.[75] With their central economic demand met, appeals to veterans' wartime memories lost their potency, and a significant portion of the North's former soldiers drifted from the Republican camp. During the presidential election of 1892 the GAR leadership sensed a loss of public support and adopted a nonpartisan stance. In the key midwestern states of Illinois, Indiana, and Wisconsin, all of which went for Democratic candidate Grover Cleveland, a significant number of veterans voted Democrat. In addition, by the mid-1890s the membership of the GAR had declined, not because older veterans were dying but because many members had quit the organization. In 1895 the rolls of the GAR dropped by 56,956, and of that total only 7,368 had died.[76]

Despite the apparent weakening of the alliance between veterans' organizations and the Republican Party, the machinery necessary to connect the two remained in place and was easily reactivated once a Bryan presidency began to seem real. Soon after Bryan's nomination two experienced veterans' organizers, L. Edwin Dudley and Daniel Sickles, joined together to form the Veterans' National Committee. Sickles was soon busy making speeches throughout the country on behalf of McKinley, and his remarks were reprinted in circular form and distributed throughout the nation by Dudley. Branches of their Union Veterans' Patriotic League appeared all over the country. In late August Dudley wrote, "The veterans and sons of veterans are responding in the most enthusiastic manner. . . . We are appealing to the old sentiments of loyalty and patriotism and especially to the love and affection which the old veterans have for their comrade, Major McKinley."[77]

In appealing to this key voting bloc of veterans, McKinley once again combined the tried-and-true tactic of evoking wartime memories and padding the pocketbooks of the North's former soldiers. Meeting with a delegation of veterans who came to his Canton home, McKinley noted that the total number of Union soldiers receiving federal pensions was higher than the total number of American soldiers who had served in the nation's army between 1776 and 1860, and he remarked that Union veterans were the "largest creditors of the government." But, he warned, the inflationary monetary policies of Bryan threatened to depreciate the value of soldiers' pensions.[78] The charge that Bryan's commitment to the free coinage of silver would result in a repudiation of the nation's debt to its creditors, including veterans, was a common theme among Republican spokespersons. The *Chicago Tribune*, for instance, noted that the "veterans recognize the danger arising from the conspiracy of the Populists, Popocrats, and free silver Republican bolters against the credit of the Nation."[79]

For rational economic reasons of their own, Union veterans proved a very attentive audience to the Republican message. For many old soldiers the pro-silver policies of the Democratic platform were deeply problematic. By 1896 940,000 veterans and their dependents were receiving just under $140 million in pension payments annually. The Democratic platform promised to "recognize the just claim of old soldiers," but the *Chicago Tribune* argued that veterans should consider that promise "a contemptible falsehood."[80] Republican editors and politicians argued time and again that the free coinage of silver at the ratio of sixteen to one with gold would halve the purchasing power of veterans' pensions. "Great numbers of the old soldiers are wholly or partially dependent on the pension they receive for their past services," the *Chicago Tribune* reminded its readers in mid-July. If Bryan's monetary policies were enacted, the newspaper's editors warned, "the purchasing power of all the pensions will be cut down one-half. The pensioners will get 140 million 50-cent dollars instead of 140 million 100-cent dollars." The editors cautioned Union veterans about the dangers they faced if Southern political leaders such as Ben Tillman gained control of the federal purse: "The Southern fire-eaters . . . have no love for the old Union soldiers. Those fire-eaters would take away their pensions altogether were it possible. As that cannot be done, it is proposed to cheat them out of half of the money which a million old soldiers, or their wives and children, are receiving from the government. . . . They will feel that they have punished the old Union soldiers who licked them."[81] Like any aging cohort living on a fixed income, veterans viewed inflationary policies with a jaundiced eye. In 1896, then, the McKinley campaign worked to combine economic unease about Bryan's free-silver policies with the historical memory of 1861 as a means of gaining support among the large voting bloc of former soldiers living in the battleground states of the Midwest.

During the campaign Bryan, who had been far too young to serve in the Union military during the 1860s, proved unwilling or unable to mount an effective appeal to veterans, either emotional or economic. Unlike their opposition, Democratic Party members refused to cultivate Union veterans as an interest group. A rare occasion when Bryan attempted to utilize historical memory to gain the support of Northern veterans came during a campaign stop in Milwaukee in early September. Beginning in an obviously reluctant tone—"You say you want to hear a little about the old soldiers"— Bryan argued that the "question before the country now appeals to the old soldiers as much as it did in 1861. . . . I am not afraid that the men who were willing at that time to endure the dangers of war because they believed the black men should be free, I am not afraid that these men are going to allow the hosts of the gold standard to enslave 70 millions of people, whites and blacks, in this country."[82] An interesting irony of the 1896 campaign, then, is that it was the Democratic candidate who employed the memory of emancipation, however briefly and clumsily, to gain the veteran vote. Given the Democratic Party's continued strength among white Southern voters and Bryan's political alliance with avowed racists such as Tillman, however, Bryan's version of an emancipationist vision of the Civil War proved an evanescent moment. After this half-hearted attempt at winning the veteran vote by linking free silver with the freedom of the nation's slaves, Bryan seldom attempted to assuage Union soldiers' concerns about the impact of his monetary policies on their pension checks. In 1896, for one last time, the generation-long effort of the Republican Party to create a client group out of Union veterans by linking historical memory of the Civil War with a generous package of federal benefits paid enormous political dividends in a presidential campaign.

In early September the McKinley-Hanna organization began a focused and determined campaign to win the veteran vote in the Midwest. At the heart of this effort was the Republican Party's argument that a Bryan presidency endangered the economic self-interest of the North's old soldiers in addition to threatening to divide the nation along class lines. The active support that the GAR offered the GOP in this effort proved crucial. The involvement of many of the Union army's most famous surviving generals played an instrumental role in the party's effort to construct and disseminate a Civil War memory designed to stigmatize the Bryan campaign as a modern threat to the nation's unity. In early September 1896 the GAR held its national encampment in St. Paul, Minnesota, a happy coincidence for McKinley because the city was the corporate headquarters of James J. Hill's Great Northern Railroad. Hill fought the Bryan campaign with all his possible means, which were considerable.[83]

In addition to instigating Ireland's attack on Bryan, Hill helped finance a tour of Union generals who barnstormed on McKinley's behalf in states throughout the Midwest. During the national encampment Russell Alger—a former commander-in-chief of the GAR, a former governor of Michigan, and McKinley's future secretary of war—lined up a group of Union veteran all-stars to promote the Republican candidate. Hill immediately agreed to help. At the conclusion of the encampment an official of the Great Northern Railroad wrote Alger, "Mr. Hill told me to tell you that he will gladly haul you anywhere on his system at any time on the cause you are representing." Hill also discussed the veterans' tour with other railroads, and the official further informed Alger that the head of the Chicago Great Western Railroad had "evinced equal interest" in the proposed tour of Union veterans, "and gladly extends to you the courtesies of his line."[84]

"Patriotism akin to the spirit of '61 will flame in the city this evening" the *Chicago Tribune* announced to its readers on September 21. That evening the participants in what soon became known to the nation as the Patriotic Heroes' Battalion—the most prominent among them former Union generals Daniel Sickles, O. O. Howard, and Russell Alger—gathered together at a giant rally at the Chicago Auditorium in preparation of their Midwest tour. "Every seat was taken," the *Tribune* reported on its front page the following day, "and hundreds stood in the side aisles and galleries." The famous old veterans onstage made quite a sight, with the *Tribune* noting that "Howard has just as many arms as Gen. Sickles has legs." In his speech Sickles, a colorful figure who was always a crowd favorite, set the tone of their expedition when he declared, "Up until the day of the Chicago [Democratic Party] platform no party in this country ever dared to present for the approval of the American peoples the doctrines of anarchy, repudiation, and mob rule."[85] After this rousing send-off, the old veterans began their tour. The campaign of the Patriotic Heroes' Battalion was aimed at more than just Union veterans. "The time was due," Richard Jensen in his classic study of the 1896 election wrote of their effort, "for a demonstration that the silent masses of the people did not support Bryan but stood behind sound money, law and order, and McKinley."[86] Aimed as much at defining the country's future as at memorializing its past, this memory of the Civil War articulated the party's notion of a patriotic nationalism that legitimated the rights of property over the rights of labor.

During the last weeks of the 1896 campaign the Patriotic Heroes' Battalion, a group of veterans who quite literally embodied the historical memory of the Civil War, moved rapidly and in tight formation around the countryside demanding that midwestern voters reject the Democratic Party and its presidential candidate. Although the McKinley campaign kept its role in the tour quiet—some newspapers speculated that Alger paid for it out of his own pocket—its complicated logistics were handled by William Beer, a young Republican Party official. William Hahn, head of the Republican National Committee's Speakers Bureau, ordered Beer to "transact all matters of business" pertaining to the veterans' "combination . . . in conjunction with the Committees of the states through which the party passes." Before the tour ended in early November the old veterans had covered an astounding 8,448 miles, speaking at 276 meetings in 255 separate locations. O. O. Howard later wrote that the campaigning began at seven in the morning and often did not end until eleven at night.[87]

The cars of the Patriotic Heroes' Battalion train were decorated with American flags, two thousand yards of red, white, and blue bunting, and giant pictures of McKinley. The flat car at the end of the train was used for speeches. Giant banners on each side of the train offered the countryside the following messages:

1896 is as vitally important to our country as 1861.

We are Opposed to Anarchy and Repudiation.

The State of Lincoln will Never Surrender to a Champion of Anarchy.

The tour was front-page news in the Midwest and closely followed by newspapers throughout the nation, even in Southern states. On October 10, for instance, the *Galveston Daily News* reported that the "famous soldiers' combination" had spoken to a crowd of ten thousand in Rushville, Indiana. In South Bend, Indiana, Alger denounced Bryan's political allies as "a dirty set. . . . They represent the red flag." In Indianapolis Alger claimed that Bryan's "assault upon the integrity of nation and upon the old flag has stirred up again the patriotic fire that called you to the front in 1861." Writing about his experience on the tour in a Boston newspaper, one of its participants, O. A. Marden, wrote, "We believe that we have done something in stirring up the old veterans in a lively sense that a crisis is pending hardly second to that of 1861 to 1865."[88]

The tour of generals was a rousing success. Writing from McKinley national campaign headquarters in Chicago, Hahn informed Beer, "I feel assured that the result of the labors of these old war worn soldiers will be of the greatest benefit to our party." He continued, "I wish you would extend to them my congratulations, and on my behalf and in behalf of the National Committee thank them for their labors they have already performed."[89] By the end of the tour the veterans had spoken to an estimated 1 million voters and caused what one Republican weekly called "considerable consternation" among Bryan supporters.[90] "Coin" Harvey, one of the most vocal proponents of free silver, called the veterans' campaign the "old wrecks of the rebellion who have lost all their honor and patriotism . . . [and are] the tool of political Shylocks."[91] Harvey's comments, predictably, backfired and served to increase the popularity of the old generals, but his frustration, as well as the frustration of Bryan supporters, was understandable. A full generation after the Confederate defeat, the Republican Party was able, yet again, to utilize the link between Union veterans, public memory of the Civil War, and a Republican candidate to elect a president.

In the last weeks of the campaign GOP officials grew confident that McKinley would prevail in the election, yet continued to use Union veterans to rouse the public's remembrance of secession. The continued appeal by Republicans to Civil War memory is, one scholar suggests, best explained by the party's larger and more enduring objective in 1896, "to merge the Republican Party's past defense of the nation with contemporary notions of patriotism itself." "Such an approach," Lawrence Goodwyn continued, promised to fashion a "blend of the American flag and Grand Old Party that might conceivably cement a political bond of enduring civic vitality." As Cecilia Elizabeth O'Leary noted, by the mid-1890s the GAR was at the center of a drive to create a "nationalist consciousness" in the United States.[92] Among the rights and rituals of the GAR's "martial patriotism" was the organization's attempts to fly the American flag over every schoolhouse, have every schoolchild recite the Pledge of Allegiance, and create a national flag day.[93] Hanna, who had chosen the American flag as the symbol for the McKinley campaign, borrowed from the GAR and decided to have the McKinley campaign sponsor a flag day of its own on the Sunday before the election.

On October 30, 1896, the day before New York's great flag day parade, forty Union generals gathered at Carnegie Hall in Manhattan for a rally of the Union Veterans' Patriotic League. Many generals—Sickles and Howard most prominent among them—had campaigned as part of the Patriotic Heroes' Battalion. They gathered in Carnegie Hall to offer McKinley a final show of support. Presiding over the meeting, as he would over the following day's parade, was former Union general Horace Porter. Offering the now familiar attack against Bryan, that the Democratic candidate "stood for revolution and anarchy," Porter noted: "We are assembled here to greet the veterans of the war—the men who went to the front in 1861 to save the Nation's life, and who are going to the polls in November to save the Nation's honor."[94] The next day three-quarters of a million New Yorkers marched on their streets. The *New York Tribune* reported that "many of those who marched yesterday have known what it is to march in war under the same flag that covered the city in its folds yesterday all day long." That same day in Des Moines, Iowa, ten thousand citizens marched in celebration of the American flag, with five hundred Union veterans afforded the honor of leading the procession. A local newspaper reported, "The veterans were greeted with shouts and tears along the line; their progress was a moving triumph from first to last."[95] In the election of 1896, then, the symbolic use of Civil War veterans was combined with the Republican Party's restructuring of Civil War memory to produce a bellicose patriotism based on the cult of the flag. For one historian the central question of American nationalism in the late nineteenth century was to "what extent would militarism and claims of safeguarding the nation-state take priority over democratic demands for social equality."[96] By election day 1896, the answer to that question was clear.

In a final appeal to veterans on the day before the election, the *Chicago Tribune*'s editors urged: "STAND TO YOUR GUNS, OLD SOLDIERS." "Time was," the editors reminded soldiers, "when some of you, moved by generous impulses, voted with the Democratic Party. That occasion no longer exists. . . . The call to the peaceful battle of the ballots is to meet an insidious foe . . . whose success augurs as much disaster to your country as the ravages of bloody battles could entail." The Republican Party, the *Tribune* editors argued, was the "natural home and rally point of the Union soldier. Never, since the rough edge of battle joined in 1861 were loyalty and honor more justly appealed to than now." And, this editorial concluded: "Your own interest, the interest of your immediate families and friends . . . all demand at this crisis the decided triumph of the Republican party at the polls. You were true to the Republic in the past, comrades, you will be true to her now."[97]

McKinley, of course, won the presidency in 1896, and the key battleground states of the Midwest fell into the Republican camp, including states such as Illinois and Indiana that Cleveland had claimed in 1892. Bryan won only four out of the forty-two electoral votes at stake in this region, and in Minnesota, home of Archbishop Ireland, McKinley won by 60,000 votes out of 340,000 cast.[98] There are no exact records illustrating which candidate the Midwest's veterans supported, but veterans' newspapers boasted of the North's former soldiers' contribution to the election result. The *National Tribune* of Washington, D.C., declared, "Never since the war were the veterans so thoroughly united . . . on one side of a political question."[99] McKinley won the watershed election of 1896 for a number of significant reasons: the Republican Party's superior financial and organizational resources, a weak and divided Democratic Party, a slight recovery in the prices of agricultural goods just prior to the election, and the reluctance of urban workers to gamble on Bryan's free-silver monetary policies. Among the many factors contributing to McKinley's success, however, was the campaign of memory waged by Republicans against Democrats. By firmly linking the Republican Party to the values of "stability, nationalism, business prosperity and law and order," the McKinley campaign's deployment of the memory of secession helped create the formula that, in the words of one scholar, would allow the GOP to "dominate national politics for more than thirty years."[100]

In the early 1890s the Democratic Party seemed on the verge of gaining control of U.S. national politics. The depression of 1893 halted this brief Democratic ascendancy, and the election defeat of 1896 hammered the final nail in its coffin. The election of McKinley, in addition, essentially ended the Populist insurgency, a movement that one scholar has called "nothing less than the last significant American challenge to industrial capitalism as a system of social, economic and political power."[101] After 1896 the Republican Party regained its position as the "dominant voice of industrial, middle class America" and maintained effective control of national politics for a generation.[102] A central component of the victorious 1896 Republican presidential campaign strategy was the selective retrieval and mass distribution of, in Archbishop Ireland's words, public memory of the "secession of 1861." In 1896 a new generation of Republican political leadership offered the nation a restructured remembrance of the Civil War. In addition to continuing the process of disengaging the party as the guarantor of the political and civil rights of African Americans, this restructured memory solidified the party's commitment to the country's industrial-capitalist order, stigmatized political critiques of class and class inequality as unpatriotic, and intensified a bellicose conception of a nation-state united along sectional and class lines just at the moment when the United States stood ready to enter as an aggressive player on the world stage.

NOTES

1. See Xi Wang, *The Trial of Democracy: Black Suffrage and Northern Republicans, 1860–1910* (Athens: University of Georgia Press, 1997); and Stanley P. Hirshson, *Farewell to the Bloody Shirt: Northern Republicans and the Southern Negro, 1877–1893* (Bloomington: Indiana University Press, 1962).

2. McKinley quoted in *New York Times*, October 12, 1896.

3. *New York Times*, October 24, 1896.

4. Lodge quoted in Stanley L. Jones, *The Presidential Election of 1896* (Madison: University of Wisconsin Press, 1964), 293.

5. William E. Chandler, "Issues and Prospects of the Campaign," *North American Review* 163, no. 2 (August 1896): 182.

6. William Jennings Bryan, *The First Battle: The Story of the Campaign of 1896* (Chicago: W. B. Conkey, 1896), 205.

7. Ireland quoted in *Des Moines Leader*, October 13, 1896; Porter quoted in *Chicago Tribune*, October 31, 1896.

8. David W. Blight, "They Knew What Time It Was: African Americans and the Coming of the Civil War," in his *Beyond the Battlefield: Race, Memory, and the American Civil War* (Amherst: University of Massachusetts Press, 2002), 28–52 (first quote on 30; Smith quoted on 48); David W. Blight, *Race and Reunion: The Civil War in American Memory* (Cambridge, Mass.: Belknap Press of Harvard University Press, 2001), 2.

9. Douglass quoted in Blight, *Race and Reunion*, 132.

10. Ibid, 2.

11. Bryan, *The First Battle*, 205.

12. Blight, *Race and Reunion*, 2.

13. Paul Kleppner, *Cross of Culture: A Social Analysis of Midwestern Politics, 1850–1900* (New York: Free Press, 1970), 179–92.

14. Ibid. For a discussion of the monetary question, see Gretchen Ritter, *Goldbugs and Greenbacks: The Antimonopoly Tradition and the Politics of Finance in America* (Cambridge: Cambridge University Press, 1997). For works on the Populist movement, see Elizabeth Sanders, *Roots of Reform: Farmers, Workers, and the American State, 1877–1917* (Chicago: University of Chicago Press, 1999); Catherine McNicol Stock and Robert D. Johnson, eds., *The Countryside in the Age of the Modern State: Political Histories of Rural America* (Ithaca: Cornell University Press, 2001); Lawrence Goodwyn, *The Populist Moment: A Short History of Agrarian Revolt in America* (Oxford: Oxford University Press, 1978); and Robert McMath, *American Populism: A Social History* (New York: Hill and Wang, 1993).

15. Stephen Kantrowitz, *Ben Tillman and the Reconstruction of White Supremacy* (Chapel Hill: University of North Carolina Press, 2000), 245 (first and second quotes), 251 (third quote).

16. Tillman quoted in *Nation*, July 16, 1896.

17. Kantrowitz, *Ben Tillman*, 251.

18. *Chicago Tribune*, July 9, 1896.

19. *Chicago Chronicle* quoted in ibid.

20. Telegraph quoted in J. Rogers Hollingsworth, *The Whirligig of Politics: The Democracy of Cleveland and Bryan* (Chicago: University of Chicago Press, 1963), 87.

21. Hanna quoted in Malcolm Charles Moos, *The Republicans: A History of Their Party* (New York: Random House, 1956), 215; Josiah Quincy, "Issues and Prospects of the Campaign," *North American Review* 163, no. 2 (August 1896): 194.

22. In his excellent discussion of the election of 1896, Richard Jensen defines the McKinley campaign as a "classic counter-crusade." See *The Winning of the Midwest: Social and Political Conflict, 1888–1896* (Chicago: University of Chicago Press, 1971), 284 (quote), 288–89.

23. Elizabeth Sanders estimates that the GOP raised from $4 million to $16 million for its 1896 "educational fund." See Sanders, *Roots of Reform*, 140.

24. Hill quoted in Joseph Gilpin Pyle, *The Life of James J. Hill*, vol. 1 (Garden City, N.Y.: Doubleday, Page, 1917), 496; Herbert Croly, *Marcus Alonzo Hanna: His Life and Work* (New York: Macmillan, 1919), 219.

25. Croly, *Marcus Alonzo Hanna*, 219.

26. Morton Keller, *Affairs of State: Public Life in Late Nineteenth Century America* (Cambridge, Mass.: Belknap Press of Harvard University Press, 1977), 583.

27. Rockefeller quoted in Ron Chernow, *Titan: The Life of John D. Rockefeller Sr.* (New York: Random House, 1998), 388. For the House of Morgan contribution, see LeRoy Ashby, *William Jennings Bryan, Champion of Democracy* (Boston: Twayne, 1987), 67.

{ PATRICK J. KELLY }

28. Roosevelt quoted in Thomas Beer, *Hanna* (New York: Alfred A. Knopf, 1929), 165.

29. Ashby, *William Jennings Bryan*, 68.

30. *New York Times*, July 12, 1896.

31. Sanders, *Roots of Reform*, 144.

32. Bryan quoted in *Chicago Tribune*, July 18, 1896.

33. Polk quoted in Lawrence Goodwyn, *Democratic Promise: The Populist Movement in America* (New York: Oxford University Press, 1976), 259.

34. *Omaha Morning World-Herald*, July 5, 1892.

35. Sickles quoted in *Chicago Tribune*, September 19, 1896.

36. Sickles quoted in *Chicago Tribune*, September 22, 1896.

37. Sickles quoted in *Sioux City Journal*, September 27, 1896.

38. Lincoln quoted in James McPherson, *Ordeal by Fire: The Civil War and Reconstruction* (New York: Alfred A. Knopf, 1982), 269.

39. Charles S. Olcott, *The Life of William McKinley*, vol. 1 (Boston: Houghton Mifflin, 1916), 225.

40. *Freeman: An Illustrated Colored Newspaper* (Indianapolis), September 12, 1896; Olcott, *The Life of William McKinley*, 226.

41. *New York Times*, October 24, 1896. If McKinley's reconciliationist stance was a cynical ploy designed to gain him electoral votes in the South, his hopes remained unfulfilled: in 1896 he lost to Bryan in all former Confederate states. Yet the future shows that McKinley was sincere in his desire for sectional reconciliation. Even after losing the South McKinley continued his determined, if racially insensitive, attempt at nation rebuilding. During the Spanish-American War he appointed two prominent Confederate veterans, Fitzhugh Lee, Robert E. Lee's nephew, and Joseph Wheeler of Alabama, as major generals in the U.S. Army. Soon after the war's end he traveled throughout the South promoting "the peace treaty and America's new territorial acquisitions in the Caribbean and the Pacific." Blight, *Race and Reunion*, 351.

42. Blight, *Race and Reunion*, 351.

43. A good discussion of Bryan's attempt to create a farmer-worker coalition and why it failed is in Sanders, *Roots of Reform*, 139–47.

44. Bryan, *The First Battle*, 205.

45. Hanna quoted in Hollingsworth, *The Whirligig of Politics*, 87.

46. "The Triumph of Sectionalism and Communism," *Harper's Weekly*, July 18, 1896, 698; *New York Mail and Express* quoted in H. W. Brands, *The Restless Decade: America in the 1890s* (New York: St. Martin's Press, 1995), 282.

47. *New York Times*, October 13, 1896.

48. "Mr. Bryan's Sectional and Class War," *Harper's Weekly*, October 10, 1896, 995–96.

49. Keller, *Affairs of State*, 581.

50. Altgeld quoted in Ray Ginger, *Altgeld's America: The Lincoln Ideal versus Changing Reality* (New York: Funk and Wagnalls, 1958), 156.

51. *Philadelphia Telegraph* quoted in Brand, *Reckless Decade*, 153; *Indianapolis American Tribune* quoted in Mary R. Dearing, *Veterans in Politics: The Story of the G.A.R.* (Baton Rouge: Louisiana State University Press, 1952), 442–43.

52. Altgeld quoted in Bryan, *The First Battle*, 408.

53. *New York Times*, November 1, 1896; "What Kind of Government Would Mr. Bryan Have," *Harper's Weekly*, September 26, 1896, 938.

54. Jones, *The Presidential Election*, 290. McKinley's effort with Catholics, however, much like his appeals to Southern voters, failed. Jensen notes, "The Catholics stayed with the Democrats in their hour of crisis, not in the hope of seeing Bryan in the White House, but with the intention of capturing full control of the party they had worked so long to build." Jensen, *The Winning of the Midwest*, 296.

55. Ireland quoted in *St. Paul Pioneer Press*, October 11, 1896. For a description of the reaction to the Paris Commune in the United States, see Philip Katz, *From Appomattox to Montmartre* (Cambridge, Mass.: Harvard University Press, 1998).

56. Minister quoted in James H. Moynihan, *The Life of Archbishop John Ireland* (New York: Arno Press, 1976), 261.

57. Marvin R. O'Connell, *John Ireland and the American Catholic Church* (St. Paul: Minnesota Historical Society, 1988), 426–27.

58. John Bodnar, "Public Memory in an American City: Commemoration in Cleveland," in *Commemorations: The Politics of National Identity*, ed. John R. Gillis (Princeton: Princeton University Press, 1994), 75–89 (quote on 75).

59. Hill quoted in Pyle, *The Life of James J. Hill*, 497; Hill quoted in O'Connell, *John Ireland*, 426.

60. O'Connell, *John Ireland*, 426–28 (quotes on 426).

61. Moynihan, *The Life of Archbishop John Ireland*, 261.

62. *New York Times*, October 13, 1896.

63. W. Fitzhugh Brundage, "No Deed but Memory," in *Where These Memories Grow: History, Memory, and Southern Identity*, ed. W. Fitzhugh Brundage (Chapel Hill: University of North Carolina Press, 2000), 1–28 (quote on 12).

64. "In Missouri and Illinois," *Review of Reviews*, November 1896, 525.

65. Hanna quoted in *New York Times*, October 7, 1896.

66. Jensen, *The Winning of the Midwest*, 23. Jensen estimates that four hundred thousand Union veterans lived in the Midwest in 1888.

67. Abraham Lincoln Post Ninety-one members quoted in *New York Times*, July 10, 1894.

68. *Chicago Tribune* quoted in Dearing, *Veterans in Politics*, 444.

69. Phillip S. Paludan, "The American Civil War Considered as a Crisis in Law and Order," *American Historical Review* 77, no. 4 (October 1972): 1013–34 (quote on 1017).

70. Veteran quoted in *Chicago Tribune*, September 22, 1896.

71. Stuart McConnell, *Glorious Contentment: The Grand Army of the Republic, 1865–1900* (Chapel Hill: University of North Carolina Press, 1992), 212, 223.

72. *Chicago Tribune*, July 26, 1896, October 9, 1896 (Sigel quote); "Mr. Bryan's Sectional and Class War," 995.

73. William Evan Davies, *Patriotism on Parade: The Story of Veterans' and Hereditary Organizations in America, 1783–1900* (Cambridge, Mass.: Harvard University Press, 1955), 189.

74. Jensen, *The Winning of the Midwest*, 25. For figures on veterans' pensions, see Theda Skocpol, *Protecting Soldiers and Mothers: The Political Origins of Social Policies in America* (Cambridge, Mass.: Belknap Press of Harvard University Press, 1992), 109. For veterans' institutions, see Patrick J. Kelly, *Creating a National Home: Building the Veterans' Welfare State, 1860–1900* (Cambridge, Mass.: Harvard University Press, 1997).

75. McConnell, *Glorious Contentment*, 153 (quote); *Chicago Tribune*, September 22, 1896.

76. Dearing, *Veterans in Politics*, 434–35, 445–46.

77. Dudley quoted in ibid., 457. McKinley enjoyed a distinguished record of service. Newspapers friendly to the Republican Party invariably referred to him as Major McKinley, the rank he had attained before leaving the army.

78. McKinley quoted in *Galveston Daily News*, September 30, 1896.

79. *Chicago Tribune*, July 26, 1896.

80. *Chicago Tribune*, July 9, 1896.

81. *Chicago Tribune*, July 18, 1896 (first quote), July 9, 1896 (second and third quotes).

82. Bryan quoted in *Galveston Daily News*, September 6, 1896.

83. Pyle, *The Life of James J. Hill*, 496.

84. M. C. Helion to Russell Alger, September 7, 1896, folder 15, box 56, William C. Beer Correspondence, September 1896, Beer Family Papers, Yale University Library, New Haven, Conn.

85. *Chicago Tribune*, September 21, 1896, September 22, 1896.

86. Jensen, *The Winning of the Midwest*, 290.

87. William M. Hahn to William C. Beer, September 21, 1896, folder 15, box 56, William C. Beer Correspondence, September 1896, Beer Family Papers; O. O. Howard, *Autobiography of O. O. Howard, Major General, United States Army* (New York: Baker and Taylor, 1907), 569. For William Beer's involvement, see Thomas Beer, *Hanna, Crane, and the Mauve Decade* (New York: Alfred A. Knopf, 1941), 66–67.

88. *Galveston Daily News*, October 10, 1896; Alger quoted in *South Bend Daily Tribune*, October 15, 1896; Alger quoted in *Indianapolis Journal*, October 14, 1896; O. A. Marden, *Boston Morning Journal*, October 28, 1896.

89. William C. Hahn to William C. Beer, October 2, 1896, folder 16, box 57, William C. Beer Correspondence, October 1986, Beer Family Papers.

90. "The Campaign Tour of the Union Generals," *Harper's Weekly*, October 31, 1896, 1084.

91. Harvey quoted in Howard, *Autobiography of O. O. Howard*, 569.

92. Goodwyn, *Democratic Promise*, 528; Cecilia Elizabeth O'Leary, *To Die For: The Paradox of American Patriotism* (Princeton: Princeton University Press, 1999), 5.

93. O'Leary, *To Die For*, 150–52. For a discussion of the GAR's creation of a national flag day, usually held on June 14, see Dearing, *Veterans in Politics*, 408.

94. Porter quoted in *New York Times*, October 31, 1896.

95. *New York Tribune* quoted in Jones, *The Presidential Election*, 292; *Des Moines Register*, October 31, 1896.

96. O'Leary, *To Die For*, 8.

97. *Chicago Tribune*, November 3, 1896.

98. O'Connell, *John Ireland*, 426.

99. *Washington, D.C., National Tribune* quoted in Dearing, *Veterans in Politics*, 466.

100. Ashby, *William Jennings Bryan*, 69 (quotes). For an analysis of election results, see Sanders, *Roots of Reform*, 145–47.

101. Walter Dean Burnham, "The System of 1896: An Analysis," in *The Evolution of American Electoral Systems*, ed. Paul Kleppner, Walter Dean Burnham, Ronald P. Formisano, Samuel B. Hays, Richard Jensen, and William G. Shade (Westport, Conn.: Greenwood Press, 1981), 147–202 (quote on 195–96).

102. Keller, *Affairs of State*, 586.

LeeAnn Whites

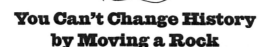

You Can't Change History by Moving a Rock
Gender, Race, and the Cultural Politics of Confederate Memorialization

On August 16, 1974, in the Missouri summer heat and when most university students were far from campus, the city of Columbia quietly removed a five-and-a-half-ton Confederate memorial from the center of the University of Missouri campus. Placing the pink granite boulder on a flatbed truck trailer, workers transported it to an outlying weed-infested field in a city park. There it stood, its original 1935 bronze plaque in dedication to the "valor and patriotism of Confederate Soldiers of Boone County" virtually obscured by the spray paint and graffiti of a younger generation of students.[1] This ignominious end was hardly the future that the local members of the United Daughters of the Confederacy (UDC) envisioned for the Rock when they first unveiled it with great pomp and ceremony some forty years earlier. With their eyes trained firmly on the past, as their motto "lest we forget" would indicate, the women of the UDC hoped that the Confederate Rock would continue to bind the following generations to a memory of what was for them, even in the early twentieth century, a lived experience of the Civil War and Civil War loss.[2]

What they could not imagine in 1935 was that the threat to their memories would arise from the members of a younger generation of university students. Not only would some white students forget the sacrifices of their Confederate forebears but also some students would not be white. By the late 1960s African American students had arrived on the University of Missouri campus in sufficient numbers to present an alternative view of the Confederacy's "valor and patriotism" that the Rock was intended to perpetuate. The struggle that emerged concerning the proper location of the Confederate Rock was therefore in many ways part of a larger cultural struggle over how and in what ways the campus in particular, and the

Members of the John S. Marmaduke chapter of the Columbia UDC with Confederate veterans from the Missouri Confederate Soldiers Home at the dedication of the Confederate Rock on June 3, 1935. (Courtesy of the United Daughters of the Confederacy, John S. Marmaduke Chapter, Scrapbook, 1935–36, Western Historical Manuscript Collection, Columbia, Mo.)

surrounding community more generally, would be racially integrated. Could or would the legacy of the white South continue to be the university's largely unquestioned hegemonic culture? Could or would the culture of white slave holders' descendants simply coexist with the cultural legacy of former slaves' descendants? And what role would white women play in this moment of potential cultural renegotiation? For when the UDC members placed the Rock at the campus center in 1935, they acted out of their position as cultural arbiters, as keepers of the public memory through their role as guardians of the white male Confederate past. Would a younger generation of white women choose to perpetuate this strategy or would they use the new cultural configuration offered by the change in the racial order to establish a new and more autonomous race and gender politics for white women?[3]

The Columbia chapter of the UDC was formed in 1903. Of the thirty founding members, twenty-three had fathers, or some other male relation, who actually had fought for the Confederacy. The chapter was named after John S. Marmaduke, a distinguished Confederate general who hailed from the region and whose niece was a member of the group. A poem written in 1925 by one Columbia chapter charter member reveals the ways in which this chapter's naming was more than an effort to honor one man. "UDC Ideals" points out the noble and manly qualities of all the men from Missouri who served the Confederate cause:

John S. Marmaduke, noble man
Among Missouri's best he stood
Brave and true, as all men are
Who love their country and their God:

Leader of men he was born to be
With his heaven endowed capacity
Of brain and blood, he dared to show
What men were made of sixty years ago

John S. Marmaduke, Oh how souls are thrilled
Every UDC Heart is filled
With renewed zeal the torch to wave
Borne by hands of men so brave.

The last two stanzas made the daughters' claim to their father's war, which became a central tenet of the organization.

Drooped and flickered tho ne'er
Trailed in the dust,
Caught up by hands true to the trust
Held aloft in the hearts and lives
Of the Daughters in Nineteen twenty five

The Children too shall know the truth
and point to All, in North or South
The Path that noble manhood trod
And leave the victory with our God.[4]

The fathers, despite their courage and valor, may have nearly "trailed" the Confederate flag in the dust, but now their daughters would keep it aloft and even pass it on to their children. Here the UDC proposed to do on a cultural level what their fathers had failed to do: win the war for the South. This white cultural war began formally as soon as the military war was lost, with the formation of such groups as ladies' memorial associations across the South. These associations were dedicated to the proper burial of Confederate soldiers and ceremonies rich in respectful symbolism.

This informal cultural war can be traced back even further to the experiences of Confederate civilians on the home front, a "second front" upon which the war was fought. The women who initially formed the Columbia UDC in 1903 had particularly strong reasons to feel that Missouri women had made significant wartime contributions to this second front. Columbia, located along the Missouri River in the heart of Boone County, was a major slaveholding area of the state where a majority of its white men fought for the Confederacy. While their men were off in the battlefields of the "first front," women were left to deal with their own sort of war. Their town and their county were contested territory, with occupying Union troops and Confederate guerrillas, or bushwhackers, pitted against one another.[5]

The story of Mary Tucker, a member of the Columbia UDC in the 1920s, illustrates this two-front experience of war in Missouri. While her father was off fighting with the Missouri State Guard against the advancing Union forces in the summer of 1861, Union troops were sacking her family home before the battle of Carthage. She was forced to flee with her mother to St. Louis after their home was burnt to the ground and their town's stores destroyed. In the following summer her father was killed at the battle of Pea Ridge, the last serious effort of the Missouri Confederate forces to control the state. By the end of the war Tucker had also lost her husband and her brother. Perhaps not surprisingly, Tucker and her mother became militant members of the second-front war and were arrested, imprisoned, and eventually banished from St. Louis for aiding Confederate spies.[6]

In the early twentieth century the Missouri UDC took up the task of preserving home front stories of Confederate sympathizing Missouri women like Mary Tucker. Their more public efforts were devoted to memorializing their men's experiences on the first front. They worked hard to secure their men's reputation based on stories of honorable battlefield behavior. In addition UDC women stressed women's valor on the second front, focusing on the ways in which women's commonplace daily activities were transformed into important political and public acts. They told the story, for instance, of a neglected grave on a farm some seven miles northwest of Columbia marked only with the single word "Benedict." Benedict was the name of a commissioned officer of the Confederate army who fell ill while on a recruiting mission in the Columbia area. He was hidden on a Confederate sympathizers' farm, where despite the diligent efforts of the family's women to nurse him back to health he died. According to the UDC's telling, the county was so "overrun" by "federals" it was impossible to give the man a decent public burial and instead the immediate neighbors were forced to gather together secretly, during the dead of night, and convey the body to its final resting place, marking it with a stone engraved only with "Benedict."[7]

Not only did the UDC lay claim to Confederate sympathizers' valor and courage on the second front but they also demanded recognition for the loss of life that fighting on the second front had cost its participants. Just as their men had sacrificed their lives on the battlefield, civilians on the home front also lost members of their families and their community to guerrilla warfare. In a paper she read before the Columbia UDC in the 1920s Ann Hickam recounted the deaths of four close neighbors at the hands of Union troops. The first, she claimed, was a "young man not yet out of his teens" who was "shot through his heart, and in the agonies of death was pierced through the throat by a bayonet and left dead and unburied." According to Hickam, friends of the family "risked their lives" to bring his body home to his sisters. "We were," as she put it, "almost afraid to bury our dead in those troubled times." The next victim was her nearest neighbor. Union soldiers also met him on the road and even though he pleaded with them to spare his life, if only because of his wife and six children, they shot him. A few days later another man was killed, also the father of a large family, and a few days later his wife died of a broken heart. Obviously these were the kind of immediate, devastating, personal experiences that people could not easily forget. The experiences were fused in a particularly intense way with women's traditional domestic activities. Hickam concluded in her account almost sixty year later, "All these sad and harrowing things happened in the small circle of our own neighborhood."[8]

After the war officially ended, former Confederate women across the South converted their wartime soldiers' aid societies, which had fed, clothed, and nursed soldiers during the war, into Ladies' Memorial Associations, which memorialized the dead. Missouri women, in contrast, found it difficult to form such organizations. This difficulty arose because the state had remained in the Union and had been convulsed by guerrilla warfare. Only in St. Louis, where large numbers of Confederate prisoners of war died in local hospitals, and in Springfield, where the state's one major formal battle, the battle of Wilson's Creek, created more than a thousand casualties, were women able to start public memorial organizations. As was the case elsewhere in the South, the Springfield Monument Association struggled to reinter the dead. Its members sought to move bodies from a temporary location in an open field in front of the county courthouse, where they had been hastily buried in the August heat. The association raised the funds successfully for a Confederate cemetery and later acquired standard grave markers. In the rest of the state commemoration of the war dead was necessarily observed as a private matter because guerrilla fighting tended to result in the dead, frequently civilians, being scattered across the landscape.[9]

It was not until the late nineteenth century that Missouri former Confederate women found the necessity and the opportunity to publicly organize and memorialize their wartime experiences. In the 1890s these women formed the first chapter of the Daughters of the Confederacy in their state to help secure the construction of a Confederate soldiers' home. Perhaps in recognition of the extent of Missouri civilians' involvement in warfare, the Missouri Confederate Home would be the only soldiers' home in the country to admit women. By the turn of the century mounting problems associated with the proper memorialization of this Confederate generation spurred Missouri chapters of the Daughters of the Confederacy to consolidate their resources to form the United Daughters of the Confederacy. In 1901, forty years after the battle of Wilson's Creek, the Missouri UDC erected the first public monument to the Confederate dead in the state.[10]

Confronted by aging and death, UDC members were acutely aware that they needed to not only care for the aging veterans but also preserve the memory of the Confederate generation that was passing away before their eyes. They needed lasting gravestones and monuments to stand as testaments to their vision of the past. Perhaps more important, they needed to transmit their stories to the younger generation, which was quickly losing contact with firsthand war accounts. At the dedication of the Confederate Rock on June 3, 1935, the Columbia UDC brought veterans, the youngest of whom was eighty-seven, from the Confederate Soldiers' Home some forty miles away in Higgensville to have living war participants present. By this point even the Confederate "daughters" were passing on. The officers of the organization who stood beside the aging denizens of the Confederate home were the granddaughters of noted war heroes. Columbia's mayor, R. Searcy Pollard, who pledged at the dedication that the city would always keep a light burning over the monument, was himself a grandson of J. J. Searcy, who in the summer of 1861 led the Columbia Home Guard against the Union at the battle of Boonville.[11]

These grandsons and granddaughters hoped that the placement of the Confederate Rock on the University of Missouri campus would perpetuate the memory of their families' wartime sacrifices long after the war's participants were gone. Indeed, the 1935 dedication was the culmination of a generation of successful effort by these women not only to care for, bury, and memorialize the passing of the Confederate generation but also to affect their descendants. There was, for example, the local elementary school, Robert E. Lee Elementary, home of the "Patriots," which they decorated with pictures of Lee and Jefferson Davis and provided with approved Civil War histories. At the University of Missouri the UDC formed a close relationship with the Kappa Alpha fraternity, meeting at the fraternity's chapter house to celebrate Lee's birthday and other significant dates on the Confederate calendar. At one such event Mr. Crowe, a grandson of a Confederate soldier, extended a particularly warm welcome to the UDC and formally extended to its members the use of the Kappa Alpha's chapter house any time. As the UDC secretary noted in the minutes of the next meeting, "the cordial welcome and evident care in decorating for our coming gives the Kappa Alpha Boys a warm place in the hearts of the 'Daughters.'" The UDC members expressed the warmth of their affection for the Kappa Alpha men by passing a motion to have a Confederate flag made for them.[12]

Admittedly not all the UDC's efforts at cultural preservation succeeded. The members petitioned the state legislature to designate a Gray and a Blue wing at the university's main library. It remained unnamed, but the Missouri Historical Society, housed in what the UDC intended to be the Gray wing of the library, labored tirelessly throughout the 1930s to collect over fifteen hundred service records of Missouri Confederate soldiers. Floyd Shoemaker, the secretary and librarian of the State Historical Society and editor of the *Missouri Historical Review*, was himself an avid supporter of Confederate memorialization, as was his wife, who was a member of the Columbia UDC. At a speech he gave in 1941 at the unveiling of a monument to three of Missouri's leading Confederates on the state capitol grounds, Shoemaker suggested that despite the monument they were gathered to dedicate on that day, Confederate military experiences remained largely unmarked in the state. It waš rather the lived cultural tradition, "pride in southern tradition and southern ancestry," as he put it, that "binds to the present the spirit of the days of the Confederacy." Evidence of Southern tradition could be found in "the love Missourians have for the strains of 'Dixie' " or in "the high columned porch so often associated with memories of old southern homes." It was then in the survival of these cultural forms, "the music, literature, legends, and architecture of the South, (that) we find the South of tradition living today."[13]

A generation later, in the early 1970s, students wondered how a memorial like the Confederate Rock, which they viewed as inappropriately political and arguably racist, could have been located on the campus in the first place. In 1935, however, women of the UDC thought that the world had finally righted itself. Through their public organizational work in honoring their men, they had honored themselves, their families, and their Southern culture more generally. They had finally won the battle of the second front. They had secured what they saw as an appropriate level of respect and recognition, of public space, for white Southern descendants and their cultural forms in the state.

Then, in 1939, an African American named Lloyd Gaines won a suit against the university and gained admission to the school as its first black student. There was a place for African Americans in the world of the UDC, but it was not as students at the university. Indeed, every year on Memorial Day the local UDC members even decorated the grave of one African American, "Uncle Jack Coates," along with white Confederate soldiers' graves. But "Uncle Jack" was honored as a loyal body servant to his master, not as a soldier in his own right. In a sense the "place" the UDC members envisioned for African Americans was not dissimilar to the position the women envisioned for themselves: as loyal supporters of white men and as avid supporters of the second-front war. Of course the difference was that their men really were *their* men, while for their slaves their owners were in

{ LEEANN WHITES }

fact no "real" kin of theirs and this despite the "Uncle" in Jack Coates or even the "Aunt" in Aunt Harris, "our black mammy," who was buried with her white owners in the same cemetery as Uncle Jack.[14]

Although the UDC continued to celebrate those African Americans who appeared (at least to them) to be like members of their families, even advocating that a special pension be established for slaves who remained loyal to their owners during the Civil War, the black community in the state worked diligently to establish itself as a truly free people. As defeated white Confederates of the county and the state looked to their kin and community to perpetuate their culture, African Americans in central Missouri looked to their kin and community for the same purpose. As white women of the UDC asserted the honor and valor of their defeated men, and therefore the honor and worthiness of their white Southern culture more generally, the black population struggled to acquire an equal place for itself in the public cultural life of the state.[15]

This struggle on the part of the state's African Americans sprang from their experiences of the Civil War, particularly its guerrilla warfare, in the same households that the UDC were so intent upon memorializing. Lloyd Gaines's admission as a student to the university represented two trends. The first was simple: that a racially exclusionary society could no longer be maintained at public institutions such as the University of Missouri. Second, it represented something arguably of much wider cultural and social significance. For intertwined with the recognition of a more racially egalitarian future was the emergence of a more racially egalitarian past. The public acknowledgment of a different past cut right to the heart of white Confederate memory.

Just as the UDC was establishing a hegemonic place for the cultural politics of the second-front war, the admission of black students to the university represented the possibility that the black story would be presented in a form that white people in the state would hear. What that black story would reveal was that the war in central Missouri was actually a three-front war, fought not only on the battlefields and in white households but also in black households. At the war's beginning, of course, black slaves lived with their white owners. Their dispersal throughout the white community created the basis for the white women at the time, and the UDC ever afterward, to cling to their single-minded vision of African Americans as servants and thus as loyal participants in their second-front war.[16]

In many ways slaves' experiences in Boone County during the war were similar to those of their owners. The African American third-front war emerged from the fortunes of the second-front war. Until 1863 slaveholding households were largely stable in the area thanks to the Union troops stationed in Columbia. However much Confederate sympathizers may have resented the presence of these soldiers and conspired against them, they had to recognize the usefulness of the Union military's commitment to upholding slavery in Missouri's formally "loyal" border area. Beginning in the fall of 1863, however, the Union military began actively recruiting slaves by offering them freedom in exchange for their service as soldiers. Union officials sent out recruiting agents from St. Louis into the heart of slaveholding regions like Boone County.[17]

This shift in Union policy marked the beginning of the end of slavery in the county and opened the war's third front. General Order 135 opened the door to black enlistment in Missouri in November 1863, and opposition by white slaveholders was strong. In Boone County the provost marshal refused to accept black enlistees and the recruiting agent returned to St. Louis in disgust. Local bushwhackers, some of whom were members of prominent slave-owning families, threatened black men with death if they enlisted. Nonetheless, that fall more than two hundred of the county's slaves ran away to the next county, where the Union accepted their enrollments. By May 1864, 387 slave men of the county had enlisted. That number represented 69 percent of black males between twenty-one and forty years of age in Boone County as of 1860. The overwhelming majority of these black enlistees would never return to their families, as the mortality rate of their regiment was above 75 percent.[18]

There were striking similarities between the white and black experiences of the war in Boone County. Like their mistresses, slave women suffered the loss of their men at the front. These black men, like their owners, had often been forced to run away in the dead of night to fight a war to uphold their beliefs. For the UDC, the story of Benedict the Confederate recruiter epitomized the secrecy and danger that accompanied Confederate recruiting efforts in the county because of Union occupation. For slaves, white slave owners and white support for slavery turned enlistment into a similarly dangerous proposition. And just as white Confederate owners, who were serving at the battlefront, left behind women and children, so too did slave men leave behind women and children to deal with a hostile occupying force. But while Confederate sympathizing women had to fear the random violence of the occupying Union forces, slave women faced possible violence from both their owners and the bushwhackers.[19]

Two stories of slave women's activities illustrate the dangers they faced.

As with the white women of Boone County who aided and assisted Confederate recruiters like Benedict, black slave women assisted the Union forces by providing critical information. The occupying Union military could count on the loyalty of the black population only because Confederate sympathy was so widespread among whites. Slaves carried out this assistance at great personal risk. One slave woman, Easter, came to Columbia with her daughter to look for protection after bushwhackers left a threatening note in the kitchen of her owner, a Mr. Samuel Davis, which read: "From Camp Dixie, Boone County, Mo. Addressed to Samuel Davis' Black woman Easter. As you are known to be a notorious reporter, this is to inform you that if you are found in this county one-month after receiving this notice you will pull a rope. You must take all your brood with you and skedaddle like hell. We are determined to have no more of your damned reporting."[20]

Easter did indeed "skedaddle like hell" and was fortunate enough to reach the safety of the Union military outpost with her daughter and two other women. Another slave woman, identified in the military record only as "a negro woman slave of Edward Graves," was not so fortunate. She had taken advantage of the county's increasingly chaotic conditions to run away to the town of Sturgeon. In the fall of 1864 she attempted to return to help some slaves from her former household escape. She started back to Sturgeon with a woman, a girl, a boy, and two small children. After proceeding several miles the group was overtaken by three men disguised in Union uniforms. They forced the slaves a distance into the woods, hung one woman before they shot her, shot the other slaves, and then returned the bodies of the two small children to their white owner. The master was taken into custody by Union officials and charged with complicity in the killing.[21]

As these stories would indicate, during the last year of the war as the second front began to collapse guerrilla activity aimed at the slave population increased sharply. In the fall of 1863, when the new Union policy encouraged slave men to enlist in the army, local bushwhackers responded by threatening with death any slave they caught attempting to join up. By 1864, however, the institution of slavery was in such tatters that the state legislature voted for gradual emancipation, and by January 1865 it voted for immediate abolition. Boone County bushwhackers responded to the news of emancipation by posting notices that blacks who sought paid work and whites who hired them would be lynched. The guerrillas gave the black population two weeks to leave the countryside and insisted that all able-bodied adult men had to enlist in the Union army. They apparently feared the continued presence of adult black men in the county now that they were free. They made good on their threats by lynching several freedmen who remained in the county's rural areas. As one Union officer described the situation, "I blush for my race when I discover the wicked barbarity of the late masters and mistresses of the recently freed persons of the counties heretofore named. I have no doubt but that the monster, Jim Jackson, is instigated by the late slaveholders to hang or shoot every negro he can find absent from the old plantations. Some few have driven their black people away from them with nothing to eat or scarcely to wear. So between Jackson and collaborators among the first families, the poor blacks are rapidly concentrating in the towns."[22]

Even with the close of the war in 1865 the freedpeople and Confederate sympathizers continued to share a conflicted history. Both would have their stories of valor and sacrifice suppressed. In the war's immediate aftermath the overwhelming majority of the county's white male citizens were disenfranchised because of their pro-Confederate stance. They found themselves living in a county and a state firmly in the hands of their wartime enemies, the Radical Republicans. For the few black soldiers who returned to their families and for the much larger number of their wives, parents, and children who lived through the war's harrowing years on the home front, the postwar era offered even fewer opportunities to publicly celebrate their sacrifices to the triumphant Union war effort than had the months immediately following the war. The demands of fighting the war had destroyed the institution of slavery that had undergirded the county's white households. But immediately after Lee's surrender the racial hierarchy was quickly reestablished through a system of de facto segregation.[23]

The Union's military victory was followed shortly by political domination of Missouri by the Republican Party. Faced with a political situation in which they had little power, former Confederates could at least attempt to retain control over the private relationship between themselves and their former slaves. They also sought to control the memory of the war. Many white citizens of Boone County claimed to respect and feel genuinely fond of their former slaves. Some whites even assisted freedpeople in their efforts to build separate communities, churches, and schools. Whites were at the same time militantly opposed to anything resembling racial equality. Although they might be happy to celebrate the loyalty of their family retainers, whose faithfulness began in earnest with the test of the Civil War and persisted into emancipation, they clung to their vision of the freedpeople as extensions of themselves. In their view the war did not move beyond the

{ LEEANN WHITES }

second front. They created a narrative of the war that privileged their own experience, even though blacks had demonstrated the same kind of wartime valor and sacrifice. Simply put, Boone County's Confederate daughters and sons claimed the power to commemorate the war on their own terms as a story of white sacrifice and white valor.[24]

The death of the white Confederate generation fueled the rise of Confederate demoralization in Boone County. The death of the "old family retainers," the slavery generation, also fueled the rise of militancy among African Americans. Empowered by the struggles of the older generation to provide them with education and material opportunities, this younger generation formed the NAACP in the first decades of the twentieth century and began to press for greater social and economic opportunities for African Americans. A few years after the dedication of the Confederate Rock they had finally found in the person of Lloyd Gaines the possibility of breaching the highest bastion of exclusionary public education, the University of Missouri.[25]

Shortly after winning his case and being formally admitted to the university, Lloyd Gaines disappeared while traveling on a train to enroll at the school. His body was never found. The message was clear: blacks were not welcome at the University of Missouri. No African American attempted to attend the university again until the 1950s, and even then only a handful did. Black enrollment swelled in the late 1960s, but on campus students found an entrenched white Southern and Confederate culture. The Kappa Alphas still flew the Confederate flag and read the Ordinances of Secession at "Old South Days" every year, the band played "Dixie" at Tiger football games, and women regularly posed on the Confederate Rock for pictures in the school annual.[26]

A particularly hostile encounter between black and white students centered on the Confederate flag and led to the formation of the first black student organization in the 1968–69 school year. By that time African American students numbered between three and four hundred on campus. At a Tiger football game a few black students responded to the custom of waving Confederate flags by waving a black flag. The response to their gesture was a small riot. At some point in the brawl a university police officer drew a gun on one of the black flag wavers and said, "We don't do things like this here" (or, according to another account, "You SOB, you drop that flag or I'll blow your brains out"). After the incident African American students formed the Legion of Black Collegians. The following fall they established the *Black Out*. In this publication black students explained why they thought it necessary to form a separate organization. As one writer explained, black students were tired of being "constantly regarded as a silent minority . . . ignored by the main stream of campus life." Another offered a more militant explanation, describing the University of Missouri, "alias 'Little Dixie,' " as a "society of Racism." According to this writer, "If George Wallace were to walk though the dorms of this University his heart would be overflowing with pride. The number of Confederate flags that would meet his eyes could make an old veteran bigot glad. . . . The monument rock dedicated to the Confederacy would fill his eyes with tears of happiness and make him want to embrace the white faculty and staff of this University, who are all his loyal comrades."[27]

This writer went on to describe the university as one large plantation. He called the central administration building "The Big House," which "stands in all its old southern splendor and basks in its deep southern environment." The "overseers" of this plantation, "otherwise known as the 'security police' still have their guns. . . . They fit perfectly into the system and have no qualms about doing the jobs 'Big Massa' calls down for them. The security police don't know that this is 1969 and slavery ended one hundred and three years ago." Black students were, according to this writer, "125 miles from nowhere" and therefore in no position to fight the sort of "political revolution" that was going on in major urban areas.[28]

Here this *Black Out* writer referred to the university's distance from Kansas City and St. Louis, major urban centers with large African American populations. Ironies abound here since in the nineteenth century the river counties in the center of the state had constituted the center of the black population. At the time of the Civil War, for instance, slaves constituted 25 percent of the population of Boone County. After the war freedpeople left rural areas and moved to local towns and eventually to big cities such as St. Louis, Kansas City, and Chicago. Thus, by the time African Americans were able to return to central Missouri as students at the university they faced an area with a powerful slave-holding tradition and almost devoid of permanent black residents. Recognizing the impossibility of a direct "political revolution," the *Black Out* writers quite astutely proposed to foment a "revolution of cultural change" and proceeded to take aim at the very aspects of Southern culture that the UDC had labored so diligently to promote.[29]

Black students expected to find no "reinforcements" among white students, but they were, in fact, forthcoming and from an unlikely place: white women. Some white women of the younger generation abandoned the older generation's role as keeper of white men's reputation for honor and valor in the war. Instead, the younger group tried to establish women's rightful place on campus. The demands of African American and white women students converged in the early 1970s, as both groups demanded more women and black faculty as well as course work that focused on the contributions of women and minorities to the culture at large. The fall of 1971 marked a banner time for both groups, as a black studies minor was established along with the first course that focused entirely on women. In connection with this nascent women's studies program the Association of Women Students brought in a series of speakers. The first were Gloria Steinem, by this time a well-known spokesperson for the women's movement, and Dorothy Pitman, a pioneer in establishing New York City's child day care program. Steinem did not disappoint her audience as she proceeded to "tear down every myth held sacred by oppressors of women." She expressed amazement that "a school of close to 20,000 students still has only one black faculty member and a handful of female professors." She called for a coalition of blacks and white women on campus because, as she put it, "together you can work some changes, but if you don't get together the establishment will try to run you against each other."[30]

Steinem argued, "It is up to us to make the white male more aware of the intrinsic value of the individual. . . . Only then will the human race stop dividing itself because of outward differences." She assumed white men were responsible for racism because they refused to recognize the "individuality" of white women and blacks. Through their support of feminists such as Steinem and the women's studies program, these young white women appeared to renounce the UDC's goals. Rather than viewing male honor as something to be cherished, many of these white women regarded it as highly suspect. Instead of "standing by their men," this younger generation attempted to ally itself with blacks and other social groups subordinated to white male dominance. As Steinem claimed, "(white) women have more empathy with blacks because both have been victims of the white man's discrimination." Steinem did acknowledge that the parallel between African Americans and white women was not complete, since "women may have lost their identities, but blacks are losing their lives."[31]

In her speech Steinem singled out the Confederate Rock and the Rebel flag waving over the Kappa Alpha fraternity house as two symbolic manifestations of the racial exclusion blacks faced on campus. She followed the lead of black students who had published a full-page picture of the Confederate Rock in *Black Out* the previous year with the caption "Is Racism

Fostered Here?" This query apparently received little attention from the overwhelmingly white student body. On October 6, however, less than a week after Gloria Steinem had castigated the Rock, the student senate passed a resolution calling the monument "offensive and insulting to blacks and to all who sincerely desire an end to black oppression." The senate members asked the city to remove the offending boulder as soon as possible. According to coverage in the town newspaper, this resolution constituted a "belated controversy" surrounding a "long ignored red granite boulder" and had taken other Columbia residents "by surprise." Of course, the citizens referred to were not among the 10 percent of the population who were black and certainly were not readers of the *Black Out*.[32]

News stories covering the student senate motion contributed to controversy brewing among the townspeople. "Party Line," an audience participation program on a local radio station, was flooded with calls about the Confederate Rock. The student senate president claimed to have received "menacing and obscene phone calls" in response to the students' request. Citizens wrote numerous letters to the editor and offered a whole range of reasons to keep the Rock on campus. Townspeople believed that the Rock stood for public recognition of their heritage. Anyone else offering an opinion were outsiders in their view. Gloria Steinem came in for criticism on this score. As one writer asserted, "Here's an astounding example of a New York City resident, an acknowledged traveling rabble rouser, coming into Columbia, being paid by the student government association to sound off, who then tells people in the Central Missouri city how they should handle their historical monuments." Even the students were viewed as "transients" by some townspeople. As one letter concluded, "How ridiculous can one get? If the Student Senate has nothing better to do than try to stir up ill feeling between the races—they should go home."[33]

What the younger generation of white women students began, black women completed. In 1971 the Rock remained in place despite the first formal request to remove it. Another protest soon followed but it, too, failed. In 1974, however, Angela Davis came to speak on campus. After her speech the Legion of Black Collegians sent a list of demands to the university's administrators that included removing the Confederate Rock from campus and warehousing it out of public view. That summer the Rock was regularly defaced, and some townspeople formed a patrol to guard it at night. Authorities became concerned that serious conflict between students and townspeople seemed likely to break out. Late in the summer of 1974,

{ LEEANN WHITES }

before the students returned to campus, the city sent workers to remove the rock to a remote field in an outlying city park.[34]

This move was not, of course, exactly what the black students had demanded. The Rock was still in public view, however far off the beaten track. The move was also not acceptable to at least some of the townspeople, especially members of the UDC and the county's historical society. These groups hired a lawyer and joined forces with the townspeople most concerned with preserving the (white Southern) "history" of the town. They first arranged to have the Rock moved to the grounds of the historical society and finally, after a formal hearing before the county judge, to have the Rock, at public expense, permanently relocated in front of the county courthouse. No students appeared at the hearing to contest the placement of the Rock in front of the courthouse, and it rests there to this day. Apparently, removing this marker of a certain kind of race and gender politics from university grounds was change enough. In having the Rock moved these students asserted the existence of a different kind of university "family," one in which African Americans were students and faculty rather than slaves and servants and in which white women were equals rather than subordinates as their father's daughters or their husband's wives.[35]

This new but fraught alliance between white women and black people would bring substantial changes to the university in the years to come by enhancing black and women's studies programs and increasing the numbers of black and women faculty, staff, and students. The Rock, for the moment, appeared not to be an issue. Its former location on campus was converted into an open circle where all were free to speak.

But in the 1980s memorialization of the Civil War was revitalized in Missouri. The Sons of Confederate Veterans was formed anew in the state and began to spearhead memorial activities such as Civil War battle reenactments, the placement of new markers on Confederate graves, and the annual celebration of Decoration Day. In Columbia the organization's members arranged to have a concrete walkway built up to the Confederate Rock to make it more accessible to the public and began to gather at it to memorialize the county's Confederate dead. In 1988 the United Confederate Veterans in Columbia paid to have a ramp built to the Rock to allow even better public access to it. And in the early nineties some townspeople once again began to celebrate Memorial Day at the Rock, not unlike the ceremony on June 3, 1935.[36]

By the early nineties, however, the resurgence of Confederate commemorative activities met with organized resistance from Missouri's African Americans. The state NAACP chapter actively opposed celebrations of Confederate heritage, pointing out that what represented valor and courage of the common soldier to heritage groups represented a history of slavery and oppression to African Americans. By 1994 pressure from the NAACP and other groups and individuals who viewed the Confederate memorialization as inherently racist caused officials at William Jewell College to refuse to allow the ceremony honoring the reburial of Jesse James to be conducted on their campus in Liberty, Missouri. The issue was not so much the reburial of a notorious Civil War guerrilla and postwar outlaw as it was the use of the Missouri Confederate flag, with which the organizers proposed to drape the casket. According to campus officials, the dark blue Missouri Confederate battle flag, while "not resembling the more familiar and controversial 'stars and bars,'" was "still judged by school officials to be a 'racially inflammatory symbol.'" School policy, according to one official, "equated Confederate flags with Nazi uniforms and Ku Klux Klan attire."[37]

The appropriateness of Confederate memorialization was questioned again on the University of Missouri campus in the fall of 2001 when two students decided to hang a three-by-four-foot Confederate flag in their dorm window. Other students on their floor protested and a petition was circulated and signed. Passersby frequently responded to the flag with calls of "racist." Nonetheless the two undergraduates persisted, arguing along with the larger Confederate memorial movement in the state that the flag represented "southern pride and rebellion," not, as their neighbor on the floor suggested, "oppression and prejudice." University officials hesitated to take action against the students because they feared a "tough legal battle" if they tried to force them to remove the flag. More to the point, one administrator noted, the problem was one of "differing cultural views trying to live peacefully together."[38]

And so we might ask, what has changed? Can you change history by moving a rock? This question was taken up by the school's town newspaper when the students first proposed the idea in 1971. As they put it, "A rock is a rock. It just sits there minding its own business . . . probably not even aware that it is racist. How much can you expect of a rock? The rock can symbolize racism, or anything else a passerby wants it to. . . . You can't change history by moving a rock." Insofar as the Rock's removal reflected larger social changes in the racial and gender climate of the University of Missouri, it at least suggested a change in the perception of Civil War history. Across the state in the 1990s Confederate memorialization met stiff resistance or defeat, indicating that the public culture had indeed restructured its telling of the past. In this new racial climate today we might expect the Rock to receive the same negative response as the Confederate flag hung in the dorm window. We might expect a return to the kind of pitched battle that created the need to move the Rock in the seventies. Instead, we find little renewed protest against the Rock and its rememorialization and even the addition of a new Civil War monument alongside it.[39]

In October 2001 while students were breaking into the dorm room in Gillette Hall and throwing a broken television through the window where the Confederate flag was hung, Civil War reenactors lined up on the courthouse square waving Confederate and Union flags to dedicate the new Civil War monument. Photo coverage of the event shows a young black girl laying a wreath from all the black school children in the county at the base of the monument and black members of the town's citizenry sitting in the front row of the audience. What this reveals is not simply a change in the memorializing event itself but a revision of the history that undergirds it. The Confederate Rock was originally dedicated solely to the white dead of the county, but the new monument includes the names of twenty-six black soldiers who gave their lives in the Union war effort, a number that surpasses the twenty-four white Union dead. The recognition and inclusion of the third front has transformed the meaning of memorial events like the dedication of Columbia's new Civil War monument.[40]

This is not to say that all is race happiness in central Missouri. Even the new monument, while including the black Union dead, critically undercounts the participation of African Americans in the war. There were, for instance, all those slaves who ran away to enlist in the nearby county because Boone County was too conservative to have its own military recruiter. It seems likely that if their names are added to the monument, the county's black Union dead will not just outnumber the white Union dead but will outnumber the total white dead, both Union and Confederate. When bounded by the experience of the UDC's white women and the standpoint of the second front, what appeared to be a white southern story in 1935 turns out, with the collapse of the tight weld between the first and second front and the politics of standing by your man, to have been a black story all along. Who knows what the Civil War and its memorialization will become in Columbia and the former slaveholding states more generally as we move ever further away from the patriarchal slaveholding households and the race and gender politics of those households that generated secession and war.[41]

NOTES

1. The use of such stone markers was commonplace in central Missouri in 1935. The UDC erected almost identical commemorative stones at the Confederate Soldiers' Home in Higgensville and also at the state capitol in Jefferson City. While official UDC records do not discuss the reason for the use of granite boulders, the placement of a photo of Columbia's stone unveiling next to a large photo of the Rock of Gibraltar in the Columbia chapter's scrapbook is suggestive. While the Rock of Gibraltar had stood unconquerable since ancient times, speculation in 1935 was that it would fall to the modern technology of German warfare, much as the Confederacy was alleged by the UDC to have fallen because of the superior industrial might of the North, despite its stalwart and "rock like" defense. John S. Marmaduke Chapter scrapbook, 1931–35, Belle Troxell Collection, Western Historical Manuscripts, University of Missouri, Columbia. For a further discussion of Confederate monuments in the state, see Sarah Guitar, "Monuments and Memorials in Missouri," *Missouri Historical Review* 19, no. 4 (July 1925): 555–603; and "Civil War Monuments and Battle Sites," Vertical File, Missouri State Historical Society, Columbia.

2. On the history of the UDC, see Karen L. Cox, *Dixie's Daughters: The United Daughters of the Confederacy and the Preservation of Confederate Culture* (Gainesville: University Press of Florida, 2003), and Mary B. Poppenheim, Maude Blake Merchant, Mary M. Faris McKinney, Rassie Hoskins White, Eloise Welch Wright, Anne Bachman Hyde, Susie Stuart Campbell, Charlotte Osborne Woodbury, and Ruth Jenning Lawton, *The History of the United Daughters of the Confederacy* (Raleigh, N.C.: Edwards Broughton, 1925). See also Fred Bailey, "Mildred Lewis Rutherford and the Patrician Cult of the Old South," *Georgia Historical Quarterly* 78, no. 2 (Summer 1994): 509–35; Fred Bailey, "The Textbooks of the 'Lost Cause': Censorship and the Creation of Southern State Histories" *Georgia Historical Quarterly* 75, no. 2 (Summer 1991): 507–33; John M. Coski and Amy R. Feely, "A Monument to Southern Womanhood: The Founding Generation of the Confederate Museum," in *A Woman's War: Southern Women, Civil War, and the Confederate Legacy*, ed. Edward D. C. Campbell Jr. and Kym S. Rice (Charlottesville: University of Virginia Press, 1996), 131–63; and Angie Parrott, "Love Makes Memory Eternal?: The United Daughters of the Confederacy in Richmond, Virginia, 1897–1920," in *The Edge of the South: Life in Nineteenth Century Virginia*, ed. Edward Ayers and John Willis (Charlottesville: University of Virginia Press, 1991), 219–38.

3. On the role of monuments and memorialization more generally in mediating contemporary social conflicts, see David W. Blight, *Race and Reunion: The Civil War in American Memory* (Cambridge, Mass.: Belknap Press of Harvard University Press, 2001); John Bodnar, *Remaking America: Public Memory, Commemoration, and Pa-*

triotism in the Twentieth Century (Princeton: Princeton University Press, 1992); John Bodnar, ed., *Bonds of Affection: Americans Define Their Patriotism* (Princeton: Princeton University Press, 1996); and W. Fitzhugh Brundage, ed., *Where These Memories Grow: History, Memory, and Southern Identity* (Chapel Hill: University of North Carolina Press, 2000).

4. Mrs. Foster Martin to Mrs. S. C. (Margaret Blight) Hunt, March 12, 1925, Hunt Family Papers, Western Historical Manuscripts, University of Missouri.

5. On the Ladies' Memorial Association, see Gaines M. Foster, *Ghosts of the Confederacy: Defeat, the Lost Cause, and the Emergence of the New South, 1865 to 1913* (New York: Oxford University Press, 1987), 36–46; LeeAnn Whites, *The Civil War as a Crisis in Gender: Augusta, Georgia, 1860–1890* (Athens: University of Georgia Press, 1995), 160–98; LeeAnn Whites, " 'Stand by Your Man': The Ladies' Memorial Association and the Reconstruction of Southern White Manhood," in *Women of the American South: A Multicultural Reader*, ed. Christie Anne Farnham (New York: New York University Press, 1997), 133–49; and Catherine Bishir, "A Strong Force of Ladies: Women, Politics, and Confederate Memorial Associations in Nineteenth Century Raleigh," *North Carolina Historical Review* 77, no. 4 (October 2000): 455–91.

6. Mary Tucker clipping, scrapbook 1, John S. Marmaduke Chapter, United Daughters of the Confederacy Collection, Western Historical Manuscripts, University of Missouri. On guerrilla warfare in Columbia, see William Switzler, comp., *History of Boone County, Missouri* (St. Louis: Western Historical, 1882), 43–53; and Thomas Prather, "Unconditional Surrender: The Civil War at the University of Missouri–Columbia, 1860–1865," April 10, 1989, Missouri State Historical Society. On guerrilla war in Missouri, see Gerald Fellman, *Inside War: The Guerrilla Conflict in Missouri during the American Civil War* (New York: Oxford University Press, 1989); Richard S. Brownlee, *Gray Ghosts of the Confederacy: Guerrilla Warfare in the West, 1861–1865* (Baton Rouge: Louisiana State University Press, 1958); and Albert E. Castel and Thomas Goodrich, *Bloody Bill Anderson: The Short, Savage Life of a Civil War Guerrilla* (Mechanicsburg, Pa.: Stackpole Books, 1998).

7. Missouri Division, United Daughters of the Confederacy, comp., *Reminiscences of the Women of Missouri during the Sixties* (Jefferson City: Hugh Stevens, 1912); Benedict clipping, scrapbook 1, John S. Marmaduke Chapter, United Daughters of the Confederacy Collection.

8. Ann Hickam clipping, scrapbook 1, John S. Marmaduke Chapter, United Daughters of the Confederacy Collection.

9. *The Confederated Memorial Association* (New Orleans: Graham Press, 1904), 215–26.

10. *Minutes of the Third Annual Meeting of the Missouri Division of the United Daughters of the Confederacy* (Fayette, Mo.: Press of the Democrat-Leader, 1900), 1–6; R. B. Rosenberg, *Living Monuments: Confederate Soldiers' Homes in the New South* (Chapel Hill: University of North Carolina Press, 1993). Although monuments to many Union generals, including Ulysses S. Grant, Nathaniel Lyon, and Frank Blair,

were erected in the state as early as 1873, there were no major Confederate monuments until the first decade of the twentieth century. Vertical File, Civil War Monument and Battle Sites, Missouri State Historical Society, Columbia.

11. John S. Marmaduke Chapter scrapbook, 1931–35, Belle Alexander Troxell Collection.

12. Minutes of the Marmaduke Chapter, April 1924, United Daughters of the Confederacy Collection.

13. Floyd C. Shoemaker, "Missouri—Heir of Southern Tradition and Individuality," *Missouri Historical Review* 36, no. 4 (July 1942): 438–46.

14. Delia Crutchfield Cook, "Shadow across the Columns: The Bittersweet Legacy of African Americans at the University of Missouri" (Ph.D. diss., University of Missouri at Columbia, 1996); Uncle Jack clipping, scrapbook 1, John S. Marmaduke Chapter, United Daughters of the Confederacy Collection.

15. On the African American experience in Missouri, see Lorenzo Greene, Gary R. Kremer, and Antonio Holland, *Missouri's Black Heritage* (Columbia: University of Missouri Press, 1993).

16. On the wartime experience of African Americans in the state, see Ira Berlin, Barbara J. Fields, Steven F. Miller, Joseph P. Reidy, and Leslie S. Rowland, *Slaves No More: Three Essays on Emancipation and the Civil War* (Cambridge: University of Cambridge Press, 1992), 60–76; Greene, Kremer, and Holland, *Missouri's Black Heritage*, 62–87; Michael Fellman, "Emancipation in Missouri," *Missouri Historical Review* 83, no. 1 (October 1988): 36–56; John W. Blassingame, "The Recruitment of Negro Troops in Missouri during the Civil War," *Missouri Historical Review* 68, no. 3 (April 1964): 326–38; and Suzanna Maria Grenz, "The Black Community in Boone County, 1850–1900" (Ph.D. diss., University of Missouri at Columbia, 1979).

17. Switzler, *History of Boone County*, 433; Blassingame, "The Recruitment of Negro Troops."

18. Grenz, "The Black Community in Boone County," 27, 172.

19. For a further discussion of the particular experience of black slave women in the Civil War, see Jacqueline Jones, *Labor of Love, Labor of Sorrow: Black Women, Work, and the Family from Slavery to the Present* (New York: Basic Books, 1985); Leslie Schwalm, *"A Hard Fight For We": Women's Transition from Slavery to Freedom in South Carolina* (Urbana: University of Illinois Press, 1997); and Thavolia Glymph, "This Species of Property: Female Slave Contrabands in the Civil War," in *A Woman's War*, 55–71.

20. *Missouri Statesman*, July 22, 1864.

21. *Missouri Statesman*, November 25, 1864.

22. Union officer quoted in Greene, Kremer, and Holland, *Missouri's Black Heritage*, 91.

23. In the 1868 registration of voters, only 411 of the county's 3,411 white men were allowed to vote; the other 3,000 were disqualified for their wartime Southern sympathies. Switzler, *History of Boone County*, 495–96. They would not regain the vote until

1871 and by that time the regional orientation of the state had been fundamentally altered. See Fellman, *Inside War*, 231–66.

24. Grenz, "The Black Community in Boone County," 30–37. The historical work that perhaps best depicts this white cultural hegemony is the only monograph on slavery in the state, Harrison A. Trexler, *Slavery in Missouri, 1804–1865* (Baltimore: Johns Hopkins University Press, 1914). Based in large part on the recollections of slave owners or their descendants, Trexler argues that the close and harmonious relations between master and slave that persisted into the postwar era characterized Missouri as a small slaveholding state.

25. Greene, Kremer, and Holland, *Missouri's Black Heritage*, 140–57.

26. "Student Activism," Vertical File, University of Missouri Archives, University of Missouri.

27. *Black Out*, November 20, 1969, Legion of Black Collegians Collection, University of Missouri at Columbia College Ephemera, Collection 3628, Western Historical Manuscripts, University of Missouri; interview with Tommy Mendenholl, August 3, 1999, Columbia; interview with William Berry, October 8, 1999, Columbia.

28. *Black Out*, November 20, 1969.

29. *Black Out*, November 26, 1970.

30. Steinem quoted in *Columbia Daily Tribune*, October 5, 1971.

31. Ibid.

32. *Black Out*, November 26, 1970.

33. *Columbia Daily Tribune*, October 12, 1971.

34. *Columbia Missourian*, April 5, 1974, April 26, 1974; *Columbia Daily Tribune*, April 26, 1974, April 30, 1974, August 16, 1974; *Columbia Missourian*, August 17, 1974.

35. *Columbia Daily Tribune*, October 29, 1974, November 5, 1974, December 4, 1974; *Columbia Missourian*, December 6, 1974.

36. *Columbia Daily Tribune*, March 30, 1988.

37. *Columbia Daily Tribune*, October 21, 1995. See also *Columbia Daily Tribune*, October 29, 1995.

38. *Columbia Daily Tribune*, October 21, 2001. See also *Columbia Daily Tribune*, October 16, 2001, October 29, 2001, November 6, 2001, November 8, 2001, November 10, 2001, November 13, 2001, November 20, 2001, and December 7, 2001.

39. *Columbia Missourian*, October 15, 1971.

40. *Columbia Daily Tribune*, October 8, 2001. See also *Columbia Daily Tribune*, April 6, 2001.

41. According to the local NAACP, the flying of the Confederate flag from the students' dorm room window continues to be a kind of litmus test of local race relations. "The atmosphere at the University that makes a student comfortable flying a rebel flag, brings again the question of how the University of Missouri is actually doing in the area of race relations? Not very good in my opinion." *Columbia Daily Tribune*, December 7, 2001. In contrast, no one publicly expressed opposition to the

flying of Confederate flags at the dedication of the new Civil War memorial in the town, perhaps partly because the monument committee, made up largely of local Sons of Confederate Veterans members, made a point of collecting the names of the county's black as well as white Civil War dead. The monument itself was designed to accommodate the addition of more names, pointing to the very real possibility of an even more inclusive memorial tradition to come in Boone County. Interview with William Berry, chairman, Boone County Civil War Monument Committee, January 23, 2002, Columbia.

Jon Wiener

Civil War, Cold War, Civil Rights

The Civil War Centennial in Context, 1960-1965

"If the South has lost the Civil War, it is determined to win the centennial."[1] So said a West Virginia critic of the centennial observances quoted in the *New York Times* in 1961. The reference, of course, was to the renewal of the civil rights movement, especially the dramatic sit-ins that had begun during the spring of 1960. The sit-ins had started at a segregated lunch counter in Greensboro, North Carolina, in February and spread rapidly. By October four national chains capitulated and announced the integration of 150 stores in 112 cities, and by the end of the year the sit-in movement had involved 70,000 participants sitting-in in 100 cities, resulting in 3,600 arrests—making them the largest direct action protests in American history. In this context Civil War commemoration became a political battlefield, an opportunity for supporters and opponents of civil rights, and for the president and others uncommitted on the issues, to reconsider and redefine the meaning of the Civil War, to find heroes and villains, to decide, in the words of David W. Blight, "what was lost and what was won."[2]

The dominant memory of the Civil War had changed little since the fiftieth anniversary observances in 1913, which, as Blight has shown, had been a celebration of white reconciliation and white supremacy. This is the version that had subsequently dominated the history books and the school curriculum as well as public and political life. What had been lost was the emancipationist vision of the war rooted in African Americans' memories of their own fight for freedom, in the politics of radical Reconstruction, and more generally in the notion that the war, by winning citizenship and constitutional equality for blacks, had reinvented the republic and advanced democracy. That reality had been repressed by a sentimental and romantic racism that, in Blight's words, served as "a mother lode of nostalgia" for the white supremacist ideology that had dominated the national memory every since.[3]

But the civil rights movement made it clear that the centennial would be an occasion for contesting once again the meaning of the war, for reasserting the emancipationist vision. As Robert Penn Warren put it in 1961, "Slavery looms up mountainously" in the story of the war "and cannot be talked away."[4]

The use of Civil War commemoration to express defiance of the U.S. government's efforts to change "the Southern way of life" was especially significant in the crucial first year of the centennial, which began with three key anniversaries: the founding of the Confederacy in Montgomery in February, the firing on Fort Sumter in April, and the Confederate victory in the battle of Bull Run in July.

The lines were already clear in February 1961 when a "week of pageantry" in Montgomery marked the hundredth anniversary of the Confederacy's founding. The festivities opened with the ringing of bells and the reenactment of the secession debates in the State House of Representatives' chamber. It culminated with a swearing-in ceremony featuring a Jefferson Davis look-alike.[5]

The oath of office was administered by Judge Walter B. Jones, best known as the judge who had issued an injunction in 1956 outlawing the Alabama NAACP. At the same time as the Confederacy birthday celebration Judge Jones was presiding in the second libel trial of *Sullivan v. New York Times*. Sullivan was the police commissioner of Montgomery who sued four leaders of the local civil rights movement and the *New York Times*, claiming he had been libeled in a fund-raising ad that appeared in the paper placed by the Committee to Defend Martin Luther King. At the trial five members of the all-white jury were wearing beards grown for the centennial celebrations. The defense objected that these obvious Confederate symbols created a prejudicial atmosphere. But Judge Jones overruled the objection and went on to enforce strict segregation in the courtroom.[6] (After the Montgomery court found for the white plaintiffs and ordered local civil rights organizations to pay them half a million dollars, the defense appealed to the Supreme Court, which eventually issued a landmark ruling greatly broadening the freedom to criticize public officials.)

The Montgomery celebration was not part of the official program of the Civil War Centennial Commission, created by Congress in 1957.[7] The official national centennial observations were scheduled to begin, appropriately enough, at Fort Sumter on April 12. Civil rights promptly became the central issue in the preparations when delegates to the event learned that the hotel in Charleston chosen by the commission to serve as its headquarters was segregated and that black delegates would thus be barred from attendance. Apparently there was only one black delegate: Madeline A. Williams, the Essex County registrar and a former New Jersey assembly member.

The New Jersey legislature promptly passed a resolution boycotting the opening ceremonies and urging all other states to do the same. The New York Centennial Commission quickly followed New Jersey's lead—its vice chair was John Hope Franklin, then teaching at Brooklyn College, and its chair was Bruce Catton. He issued a statement declaring it was unacceptable to participate in ceremonies that "will in effect be closed to Negro citizens" because "we do not believe that any bigotry belongs in any Civil War centennial ceremony."[8] Catton said the New York commission would hold a separate observance of the firing on Fort Sumter: the laying of a floral wreath, "dedicated to the soldiers of both armies, to be deposited . . . at the monument to Col. Robert Gould Shaw on Boston Common." That was a potent symbol, as the *New York Times* explained in its page one story: Shaw, "who was white, led a regiment of Negro troops in the war. He was killed in action."[9]

Illinois also joined the boycott. Governor Otto Kerner declared, "We cannot ignore the fundamental precept of equality for all people and still represent Illinois, the state of Abraham Lincoln." California became the fourth state to join the boycott. The head of the state's three-man delegation said simply, "We wouldn't go there because of the South Carolina people's attitude against colored people." Despite the boycott the national commission, chaired by Major General Ulysses S. Grant III, grandson of the Union general, refused to budge, declaring that it had "no authority or jurisdiction by which it can dictate" to the "owners and operators of the hotels concerned."[10]

John F. Kennedy had been in office for only two months, and this controversy became the first civil rights issue he decided to take on. His statement at a press conference made page one news in the *New York Times*: "President Tells Civil War Unit Not to Hold Segregated Meeting." The president announced he was going to tell Grant that "a Government body, using Federal funds, should hold its meetings at places free of racial discrimination."[11]

But the commission's executive committee responded with a statement agreeing with Grant and declaring it had "no authority or jurisdiction" to require hotel keepers to provide "rooms for Negroes." That statement was criticized by an Iowa Republican member of Congress who served on the commission and who threatened "a modern secession" unless blacks received equal treatment. A New Jersey member of Congress, Democrat Hugh Addonizio, urged the commission to cancel its meeting in Charleston. He said it was "inconceivable that an official federal agency would acquiesce in discriminatory practices in direct conflict with national policies." South Carolina governor Ernest F. Hollings was "unavailable for comment."[12]

Two days after Kennedy's press conference the centennial was back on page one: "Civil War Parley Bows to Kennedy, Will Hold Meetings in April at Navy's Desegregated Base in Charleston."[13] That decision meant that delegates would be housed at the base and that the commission's official meeting would be integrated, along with lunch and dinner. Most states that had objected agreed to end their boycott and participate, but the *Charleston News and Courier* quoted the head of California's three-man delegation saying they still would not go because of "the South Carolina people's attitude against colored people." And the secretary of the Illinois commission declared, "We're going to be commemorating Civil War events for the next four years and we might as well get this thing straight right now. There can be no compromise on this."[14]

On the other side, Representative Mendel Rivers of South Carolina said that Kennedy's decision "will be highly satisfactory to the National Association for the Advancement of Colored People and to the Americans for Democratic Action." He called it "a very dangerous precedent" and concluded that "the president has made a serious mistake." Grant, according to the *Charleston News and Courier*, had "supported the South by backing segregated housing for the Charleston assembly." Grant "made it plain that the shift of the official headquarters . . . resulted only from President Kennedy's insistence." The local paper quoted the head of the Greater Charleston Chamber of Commerce, saying, "We had to stand our ground" and that "the whole thing was strictly political."[15] Local hotel officials were quoted as saying that the tens of thousands of tourists expected to attend the events would fill the hotels anyway, so they would suffer no loss of income.

The *News and Courier* emphasized in a page one headline that the integrated housing for the commission members at the naval base would be "austere." Delegates would be housed in barracks "divided into cubicles each of which houses four persons. 'They'd have to do a lot of doubling up,'" a base spokesperson remarked. According to the paper, delegates to the commission would also "miss some of the important commemorative events in town" because the base was outside town.[16]

{ JON WIENER }

But Kennedy's order moving the site was hardly the end of the issue. The South Carolina Confederate Centennial Commission, host of the event, seceded from the national organization in protest. The Fort Sumter event itself was an innocuous fireworks display over the site, but prosegregationist sentiments were trumpeted at a segregated luncheon held the same day by the South Carolina Confederate Centennial Commission. Ashley Halsey Jr., a Charleston-born associate editor of the *Saturday Evening Post*, declared that the Fourteenth and Fifteenth Amendments had been "railroaded into our Constitution" and underlay "our present racial unrest."[17] The same evening the same Halsey spoke at an integrated event at the national commission's observance at the Charleston navy yard. "Halsey included a tasteless though humorously intended remark about Lincoln," *Newsweek* reported; "he dropped the parts suggesting that school integration should be decided by popular vote, and criticism of the use of Federal troops at Little Rock—but complete texts of the speech had already been distributed to guests and newsmen."[18]

New Jersey delegation leaders demanded the right to reply, but Grant ruled all comments out of order. The New Jersey group then held its own press conference to denounce the opening observance of the centennial for having been sabotaged by remarks "calculated to incite bitterness and to open old wounds." *Newsweek* concluded its coverage of the event by asking whether future observances of the Civil War centennial would be "worth it." Shortly thereafter, the commission's director, Karl S. Betts, resigned.[19]

Kennedy learned his own lesson from his efforts: it seemed to him that the opening centennial observance demonstrated that civil rights involved petty squabbles over minor issues like hotel accommodations and that the political damage he suffered among white Southerners was not balanced by any significant gains among liberals and blacks. The Fort Sumter centennial controversy reinforced his conviction that civil rights was a source of trouble and a peripheral issue for him. What he saw as the inflamed passions and emotional commitments of the civil rights activists seemed damaging to his public standing, something to be avoided whenever possible.[20]

:::

The Reenactment Problem

Civil rights supporters raised new concerns after the Charleston fiasco about plans for the reenactment of the battle of Bull Run to be held on July 18. They anticipated thousands of Southern white men waving Confederate flags and giving the "Rebel yell" in celebration of the defeat of Union troops before an audience of tens of thousands of cheering segregationists. Concern was first expressed publicly at the Charleston luncheon for delegates from the former Confederate states by James F. Byrnes, former governor of South Carolina and former secretary of state. He criticized the plans for battle reenactments: "There can be no doubt of the good intentions of the sponsors," he said, "but in my opinion it was a mistake. . . . Our Civil War was the greatest tragedy in the history of any country. After two centuries its battles MIGHT be commemorated, but one century is a short period in the history of a country and I fear it is quite impossible to relive the four years of our Civil War without recalling experience that will be unpleasant to the people of both North and South."[21]

The *New York Times* reported on "the discussion that has developed over the economic and psychological merits of Civil War observances." Many people, according to the *Times*, "believed the centennial observances were likely to provide both a pretext and a platform for extremists on both sides of the segregation issue."[22] The *Times* did not explain who the "extremists" on the civil rights side were.

One month after the Fort Sumter centennial and two months before the Bull Run reenactment, the "extremists on both sides" recaptured the headlines as they learned of the vicious mob attacks on Freedom Riders in Alabama. Between May 15 and May 20 the Freedom Riders' buses were attacked in three cities in Alabama. They were firebombed in Anniston; passengers in Birmingham were beaten for ten minutes by white militants with iron pipes before police arrived; in Montgomery they were attacked by a mob of one thousand. Kennedy dispatched 350 marshals to Montgomery to protect them and the city was put under martial law. That proved inadequate on May 21, when the National Guard had to be called to protect a black church meeting besieged by a mob of one thousand whites.

The attacks on the Freedom Riders provoked new criticism of the Civil War centennial. A month after the Freedom Riders returned to Montgomery the *New York Times* featured the head rabbi of Reform Judaism calling the centennial observance a "blasphemy and a disgrace" that was "glorifying a romantic episode in so carefully balanced a way that no one's sensibilities shall be ruffled. The general line which the celebration is taking seems nothing less than alarming," he said. "The war was in vain . . . if a century later the Negro's right to full equality may still be limited by prejudice enacted into law or perpetuated by custom." Dr. Bernard J. Bamberger, president of the Central Conference of American Rabbis, "expressed approval of the Freedom Riders for acting on the basis of what he called 'this great ethical principle.' "[23]

Memories of the mass attacks on Freedom Riders in Alabama were still fresh a month later in July, when reenactors took to the fields of Manassas to restage the battle of Bull Run. Between fifty and seventy-five thousand people paid as much as $3.50 to sit in the bleachers during the two-and-a-half-hour event. The *Washington Post* reported that the crowd greeted Union troops with "jeers" and that "the biggest applause, laced with Rebel yells, came at the battle's end when the last Federal forces were driven into the woods."[24]

Civil rights supporters again objected. *New York Times* drama critic Brooks Atkinson wrote a column criticizing the festive atmosphere that prevailed in Manassas. "As for the Civil War, why not drop it as a spectator sport?" he wrote. He quoted from Mary Chesnut's diary, recently published: the war was "the dreadful work of death." Reading Chesnut's diary led him "to realize that many of the problems the Civil War left unsolved have only been papered over; and every day we are reminded that the Negro is not yet free." Instead of the reenactors' "air of celebration," he concluded, "mourning would better become public recognition of our most grievous national experience."[25] Alfred Kazin also objected to the celebration. To read about the horrors of the war was "to realize at once the frigid emptiness of all this current play acting," he wrote in the *Reporter*. He too ended by noting the lack of freedom for "the Negro in America."[26]

Behind the scenes at the Civil War Centennial Commission, battle reenactments were being challenged. Grant resigned as commission chair in October, complaining about what he called "arbitrary and inconsiderate demands" made on him. The *New York Times* reported that "a series of disagreements" about "the commission's participation in battle reenactments" prompted his decision. To replace him, Kennedy appointed Allan Nevins, a Pulitzer Prize–winning historian of the Civil War. Seventy-one years old at that point, Nevins had written the foreword to Kennedy's book *Strategy for Peace*. Nevins's first action as chair was to announce a "de-emphasis on battle re-enactments." "If the National Commission tries to reenact a battle," he declared, "my dead body will be the first found on the field."[27]

: : :

The Centennial in Life *Magazine*

While segregationists were rallying around the centennial of the Confederacy to challenge the civil rights movement, *Life* magazine published a lavish six-part illustrated series on the war that carefully avoided presenting slave emancipation as the conflict's great achievement. The first episode featured text by Bruce Catton and a dozen pages of "specially commissioned paintings" with scenes "portrayed with historical accuracy" by "distinguished American artists." Text and paintings together "describe[d] the war's acts of heroism." Catton's lead piece bore the modest title "Gallant Men in Deeds of Glory." It was dedicated to the thesis that, North and South, "all the brothers were valiant."[28] None of the valiant brothers portrayed in the illustrations was black.

The men who fought for slavery and treason received admiring and affectionate coverage. The section entitled "Youngsters' Hour of Glory" was all banners and bayonets as teenage cadets from the Virginia Military Institute took a Union battery in hand-to-hand combat, "halting, for the first time, the Union invasion."[29] In a strange, full-page, full-color illustration entitled "The Impudent Raider," Rebel John Singleton Mosby was shown at the moment he broke into the bedroom of Brigadier General Edwin Stoughton, woke him with "a wicked grin" and "a slap on the rump"—surprised as he was taken from behind—an illustration intended to be amusing.[30]

Following "Gallant Men in Deeds of Glory," part 2 was entitled "Now History, the Battles." Part 3 was "The Soldier's Life, North and South," written by Bell Irvin Wiley. Part 4 was "Great Advances that Changed War" by Lieutenant General James M. Gavin, who wrote about the "revolution in military technology." Part 5 was "The Home Front," written by Margaret Leech, who had received two Pulitzer Prizes for history in 1941 and 1959.[31]

The finale, entitled "A Mark Deep on a Nation," was written by Robert Penn Warren. This essay took up the delicate question of Civil War memory. Photos gave equal treatment to the reenactments of Jefferson Davis taking the Confederate oath of office in Montgomery and Lincoln at his first inaugural address. For the first and only time in the six-part series a black man appeared in an illustration—not one of the lavish full-color battle scenes but a smaller black-and-white news photo of a man born in slavery honored in New Jersey as part of that state's centennial celebration.[32]

The *Life* magazine treatment of the centennial, offering the most traditional and conservative constructions of the war's meaning and significance, had some striking similarities to the mid-nineteenth century treatment of the war as described by Alice Fahs in *The Imagined Civil War*. In 1961 as in 1861 many national publications based in New York tried to appeal to a Southern as well as a Northern audience with attempts at "neutrality" aimed at maintaining Southern readership. In 1961 as in 1861 periodicals published lavishly illustrated accounts of the battles. Periodicals emphasized the authenticity of their paintings, drawings, and photos. Lavish illustration intended for the whole family was characteristic of both periods.[33]

Life magazine's construction of the Civil War story along conservative lines in 1961 did not go unchallenged. Allan Nevins had recently published a two-volume history of the war. He wrote in the *Saturday Review* lamenting the focus on "military topics and leaders, on . . . the floating banners, the high-ringing cheers, the humors of the camp, the ardors of the charge, the whole undeniable fascination and romance" of the war. He called instead for "attention to its darker aspects, and [to] examine more honestly such misrepresentations as the statement it was distinguished by its generosity of spirit."[34]

: : :

The International Context

Although the burgeoning civil rights movement provided the most significant and intense context in which the Civil War centennial was understood, a new intensification of the Cold War also framed the events and provided some novel interpretations.[35] The same day as the anniversary of Fort Sumter, April 12, the USSR put the first man in space: Yuri Gagarin, who traveled one orbit in 108 minutes. A week later CIA-trained forces landed in Cuba at the Bay of Pigs. All fifteen hundred invaders were killed or captured within three days, making the operation the greatest defeat for the United States in the Cold War and a humiliation for the new president.[36] Two months later in the summer of 1961, as Civil War reenactors geared up for the centennial of Bull Run, the Berlin crisis began. Growing threats from the USSR culminated in the building of the Berlin Wall beginning August 13. And on December 11 the first U.S. troops—four thousand—arrived in South Vietnam.

Against the background of growing confrontation with communism on three continents, *Look* magazine published a sensational cover story, "If The South Had Won the Civil War" by Pulitzer Prize winner McKinley Cantor.[37] The author has Texas seceding from the Confederacy, the South engaging in gradual emancipation in the 1880s, and Wilson winning the presidency of the Confederacy in 1912 while Theodore Roosevelt returns for a second term in Washington.

Look *magazine cover, November 22, 1960.*
(Courtesy of the Library of Congress, Prints and Photographs Division, Look
Magazine Photograph Collection)

The Cold War makes for a stunning denouement: the weakened government in Washington never has the vision or resources to purchase Alaska, which becomes at midcentury "the colossal menace of Russian America." The three separate nations are too weak to defend themselves against the "somber threat of Communist domination," which "spread[s] like a cold fog across the oceans and chill[s] the hearts of North Americans." Meanwhile in Soviet Alaska, "airstrips were being extended, missile bases were gouged, tank brigades were deployed on maneuvers."[38]

The Soviet threat in Alaska leads to the rise of a "consolidationist" movement in each of the three nations: in the "persuasive heat of common peril, the rains of angry determination brought the plant into flower." Consolidationists in the three countries succeed in introducing legislation simultaneously in each capital in 1959 "to set up machinery for that reassembling of American power which had become an almost religious necessity." The president of the Confederacy takes the lead, declaring, "Our three countries must not only make common cause in the present world crisis, but must abide by a common law and be inspired by the original American dream. If we have lost a century of mutual endeavor, we shall rectify that loss by a devotion more concentrated and an effulgence unique in the annals of mankind." On December 20, 1960—the one hundredth anniversary of South Carolina's secession—the reunion is accomplished—"televised internationally at nine p.m. eastern standard time."[39] The end.

Although the happy ending laid the groundwork for a common defense against the Soviets, letters to the editor expressed anxiety over the reunion's late date. Upton Sinclair wrote a letter, and so did Harry Truman. Truman was confident that after a Union defeat, "the Northwest would have seceded from the Northeast." He also thought a Mexican empire would have controlled California, Utah, Arizona, and New Mexico. The existence of four nation-states—the northeastern United States, the northwest republic, the Confederacy, and the Mexican empire—would have left all of them even weaker in the face of the Soviets in Alaska, and the problem would have been even more stark since the Soviet Union would "in all probability have taken all Northwest Canada."[40]

"What then?" Truman asked. The Soviet Union could easily have conquered the northwestern states from Washington and Oregon east across the plains. The best that could have been hoped for was that the Northeast and the Confederacy "could have created an alliance and held the Russians at the Mississippi." Truman found a decisive lesson in his version: he concluded that although "my sympathies and all my family were on the side of the South," this alternative scenario, with the Soviets expanding from Anchorage all the way to New Orleans, demonstrated that the Union was "worth all the sacrifices made to save it."[41] Thus the Cold War was invoked to explain to Southerners why they should accept the Union victory—despite the threat to the Southern way of life the civil rights movement had recently inaugurated. And thus both *Life* and *Look* told stories about the Civil War and its significance that omitted "the Negro" and thereby avoided coming to the conclusion that the war's tasks remained unfinished.

:::

The Centennial of Emancipation

Throughout 1962 the upcoming centennial of emancipation—January 1, 1963—provided the civil rights movement with a target date for action and public commitment. The Civil War Centennial Commission held a commemorative event at the Lincoln Memorial in September, the centennial of the issuance of the proclamation, but Kennedy did not attend.[42] Instead, he sent Adlai Stevenson, his United Nations ambassador, to deliver the principal address. Martin Luther King and other black leaders called for a boycott of the event in protest against the absence of "a Negro speaker on the program."[43] The proceedings, with Allan Nevins presiding, included a speech by Governor Nelson Rockefeller of New York and songs by Mahalia Jackson. Kennedy's remarks were presented on audiotape.[44] Kennedy declared, "Much remains to be done to eradicate the vestiges of discrimination," but he failed to specify what those tasks were. He praised blacks for rejecting "extreme or violent policies"—a thinly veiled criticism of Malcolm X.[45]

In contrast to the national event that day, the American Negro Emancipation Centennial Authority of Chicago held a ceremony at Lincoln's tomb in Springfield, Illinois. The keynote speaker was a black judge from Chicago, James Parsons, who declared that America had to offer blacks more than a "pretense toward equality." He claimed that the "democratic process" was still a "farce" in cities that remained "patchworks of ethnically separated peoples who have retained their ideas of group superiority and hatred."[46]

Kennedy's absence from the commemoration of the Emancipation Proclamation had been glaring. On the day of the Washington observances civil rights supporters called on the president to "honor the anniversary by fulfilling his campaign pledge to sign an Executive Order forbidding racial discrimination in federally aided housing projects."[47]

Kennedy refused—a refusal that was widely noted. The *Nation* magazine suggested in December 1962 that the president missed a unique opportunity in an article aptly entitled "Kennedy: The Reluctant Emancipator." A hundred years earlier, as author Howard Zinn pointed out, Lincoln had proclaimed that, as in the North, within the Confederacy slaves were henceforth "forever free." Martin Luther King, Zinn reported, now hoped Kennedy could be persuaded (or pressured) into saying something similar about blacks living under segregation. King had already lobbied the White House, arguing that Kennedy should issue what he called a "Second Emancipation Proclamation."[48]

The White House was opposed to the idea. Kennedy's director of the budget declared privately that "practical considerations" made it "undesirable to use the Civil War Centennial Commission as a vehicle for observance." The "practical considerations" consisted of "threats of protest by the Southern State Centennial Commissions."[49] The White House had such a limited response to King's proposal for a second Emancipation Proclamation that King's advisors wanted him to march on the White House himself to deliver a proclamation to Kennedy, perhaps with Lincoln's biographer Carl Sandburg at his side.

Meanwhile, inside the White House Arthur Schlesinger was conferring with other officials about King's proposal. Pierre Salinger was given the draft for the "Second Emancipation Proclamation" on December 26 to present to Kennedy for a final decision. The draft was short, but it preserved the notion of a presidential commitment:

> Whereas Negro citizens are still being denied rights guaranteed by the Constitution and laws of the United States, and the securing of these rights is one of the great unfinished tasks of our democracy:
>
> Now, therefore, I, John F. Kennedy, President of the United States of America, do hereby proclaim that the Emancipation Proclamation expresses our Nation's policy, founded on justice and morality, and that it is therefore fitting and proper to commemorate the centennial of the historic Emancipation Proclamation throughout the year 1963.[50]

Kennedy refused to issue this statement. Although his civil rights advisor at the time—Lee White—told Salinger that "not to issue some statement would be regarded as a minor disaster," Kennedy would not do it. He still did not consider civil rights a major issue, and he was dependent on segregationist Southern Democrats for other policies he considered more important. Schlesinger supported an alternative proposal: instead of issuing a second Emancipation Proclamation Kennedy would invite black leaders to a White House reception on Lincoln's birthday. That would get good publicity for the president in *Ebony* and *Jet* and not bother Southern white Democrats too much. Kennedy's real interests that month were Fidel Castro and the deteriorating situation for the United States in Vietnam.[51]

So on New Year's Day instead of issuing a second Emancipation Proclamation in Washington, Kennedy attended the Orange Bowl game in Miami, puffing on a cigar as he watched a young quarterback named Joe Namath bring victory to the segregated University of Alabama.[52] White students had rioted at Alabama in 1956 when courts ordered the school to admit Autherine Lucy as the first black student; the school had responded by suspending her rather than the students responsible for the riot. When Governor George Wallace declared he would "stand in the schoolhouse door" to block black students from enrolling, he was talking about the University of Alabama.

With the president's failure to act on the anniversary of emancipation, the most important Civil War centennial observance came to an ignominious end.[53] Just two weeks after the centennial of emancipation J. Edgar Hoover received a memo from one of his most trusted lieutenants about Martin Luther King: "The fact that he is a vicious liar is amply demonstrated by the fact that he constantly associates with and takes instructions from Stanley Levison who is a hidden member of the Communist Party in New York." That was false, but Hoover wrote at the bottom of the memo, "I concur."[54] Thus instead of issuing a second Emancipation Proclamation, as suggested by Martin Luther King, Kennedy gave permission to the FBI to wiretap King, as suggested by J. Edgar Hoover.

A few state observances, however, firmly reasserted that slave emancipation provided the Civil War's greatest legacy. The most notable came in 1963, as Edward Tabor Linenthal has shown, when the battle of Gettysburg's centennial commemoration was organized by the state of Pennsylvania. The state's policy had been declared back in 1961, when the Charleston celebration of the firing on Fort Sumter had included denying a hotel room to a commission member from New Jersey who was black. The Pennsylvania Centennial Commission declared at that time that it would "insist upon the equality of opportunity . . . in connection with Civil War Centennial observances" at Gettysburg.[55]

Pennsylvania held its Gettysburg commemoration beginning June 30, 1963. Former president Eisenhower opened the event with a conservative call for a revival of "the sturdy self-reliance" he somehow found invoked in the Gettysburg Address.[56] On July 1 Kennedy's assistant secretary of the interior, John A. Carver Jr., described Gettysburg as the place where "the ideals expressed by the Emancipator became possible of realization." He added that "the equality defined on this field has been withheld from millions of our fellow citizens."[57]

That emancipationist view did not go unchallenged. Governors of twenty-seven of the twenty-nine states that had sent troops to fight at Gettysburg took part in wreath-laying ceremonies on July 1. Notable among them was George Wallace of Alabama, who had gained national notoriety as the most prominent enemy of the civil rights movement. He spoke on July 2 and declared that Americans "look to the South to restore . . . the rights of states and individuals." Ross Barnett of Mississippi lived up to his reputation as a segregationist by declaring in his speech that limited state sovereignty should be "fully preserved."[58]

Liberal governors from the North replied by reasserting the significance of emancipation: Harold Hughes of Iowa declared that some issues over which the battle had been fought were still alive, including "strife between men of differing races." The goal of equality, he remarked, "for which so many men fell at Gettysburg, eludes us." Edmund G. "Pat" Brown of California said we should "remind ourselves that peace between the races . . . has not been secured"—which was not quite the same as saying racial justice had not been secured.[59]

At the observances at Gettysburg on July 3, 1963, the state commission offered a unique solution to the reenactor/Rebel yell problem. In front of an audience of forty thousand people five hundred Confederate reenactors "crossed the famous field" where the Pickett-Pettigrew charge had taken place, "stopped[,] and lowered their flags in tribute to those who had died." Then, instead of the reenactors giving the Rebel yell, the audience heard "pre-recorded sound effects" of the Rebel yell, along with a soundtrack of rifle fire and music. Then the Confederate troops proceeded to the Angle, where the sound effect tape was turned off and there was a "sudden silence." The official report of the state commission explained the culmination of the event: over the low stone wall "the men who had been representing both sides became 'present day' Americans." Together they marched to the Armistead marker, where they joined in a salute and sang the national anthem together. The program explained that the men had "joined in brotherhood and amity to pledge their devotion to the symbol of their common unity—the Stars and Stripes!"[60]

The Gettysburg centennial observance provides a sharp contrast to the commemoration fifty years earlier on the same site. David W. Blight described the 1913 reunion of veterans at Gettysburg as "a ritual like none other that had occurred in America." The official theme was sectional reconciliation. The states appropriated almost $2 million to pay for the transportation of any Civil War veteran from anywhere in the country. The offer of free tickets to Gettysburg had a massive response: more than fifty-three thousand veterans attended the reunion. Spectators also showed up in enormous numbers, estimated at more than fifty thousand. President Woodrow Wilson spoke. Amazingly, he declared it an "impertinence to discourse upon how the battle went, how it ended," or even "what it signified." He claimed that the "quarrel" had been "forgotten" except for "the splendid valor" and "the manly devotion" displayed by both sides. Blight concluded that the fifty-year Gettysburg commemoration had been "a Jim Crow reunion, and white supremacy might be said to have been the silent, invisible master of ceremonies."[61]

The centennial of the war's end was marked early in 1965 when the North Carolina Centennial Commission observed the anniversary of the surrender of ninety thousand Confederate troops to William Tecumseh Sherman. Vice President Hubert Humphrey, who had first come to national prominence in 1948 as a spokesperson for civil rights, issued a statement calling for social order and unity—an implicit criticism of civil rights activism. He sought to soothe white Southern feelings by claiming that the "radicalism" that dominated the Reconstruction era was an example of the "senseless, revengeful extremism that even today, if left unchecked, could bring our great democracy to its knees." And he called for an end to the "senseless struggle" of "race against race."[62]

The Civil War's centennial commemoration came to a conclusion in official ceremonies held in Washington in the spring of 1965. They included a parade down Pennsylvania Avenue in February and in March a reenactment of Lincoln's second inaugural address—with Henry Fonda playing Lincoln. That same month civil rights marchers in Selma were attacked and beaten by state police. Five months later the Watts riots would underscore the national dimension of the nation's racial crisis. Meanwhile the *New York Times* article "Civil War Centennial Ends" listed highlights of the four-year observance: at the top of its list was "the spectacular reenactment of the Battle of Bull Run."[63]

One legacy of the Civil War centennial has survived to the beginning of the twenty-first century: the flying of the Stars and Bars, the Confederate

{ JON WIENER }

battle flag, as a symbol of white resistance. The practice began in 1961, when the state legislatures of South Carolina, Alabama, and Mississippi started flying the Confederate battle flag over their state capitols, ostensibly as part of the centennial observances. The Stars and Bars had not figured prominently as a segregationist symbol before 1961.[64] But in 1965, when the centennial ended, none of the states took the flags down. Twenty-two years later, in 1987, the NAACP sued those states to get them to remove the flags, and in 1999 the NAACP called for a national tourist boycott of South Carolina for its refusal to stop flying the Stars and Bars over the state capitol. Although the battle flag was removed from over the capitol building in 2000, a similar flag was positioned on the grounds nearby over a monument to Confederate soldiers. The continuing popularity of the Confederate flag as a symbol of white defiance of black rights remains the most significant legacy today of the Civil War centennial.[65]

NOTES

1. "War Centennial Critic," *New York Times*, May 1, 1961.

2. David W. Blight, *Race and Reunion: The Civil War in American Memory* (Cambridge, Mass.: Belknap Press of Harvard University Press, 2001), 19.

3. Ibid., 4. "Emancipationist vision" is Blight's term.

4. Robert Penn Warren, *The Legacy of the Civil War* (1961; reprint, Cambridge, Mass.: Harvard University Press, 1983), 7.

5. For a description, see Alfred Kazin, "And the War Came," *Reporter*, May 11, 1961, 36.

6. Taylor Branch, *Parting the Waters: America in the King Years, 1954–63* (New York: Simon and Schuster, 1988), 391.

7. The commission consisted of twenty-five members, including President Eisenhower, Vice President Nixon, House Speaker Sam Rayburn, four senators, four representatives, and two representatives of the Department of Defense. The historians Eisenhower named to the commission were Bruce Catton, Avery O. Craven, and Bell Irvin Wiley. Their first meeting was held at the end of 1957, when they began planning for the first festivities to be held in 1961. U.S. Civil War Centennial Commission, *The Civil War Centennial: A Report to the Congress* (Washington, D.C.: GPO, 1968), 7–8, 10–11. On the politics of the creation of the commission, see Richard M. Fried, *The Russians Are Coming! The Russians Are Coming!: Pageantry and Patriotism in Cold-War America* (New York: Oxford University Press, 1998), 124–25.

8. "Civil War: Legacy of the Conflict," *Newsweek*, March 20, 1961, 28; "President Tells Civil War Unit Not to Hold Segregated Meeting," *New York Times*, March 24, 1961.

9. "President Tells Civil War Unit Not to Hold Segregated Meeting."

10. "Civil War Parley Bows to Kennedy, Will Hold Meetings in April at Navy's Desegregated Base in Charleston," *New York Times*, March 26, 1961.

11. "President Tells Civil War Unit Not to Hold Segregated Meeting."

12. "Kennedy Critical of Panel," *Charleston News and Courier*, March 24, 1961 (first and second quotes); "Iowan Wants Site of Meeting Moved," *Charleston News and Courier*, March 24, 1961 (third, fourth, and fifth quotes). Addonizio later gained notoriety as the mayor of Newark during the 1968 riots there; Hollings went on to the Senate.

13. "Civil War Parley Bows to Kennedy."

14. "Centennial Panel Switches Meeting to Naval Station," *Charleston News and Courier*, March 26, 1961.

15. "Kennedy Himself Ordered Shift in Centennial Site," *Charleston News and Courier*, March 24, 1961.

16. "Naval Base Says Housing to Be Austere," *Charleston News and Courier*, March 26, 1961; "Move May Cause Visitors to Miss Events," *Charleston News and Courier*, March 26, 1961.

17. Halsey quoted in Fried, *The Russians Are Coming!* 131.

18. "Please Don't Start Another War," *Newsweek*, April 24, 1961, 40.

19. Ibid. In its 1968 report the commission described what it called "the Charleston blunder" as the result of "a deplorable lack of vigilance" by its leaders. U.S. Civil War Centennial Commission, *Civil War Centennial*, 12. Edward Tabor Linenthal reports that "Edwin C. Bearss, chief historian of the NPS, noted that there had been a 'long standing practice in Charleston to permit Black delegates attending predominantly white functions to have rooms and eat at banquets in hotels . . . but their presence would be low profile, i.e. they would not enter or leave by the front entrance. The National Centennial Commission mistakenly believed that the black lady member of its New Jersey Commission would adhere to this covert practice and it boomeranged." Letter to the author quoted in *Sacred Ground: Americans and Their Battlefields* (Urbana: University of Illinois Press, 1991), 120.

20. Branch, *Parting the Waters*, 398; Victor Navasky, *Kennedy Justice* (New York: Atheneum, 1971), 96–97.

21. " 'Reliving' of War Feared by Byrnes," *New York Times*, April 16, 1961.

22. Ibid.

23. Bamberger quoted in "War Centennial Called 'Disgrace,' " *New York Times*, June 21, 1961. The same qualities can be found in Civil War battle reenactments today: "Some unreconstructed Confederates even tried to rewrite history by turning reenactments of Southern losses into latter-day rebel victories." Tony Horwitz, *Confederates in the Attic* (New York: Random House, 1988), 135.

24. "Traffic Jammed for Hour after 'Battle,' " *Washington Post*, July 22, 1961.

25. Brooks Atkinson, "Critic at Large: Air of Celebration Attached to Civil War Centennial Belies Tragedy of Conflict." *New York Times*, September 19, 1961.

26. Kazin, "And the War Came," 36–40.

{ JON WIENER }

27. "Nevins Appointed to Civil War Unit," *New York Times*, October 14, 1961; "Nevins Heads Civil War Commission," *New York Times*, December 5, 1961; U.S. Civil War Centennial Commission, *Civil War Centennial*, 14.

28. Bruce Catton, "Civil War Part 1: Gallant Men in Deeds of Glory," *Life*, January 6, 1961, 50.

29. "Youngsters' Hour of Glory," *Life*, January 6, 1961.

30. "The Impudent Raider," *Life*, January 6, 1961.

31. "Civil War Part 2: Now History, the Battles," *Life*, January 20, 1961; Bell Irvin Wiley, "Civil War Part 3: The Soldier's Life, North and South," *Life*, February 3, 1961, 84–89; James M. Gavin, "Civil War Part 4: Great Advances that Changed War," *Life*, February 17, 1961, 66–67; Margaret Leech, "Civil War Part 5: The Home Front," *Life*, March 3, 1961, 68–69.

32. Robert Penn Warren, "Civil War Part 6: A Mark Deep on a Nation," *Life*, March 17, 1961, 82–83; "Honor for Ex-Slave" appears on 88.

33. Alice Fahs, *The Imagined Civil War: Popular Literature of the North and South, 1861–1865* (Chapel Hill: University of North Carolina Press, 2000).

34. Allan Nevins, "The Glorious and the Terrible." *Saturday Review*, September 2, 1961, 48.

35. For this connection, see Fried, *The Russians Are Coming!* 122–37, and Mary Dudziak, *Cold War Civil Rights* (Princeton: Princeton University Press, 2000).

36. Castro had marched into Havana on January 1, 1959. On January 1, 1961, the United States had broken diplomatic relations with Cuba. Kennedy was inaugurated on January 20.

37. McKinley Cantor, "If the South Had Won the Civil War," *Look*, November 22, 1960, 29–62. The essay was published as a paperback in 1961 and republished in 1965 for the centennial of the end of the war (1961; reprint, New York: Bantam Books, 1965).

38. Ibid, 62. In contrast, Cantor has the Confederacy annexing Cuba at the end of the nineteenth century, which prevented communism from gaining a foothold there.

39. Ibid., 61–62.

40. Harry S. Truman, "History in Reverse," *Look*, January 3, 1961, 4.

41. Ibid.

42. On Kennedy's withdrawal, see Fried, *The Russians Are Coming!* 134–35. In this context, see Scott A. Sandage, "A Marble House Divided: The Lincoln Memorial, the Civil Rights Movement, and the Politics of Memory, 1939–1963," *Journal of American History* 80, no. 1 (June 1993): 135–78.

43. "Negroes' Boycott in Capital Stands," *New York Times*, September 18, 1962. In its official report the commission did not note that King and others had called for a boycott of the event; it lamented that "too little demand was manifest for study and appreciation of the great Emancipation," which it saw on a par with "the Homestead Act, the Pacific Railroad Act, and the Land-Grant College Act." U.S. Civil War Centennial Commission, *Civil War Centennial*, 17–19, 5.

44. "Centennial Rites Hail Emancipator," *New York Times*, September 23, 1962.

45. Kennedy quoted in Branch, *Parting the Waters*, 685; "Text of Kennedy Emancipation Message," *New York Times*, September 23, 1962.

46. "Negro U.S. Judge Finds a Lag in Emancipation after Century," *New York Times*, September 22, 1962. The commission added federal judge Thurgood Marshall to the program in response. Nevins later reported to Congress that 12 million people had watched the proceedings on television. Fried, *The Russians Are Coming!* 135.

47. "Rabbis Set Goal of Emancipation," *New York Times*, September 23, 1962.

48. Howard Zinn, "Kennedy: The Reluctant Emancipator," *Nation*, December 1, 1962, 373–76. See also Branch, *Parting the Waters*, 685–86. African American criticism of Lincoln being dubbed the Great Emancipator did not appear in these reports. Kennedy had deeply disappointed all friends of civil rights the preceding year when he had failed to use federal power to protect black rights in Albany, Georgia, the site of prolonged and unsuccessful demonstrations led by King and the Southern Christian Leadership Conference.

49. Director of the budget quoted in Branch, *Parting the Waters*, 685.

50. Proclamation quoted in ibid., 686.

51. Ibid., 398–99, 587, 686. White had been an oil and gas lawyer on Theodore Sorenson's staff who took over the duties that had been held by Harris Wofford, Kennedy's special assistant on civil rights.

52. Ibid., 688. Branch judges this decision by the Kennedy administration—not to have any federal observance of the centennial of emancipation—"perhaps the most glaring of the government's withdrawals from the four-year centennial" (685).

53. Others not part of the official state commissions, however, did speak up. Nelson Rockefeller was sworn in as governor of New York for his second term on the first day of 1963. He began his inaugural address by declaring, "This is an historic anniversary. Just 100 years ago, on January 1, 1863, the Emancipation Proclamation became law" (ibid., 688).

54. Memo quoted in ibid., 692.

55. *Gettysburg 1963: An Account of the Centennial Commemoration: Report of the Commission to the General Assembly*, quoted in Linenthal, *Sacred Ground*, 98. Linenthal refers to advocacy for civil rights as "rhetorical brooding over the unfinished business" of the Civil War (99).

56. Eisenhower quoted in Fried, *The Russians Are Coming!* 135–36.

57. Carver quoted in Linenthal, *Sacred Ground*, 98.

58. Wallace and Barnett quoted in ibid.

59. Hughes and Brown quoted in ibid., 99.

60. *Gettysburg 1963* quoted in ibid., 99.

61. Blight, *Race and Reunion*, 8–9, 11 (Wilson quotes).

62. Humphrey quoted in Fried, *The Russians Are Coming!* 136, and in John Bodnar, *Remaking America: Public Memory, Commemoration, and Patriotism in the Twentieth Century* (Princeton: Princeton University Press, 1992), 224. Fried writes

that civil rights was an "irritant" in the Civil War commemorations (122). Bodnar's thesis emphasizes local and regional resistance to official intentions. In making this case for the Civil War centennial he describes civil rights as an "issue of racial divisiveness" (210) and misses the pro-Confederate theme of the battle reenactments. Resistance to civil rights in this analysis is an act of "ordinary people" who "used" the events for purposes other than "what the authorities wanted them to be" (206).

63. "Civil War Centennial Ends," *New York Times*, February 28, 1965.

64. Georgia was the exception: the state began flying the Confederate flag in 1956.

65. Horwitz, *Confederates in the Attic*, 78; "A Backward-Looking Symbol: A Confederate Flag on a State Capitol Can Bring Nothing but Pain," *Los Angeles Times*, November 29, 1996. On the NAACP calls for a boycott, see "NAACP to Boycott South Carolina," *Washington Post*, October 17, 1999. Republican governor David Beasley of South Carolina supported taking down the flag. The Myrtle Beach Chamber of Commerce called on the state to take down the Confederate flag. "Another Shot at Rebel Battle Flag," *Houston Chronicle*, October 23, 1999. The mayor of Columbia, Bob Coble, sought to remove the flag from the statehouse, as did Charleston Mayor Joseph Riley. "Memorial Suggested for Confederate Flag," *New Orleans Times-Picayune*, September 4, 1999.

The era left one other historical legacy: a flowering of historical scholarship. The same year the Civil War centennial ended James M. McPherson published *The Struggle for Equality*, George M. Fredrickson published *The Inner Civil War*, and William McFeely was working on his dissertation, "The Freedmen's Bureau: A Study in Betrayal." These works, and others that followed, transformed the history of the Civil War from the white supremacist to the emancipationist interpretation.

Stuart McConnell

❧

Epilogue
The Geography of Memory

emory has geography. L. P. Hartley's famous remark ("The past is a foreign country—they do things differently there") used a geographic metaphor to describe the strangeness of past events, the discomfort and excitement we feel when we take seriously the exotic intellectual worlds that earlier human beings—in all other respects exactly like ourselves—inhabited. Hartley meant to equate defamiliarization over time, the traditional province of the historian, with defamiliarization over space, the subject of explorers and travel writers (and more recently of anthropologists). Both kinds of travel make the passenger rethink settled cultural assumptions. Yet memory is geographical in another sense. It is a kind of map on which individuals and societies locate past events relative to one another. As Maurice Halbwachs pointed out many years ago, the only area of human memory not rooted in social experience is the dream, which for that very reason lacks structure, continuity, and orderly progression.[1] The dream, that is, lacks a map.

Until recently the study of historical memory has also lacked guideposts. The prevailing scheme is the monograph, with memory studied among discrete social groups, in particular locales, or as expressed in single memorial forms such as monuments or textbooks. Sometimes such social memories are contrasted, implicitly or explicitly, with a presumably more objective or accurate "history," of which memorial narratives are seen as corruptions.[2] But more often each historical memory is left to stand on its own, as a "version" of the past, on which the historian does not presume to pass judgment. Having absorbed the postmodern lesson that we cannot surgically remove information from the story in which it comes embedded without embedding it in some other story, we are too often content to line the stories up next to each other, like pieces of a dream, without considering their interrelation. This approach has the considerable side benefit of simplifying research, since it is easier (and safer) to report what some group believed about the past than it is to assign meaning ourselves. Thus, where the Civil War is concerned there can be Northern and Southern memories, men's and women's memories, black and white memories, Republican and Democratic memories, all peacefully coexisting without much thought given to their connections.[3]

This collection begins the important work of thinking holistically about Civil War historical memory. Some sense of the scope of this project can be seen in the wide variety of popular historical forms dissected by these authors: textbooks, formal histories, children's literature, memoirs, political speeches, commemorative rituals, and monuments ranging from a bronze John Calhoun to a painted rock. Even this cornucopia hardly exhausts the list of memorial forms. The Civil War has also been remembered through visual art, sermons, popular songs, cemeteries, genealogies, relic collections, reenactments, private letters, legislation, folklore, advertising, movies, tourist souvenirs, and even the physical landscape envisioned by organizations such as the Gettysburg Battlefield Memorial Association. When memory takes such disparate forms it can become unwieldy as an object of study. Small wonder, then, that historiographers have tended to acknowledge only the arguments made by professional historians in books, consigning the rest to the realm of myth and popular culture.[4]

Consider, however, that more people have seen a single fictional Civil War film, *Gone with the Wind*, than have read the works of all professional Civil War historians combined. The notion of "history" as something written by a few hundred people in universities, often largely for each other, while the understandings of the multitude are "historical memories" is an odd one, but it is the product of a particular cultural moment—a moment characterized by stark class divisions, strong professionalism, and a thoroughly commercial popular culture. If we wish to understand the geography of earlier memories, we must follow the lead of the authors in this collection and look backward at previous relations of power and cultural space.

To begin with, a simple taxonomy of memorial forms disguises the uneven physical, cultural, and political space in which those forms exist. Virtually all memorial forms are more available to some social groups than to others. This uneven landscape is most visible in fights over actual physical space, as in the siting of monuments. Karen Fields's African American ancestors, for example, could vandalize the Charleston statue of "Calhoun and He Wife," but they were not in a position to erect one of their own to Nat Turner (or even to prevent the scowling Calhoun from being plopped down in their neighborhood). Thomas J. Brown has elsewhere shown how a campaign to erect a monument to "the common soldier" in Boston was also a political victory for the city's Irish working class, who seized a public square formerly reserved for Brahmins.[5] LeeAnn Whites's essay in this volume describes a political coming-of-age story among black citizens of Columbia, Missouri, over the 1974 uprooting of a Confederate rock. And across the South in the 1990s came drives by African American leaders, empowered by political changes and the economic clout of tourism, to remove Confederate flags from state capitol buildings, as Jon Wiener notes in his essay.

Arguments about physical public spaces such as courthouse lawns and public squares are won by those with political muscle and are not infrequently tied up with economic interests such as real estate values or downtown development. Logan Circle in Washington, for example, owes as much to the ambitions of real estate developers as to the Civil War heroics of General John Alexander Logan. Elsewhere, the white elite that controlled nineteenth-century city development has shown remarkable staying power. Neither the Southern statehouse flags nor the Columbia rock was actually removed; rather, they were resituated on marginally less symbolic ground. Still, the difference between sacred and semisacred space is important and becomes more so as the nation centralizes. It was once enough to erect a public monument in Washington, D.C. Now, that monument must be on the Mall, which, as a site of memorial battle, has become to the twenty-first century what Gettysburg was to the nineteenth.[6]

Monuments demonstrate forcefully in physical space the same sorts of tensions that less obviously characterize cultural and political space. In the nineteenth century, for example, the textbooks analyzed by James M. McPherson in this volume were universally written by genteel white men. Whereas immigrants such as the Boston Irish might be able—through sheer political muscle—to build a monument, they had no access to the universities, publishing houses, and school boards that controlled academic history writing and textbook dissemination. Catholic immigrants were also uncomfortable with Memorial Day (which, once its African American origins detailed here by David W. Blight were forgotten, became a Protestant holiday) and with the Republican Party's use of war issues to attack Democrats. On the other hand, immigrants had full access to the realm of popular culture, in songs such as "Who Will Care for Paddy Now?" (a parody of the WASP weeper "Who Will Care for Mother Now?"), in folklore, and in the

{ STUART MCCONNELL }

quasi-minstrel "Tom shows" that gradually perverted *Uncle Tom's Cabin* on stage throughout the late nineteenth century.[7]

Similarly, women were barred from the ranks of academic historians and textbook authors and appeared in memorial statuary only as abstract allegorical figures or on the sponsors' plaque. Yet women had an avenue of remembrance that was not available to immigrant men and only secondarily even to their native-born male counterparts: the realm of sentimental fiction. Long established as a female enterprise, the writing of sentimental fiction allowed women to remember the Civil War as a time of suffering rather than heroism, of joint sacrifice rather than manly valor. Lyde Cullen Sizer points out elsewhere that Elizabeth Stuart Phelps's novel *The Gates Ajar*, one of the best-selling books of the late nineteenth century, imagines a heaven for women only in recompense for the double loss women suffered during the war—the loss of a loved one, followed by grieving.[8] This message of female forbearance subverted the dominant memorial discourse of the Gilded Age, which was one of white masculine heroism (exemplified by the children's fiction Alice Fahs examines here). But it may be that sentimental fiction could offer such a vision only because it "flew beneath the radar" of cultural authorities, occupying a metaphorical side street rather than the courthouse lawn. In any case, it was a piece of twentieth-century romantic fiction by Margaret Mitchell that would eventually, in cinematic form, dominate popular memory of the Civil War.

Every other form of remembrance existed within the same kinds of cultural boundaries. Pensions were available to men but not to women (or, more accurately, to women only as the dependents of men) and to Union veterans but not to former Confederates. The *Century* series of Civil War articles was open to tales of "battles and leaders" (most famously those of Ulysses S. Grant, which, as Joan Waugh notes in this volume, became the basis of Grant's best-selling *Personal Memoirs*) but not to those of war prisoners or Sanitary Commission volunteers. Genealogy was easier for whites to practice than it was for blacks in the wake of slavery's devastation of families. Cemeteries and battlefield parks required land, letters and memoirs required literacy, "high" arts such as painting required a trained eye. And when remembrance was part of an explicitly commercial enterprise it was limited to those with stories that large numbers of paying customers wanted to hear. In the nineteenth century—and, actually, well into the twentieth—the stories that sold best were military exegeses (such as Grant's *Personal Memoirs*), romantic sagas (such as *Gone with the Wind*), and paeans to manly valor. Commercial taste may have shifted somewhat since the civil rights movement and the Vietnam War, with directors such as Ken Burns (*The Civil War*) and Edward Zwick (*Glory*) finding mass audiences for tales of tragedy and racial reconciliation. But as Jon Wiener's essay in this volume suggests, the transition to a civil rights narrative of the war in mainstream culture has been anything but smooth and complete. In any case, making and distributing films on a mass scale requires resources to which few citizens less wealthy than General Motors have access.

Simply to show that groups have differential access to certain memorial forms, however, may imply that all forms carry the same cultural weight, which they certainly do not. A relic collection is less important than a best-selling history; a genealogy will have nowhere near the reach of *The Civil War*. Indeed, dominant forms influence the ways in which peripheral forms are understood—as with the relic collector who sees in his Robert E. Lee autograph the grim determination sketched by Douglas Southall Freeman (among Gary W. Gallagher's concerns here) or the genealogist who reads in her distant ancestor's letters the wistful romanticism of Sullivan Ballou. Here we arrive at the nub of the problem, which is to describe not just relations of cultural space but relations of cultural power. Memorial forms have a hierarchy, albeit one that shifts over time.

For the Gilded Age it seems safe to say that politics was primary. This was a culture in which fraternal orders fought furious battles over offices such as grand sachem; in which men displayed their partisan affiliations in civic gazetteers and obituaries; in which national elections provoked torch-light parades, fistfights, record turnouts, and speeches that doubled as popular entertainments.[9] Because political power was seen as the root of all else, nineteenth-century politicians were sometimes willing to settle for politically symbolic but practically empty victories. The Reconstruction amendments to the Constitution (Thirteenth to Fifteenth Amendments), for example, proved hollow reeds in the absence of Southern economic reforms and federal enforcement. Earlier, during the sectional crisis, Southern whites repeatedly dug in their heels on issues (such as a slave code for Kansas) that were of no practical benefit. Thus when it came to remembering the Civil War, actions in the political sphere regularly trumped cultural productions. Many more Gilded Age Americans could have discoursed on such now forgotten political incidents as Anna Dickinson's 1872 apostasy (J. Matthew Gallman's subject in this volume) or Grover Cleveland's 1887 "battle flag order" than on the origins of Memorial Day or the novels of Thomas Nelson Page. As Patrick J. Kelly shows in his discussion of the

{ STUART MCCONNELL }

1896 presidential campaign here, war memories had remarkable staying power when explicitly politicized.

At the same time the primacy of politics in the Gilded Age allowed nonpolitical sites of memory to flourish offstage, relatively undisturbed. Women's sentimental fiction has been mentioned as one form that flew beneath the political radar. Another might be the textbook, where McPherson's analysis suggests that the Northern public offered little resistance to Lost Cause textbook authors of the 1880s and 1890s. Perhaps Northerners paid less attention to Southern revanchism in the schools because it was a cultural offensive taking place off to one side of the political stage. Other forms of memory fell into line behind politics, with folklore of the most outcast groups—those with no access to political power at all—bringing up the rear. We will wait a long time, I think, for *The Draft Dodger's Civil War* or *The Irish Rioter's Civil War* (though with the voracious appetite of the Civil War publishing industry, one learns never to say never).

This is not to say that cultural forms of memory are inherently less important than political forms or that women's activities are less important than those of men. Indeed, within our early-twenty-first-century landscape of memory culture frequently looms larger than electoral politics, and much excellent scholarship has gone to unearthing sites of cultural memory that the Gilded Age neglected or hid.[10] It is only to argue that we must map the landscape of memory as it appeared to the late Victorian Americans we are studying. We need to delineate the memorial forms through which they understood the past, the importance they attached to each of those forms relative to the others, and the differential access that important social groups had to each form. We may abhor the Victorians' penchants for blind partisan politics, mawkish sentimentality, reactionary jurisprudence, or racist social thought. Yet these were the landmarks around which all late-nineteenth-century Civil War memories arranged themselves.

In the years since 1900 the geography of Civil War memory has changed in several ways. To begin with, the members of the Civil War generation have all died. Halbwachs and other theorists of memory insist on the great difference between social memory, in which living people impose constraints on us, and "personal memory," in which we may roam freely among the dead under "the illusion of living in the midst of groups which do not imprison us, which impose themselves on us only so far and so long as we accept them."[11] Without the presence of those who lived through the war certain practices that were cornerstones of Victorian war memory—the marking of Memorial Day as a sacred holiday, for example—faded away.

Other once-popular memorial activities, such as the singing of war songs and the use of cemeteries as picnic grounds, fell victim to changes in middle-class taste.

More significantly, the highly political Gilded Age gave way to a twentieth century whose culture put ever more stress on commercial entertainment, consumption, and tourism. By the late twentieth century film and television dominated popular memorial forms to the point that memory itself came to be seen as a kind of entertainment (rather than, as in the nineteenth century, a political weapon). Civil War battlefields hired reenactors and built attractive gift shops, Lincoln impersonators sold cars on Presidents' Day, and memorial forms such as academic history, which had carried authority in the nineteenth century partly because they were stodgy and serious, now lost caste for the same reasons. The modern consumer would have trouble sympathizing with the Union veteran who in 1889 complained of a plan to relocate monuments in Gettysburg Battlefield Memorial Park: "These monuments were erected in the interests of history, and not for the convenience of tourists."[12] In short, a map of twentieth-century historical memory would be centered on Mount Diversion, with other memorial forms arrayed in the foothills before it.

Finally, and apropos of this volume, something happened late in the twentieth century that suddenly made "historical memory" visible as an object of study. It was not a term in common scholarly use until about fifteen years ago. Coinages such as "popular history" and "public history" referred to works by professional historians (or journalists) who were trying to reach a broader audience. The "myth and reality" school of American studies in the 1950s acknowledged in a backhanded way the power of popular misinformation. But the idea that audiences might have their own valid models of the past was not something historians cared to ponder until events drove them to it. The great wave of democratization unleashed by the 1960s started historians on the path of studying "ordinary people," writing narrative "from the bottom up," and taking seriously the histories of previously neglected groups. When these new actors told a rash of stories that did not fit existing master narratives of U.S. history particularly well, what followed was an attack on those master narratives, which led in turn (through the instrumentality of literary postmodernism) to an attack on the whole idea of master narratives. By the 1980s it was a commonplace of scholarly discourse that there are many versions of the past, all potentially true from somebody's point of view, and that the imposition of a master narrative is little more than an arrogation of power on the part of the historian.

Meanwhile, the commercial culture of the twentieth century rolled on, churning out imagined pasts that entertained the multitudes but struck many professional historians as spurious. An ersatz "Tara" appeared as a tourist attraction; in the film *Mississippi Burning* the FBI was on the side of the civil rights marchers. Still, if every history was just text—just a "version," just a different story told about the past—what basis did professionals have for imposing their own narratives? One could no longer dismiss the myths dear to ordinary people as "misinformation." However, one could not let them inside the professional tent, since what would be the use of a historical profession if Everyman (or Everywoman) really *was* his/her own historian? Popular memories had to be treated with respect, but they also had to become the objects of study, not the study itself. And thus was born the nascent field of "historical memory" in a landscape marked by consumerism, multicultural democracy, and professional self-doubt. A thousand versions would bloom, but only under the watchful eye of the historical profession.

This brings us back to the question of why studies of historical memory so often avoid the analytical forest to tend the monographic trees. To map the geography of memory is to reimpose narrative on a sprawling democracy of versions. It is also to grapple with the memorial geography of one's own time, the ways in which even the designation of somebody else's past as "historical memory" represents a kind of gesture in a professional project. Those will never be popular tasks in a culture so enamored of democracy. They will be especially difficult where the memory of the Civil War is concerned, tied up as that conflict is with ongoing problems of race, state power, and nationality. But we will enjoy the journey more if we start to take in the whole landscape.

NOTES

While I was revising this essay for publication John Higham passed away. As mentor and student John and I traded many ideas over the years and some essays—including this one. Although he disliked my geographic metaphor John was always generous and greatly helped in sharpening an argument with which I know he disagreed. This essay is dedicated to his memory.

1. Maurice Halbwachs, *On Collective Memory*, ed. and trans. Lewis A. Coser (Chicago: University of Chicago Press, 1992), 23, 41–45.

2. A good example of this old-fashioned empiricist approach is Carol Reardon, *Pickett's Charge in History and Memory* (Chapel Hill: University of North Carolina

Press, 1997); see also Stuart McConnell, "Resisting the Pickett T-Shirt," *Reviews in American History* 26, no. 4 (December 1998): 705–10.

3. A significant and remarkable exception is David W. Blight's *Race and Reunion: The Civil War in American Memory* (Cambridge, Mass.: Belknap Press of Harvard University Press, 2001), which treats the Civil War memories of discrete groups in separate chapters but integrates them elegantly in a narrative that explains how white supremacy emerged by 1900.

4. See, for example, Thomas J. Pressly, *Americans Interpret Their Civil War* (Princeton: Princeton University Press, 1954), and Eric Foner, "The Causes of the American Civil War: Recent Interpretations and New Directions," *Civil War History* 20, no. 3 (September 1974): 197–214.

5. Karen Fields, "What One Cannot Remember Mistakenly," in *History and Memory in African-American Culture*, ed. Geneviève Fabre and Robert O'Meally (New York: Oxford University Press, 1994), 156–58; Thomas J. Brown, "Reconstructing Boston: Civic Monuments of the Civil War," in *Hope and Glory: Essays on the Legacy of the Fifty-Fourth Massachusetts Regiment*, ed. Martin H. Blatt, Thomas J. Brown, and Donald Yacovone (Amherst: University of Massachusetts Press, 2001).

6. Elaine Sciolino, "Fighting for Space in Memorial Heaven," *New York Times*, June 28, 2001.

7. Stephen Railton of the University of Virginia English Department maintains a website, "Uncle Tom's Cabin and American Culture," containing a large archive of material on the "Tom shows" at http://jefferson.village.virginia.edu/utc.

8. Lyde Cullen Sizer, *The Political Work of Northern Women Writers and the Civil War* (Chapel Hill: University of North Carolina Press, 2000), 264–66; Elizabeth Stuart Phelps, *The Gates Ajar* (Boston: Houghton Mifflin, 1890).

9. Michael McGerr, *The Decline of Popular Politics: The American North, 1865–1928* (New York: Oxford University Press, 1986).

10. Blight, *Race and Reunion*, especially 300–337; Alice Fahs, *The Imagined Civil War: Popular Literature of the North and South, 1861–1865* (Chapel Hill: University of North Carolina Press, 2001); James Alan Marten, *The Children's Civil War* (Chapel Hill: University of North Carolina Press, 1998); W. Fitzhugh Brundage, ed., *Where These Memories Grow: History, Memory, and Southern Identity* (Chapel Hill: University of North Carolina Press, 2000). A fascinating twentieth-century case study of subversive teachings slipping past political censors precisely because they were located in a supposedly "peripheral" cultural site is Julia Mickenberg, *Learning from the Left: Children's Literature and Radical Politics in the United States* (New York: Oxford University Press, 2005).

11. Halbwachs, *On Collective Memory*, 50.

12. *Grand Army Record* (Worcester, Mass.), January 1889, 4.

Contributors

David W. Blight is the author of *Race and Reunion: The Civil War in American Memory*. He teaches at Yale University.

Thomas J. Brown, who teaches at the University of South Carolina, is the author of *Civil War Eras*.

Alice Fahs teaches at the University of California at Irvine. She is the author of *The Imagined Civil War: Popular Literature of the North and South, 1861–1865*.

Gary W. Gallagher has published numerous works, including *Lee and His Army in Confederate History* and *The Confederate War*. He teaches at the University of Virginia.

J. Matthew Gallman is the author of *Mastering Wartime: A Social History of Philadelphia during the Civil War*. He teaches at the University of Florida.

Patrick J. Kelly, who teaches at the University of Texas at San Antonio, is the author of *Creating a National Home: Building the Veterans' Welfare State, 1860–1900*.

Stuart McConnell's publications include *Glorious Contentment: The Grand Army of the Republic, 1865–1900*. He teaches at Pitzer College in Claremont, California.

James M. McPherson of Princeton University is the author of many books, including *Battle Cry of Freedom* and *For Cause and Comrades*.

Joan Waugh, who teaches at the University of California at Los Angeles, is the author of *Unsentimental Reformer: The Life of Josephine Shaw Lowell*.

LeeAnn Whites is the author of *The Civil War as a Crisis in Gender: Augusta, Georgia, 1860–1890* and teaches at the University of Missouri at Columbia.

Jon Wiener's most recent book is *Gimme Some Truth*. He is a contributing editor to the *Nation* magazine and teaches at the University of California at Irvine.

Index

Catton, Bruce, 6, 10, 239, 244
Cavour, Count, 146
Central Conference of American Rabbis, 242–43
Century Magazine, 5, 8, 11, 23–24, 79, 89, 261
Century Publishing Company, 23–24
Chandler, William E., 181
Charles L. Webster and Company (publisher), 6, 24, 32 (n. 12)
Charleston, South Carolina: fall of, 95–97; horse track prison in, 97; and Memorial Day, 97–98, 99, 124–25 (n. 8); and Calhoun monument, 130, 133–34, 136, 139, 259; and Civil War centennial, 238–40, 254 (n. 19); and Confederate flag, 257 (n. 65)
Cheesborough, Esther B., 135, 139, 144
Chesnut, Mary, 243
Cheves, Langdon, 147
Chicago Great Western Railroad, 202
Chicago Inter-Ocean, 122
Children: and Southern Civil War monuments, 64, 135; as living monuments, 65–66; recitations of, 66; and burning of U.S. history textbooks, 71; integration into imaginary world of war, 80; and orphans on Memorial Day, 102. *See also* Children's war novels; Education
Children of the Confederacy, 66
Children's war novels: and racial ideology of masculinity, 3, 82, 84, 86, 91, 261; for boys, 79–85; market for, 80–81, 85; and gender, 81, 82, 83–85; mothers in, 81, 82, 84; fathers in, 82, 83, 84, 87–88; for girls, 84; and reconciliation, 85–86, 89–90, 91; and slavery, 86–88,

90–91; and white supremacy, 89–91
Civil rights movement: and Civil War memory, 1; and Civil War centennial, 3–4, 237–39, 243, 245, 252, 257 (n. 62); and *Sullivan v. New York Times*, 238; and Kennedy, 241, 248–49, 256 (n. 48); and emancipation centennial, 248; as threat to Southerners, 248; and Wallace, 251; and commercial taste, 262
Civil War, The (Burns), 262
Civil War centennial: and civil rights movement, 3–4, 237–39, 243, 245, 257 (n. 62); and Bull Run reenactment, 241–43, 254 (n. 23); in *Life* magazine, 243–45; international context of, 245, 247–48; and emancipation centennial, 248–52, 255 (n. 43), 256 (n. 52)
Civil War Centennial Commission, 238–40, 241, 243, 248, 249, 253 (n. 7)
Civil War history: and military writing, 9; and battlefield reports, 10–12; and Lost Cause ideology, 15–17; Grant's influence on, 19, 26; truthfulness of, 20–21; and reconciliation, 22; Early's influence on, 39, 44, 45, 50–51, 56, 58; Freeman's influence on, 39, 47–48, 49, 51, 56, 58, 62 (n. 21); Lee's influence on, 40, 50, 51
Civil War memory: and selective memories, 1; geography of, 2, 263–64, 265; and *Personal Memoirs of U. S. Grant*, 8; and Grant's influence as president, 14–15; and Lost Cause ideology, 58, 110, 115–16, 118; and popular culture, 79; shifts in, 81; and Memorial Day, 95, 99, 123; and "bloody shirt" rhetoric,

102, 104, 109, 123, 180; and Early, 107; and African Americans, 110; and sympathy for Confederate veterans, 117; and emancipation, 119; and Holmes, 121; and Civil War monuments, 130, 132; and Dickinson, 157, 160–61, 165, 168, 169–71, 173–74; and election of 1872, 157, 169–71; and Republican Party, 173, 180, 181, 182, 183–84, 187–88, 189, 191, 196–98, 201–7; and Democratic Party, 180, 184–85, 188; and election of 1896, 180, 263; and racism, 182, 183–84, 190, 237; and McKinley, 188, 189, 191, 200–201, 206; and Bryan, 188, 189, 201; and Populist Party, 188–89; and Ireland, 194–97; Warren on, 244; forms of, 259–62

Civil War monuments: and language of memory, 2; and Union veterans, 64; and Confederate veterans, 64, 65, 107, 108, 109; in cemeteries, 105; in South, 105, 107–11; and women, 108, 132, 149, 150 (n. 3), 213, 215; in Missouri, 213, 215, 218, 219, 220, 225, 226, 227–31, 233–34 (n. 10), 236 (n. 41)

Civil War's cause, 8, 12, 14, 16, 22, 74

Civil War's meanings: legitimacy of, 2; and *Personal Memoirs of U. S. Grant*, 6; and sectional identity, 16; and Memorial Day, 95, 101, 105; and emancipation, 104, 106, 111, 112, 122, 237, 238, 244; and Civil War monuments, 107; and Calhoun monument, 139; and Dickinson, 174; and Civil War centennial, 237, 238

Claflin, Tennie C., 162

Class issues: and election of 1896, 181–82, 183, 184, 191–95, 198, 205,

207; and historical memory, 259; and monuments, 260

Clemson, Thomas Green, 144, 145

Cleveland, Grover, 184, 185, 186, 193–94, 196, 197, 199, 206, 262

Coates, Jack, 220–21

Cochrane, John, 114–15

Cold Harbor, 10, 42

Cold War, 245, 247–48

Columbia, Missouri, 213, 215, 216, 228–29, 260. *See also* University of Missouri

Columbia, South Carolina, 142, 145, 149, 257 (n. 65)

Committee to Defend Martin Luther King, 238

Compromise of 1850, 134

Compromise of 1877, 113, 114, 117

Confederacy: and Early, 39, 45; and Lost Cause ideology, 40, 44, 58; and Freeman, 45; political and social history of, 45; conflict in, 55; and U.S. history textbooks, 70; and burying of war dead, 97; Calhoun's importance to, 139; and Dickinson, 160; anniversary of founding, 238

Confederate cause. *See* Southern cause

Confederate civilians, 53–54, 216–17

Confederate flag: controversy over, 1, 4; and University of Missouri, 219, 225, 226, 227, 230, 231, 235–36 (n. 41); and Jesse James's burial, 230; and Civil War centennial, 241–42, 253; as symbol of white resistance, 252–53, 257 (n. 65); and African Americans, 260

Confederate guerillas, 216, 217, 218, 221, 222, 223–24, 230

Confederate veterans: and reconciliation, 22, 117; and *Personal Memoirs of U. S. Grant*, 32–33 (n. 15); and

Edmondston, Catherine Ann Devereux, 54
Education: public education, 67–72, 73; private education, 72; and gender, 137, 143, 144; and African Americans, 143, 213, 220, 225; and racial politics, 143–44; and United Daughters of the Confederacy, 219. *See also* U.S. history textbooks
Eicher, David J., 48
Eisenhower, Dwight D., 250–51
Elson, Henry W., 74, 75
Emancipation: and Lincoln, 11, 249, 256 (n. 48); and Civil War history, 22; Rhodes on, 73; and white ethos of reconciliation, 85; and children's war novels, 88; and Memorial Day, 94, 95, 101, 103, 123; and Civil War's meanings, 104, 106, 111, 112, 122, 237, 238, 244, 251; and "enough" doctrine, 118; and Civil War memory, 119, 183; and Republican Party, 180; and election of 1896, 190, 201; in Missouri, 223; centennial of, 248–52; and Second Emancipation Proclamation, 249
Emancipation Proclamation, 73, 158
Encyclopedia Britannica, 70
England, 16, 54, 56, 107–8
Ethnic diversity: and Memorial Day, 103–4
Evans, Clement Anselm, 52
Everett, Edward, 104

Fahs, Alice, 2–3, 244, 261
Family: and children's war novels, 81, 82, 84, 85
Fathers: in children's war novels, 82, 83, 84, 87–88
FBI, 250, 265
Field, James G., 189
Fields, Karen, 259

Fields, Mamie Garvin, 148
Fifteenth Amendment, 104, 109, 111, 161, 241, 262
54th Massachusetts, 99
Finch, Frances Miles, 111
Fisk, Wilbur, 53
Five Forks, battle of, 29
Foley, T. H., 107, 108
Fonda, Henry, 252
Force Bill, 180, 191
Fort Sumter, battle of, 73, 238
Fosdick, Charles Austin, 80
Foster, Gaines M., 40, 50, 106
Fourteenth Amendment, 111, 241, 262
France, 54
Franklin, John Hope, 239
Frederickson, George M., 257 (n. 65)
Freedom Riders, 242–43
Freeman, Douglas Southall: and Union's numerical superiority, 39, 47, 50, 56; and Civil War history, 39, 47–48, 49, 51, 56, 58, 62 (n. 21); and Lee, 45, 47–48, 50, 262; critiques of, 49, 51, 52; and Lost Cause ideology, 58
Fremont, John C., 114
Fuller, Margaret, 133

Gaines, Lloyd, 220, 221, 225
Gallagher, Gary W., 2, 262
Gallman, J. Matthew, 3, 262
Garnet, Henry Highland, 114
Garrison, William Lloyd, 96, 97, 140, 158, 170, 174
Gavin, James M., 244
Geertz, Clifford, 123
Gender: and children's war novels, 81, 82, 83–85; and cult of manliness, 121; and Civil War monuments, 132, 135, 150 (n. 3); and education, 137, 143, 144; and Dick-

inson's lectures, 165. *See also* Women

Genealogy, 261, 262

Geography of memory, 2, 258, 263–64, 265

Gettysburg, battle of, 53, 55, 250–52

Gettysburg Address, 111, 251

Gettysburg Battlefield Memorial Association, 259

Gillmore, Quincy A., 96

Gilmer, John A., 111–12

Gilmore, Joseph A., 158

Glory (film), 262

Gone with the Wind (film), 10, 259

Gone with the Wind (Mitchell), 10, 261

Goodwyn, Lawrence, 204

Gourdin, Henry, 139

Gourdin, Robert, 139

Grand Army of the Republic, 18, 19, 68, 99, 113–15, 197, 198–99, 202, 204–5

Grant, Frederick Dent, 24, 25

Grant, Ida, 24

Grant, Jesse (father), 26

Grant, Jesse (son), 24

Grant, Julia, 5, 20

Grant, Ulysses S.: and memory of Union cause, 2; financial problems of, 5; and throat cancer, 5, 24, 25; death of, 6; literary credentials of, 8; as symbol of unionism, 8; reputation of, 9–10, 15, 16, 17, 39; battlefield reports on, 11; generalship of, 11, 15, 16, 17–18, 27, 31, 55, 58; battle reports of, 11–12; writing style of, 11–12, 26; farewell message to Union soldiers, 12; "Report to Congress," 12, 13–14; and Union's numerical superiority, 13, 16, 17–18, 19, 55, 60 (n. 7), 119–20; post-war career of, 14–15; and recon-

ciliation, 17, 30, 118; and Memorial Day, 18–19; and factual information, 20–21; work methods of, 24; leadership of, 41; nobility at Appomattox, 54; and Southern children's attitudes, 65; and election of 1872, 157, 163–65, 170, 173; and Republican Party, 162; and Dickinson, 163, 164, 165, 169, 170, 171, 172, 174; and woman suffrage, 164. See also *Personal Memoirs of U. S. Grant*

Grant, Ulysses S., Jr., 24

Grant, Ulysses S., III, 239–40, 241, 243

Graves, Edward, 223

Great Bazaar, Columbia, South Carolina, 140

Great Northern Railroad, 195, 202

Greeley, Horace: and election of 1872, 3, 157, 163, 165–69, 173–74, 175; and Dickinson, 161, 164, 165–67, 168, 169, 171–72, 173, 174; and woman suffrage, 172

Greenwood Cemetery, Brooklyn, New York, 115

Guilford, North Carolina, 111

Hahn, William, 203, 204

Halbwachs, Maurice, 258, 263

Halleck, Henry, 11, 21–22

Halsey, Ashley, Jr., 241

Hanna, Mark, 180, 186–87, 192, 195, 196–97, 202, 205

Harnisch, Albert E., 145–47, 155 (n. 49)

Harper's Weekly, 139, 192, 194, 198

Hartley, L. P., 258

Harvey, "Coin," 204

Harwell, Richard Barksdale, 48

Hay, John, 161

Hayes, Rutherford B., 113

Lee, 16, 49, 52, 56; critiques of, 17, 49–50, 58–59; and Reconstruction, 17, 110–11, 118; and explanation for defeat, 39; and slavery, 40, 58, 117–18; and Early, 42–43, 58, 107; and Union's numerical superiority, 44, 50, 53; and "great man" version of history, 51; and Civil War memory, 58, 110, 115–16, 118; and U.S. history textbooks, 75–76, 263; and Memorial Day, 106, 108; and Pryor, 116–18

Lowndes, William, 147

Lumpkin, Katharine Du Pre, 64–65

Magnolia Cemetery, Charleston, South Carolina, 133, 136, 142

Malcolm X, 248

Marden, O. A., 204

Marmaduke, John S., 215

Marshall, Charles, 40, 59 (n. 2)

Marshall, Thurgood, 256 (n. 46)

Martineau, Harriet, 75

Maury, Dabney H., 17

McCall, John, 187

McConnell, Stuart, 2, 4, 198

McFeely, William, 10, 25, 257 (n. 65)

McKinley, William: and election of 1896, 180–83, 186–87, 189, 190–93, 195, 196, 198, 199–206; and class issues, 181–82; and reconciliation, 183, 190, 191, 209 (n. 41); and Civil War memory, 188, 189, 191, 200–201, 206; and African Americans, 190–91; and Patriotic Heroes' Battalion, 202–4

McKinley, Reverend William, 105

McPherson, James M., 2–3, 10, 257 (n. 65), 260

Meade, George, 12

Memoirs of soldiers, 9

Memorial Day: and racialized mean-ings of Reconstruction, 3; Grant's sanctioning of, 18–19; and emancipation, 94, 95, 101, 103, 123; and African Americans, 94, 98–99, 104, 112–13, 114, 115, 124–25 (n. 8), 127 (n. 38); evolution of, 94–95, 120; founding of, 95; and Reconstruction, 95, 105, 106, 108, 113; and reconciliation, 95, 112, 113–16, 128 (n. 40); and Charleston, 97–98, 99, 124–25 (n. 8); and women, 99, 100, 101, 104, 105, 123; and funereal orations and sermons, 100–106, 107, 125–26 (n. 17); picnics at battlefields, 101, 264; and democratic character of war, 102–3; North/South participation in, 111–12; and Douglass, 118–19, 129 (n. 53); fading of, 120, 263; and Holmes, 122

Memory: language of, 2; geography of, 258, 263–64, 265; historical memory, 258–59, 264, 265, 266 (n. 3); personal and social memory, 263; as entertainment, 264. *See also* Civil War memory

Mexican War of 1846–48, 26–27

Military writing, 9, 10, 14, 48

Mississippi Burning (film), 265

Missouri: Civil War monuments in, 213, 215, 218, 219, 220, 225, 226, 227–31, 233–34 (n. 10), 236 (n. 41); and Confederate Rock, 213, 215, 219, 220, 225, 226, 227–31, 260; United Daughters of the Confederacy in, 215–16, 218; and Confederate women's memorial associations, 218; and African Americans, 220, 221–22, 224–28; Republican Party in, 224

Missouri Confederate Home, 218, 219

Missouri Historical Society, 219–20

{ *Index* }

ciliation, 91; and Civil War memory, 182, 183–84, 190, 237

Racial equality: and whites, 75, 182–83; opposition to, 86, 90; and Memorial Day, 102–4, 123; and Compromise of 1877, 117; and Dickinson, 160–61; and Civil War memory, 183; and McKinley, 191; in Missouri, 221, 224–25; and Civil War's meanings, 237; and Civil War centennial, 238–40, 251; and emancipation centennial, 248

Racial mixing, 109

Racial politics: and Civil War symbols, 1; and Missouri's Confederate soldiers monument, 3, 220; and Jackson monument, 109–10; and enforcement of black civil rights, 112, 121, 180, 181; and Reconstruction, 118; and site for Calhoun monument, 138; and education, 143–44; and Dickinson, 160; and Republican Party, 181

Radical Republicans, 224

Randolph-Macon College, 74

Ravenal, Mrs. St. Julien, 95

Reading Railroad Company, 184

Reardon, Carol, 49

Reconciliation: and Grant, 17, 30, 118; and Civil War history, 22; and children's war novels, 85–86, 89–90, 91; and white supremacy, 85–86, 89–90, 123, 237; and nationalism, 86, 183; and Memorial Day, 95, 112, 113–16, 128 (n. 40); and Lost Cause ideology, 107; and Jackson monument, 110; and Democratic Party, 112, 163; and Pryor, 117; dissent from, 118–19; and Douglass, 119; and Holmes, 121–22; and Civil War memory, 123, 183, 190; and Calhoun monument, 147; and election

of 1896, 181, 191; and McKinley, 183, 190, 191, 209 (n. 41)

Reconstruction: racialized meanings of, 3; Grant's policies on, 15, 17, 30; and Lost Cause ideology, 17, 110–11, 118; failures of, 18; and Memorial Day, 95, 105, 106, 108, 113; and national cemeteries, 97; and Compromise of 1877, 113, 117; and white supremacy, 116; and Dickinson, 161; and Republican Party, 163, 181; and Civil War's meanings, 237; Humphrey on, 252

Redpath, James, 99, 124–25 (n. 8), 169

Reid, Whitelaw, 124 (n. 8), 161, 162, 163, 166, 167–68, 169, 173, 174

Religion: and nationalism, 100–101; and Memorial Day, 102–3; and election of 1896, 194, 195, 196, 210 (n. 54)

Republican Party: and Union veterans, 3, 18, 180, 182, 198–206; antislavery position of, 27; in South, 108, 112; and reconciliation, 112, 181; and Dickinson, 158, 161, 162, 166, 169, 170, 173; and election of 1872, 162; and Grant, 162; and woman suffrage, 172; and Civil War memory, 173, 180, 181, 182, 183–84, 187–88, 189, 191, 196–98, 201–7; and election of 1896, 180–81, 186–90, 196–97, 206–7; and Grand Army of the Republic, 198–99; in Missouri, 224; and Memorial Day, 260

Reunionism, 111–12, 119, 120, 130, 182

Rhind, John Massey, 148–49

Rhodes, James Ford, 73

Richmond, Virginia, 107–11

Riley, Franklin L., 74

Rivers, Mendel, 240

Smith, James McCune, 182–83
Snowden, Isabel, 135, 143
Snowden, Mary Amarinthia, 140, 142–44, 149
Social memory, 263
Soldiers' Monument, Greenwood Cemetery, 115
Soldiers' National Cemetery, Gettysburg, Pennsylvania, 104
Soldiers' Relief Association, 140, 142
Sons of Confederate Veterans, 64, 76, 229, 236 (n. 41)
South: Grant's judgment of, 11, 14, 27, 31; advantages of, 13; Grant's attempts at reconciliation with, 17, 163; and *Official Records of the War of the Rebellion*, 21–22; conflict in, 55; and Lee's generalship, 56; deaths during war, 94; and Memorial Day, 94, 104–12; Civil War monuments in, 105, 107–11; and election of 1872, 171; and Democratic Party, 181
South Carolina, 239, 240, 253, 257 (n. 65)
South Carolina College, 143
South Carolina Confederate Centennial Commission, 241
South Carolina Historical Society, 136
Southern Alliance, 188
Southern cause: equivalency with Northern cause, 6, 20, 22, 68; and Lost Cause ideology, 15–21; whitewashing of, 16; Grant's criticism of, 31; Lee as embodiment of, 49; and slavery, 67, 68, 75; and self-government, 68; and U.S. history textbooks, 68
Southern Historical Society Papers, 16, 17, 22, 33 (n. 15), 36 (n. 60), 50, 106, 107
Southern Magazine, 106

Southern State Centennial Commissions, 249
Southern terror, 107, 123
Southern textbook publishers, 2–3, 67–68, 69, 70, 73
Spotsylvania, 12, 42
Springfield Monument Association, 218
Standard Oil, 187
Stanton, Edwin, 11, 12, 22
Stanton, Elizabeth Cady, 157, 164, 172
Starnes, Richard D., 50
States' rights, 16
Steinem, Gloria, 227, 228
Stephens, Alexander, 142
Stevenson, Adlai, 248
Stiles, Robert, 44
Stillwater, Minnesota, 121
Stonewall Brigade, 110
Stoughton, Edwin, 244
Street and Smith's New York Weekly, 79
Strong, George Templeton, 57
Sullivan v. New York Times, 238
Sumner, Charles, 74, 147, 162, 163, 164, 166, 174
Swinton, William, 19–20, 57

Tantardini, Antonio, 146
Taylor, Walter H., 60 (n. 7)
Taylor, Zachary, 27
Thirteenth Amendment, 111, 262
35th U.S. Colored Troops, 99
Thomas, Emory M., 48
Thorstenberg, Herman J., 74–75
Tillman, Ben, 184–86, 188, 190, 192, 193, 201
Tilton, Elizabeth, 162
Tilton, Theodore, 162, 163, 167
Tourgee, Albion, 112, 122–23
Trotter, James F., 44
Trowbridge, John Townsend, 80, 82

Truman, Harry, 247–48
Tucker, Mary, 216–17
Turner, Nat, 259
Twain, Mark, 9, 24–25, 32 (n. 12)
21st U.S. Colored Regiment, 95
Tyler, Moses Coit, 166
Tyrell, Harrison, 24, 25

Uncle Tom's Cabin, 261
Union: Grant as symbol of, 8; disadvantages of, 13; and burying of war dead, 97; and Mount Vernon, 135. *See also* Union's numerical superiority
Union cause. *See* Northern cause
Union Orphan Asylum, 102
Union's numerical superiority: and Grant, 16, 17–18, 55, 60 (n. 7), 119–20; and Badeau, 19, 42; and Early, 39, 42, 50, 53, 56, 60 (n. 6); and Freeman, 39, 47, 50, 56; and Lee, 40, 41, 50, 53, 56; and Trotter, 44; and Lincoln, 54, 58; and U.S. history textbooks, 68; and Rutherford, 73
Union veterans: and Republican Party, 3, 18, 180, 182, 198–206; Grant's relationship with, 18; bravery of, 20; and *Official Records of the War of the Rebellion*, 21; and reconciliation, 22; and Civil War monuments, 64; and Memorial Day, 99, 102; and cult of manliness, 121; and election of 1896, 189, 197–99. *See also* Grand Army of the Republic; Veterans' affairs
Union Veterans' Patriotic League, 200, 205
United Confederate Veterans: and Early, 44–45; and Freeman, 45; and children's presence at reunions, 64, 65; and U.S. history textbooks, 67–70, 72–73, 75; and public and school libraries, 70; and censure of books and authors, 71; declining membership of, 76; in Missouri, 229
United Daughters of the Confederacy: and children's presence, 64; and children as living monuments, 66; and U.S. history textbooks, 67–69, 72–73, 75, 76; and public and school libraries, 70; and censure of books and authors, 71; and Memorial Day, 99; and commemorative stones, 213, 215, 232 (n. 1); and Civil War memory, 215–16; in Missouri, 215–16, 218, 225, 229; white cultural war of, 216, 221; and second-front war, 217–18, 220, 221, 231; and African Americans, 220–21
Unit histories, 9
University of Missouri: and Confederate Rock, 213, 215, 219, 220, 225, 226, 227–31, 260; and Confederate flag, 219, 225, 226, 227, 230, 231, 235–36 (n. 41); and African Americans, 220, 221, 225–28; and women, 226–29
U.S. Constitution: and U.S. history textbooks, 72; Rutherford on, 73; Fifteenth Amendment, 104, 109, 111, 161, 241, 262; and Lost Cause ideology, 111; Fourteenth Amendment, 111, 241, 262; Thirteenth Amendment, 111, 262; and Altgeld, 193, 194
U.S. history textbooks: and Southern textbook publishers, 2–3, 67–68, 69, 70, 73; and Northern textbook publishers, 67, 68, 70; laws concerning, 69–70; burning of, 71–72, 75; in Southern colleges, 71–75;

{ *Index* }

CPSIA information can be obtained at www.ICGtesting.com
Printed in the USA
LVOW10s0814231215

467589LV00005B/411/P